When There's No Place Like Home

This book is printed on recycled paper.

When There's No Place Like Home
Options for Children Living Apart from Their Natural Families

edited by

Jan Blacher, Ph.D.
Professor, School of Education
Principal Investigator, Families Project
University of California at Riverside

Baltimore • London • Toronto • Sydney

Paul H. Brookes Publishing Co.
P.O. Box 10624
Baltimore, Maryland 21285-0624

Copyright © 1994 by Paul H. Brookes Publishing Co., Inc.
All rights reserved.

Typeset by the Composing Room of Michigan, Inc.,
Grand Rapids, Michigan.
Manufactured in the United States of America by
The Maple Press Company, York, Pennsylvania.

Permission to reprint the following quotation is gratefully acknowledged:

Page 329: Quotation from *The Little Prince* by Antoine de Saint-Exupéry, copyright 1943 and renewed 1971 by Harcourt Brace & Company, reprinted by permission of the publisher.

Library of Congress Cataloging-in-Publication Data
When there's no place like home : options for children living apart
  from their natural families / edited by Jan Blacher.
     p.   cm.
  Includes bibliographical references and index.
  ISBN 1-55766-145-6
    1. Child welfare—United States.   2. Adoption—United
States.   3. Foster home care–United States.   4. Children–
Institutional care—United States.   5. Family services—United States.
  I. Blacher, Jan.
   HV741.W395   1994
362.7'34'0973—dc20   93-49692
                                                                CIP

British Library Cataloguing-in-Publication data are available from the British Library.

Contents

Contributors vii
Foreword   *T. Berry Brazelton, M.D.* ix
Preface xiii
Acknowledgments xix
Introduction xxi

I   IMPACT OF SOCIAL AND LEGAL POLICIES
    ON PLACEMENT 1

1   Intervention versus Interference: The Role
    of the Courts in Child Placement
    Sharon Gross Portwood and N. Dickon Reppucci 3
2   The Plight of Homeless Children
    Ellen L. Bassuk and Linda Weinreb 37
3   Consequences of Placement for Children
    Who Are Abused
    Virginia G. Weisz 63
4   Mental Health Policy and the Psychiatric
    Inpatient Care of Children: Implications for Families
    Charles A. Kiesler 101

II ALTERNATIVE FAMILIES 121

5   Temporary Foster Care: Separating
    and Reunifying Families
    Inger P. Davis and Elissa Ellis-MacLeod 123
6   The Casey Family Program: Factors in Effective
    Management of a Long-Term Foster
    Care Organization
    Ruth Massinga and Ken Perry 163
7   Not Under My Heart, But In It: Families
    by Adoption
    Laraine Masters Glidden 181

III	RESIDENTIAL PLACEMENT	211
8	Placement and Its Consequences for Families with Children Who Have Mental Retardation *Jan Blacher*	213
9	Comprehensive Service Programming for Children with Autism and Their Families *Stephen R. Anderson, Susan F. Thibadeau, and Walter P. Christian*	245
10	Residential Treatment for Children with Dual Diagnoses of Mental Retardation and Mental Disorder *Steven I. Pfeiffer and Bruce L. Baker*	273
IV	RECONCEPTUALIZING PLACEMENT	299
11	To Have and to Share: Culturally Constituted Fostering in Familial Settings *Janet E. Kilbride and Philip L. Kilbride*	301
12	Commentary: A Social Policy Perspective *Emmy E. Werner*	329

Index 345

Contributors

Stephen R. Anderson, Ph.D.
Vice President
Child and Adolescent Services
Metropolitan Boston Area
The May Institute, Inc.
10 Acton Street
Arlington, MA 02174

Bruce L. Baker, Ph.D.
Professor
Department of Psychology
Franz Hall
University of California at Los
  Angeles
Los Angeles, CA 90024

Ellen L. Bassuk, M.D.
President
The Better Homes Foundation
181 Wells Avenue
Newton, MA 02159-3320
and
Associate Professor of Psychiatry
Harvard Medical School
Boston, MA 02115

Jan Blacher, Ph.D.
Professor
School of Education
Principal Investigator
Families Project
University of California at Riverside
Riverside, CA 92521

Walter P. Christian, Ph.D.
President and CEO
The May Institute, Inc.
100 Sea View Street
Chatham, MA 02633

Inger P. Davis, Ph.D.
Professor and Principal Investigator
Child & Family Research Group
School of Social Work
San Diego State University
5050 Murphy Canyon Road,
  Suite 110
San Diego, CA 92123

Elissa Ellis-MacLeod, M.A.
Research Associate
Child & Family Research Group
School of Social Work
San Diego State University
5050 Murphy Canyon Road,
  Suite 110
San Diego, CA 92123

Laraine Masters Glidden, Ph.D.
Professor
Division of Human Development
St. Mary's College of Maryland
St. Mary's City, MD 20686

Charles A. Kiesler, Ph.D.
Chancellor
105 Jesse Hall
University of Missouri
Columbia, MO 65211

Janet E. Kilbride, Ph.D.
Independent Researcher/Writer
225 Cardinal Drive
Conshohocken, PA 19428

Philip L. Kilbride, Ph.D.
Professor
Department of Anthropology
Dalton Hall
Bryn Mawr College
Bryn Mawr, PA 19010

Ruth Massinga, M.S.
Chief Executive
The Casey Family Program
1300 Dexter Avenue North,
 Suite 400
Seattle, WA 98109-3547

Ken Perry, M.S.W.
Director
The Casey Family Program
Boise Division
2033 Sixth Avenue, Suite 1100
Seattle, WA 98121-2536

Steven I. Pfeiffer, Ph.D., ABPP
Executive Director
Institute of Clinical Training and
 Research
The Devereux Foundation
19 South Waterloo Road, Box 400
Devon, PA 19333
and
Adjunct Professor
 of Psychology in Psychiatry
University of Pennsylvania Medical
 School
3815 Walnut Street
Philadelphia, PA 19104

Sharon Gross Portwood, J.D.
Department of Psychology
University of Virginia
301 Gilmer Hall
Charlottesville, VA 22901

N. Dickon Reppucci, Ph.D.
Department of Psychology
University of Virginia
301 Gilmer Hall
Charlottesville, VA 22901

Susan F. Thibadeau, Ph.D.
Vice President
Child and Adolescent Services
Cape Cod and the Islands
The May Institute, Inc.
100 Sea View Street
Chatham, MA 02633

Linda Weinreb, M.D.
Associate Professor
Family & Community Medicine
University of Massachusetts Medical
 School
Worcester, MA 01655
and
Medical Director
The Better Homes Foundation
181 Wells Avenue
Newton, MA 02159-3320

Virginia G. Weisz, J.D.
Co-Director
The Interdisciplinary Graduate
 Training Program in Child Abuse
 and Neglect
and
Directing Attorney
Children's Rights Project at
 Public Counsel
601 South Ardmore Avenue
Los Angeles, CA 90005
and
Co-Director
The Interdisciplinary Graduate
 Training Program in Child Abuse
 and Neglect
University of California at Los
 Angeles
Los Angeles, CA 90024

Emmy E. Werner, Ph.D.
Professor of Human Development
Division of Human Development
 Family Studies
Department of Applied Behavioral
 Sciences
University of California at Davis
Davis, CA 95616

Foreword

Every child deserves to be born into an environment where at least one, preferably two, people are passionately in love with him.[1] I have used this as an argument for family planning, and even as an argument for the question about abortion. It is a child's right, and we as adults need to be responsible for providing him with that right. As a pediatrician, I have seen too many abused and neglected children to wish for less than a loving environment for any child. The choice for that environment should be made as early as possible, with an eye to the child's best future interests. The family who must give that child a future must be carefully consulted, evaluated, and supported. Today, a family cannot be expected to provide that environment without support. As the African proverb goes, "It takes a community to raise a child." Families need to be members of a community and they need the supports of those around them. The community and the family must consider their offspring as their foremost responsibility. Adult values must be subjugated to the well-being of the children if we are to survive as a viable society. Our future is in the hands of these children. Hence, those who are entrusted with them become responsible for our future values.

We know a lot about children and child-rearing. We know that children who feel secure about themselves can preserve values for the future and can upgrade our society. We know that a child's self-image depends on the safety, reliability, and caring of the environment in which he is raised. We know that the first few years are critical to his sense of inner security. We also know that the converse is true. If a child must be shifted from one caregiver to another in the first years,

---

[1] For economy's sake, I shall use the male pronoun for the child, the female for the parent.

he is likely to grow up with a less than optimal image of himself. When a child is given up by one caregiver and sent to another, he must blame himself: "I was no good. Those people didn't love me, because I was not a good enough person." Not only must a child resort to depression after each shift, but he must handle his feelings of inadequacy—often by provocative or negative behavior. The more depressed he is, the less likely he will be to adjust to a new family environment. Then he will act out to set himself up for another shift, and another, and another. He will make his own contribution to the failure of these "homes." Children who are raised in this kind of unreliable, shifting atmosphere are likely to be unable to develop deep attachments in their own adulthood. Violence and neglect reproduce themselves from one generation to another. Can't we begin to use this knowledge?

Our U.S. society is the least child- and family-oriented society in the world. Having spent the past 3 years as a member of the National Commission on Children, I was able to evaluate the devastating conditions for children that exist in the most affluent country in the world. Twenty-five percent are living below the poverty line. Nearly 25% are being raised by desperate single parents. Fifty percent will have lived for a significant part of their lives in a single-parent household, primarily because of divorce and depression in adults around them. Divorce rates are rising precipitously. Families are at risk. Within families, abuse both physical and sexual is escalating at a frightening rate. These are symptoms of the stress that families are unable to handle. We need to reconsider the hopelessness and helplessness in which we have placed too many families in our society. Yet our society does far too little to support stressed families and their children.

There are a few indications that this dire situation may be in a state of flux. The Clinton administration is certainly more child and family oriented than have been previous administrations. However, they need direction from all of us who are intimately involved with families and children. This volume is timely.

"Family preservation" has become a buzzword of the Divisions of Social Services in the states. The effort is being made to keep families together, and keep children in these families. In the process, the child's best interest can be ignored. There is not enough investigation into the strength and potential of these families. Our resources are often too minimal to back them up with what they need—income support, food, nutrition, jobs, safe neighborhoods, schools, child care. The effort is still in the realm of lip service and Band-Aid–like pressures to remain together. Children and their welfare may not be the concern of those who are pressing for family preservation. Far too many of these families are dysfunctional, and the children in them often deserve more secure, nurturing placements. However, we have not front-loaded existing investigations with children in mind. Home is not a home for these children. Foster placements are temporary, and children are moved from one to another until it is too late for them. Adoption is postponed hopelessly from the standpoint of the child's safety and security can be sacrificed in the guise of an empty slogan. If we mean to preserve families, we must investigate early and thoroughly. We must reinforce our decisions with the child's well-being as our goal.

The courts are responding to pressures to become more family oriented, but they are not responding with child-oriented decisions. Shared custody is not necessarily in a child's best interest. It is certainly a great idea to have both the father and mother involved, but what child can grow up secure in two households per week? I have recommended that the divorcing custodial parents move in and out of the house, to let the child remain in his own safe environment. Again, a thorough investigation of the situation with the child's interests and future development in mind easily could prevent such inadequate decisions as have plagued thousands of children of divorcing adults. We do know what a child needs to grow up healthy and secure. Let's demand it for our children's sake.

My research and teaching have been concerned with strengthening family values and offering cement to those families. All parents today are stressed—most of them beyond their capacity to meet that stress. Yet our knowledge of when and where we could back up young families to become successful in their coping strategies is enormous. We know a lot about attachment processes and how vital they are within a family and for the child's future. This volume will further our resolve to fight for all we know—and to lay out a roadmap for our leaders, who may be able to strengthen the supports for family preservation. We must be sure that our roadmaps are laid out for our children's best interests.

T. Berry Brazelton, M.D.
Children's Hospital
Child Development Unit
Boston, Massachusetts

SUGGESTED READINGS

Brazelton, T.B. (1992). *Touchpoints: Your child's emotional and behavioral development.* Reading, MA: Addison-Wesley.

Greenspan, S., & Cunningham, A. (1993, July 25). Kids who will be killers. *Washington Post,* p. 10.

National Commission on Children. (1991). *Beyond rhetoric: A new American agenda for children and families.* Washington, DC: Author.

Schorr, L.B., & Schorr, D. (1988). *Within our reach: Breaking the cycle of disadvantage.* New York: Doubleday.

Preface

"Oh, Auntie Em, there's no place like home."

Dorothy's heartfelt exclamation brings to a close the classic film adaptation of L. Frank Baum's tale, *The Wizard of Oz*. Abruptly uprooted from the place she called home, Dorothy embarked on a long and arduous quest for the way back. Oz, despite its wicked witches, was a pretty nice place, but even at its most enticing Oz wasn't, well, home.

This book explores the meanings of Dorothy's now-familiar words, along with the predicaments that result when there is, indeed, no such place for a child. Dorothy's story had a happy ending, but what is the hope that we as a nation can script happy endings for the countless other children who find themselves without parents or home?

This book is about homes for children—about supporting them, leaving them, and finding them. It is about the various situations that lead to children living apart from their natural homes. In many of the scenarios depicted in these pages, a child's placement resulted from a deliberate decision on the part of the caregiver. In others, the situation was such that existing legal and social policies left no alternative.

In this book we try to avoid a single philosophical stance about placement. We consider the issues from a broad perspective that includes both the current emphasis on family preservation and the viewpoint of parents who deliberately and thoughtfully opt for more permanent out-of-home placement.

The contributors to this book are all vitally concerned with the well-being of children. The perspectives presented reflect those of diverse professions and try to speak to a broad audience: social workers, physicians, psychologists, educators, anthropologists, lawyers, policy makers, and parents.

When There's No Place Like Home represents a collaborative effort among professionals and practitioners with diverse orientations. As a group, we identified research on factors that resulted in children being placed in circumstances in which there seemed to be "no place like home." In order to move beyond analysis into action, contributors also delineate the policy implications of their reported findings.

The chapters in this book are arranged into four sections. The first section addresses the *impact of legal and social policies* on placement. The second section focuses on *alternative families,* with particular emphasis on foster care arrangements and adoption. The third section addresses issues arising in *residential placement,* focusing on special populations that typically are served by either the mental health or special education systems. The fourth section discusses *reconceptualizations of placement.* New perspectives on the concepts of foster care, parenting, and what constitutes "home" can be linked with a more creative and coordinated policy that addresses the needs of children and families in contemporary society.

IMPACT OF LEGAL AND SOCIAL POLICIES

Without question, all children need a home that provides nurturance and guidance, particularly if they are affected by additional physical, emotional, or intellectual problems. The best home for a child is with a family, but given the necessity of temporarily or permanently placing some children apart from their families, coupled with today's overarching emphasis on family preservation, we need to ponder carefully the question: "Whose family?" This is an especially appropriate question when considering placements that are court ordered or the result of social policies. In Chapter 1, Sharon Gross Portwood and N. Dickon Reppucci consider issues of child abuse, divorce and custody, as well as delinquency and incarceration, as they apply to adolescents. Placement of these troubled youths often involves permanent removal from their homes.

Finding homes for all families and children in this country is, unfortunately, a far greater challenge than it should be. In Chapter 2, Ellen Bassuk and Linda Weinreb chronicle the origins of homelessness for children, with attention to the development of policies that will not only provide housing, but also prevent homelessness. They write that "although the routes onto the streets are as numerous as the families involved, extreme poverty combined with the lack of decent, affordable, low-income housing is the final common pathway" (p. 37). Here the search for appropriate placement involves not just the homeless child but often the entire family.

In Chapter 3, Virginia Weisz addresses the different legal and social consequences for the children who are victims of parental abuse. She outlines the complicated process that ensues when authorities must determine whether or not to remove abused children from their natural parent(s).

In Chapter 4, Charles Kiesler addresses current issues regarding psychiatric inpatient care of children and adolescents. Paradoxically, against the backdrop of decreasing institutional census, he notes the upsurge of inpatient episodes for children and youths in private hospitals. He presents sobering statistics indicating that such psychiatric inpatient episodes are increasing, almost doubling from 1980 to 1985 (Kiesler, 1993; Kiesler & Simpkins, 1991) and continuing to increase through 1989, the most recent year studied (Kiesler & Simpkins, 1993).

ALTERNATIVE FAMILIES

Foster care is the single most often used placement setting in this country, embracing children with a myriad of special needs. We can anticipate additional use of foster care in the years immediately ahead; foster care populations that are increasing include children under the age of 6, adolescents, and medically troubled children such as those born to mothers who are drug addicted or infected with human immunodeficiency virus. In Chapter 5, Inger Davis and Elissa Ellis-MacLeod speak to both the progress and problems of short-term foster care in this country. In Chapter 6, Ruth Massinga and Ken Perry detail the process of delivering long-term foster care, drawing on the prominent Casey Family Program in Seattle, Washington, as an illustration.

Adoption—providing a permanent home for children—is a popular placement option. About 61,000 nonrelative adoptions are finalized annually in the United States (National Committee for Adoption, 1989). Roughly one quarter of these children have special needs or disabilities. For this group, adoption is perhaps the most permanent form of placement, because it usually precludes further involvement from the natural family. Giving a child with special needs up for adoption takes a "lot of love," says Janet Marchese, who runs the Down Syndrome Adoption Exchange in White Plains, New York. Marchese "urges parents not to feel guilty" about their choice: it is admirable to acknowledge that "the baby needs the best and we're not the best" (Springen & Kantrowitz, 1990, p. 78). In Chapter 7, Laraine Masters Glidden describes how adoptions are arranged by public and private agencies for children of all ages, nationalities, and physical, intellectual, and behavioral characteristics.

RESIDENTIAL PLACEMENT

The 1960s marked a turning point in residential treatment of children in America. For the preceding century and a half, state and private institutions for persons with mental illness or mental retardation grew even larger. The residents typically entered as children into what would become a lifetime "home." During the last quarter-century, we have witnessed a virtual revolution in models and practices of care and treatment, with an increasing emphasis on community-based treatment and family preservation.

In Chapter 8, I consider placement for children with retardation, with particular emphasis on the correlates and consequences of such placement for the family members involved. According to the March of Dimes (Springen & Kantrowitz, 1990), approximately 250,000 children are born annually with some kind of physical or mental disability; that's about one every 2 minutes! Yet, although the majority of these children are raised at home by their natural parents, thousands of parents decide each year that they can no longer do this. Residential placement or care is one alternative for such children. Roughly 3% of the population in the United States will be diagnosed as having mental retardation at some point in their lifetimes; almost 20% of these individuals live in some form of nonfamily, licensed placement, whether institutional or community based (Seltzer & Ryff, 1994). However, these primarily constitute persons with moderate to severe levels of mental retardation.

In Chapter 9, Stephen Anderson, Susan Thibadeau, and Walter Christian expand our consideration of children with disabilities, addressing the challenging problem of autism (or pervasive developmental disorder) and the resultant service needs of these children and youths. They draw on cases from the exemplary continuum of programming options offered by The May Institute in Chatham, Massachusetts.

In Chapter 10, Steven Pfeiffer and Bruce Baker consider children with dual diagnoses of mental retardation and mental disorder. These children present particular difficulties for the family to overcome and are at especially high risk for placement. The authors note that, although residential programs traditionally have done little to involve family members meaningfully in treatment, such involvement opportunities become critical if family reunification is to be the goal.

RECONCEPTUALIZING PLACEMENT

The options for placement that exist in the United States today are largely an outgrowth of legal and social policies that may date back many years. These policies have provided a patchwork, sometimes situation-specific response to the problem of children who cannot or should not remain in their natural homes, reflecting our lack of commitment to developing a flexible, adaptive mechanism to cope with the need for placement. It is possible that, by broadening our outlook on foster care, we may improve a system that sometimes seems to do as much harm as good.

In Chapter 11, Janet and Philip Kilbride add the perspectives of time and culture to the issue of where children are best raised. They point out that, for many centuries, children have migrated from and back to their natal homes with "no detriment to the human species" (p. 301). They contrast "crisis fostering" in this country, which is relatively institutionalized and formal, to informal fostering among various societies in South America and Africa. This type of fostering, which is voluntary, purposeful, and integrated into the cultural systems of which it is a part, may provide new options for placement in our own culture as well.

As we thought and wrote about children living apart from their natural homes, we saw several common themes regarding social policy and placement emerge. In the final chapter of this book (Chapter 12), Emmy Werner articulates a social policy perspective that incorporates national and international perspectives, and draws on the suggestions made by the other contributors. Her chapter builds on a model put forth by the Children's Defense Fund (1992) that proposes that all families require adequate housing, income, health care, child care, education, and recreational services. As the needs of families increase, the model assures extra assistance that grows more specialized as a given problem increases in intensity, chronicity, and (we hope) rarity. Families whose children cannot be protected or treated at home may, ultimately, utilize residential treatment centers, therapeutic homes, or foster family homes.

Throughout this book, we have resisted the urge to oversimplify problems and solutions. We hope that the reader will agree that, regardless of whatever social policy is currently in vogue, there is a need to consider and preserve options for families and others who are faced with decisions about placement for children.

REFERENCES

Children's Defense Fund. (1992). *The state of America's children 1992*. Washington, DC: Author.

Kiesler, C.A. (1993). Mental health policy and the psychiatric in-patient care of children. *Applied & Preventive Psychology, 2,* 91–99.

Kiesler, C.A., & Simpkins, C.G. (1991). Changes in psychiatric inpatient treatment of children and youth in general hospitals, 1980–85. *Hospital and Community Psychiatry, 42,* 601–604.

Kiesler, C.A., & Simpkins, C.G. (1993). *The unnoticed majority in psychiatric inpatient care.* New York: Plenum.

National Committee for Adoption. (1989). *Adoption factbook*. Washington, DC: Author.

Seltzer, M.M., & Ryff, C.C. (1994). Parenting across the lifespan: The normative and nonnormative cases. In D. L. Featherman, R. Lerner, & M. Perlmutter (Eds.), *Life-span development and behavior* (Vol. 12, pp. 1–40). Hillsdale, NJ: Lawrence Erlbaum Associates.

Springen, K., & Kantrowitz, B. (1990, October 22). The long goodbye: When parents give a disabled child up for adoption, the pain often lingers. *Newsweek*, pp. 77–78, 80.

Acknowledgments

I have no illusion; I will never be able to acknowledge all of the people who have inspired and encouraged me, and participated in the 11 years of work on placement that undergird the rationale for this book. There are several important sources of everyday influences that I will mention here.

I owe over a decade of thanks to the National Institute of Child Health and Human Development (Grants HD14680 and HD21324) for providing me the rare opportunity to learn about placement firsthand, from so many families over such a long period of time. May the agency and its reviewers bask in the knowledge that more is yet to come.

The staff of the University of California at Riverside Families Project have given unfailingly to our research effort. The following people contributed to some of the studies cited in Chapter 8: Bruce L. Baker, Ph.D.; Barbara Bromley, Ph.D.; Paula Eberhard; Laurie Eisenberg, Ph.D.; Bob Hanneman, Ph.D.; Kathy Mattson; Rebecca Shepherd; and Margi Wild. To the other research assistants, students, and volunteers on the project (literally dozens of them since 1982!), I say "thanks" for a job that was well done and is still ongoing. I would also like to thank the families involved in our research for helping us to contribute empirical data to the ongoing debate about child placement.

I would like to acknowledge the sense of humor and competence of this book's contributors, who put up with my prodding, with my selection of cartoon-laden memos, and with the consistent demands for rewriting to further unify the purpose and content of this book. There were many individuals at Brookes Publishing who carefully nurtured the book along; special thanks to Melissa Behm for sharing in my vision and supporting it. I also appreciate the expertise and advice of David Erickson, Leslie Kahan, Victoria Thulman, Roslyn Udris, Susan Vaupel, and Megan Westerfeld.

Finally, I'd like to acknowledge the participation, support, and encouragement of my most beloved critic and colleague—my husband—Bruce L. Baker. He was the one who urged me to follow through on the idea of exploring the myriad of circumstances under which children live apart from their families. Thanks, Bruce, for maintaining humor and harmony in our home during even the most tempestuous stages of writing.

Introduction

What is "home"? The sentiment of "There's no place like home" is a familiar one, echoed by phrases such as "Home sweet home," "Home is where the heart is," and "Happy to be home." We seem to have an intuitive sense of home that goes beyond the particular people or possessions found there:

> Dorothy lived in the midst of the great Kansas Prairies, with Uncle Henry, who was a farmer, and Aunt Em, who was the farmer's wife. Their house was small, for the lumber to build it had to be carried by wagon many miles. There were four walls, a floor and a roof, which made one room; and this room contained a rusty looking cooking stove, a cupboard for the dishes, a table, three or four chairs, and the bed (Baum, 1956, p. 9).

Presumably without formal adoption, the orphan Dorothy made her home with her uncle and aunt. For her, there was no place like *it*.

It will be apparent throughout this book that "home" for a child need not be with his or her biological parents. Nor need it have the so-called material comforts of home ("Be it ever so humble..."). Home, ideally, is where there is love, nurturance, and acceptance. It is a place one returns to, after journeys both brief and extended. It is a place where one can count on a bed, food, shelter, and security.

CRITICAL ISSUES IN PLACEMENT

Whether by parental choice, unfortunate circumstances, or legal mandate, some children will not live with their natural or birth parents. Thus, the well-being of children depends, in part, on the placement *options* available to them and their families. Whatever its cause, placement has a potentially profound effect on the natural family, the child placed, and the "new" family or caregivers. A compelling impetus for writing this book was a recognition of the need to consider and preserve options for placement of children.

Four critical issues that affect placement decisions are considered here. The first is recognition of the *magnitude of the problem:* How many children are, in fact, living away from home? The prevalence of some problems that lead to placement is simply astonishing. In 1991, for example, over 2.6 million child abuse and neglect reports were made in America (National Center for the Prevention of Child Abuse, 1992, cited in Weisz, chap. 3, this volume). Many, although certainly not most, abused children enter foster care. Over half a million children are expected to be in our foster care system by 1995 (U.S. House of Representatives Select Committee on Children, Youth and Families, 1989), with some estimates as high as 840,000 (Rotheram-Borus, Koopman, & Ehrhardt, 1991). Many others, uncounted, are the runaway or "throwaway" children that slip through the formal service system.

Moreover, at least 100,000 children are homeless every night, sleeping in emergency shelters, welfare hotels, abandoned buildings, cars, or elsewhere. As many as 300,000 children find themselves homeless sometime during each year (Bassuk & Weinreb, chap. 2, this volume; Institute of Medicine, 1988).

Or consider psychiatric inpatient admissions for children and youths. These have shown dramatic increases since 1980, with roughly 368,000 episodes of hospitalization reported in 1985, as compared to 189,000 in 1980 (Kiesler, 1993). We cannot determine from these figures whether the same children are experiencing recurrent hospitalizations, or whether many more children and youths are entering the psychiatric inpatient system for the first time. In any event, the use of psychiatric inpatient care for children and youths is increasing, particularly in "largely uninvestigated and more expensive sites" (Kiesler, 1993, p. 91).

Although the prevalence of placement for other special populations is considerably lower, it is no less troublesome. Individuals with autism, severe retardation or other disabilities, and dual diagnoses of mental retardation and a psychiatric disorder are at high risk of placement during their childhood years. Hence the magnitude of the problem of children living away from home is enormous—well over a million, if we could find and count them all.

A second consideration in this book concerns the *placement decision:* Who decides? Was a particular child's placement a direct result of legislation or policy (e.g., policies regarding welfare, income supplements, and homelessness), the direct result of a court-ordered action (removal of abused children), or the private decision of the child's parents (placement of children with severe disabilities)? Actually, it is often the nature of adults' difficulties rather than the child's problem or needs that dictate such decisions. In the case of psychiatric inpatient care of children, we learn that many youths are hospitalized because their parents are substance abusers, or are themselves incarcerated in prison and are not available to be parents (Gobel & Frances, 1991).

The National Commission on Children addressed child and family policy, with emphasis on issues that either directly or indirectly affect placement decisions—poverty, teenage pregnancy, increasing drug use and the resulting number of babies abandoned to hospitals, and, of course, skyrocketing health care costs. John D. Rockefeller IV opened the Final Report with these words:

> Although many children grow up healthy and happy in strong, stable families, far too many do not. They are children whose parents are too stressed and harried to provide caring attention and guidance. They are children who grow up without the material support and personal involvement of their mothers and fathers. They are children who are poor, whose families cannot adequately feed and clothe them and provide safe, secure homes. They are children who are victims of abuse and neglect at the hands of adults they love and trust, as well as those they do not even know. They are children who are born too early and too small, who face a lifetime of chronic illness and disability. (National Commission on Children, 1991, p. vii)

Clearly, concepts of health care also must embrace the mental health needs of children and include the provision of subsistence to parents who are struggling to maintain their children with special needs at home. These practical supports are essential to move considerations of children's well-being beyond rhetoric.

Another theme concerns *placement facilities:* Where do these children go? These alternatives to "home" include facilities with formal programs (e.g., psychiatric hospitals, nursing care facilities), those with less formal programs in alternative homes (e.g., foster care, small family homes, adoption), and those with no child-oriented programs in haphazard settings (e.g., welfare hotels). The choice of placement facility may not follow logically from the child's problem; many of the youths in psychiatric hospitals, for example, are there primarily because they exhibit socially deviant behavior that is not now dealt with by the criminal justice system (Kiesler, 1993). There is nowhere else for them to go.

The choice of placement facility, of course, has enormous repercussions for the child's future. For example, it may determine how involved the child's parents can remain in his or her care. An article in *Newsweek* (Springen & Kantrowitz, 1990) on placing children with disabilities for adoption highlighted the issue: "Most child-welfare workers now believe that family settings provide the best environment for children with handicaps. But whose family?" (p. 78).

A fourth theme is that of *placement permanency:* How long will the child live away from home? The length of stay may range from one night to a lifetime, depending on the child's situation and the desired outcome. What are the goals of the placement—to reunify the child with his or her family (as in foster care), or to find the child a permanent home that both invites and fosters ongoing family involvement (as in residential placement of children with retardation), or to find the child a permanent home apart from his or her biological family (as in adoption)? These very different placement outcomes have developed from a single policy perspective on placement in which the inherent issue of permanency is seldom addressed (see Blacher, chap. 8; Davis & Ellis-MacLeod, chap. 5; Glidden, chap. 7; and Massinga & Perry, chap. 6, this volume).

The philosophy behind permanency planning is that children should, in all cases, be reunited with their natural families. If that is not possible, for whatever reason, the push is for professionals to help find routes to alternative placements that will hopefully provide more permanent homes.

Generations of readers have enjoyed *The Wizard of Oz* (Baum, 1956), cheering Dorothy on her determined course to find a way back home. After struggles with all the hardships that bad witches could put in her way, Dorothy comes, in the end, to find that she has the power to help herself in her own wishes and thoughts:

> Says the Good Witch Glinda: "Close your eyes, tap your heels together three times, and think to yourself: 'There's no place like home.'"

If only it were so!

REFERENCES

Baum, L.F. (1956). *The wizard of Oz*. Chicago: Rand McNally.
Gobel, S., & Frances, R.J. (1991). Alcohol and drug abuse: Establishing links between residential placement for youth and prisons for adults. *Hospital and Community Psychiatry, 42,* 1203–1204.
Institute of Medicine. (1988). *Homelessness, health and human needs*. Washington, DC: National Academy Press.
Kiesler, C.A. (1993). Mental health policy and the psychiatric in-patient care of children. *Applied & Preventive Psychology, 2,* 91–99.
National Commission on Children. (1991). *Beyond rhetoric: A new American agenda for children and families*. Washington, DC: Author.
Rotheram-Borus, M.J., Koopman, C., & Ehrhardt, A.A. (1991). Homeless youths and HIV infection. *American Psychologist, 46*(11), 1188–1197.
Springen, K., & Kantrowitz, B. (1990, October 22). The long goodbye: When parents give a disabled child up for adoption, the pain often lingers. *Newsweek,* pp. 77–78, 80.
U.S. House of Representatives Select Committee on Children, Youth and Families. (1989). *No place to call home: Discarded children in America*. Washington, DC: Author.

Dedicated to my sons,
Alexander Lee Baker
and
Spencer Benjamin Baker

When There's
No Place Like Home

I

IMPACT OF SOCIAL AND LEGAL POLICIES ON PLACEMENT

The chapters in Part I outline the mechanisms by which laws and social policies combine to produce the problem of children without homes. We include detailed descriptions of the legal processes resulting in out-of-home placement, as well as the social and economic factors leading to homelessness of entire families and its outcome. We also describe the unique problems of child abuse and childhood mental illness. We see that sometimes social and legal policies allow children to be deprived of their natural home, while the system is unable to ensure their return to a home.

1

Intervention versus Interference
The Role of the Courts in Child Placement

Sharon Gross Portwood and N. Dickon Reppucci

Although no exact figures are available as to the number of children whose custody or placement is decided by the courts because of abuse, neglect, divorce, delinquency, health care problems, or any number of situations that threaten the continuation of the child's current living arrangements, this number is clearly in the hundreds of thousands, if not millions (Children's Defense Fund, 1991). It is within the context of child placement that the legal system faces some of its most difficult challenges.

After outlining the basic framework that guides the courts in resolving issues concerning children, this chapter examines four specific contexts in which the courts are called on to make child placement determinations: abuse and neglect, custody after divorce, commitment in cases of mental illness, and juvenile delinquency. Although not exhaustive, relevant legal authorities, current guiding principles, and issues that continue to plague the courts in each of these arenas are discussed. In addition, some empirical findings, along with their implications for future directions in the legal system, are presented.

AN OVERVIEW OF TRADITIONAL LEGAL PERSPECTIVES

At the base of any legal dilemma involving the removal of a child from his or her "home" (defined for purposes of this chapter as "custody by the child's natural or adopted parent or parents") is an attempt to balance the needs of the child, the parents' right to family autonomy, and the interests of the state as a protector of children. Many commentators (e.g., Crosby & Reppucci, 1990; Reppucci, Weithorn, Mulvey, & Monahan, 1984) have highlighted the potential for unsatisfactory outcomes that characterizes this delicate balancing test and that, in many cases, requires that the interests of at least one entity—child, family, or state—be subordinated to the rights of another. Historically, the rights of the child have yielded to the paternalistic and protectivist roles of parent and state. Nonetheless, it is appropriate to view the legal framework within which the placement needs of children are addressed as triangular, with the interests of the state, families, and children occupying potentially competing positions. These different interests can be identified as the *parens patriae,* family libertarianism, and children's rights perspectives, each of which merits additional analysis before examining the specific issues presented in different placement dilemmas.

Parens Patriae

The more traditional view clearly favors the interests of the state through the *parens patriae* doctrine. The right of the state to intervene in the family is derived from its police power, through which it is empowered to act to promote the public welfare, and the concept of *parens patriae,* which is the limited power of the state "to protect or promote the welfare of certain individuals, including children, who lack the capacity to act in their own best interest" (Rosenberg & Hunt, 1984, p. 85). The exercise of the *parens patriae* power is limited by three principles: 1) *parens patriae* is founded on the presumption that children do not possess the mental competence and maturity of adults; 2) before intervening in the family, the state must establish that a child's parents or guardians are incapable of or unwilling to care for the child; and 3) the state's power should be exercised solely to promote the best interests of the child (Mnookin, 1978). Thus, while attempting to afford due consideration to the "interests" of the child, the state nonetheless defers to the "rights" of the parents.

Family Libertarianism

Under the principle of family libertarianism, the privacy and autonomy of the family is recognized as the paramount right. The fundamental right of parents is based on the premise that the private, autonomous family is the institution best suited to care for children (Reppucci & Crosby, 1993). This premise arises from two further presumptions:

1) parents will act in their child's best interests, and 2) parents have the maturity, experience, and judgment that a child lacks (Reppucci & Crosby, 1993).

In large part, the U.S. Supreme Court has emphasized the family libertarian perspective during this century. In 1923, in *Meyer v. Nebraska,* the Court first alluded to the right of parents to control the upbringing of their children free of state interference. In this case, the Court held unconstitutional a Nebraska statute that limited the teaching of a foreign language in part because it interfered with the right of parents to control the education of their children. Two years later, in *Pierce v. Society of Sisters* (1925), a unanimous Court invalidated an Oregon law requiring parents to educate their children in public schools. Relying on *Meyer,* the Court concluded that the Constitution protected the parents' right to "direct the upbringing and education of children under their control." Thus, the Court recognized as a guiding principle that the custody, care, and nurture of children resides first with the parents, "whose primary function and freedom include preparation for obligations the state can neither supply nor hinder." These early decisions set the stage for the Court's continuing position of respecting the private realm of family life and holding it largely free from state interference.

Although the parental right is clearly established, the extent of the right remains subject to debate. In *Prince v. Massachusetts* (1944), which arose from a conflict between the Massachusetts child labor laws and the child's alleged exercise of her religious convictions in dispensing literature for the Jehovah's Witnesses, the Court was required to reassess its strict noninterventionist position and again invoke the state's *parens patriae* power. Giving due deference to its decision in *Pierce,* the Court nonetheless held that neither religious nor parental rights are unlimited. In so doing, the Court espoused the principle that the power of the state to control the activities of children is broader than its power as to adults. The state may, under circumstances in which it is necessary to protect the child's well-being, exercise its *parens patriae* power to restrict parental control. Although there is no general rule authorizing the government to supersede parental authority, the state also may have some control over parental discretion when a child's physical or mental health is threatened. Under its *parens patriae* power, the state can intervene to protect the child when the parents cannot or will not.

Children's Rights

Recent commentators have suggested that the more traditional views, which favor primary roles for the family and the state, fail to acknowledge the rights of the children themselves. Criticizing America's apparent indifference toward children's rights, Judge Polier stated:

> While our rhetoric reflects the American mythology about children as our most precious resource, our actions conform to a pathology which allows blindness to deprivations that brand children with the stigmata of feeling neither wanted nor needed. It is this pathological blindness that alienates and destroys the capacity in children for caring for others or having hope for themselves. (1973, p. xiii)

This rationale has given rise to an advocacy movement in support of a children's rights perspective, which has gained momentum in the past decade.

Although the concept of children's rights can encompass many ideas, Wadlington, Whitebread, and Davis (1983) have suggested three possible definitions: 1) "the extension of broad freedom of personal action and decision making to children," 2) the "increased protection from governmental intrusion in matters of parental (and thus family) decision making for children," and 3) the formulation of "statements of fundamental principles to be used judicially as guidelines for interpreting or applying various laws or procedures" (p. 47). Taking a slightly different approach, Melton (1987b) divided contemporary theories within the children's rights movement into the following categories: 1) "kiddie libbers," who view children as more like than unlike adults and thus favor policies to protect the privacy and autonomy of minors; 2) "child savers," who believe that the state must become more involved to ensure children's well-being; and 3) those who assume that children are vulnerable, incompetent, and dependent and thus need "seemingly omnipotent parents for healthy development" (p. 347). Some proponents of a children's rights approach urge that all rights afforded adults should likewise be extended to children. Although several cases, starting with the landmark *In re Gault* (1967), have guaranteed children some due process rights and therefore designated them as individuals with legal standing, the Supreme Court has hesitated to adopt the view that children should be afforded rights equal to those of adults. The Court believes that, because of their age and lack of experience, children are unable or incapable of protecting their own best interests (Reppucci & Crosby, 1993). Nonetheless, the increasing popularity of the children's rights approach demands that, as the courts address issues that will affect the placement of children, they attempt to identify and respect not only the family's rights to privacy and autonomy and the state's interest in protecting its young citizens, but also the rights of the individual child.

ABUSE AND NEGLECT

Perhaps in no context is the goal of protecting the rights of the individual child more pronounced than in cases of alleged abuse and neglect. Although most cases of suspected abuse or neglect, like other placement determinations, are resolved without court intervention (Miller, Shireman, Burke, & Brown, 1982), 15%–20% of child protection cases do prompt action by the courts (Rosenberg & Hunt, 1984).[1] Cases of child maltreatment may be pursued in either the criminal or civil courts; however, because the court becomes involved in the placement of the child only in the context of civil intervention, this chapter limits its discussion of abuse and neglect to civil proceedings.

Definition of Child Maltreatment

When adjudicating cases involving allegations of abuse or neglect, the courts are presented with the threshold issue of what, in fact, constitutes abuse (Crosby & Reppucci, 1990). The definition of child maltreatment may encompass physical abuse and neglect (Wolfe, 1987), emotional abuse and neglect (Garbarino, Guttman, & Seely, 1986), and sexual abuse (Haugaard & Reppucci, 1988). Among these components, *neglect* is a particularly vague term because it is difficult to differentiate childrearing patterns that are harmful from those that are simply different from more generally accepted styles (Rosenberg & Hunt, 1984). This definitional dilemma is compounded by the Supreme Court's repeated rulings that parents have a fundamental right to raise their children as they see fit.

State laws provide varying degrees of assistance to the courts in defining abuse and neglect. Some states have adopted a broad definition of child abuse that attempts to encompass all potential forms of abuse. For example, the Pennsylvania statutes, § 6303, define child abuse as:

> Serious physical or mental injury which is not explained by the available medical history as being accidental, sexual abuse, sexual exploitation or serious physical neglect of a child under 18 years of age if the injury, abuse or neglect has been caused by the acts or omissions of the child's parents or by a person responsible for the child's welfare, or any individual residing in the same home as the child, or a paramour of the child's parents.

Other states have chosen to delineate specific types of abusive behavior. For example, § 34.02 of the Texas Family Code includes within the

---

[1] Given the estimated 1 million children who experienced abuse or neglect in 1986, according to data from the U.S. Department of Health and Human Services, approximately 150,000–200,000 cases reach the courts annually (Children's Defense Fund, 1991).

definition of abuse not only physical injury, but also mental or emotional injury resulting in impaired growth, development, or psychological functioning; causing or permitting the child to be in an injurious situation; and numerous specific acts of sexual abuse. Texas takes a similar approach in defining neglect, including within the ambit of that term placing or failing to remove a child from a potentially harmful situation, failing to provide adequate medical care for a child, and failing to provide a child with adequate food, clothing, or shelter (Texas Family Code, § 34.012).

The difficulty in resolving the numerous definitional ambiguities that plague child maltreatment cases is perhaps best illustrated by the fact that legal and mental health professionals disagree not only as to the evidence needed to prove abuse, but also as to the point at which state intervention in the family is justifiable (Rosenberg & Hunt, 1984). In a study of multiple professional groups' definitions of what constitutes sexual abuse, Atteberry-Bennett (1987) found several differences, with mental health professionals labeling more acts, such as parents being nude in front of 5- and 10-year-olds, as sexual abuse than did legal professionals.

Given the discrepancies between definitions held by different professional groups working with abused and neglected children, it appears that laypersons will have at least an equally difficult time in identifying certain acts as abuse or neglect. Nonetheless, every state now has laws that require certain persons to report suspected child maltreatment (Aber & Reppucci, 1992). These statutes detail who must or may report suspected incidences of child maltreatment, what must be reported, whether certain information qualifies as a privileged communication, sanctions for failure to report, and reporting procedures. Significant debate has been generated concerning mandatory versus permissive reporting. For example, attorneys may be prohibited by the ethical guidelines adopted by their state to ensure attorney–client confidentiality from reporting cases of suspected abuse or neglect (see *Model Rules of Professional Conduct,* § 1.6). Each state has adopted its own professional guidelines—in various forms.

Emergency Placement Determinations

Once an allegation of child maltreatment is levied, state legislation typically provides that, under certain circumstances, abused or neglected children may be taken into custody immediately. Despite the courts' continuing position favoring family autonomy and a policy of nonintervention, the parents' interest in keeping the family unit intact is not a clearly established right where there exists a reasonable suspicion that a parent may be abusing a child (*Myers v. Morris,* 1987). The guiding principle in such emergency placement is that the option selected should constitute the least drastic alternative and that every effort should be made to prevent removal and support continued placement in the home.

Although at least some courts have recognized that a child's rights may outweigh those of his or her parents in cases of suspected abuse, the courts have declined to impose a proactive duty on the state to protect children from their parents. Instead, in *DeShaney v. Winnebago County Department of Social Services* (1989), the Supreme Court expressly limited a state's responsibility for protecting a child from potential abuse.

The facts of *DeShaney* were extremely compelling. Four-year-old Joshua DeShaney was beaten so badly by his father that he lapsed into a life-threatening coma. Although he survived, Joshua sustained severe brain damage, necessitating his placement in an institution for persons with profound retardation. Despite repeated complaints and a belief that the petitioner was being beaten by his father, the Department of Social Services took no action to remove the boy from his father's custody. The petitioner alleged that, through its failure to intervene "to protect him against a risk of violence at his father's hands of which [Social Services] knew or should have known," the Department violated his liberty and due process guarantees under the Fourteenth Amendment (489 U.S. at 193). The Court rejected this contention, holding that the due process clause is designed to protect citizens from unreasonable deprivations of life, liberty, and property by the state—not by other private citizens. The court added that the due process clause is not intended "as a guarantee of certain minimal levels of safety and security"; it imposes no affirmative obligation on the state to ensure that individuals are not harmed by others.

In response, the petitioner further argued that, even if the requirements of the due process clause did not obligate the state to protect individuals from potentially harmful acts of private citizens, as well as the government, an affirmative duty to provide adequate protective services to the general public may nonetheless flow from "certain 'special relationships' created or assumed by the State with respect to particular individuals" (489 U.S. at 197). Although there was no dispute that the state was aware of the danger to Joshua and had specifically undertaken to protect him in the years prior to the incident giving rise to this suit, the Court nonetheless rejected the petitioner's argument:

> That the State once took temporary custody of Joshua does not alter the analysis, for when it returned him to his father's custody, it placed him in no worse position than that in which he would have been had it not acted

at all; the State does not become the permanent guarantor of an individual's safety by having once offered him shelter. (489 U.S. at 201)

Although, under *DeShaney,* the state has no constitutional duty to protect children from abuse, the individual states may place responsibility for such a failure to act on the state and its officials by enacting appropriate provisions in tort law.

Courtroom Proceedings

Once charges of abuse or neglect have been made and legal proceedings instituted, two critical concerns arise regarding the child's role in the courtroom proceedings: 1) Is the child competent to testify? and 2) Will testifying result in trauma to the child? These concerns have spawned many recent reforms in courtroom procedures in an effort to protect children and improve the reliability of their testimony.

A discussion of the research in the area of children's competence to testify, as well as the suggestibility of children, is beyond the scope of this chapter (Ceci & Bruck, 1993; Doris, 1991; Goodman & Bottoms, 1993; Haugaard & Reppucci, 1988; Melton, 1985); however, it is now widely accepted that most children who can contribute to a resolution of relevant issues should not be disqualified from testifying solely on the basis of age (Weithorn, 1984). In fact, the legal presumption has shifted from viewing children as incompetent to viewing them as competent, with the question of credibility going to the jury (Perry & Wrightsman, 1991). In those states that continue to require an initial showing of competence, factors such as the child's age, understanding and appreciation of the oath to tell the truth, mental capacity to recall an event independently, and ability to articulate such recollections and answer questions concerning the event are used to determine whether the child's testimony will be admitted (Bulkley, 1988; Weithorn, 1984).

In part because of the increasing number of children appearing as witnesses in cases of alleged abuse or neglect, the courts and legislatures have instituted several procedural reforms aimed at overcoming objections that the stress of testifying in a courtroom may equal the trauma of the abuse itself (Crosby & Reppucci, 1990). These reforms typically focus on limiting face-to-face contact between the defendant and the child. However, any procedure must balance the need to protect child witnesses against the defendant's Sixth Amendment right to confront witnesses (*Ohio v. Roberts,* 1980). With this potential conflict in mind, numerous states have adopted the use of two-way closed circuit television, admission of certain (out-of-court) hearsay statements, and the use of videotaped statements in lieu of live child testimony (Crosby & Reppucci, 1990).

Although, in its first case regarding the constitutionality of procedures designed to protect alleged victims of child abuse by limiting face-to-face confrontation with the alleged perpetrator (*Coy v. Iowa*, 1989), the Supreme Court rejected an Iowa statute providing that the witness be separated from the defendant by a screen, subsequent cases have supported courtroom reforms. In *Maryland v. Craig* (1990), the Court sanctioned the use of testimony by an alleged victim via one-way closed circuit television. Writing for the majority, Justice O'Connor made direct reference to the *amicus curiae* brief filed by the American Psychological Association and the literature cited in it to support her finding that the state does have a compelling interest in protecting child witnesses from physical and psychological harm. The Court held that the interest of alleged child abuse victims may outweigh the defendant's Sixth Amendment rights provided there is a showing that the particular witness requires special protection. Although *Maryland v. Craig* and its progeny suggest that the Court is amenable to the use of certain procedural safeguards where child victims are required to testify, these holdings may be limited to cases of *sexual* abuse, because the courts have yet to address these issues in a case of strictly physical abuse or neglect.

Placement After Trial

When the court determines that a parent or guardian has abused or neglected a child, several alternative placements may be considered. For example, the court may allow the child to remain with the parents subject to certain conditions or may transfer legal custody to the grandparents, other relatives, a child welfare agency, public welfare, or social services. Transfer of custody to a public service agency typically results in the child's being placed in temporary or permanent foster care. In the most extreme cases, the court may pursue termination of parental rights.

Termination of Parental Rights

The Supreme Court has recognized a fundamental right of parenthood. As noted, the Court has refused to sanction state restrictions on family autonomy through cases such as *Meyer v. Nebraska, Pierce v. Society of Sisters, Wisconsin v. Yoder* (1972), and *Stanley v. Illinois* (1972). However, the Court also has recognized that parental rights are not absolute. In extreme cases in which parental rights conflict with the best interests of the child, parental rights may even be terminated.

In termination cases, despite the circumstances or consequences to the parents, who may themselves be victims of circumstances beyond their control, the best interests of the child are paramount. However, because parental rights are deemed fundamental, they cannot be terminated absent a showing of a "compelling" state interest. Based on Supreme Court holdings that family autonomy is protected from state intervention by the Fourteenth Amendment, courts will apply a "strict scrutiny" test to any termination standard. This test requires that any infringement on the right of family autonomy must serve an "important" state interest.

Under *Santosky v. Kramer* (1982), clear and convincing evidence is required for a termination of parental rights. (At the time of the Court's opinion in *Santosky,* 15 states already required a showing of "clear and convincing evidence" or its equivalent by statute.) Citing its prior opinions demonstrating a recognition "that freedom of personal choice in matters of family life is a fundamental liberty interest protected by the Fourteenth Amendment," the Court nonetheless held that parents' fundamental interest in the "care, custody, and management" of their children "does not evaporate simply because they have not been model parents or have lost temporary custody of their child to the State" (455 U.S. at 753).

The deference afforded parents in termination proceedings is not without limitation. In *Lassiter v. Department of Social Services* (1981), the Supreme Court held that the Constitutional guarantee to due process does not mandate that counsel be appointed to represent indigent parents in every proceeding to terminate the parental relationship. In *Lassiter,* the Department of Social Services had petitioned the court to terminate the petitioner's parental rights, alleging that she had not had any contact with her child for over 2 years and had left her son in consecutive foster care during that period without making any substantial progress to correct the conditions that led to his removal from the home, to show a positive response to the assistance offered by the Department of Social Services, or to develop any constructive plan for the future of her child. Ms. Lassiter, who was serving a sentence for second-degree murder, made no attempts to obtain counsel to represent her at the hearing and later urged that the trial court had erred in not requiring the state to appoint counsel for her as an indigent because the due process clause of the Fourteenth Amendment entitled her to the assistance of counsel. The court noted:

> This Court's decisions have by now made plain beyond the need for multiple citation that a parent's desire for and right to "the companionship, care, custody, and management of his or her children" is an important interest that "undeniably warrants deference and, absent a powerfully countervailing interest, protection." [Citation omitted.] Here, the State has sought not simply to infringe upon that interest, but to end it. If the State prevails, it will have worked a unique kind of deprivation. [Citation

omitted.] A parent's interest in the accuracy and justice of the decision to terminate his or her parental status is, therefore, a commanding one. (452 U.S. at 27)

Noting that, because of its own "urgent interest in the welfare of the child," the state shares parents' interests in accurate judicial decisions, the Court reasoned that the interest of both parties might be served best by a hearing in which both were represented by counsel. Although the state has an additional interest in judicial economy (i.e., avoiding unnecessary time and expense in the resolution of legal conflicts), this pecuniary interest does not outweigh the private interests at issue. Nonetheless, the state's interests must be afforded some consideration. Thus, constitutional requirements may be satisfied in parental rights termination proceedings even when some procedures are mandated only on a case-by-case basis, rather than generally.

One of the primary bases for seeking a termination of parental rights is to emancipate the child for legal adoption. In essence, dissolution of the biological family is simply a means of placing the child in an intact family. Because adoption is controlled by the laws of the various states, a full discussion of the procedures and guidelines is beyond the scope of this chapter. However, it should be noted that, although the courts may serve as an overseer in adoption proceedings, primary determinations of parental fitness have been left largely to social service agencies.

A recent potential development in the context of adoption and termination of parental rights merits note. In the 1992 case of *In re Gregory K.*, a Florida state court allowed a 12-year-old boy to institute suit to have his mother's parental rights terminated in order that he could be adopted by his foster family. This case was significant in that it represented a recognition of children's legal standing to petition the court to make a placement determination, at least in cases of alleged neglect. Although widely touted by the media as a step in advancing the cause of children's rights, the court's ruling is not binding on other state or federal courts. Nonetheless, the apparently favorable public response may support further movement toward allowing children to play a greater role in their own placement determinations.

Summary

The courts face many challenges when presented with cases involving abuse and neglect. A court initially must determine whether *any* intervention, and the violation of family autonomy that it entails, is merited. This decision is complicated by the difficulty in distinguishing between acts or omissions that should be characterized as abuse or neglect and those that simply represent more nontraditional parenting behavior. When the court does decide to act, it will continue to give great deference to the rights of the parents, attempting to maintain the child's placement in the home whenever possible. However, recent cases have held that, when there is a threat of danger to the child, his or her rights may supersede the parents' right to privacy. Despite several encouraging steps toward protecting children, the courts have remained hesitant to place the rights of children before those of parents or other adults accused of abuse or neglect.

CUSTODY AFTER DIVORCE

Whenever a family is separated by divorce, the courts are involved to some extent in the placement of the family's children. Again, there is a triangular framework of competing interests—the state's interest in protecting the child, the parents' right to raise their child as they deem appropriate and to confront all relevant evidence, and the child's interest in contributing to a decision as to his or her placement (Scott, Reppucci, & Aber, 1988). In the majority of cases, the court's role is simply to sanction the agreement of the parents. However, with the increase in the number of fathers asserting a right to custody, the courts are faced with a growing number of cases in which they must determine appropriate custody arrangements. It is estimated that 60% of all divorces involve children (Emery, 1988), and that, of these, 10%–15% give rise to contested custody cases (Reppucci, 1984). Although this percentage may appear to be small, when absolute numbers are considered, it becomes clear that a large number of children are involved in this form of legal proceeding. In these contested cases, the ambiguous standard of "the best interests of the child" continues to be the most widely used approach (Reppucci, 1984). Although this standard has been widely criticized, the legal system as a whole has yet to identify or adopt a more appropriate test.

Initially, the American legal system relied on English common law, which included the doctrine of *parens patriae,* when making custody determinations (Weithorn, 1987). This body of law included a paternal preference rule, which arose from a belief that the father was the best custodian of the child because of his superior ability to provide for the child's economic support (Derdeyn, 1976). Not until the early 1900s did this rule yield to a new philosophy, the tender years presumption (Reppucci, 1984), based on the idea that, during their youth, children should be placed in the custody of the parent who could best provide the extraordinary care required to ensure the child's proper development into a productive adult. In most cases, this parent was believed to be the mother. Although both the paternal and maternal preference presumptions provided judges with an unambiguous standard for determining custody, by the 1960s they had begun to be replaced by the more flexible best interests standard, under which both parents are afforded more equal protection (Freed & Walker, 1988). Although the previous standards were based on a presumption that they served the best interests of the child, the new standard expressly dictated that the child's welfare was to be the primary consideration in custody disputes.

Factors Affecting Custody Decisions

In an attempt to clarify the admittedly vague requirements of the best interests standard and to effect more consistent application, the Uniform Marriage and Divorce Act was proposed in 1970. Under § 402 of the Act, when applying the best interests standard, the court is to consider all relevant factors, including: 1) the wishes of the child's parents; 2) the wishes of the child; 3) the child's interaction and interrelationship with his or her parents, siblings, and other individuals who may have a significant effect on the child's best interests; 4) the child's adjustment to his or her home, school, and community; and 5) the mental and physical health of all the individuals involved. The court is not to consider any conduct of a proposed custodian that does not affect his or her relationship with the child. Although many states have adopted either the Uniform Act or a modified version of it, others (e.g., Arkansas) rely solely on case law to set forth the criteria for making a custody determination. These various criteria offer some guidance to judges, but they fail to outline the weights to be given to the various factors, and, thus, application of the best interests standard remains largely a matter of judicial discretion.

Despite the courts' continued adherence to the best interests standard, in the past decade, a growing trend has developed toward the consideration of psychological, as well as biological, bonds in defining family relationships (Rosenberg & Hunt, 1984). In their book *Beyond the Best Interests of the Child,* Goldstein, Freud, and Solnit (1973) proposed an alternative set of standards based on psychoanalytical concepts. The key to this approach is to place the child in the least detrimental alternative by focusing on three criteria aimed at determining which adult is or is most likely to become the child's "psychological parent." These criteria are: 1) a determination that ensures continuity of the child's relationship with his or her psychological parent, 2) an adjudication that proceeds according to the child's sense of time, and 3) the state's inability to supervise interpersonal relationships and the limits of making long-term assessments of the future needs of children and parents. Although this approach is notably influential, criticisms include its lack of validity, its basis in theory rather than empirical findings, and its failure to address conflicting evidence (Reppucci, 1984).

While adhering to traditional standards in making custody determinations, the courts have shown a trend toward increased consideration of child preference, especially among adolescents. To date, 46 states have made provisions through statutory or case law for children to participate in custody determinations. However, the merits of such a system remain in dispute (Reppucci, 1984). Some authors note that having to choose between two parents may cause a child to feel guilty or depressed and may subject him or her to pleading and manipulation by the parents (Franklin & Hibbs, 1980). In contrast, Wolman and Taylor (1991) found that some aspects of a custody dispute actually may benefit the child through the development of adaptive coping strategies that maintain or enhance the child's view of both self and family. Zimring (1982) has suggested that older children in particular may benefit from participating in the custody decision through increased self-esteem and feelings of autonomy.

Although the state legislatures have adopted various standards in regard to the weight to be afforded a child's custodial preference, the emergent theme in recent appellate court opinions is that, in order for the preference to be meaningful to the courts, a child must be "of sufficient age and mental capacity to form a rational judgment" or "an intelligent choice," or the child's preference must be founded on "sound reasoning" (Weithorn, 1984, citing Siegel & Hurley, 1977). Interestingly, however, the law has been more clear in articulating which factors do *not* provide an acceptable basis for a reasonable preference than in identifying which types of reasons are sufficient (Weithorn, 1984).

A series of studies by Barnard and Jensen (1985) and Lowery (1981, 1984) indicate that the most important factors in determining custody include mental stability of each parent, each parent's sense of responsibility to the child, each parent's ability to provide a stable community environment, and the biological relationship when one parent is a stepparent, with judges affording increasing weight to children's preferences.

From a strictly legal standpoint, the fundamental determination in the child's expressing a preference is whether he or she recognizes the nature and consequences of the question being asked, particularly when young children are involved. Thus, it is not surprising that judges appear to accord different roles to the child's preference depending on the child's age. In a survey of attitudes and practices, Virginia juvenile and circuit court judges reported that the wishes of children age 6 and under were irrelevant to the custody decision, although it was common practice to ascertain the preferences of older children (Scott et al., 1988). In fact, Scott et al. (1988) found that 90% of judges surveyed believed that the preference of a child age 14 or older was either dispositive or extremely important, as did 54% who gave this same rank to the preferences of children ages 10–13. The judges suggested that older children should have the freedom to associate with the parent of their choice and that their preferences were stronger and more mature.

In evaluating children's competence to participate in custody decisions, Garrison (1991) asked domestic relations judges to compare the preferences and supporting reasons of children ages 9–14 to those of a group of 18-year-olds. She found that 14-year-olds were viewed as being as competent as 18-year-olds under the applicable legal standards and that 9-year-olds were similar to controls on two of the criterion measures. Although the fact that all the children rated came from intact families may limit the generalizability of these results, Garrison concluded that her results provide empirical support for granting significant weight to the custodial preferences of children ages 14 and older. However, only Georgia has adopted a statute dictating that the preference of a 14-year-old shall be controlling.

Assuming that children's preferences should be obtained, there are many unanswered questions regarding the procedural options available to judges when ascertaining a child's custodial preference. Typically, these determinations are made based on a *voir dire* examination or interview of the prospective child witness by the judge (Weithorn, 1984). However, the relative merit of this practice remains the subject of debate. For example, some have questioned whether the judge should interview the child or whether this task should be given to the attorneys or mental health professionals (Benedek & Benedek, 1979). Other questions include where the interview should be conducted (e.g., in the courtroom, in the judge's chambers); who should be allowed to be present (e.g., the parents' attorneys, the court reporter); and when the child's preference should be ascertained (e.g., pretrial, posttrial).

One alternative to the emotionally wrenching dilemma of choosing between parents is joint custody. For the past 15 years, the judiciary has moved toward an assumption of joint custody, which endows both parents with equal power and authority in their children's upbringing and general welfare, because it appears to be in the best interests of the child (Reppucci, 1984). Although many observers now recognize that joint custody is not a panacea for all, it does provide a previously unused option.

Finally, several commentators (Gendon, 1975; Inker & Peretta, 1971; Podell, 1973) have proposed that the appointment of a guardian *ad litem,* an attorney who would provide independent representation for the child, could serve to ensure that all considerations regarding the best interests of the child would be presented to the court and that the child would be the focus of the custody decision. Several states (e.g., Wisconsin) have adopted statutes mandating the appointment of a guardian *ad litem* in contested custody cases. In fact, there is some authority (*Mathews v. Eldridge,* 1962) to suggest that children have a constitutional right to representation in these cases under the Constitution's Fifth and Fourteenth Amendments. However, some (e.g., Speca, 1980) have objected to independent representation, noting that the guardian *ad litem*'s recommendations may prejudice the judge and add to the tension between the parties by increasing the adversarial nature of the process.

Summary

Typically, the courts will intervene in custody decisions only when the parents have failed to reach an agreement and the court must step in as *parens patriae.* Having discarded prior presumptions of paternal and then maternal preference, the courts now adhere to the "best interests of the child" standard in making custody determinations. Attempts to elucidate this standard have met with only limited success as custody continues to remain a discretionary matter with the judge. This discretion encompasses not only the final determination, but also the procedures to be used in developing the relevant factors to be considered, particularly the preference of the child. Although the limited research has offered some insight into the process, no empirical data exist regarding the important psychological issues surrounding custodial preference—more particularly, the child's capacity to participate in custody determinations, the effects of participation on the child's well-being, and the appropriate procedures to use in ascertaining the child's preference.

COMMITMENT IN CASES OF MENTAL ILLNESS

When addressing issues involving minors and mental health, again one of the primary concerns is competence. In the context of voluntary mental health treatment, the question is whether the potential benefits of mental health treatment outweigh children's or adolescents' possible incompetence to make such decisions; when involuntary commitment is at issue, the question becomes whether the potential benefits of treatment outweigh constitutional guarantees against deprivation of liberty without due process (Crosby & Reppucci, 1992).

Voluntary Commitment

The Supreme Court has not addressed whether minors have a constitutional right to seek mental health services that supersedes the right of parents; however, the Court's precedents on abortion and contraception indicate that adolescents may have a qualified right to seek psychological counseling without obtaining the consent of their parents (Crosby & Reppucci, 1992). At present, several states provide for juveniles' admission to inpatient mental health services without parental consent—provided the child is at least 14 years of age (see Colorado Revised Statutes, § 27-10-103; Massachusetts General Laws Ann., Ch. 123.10; New York Mental Hygiene Law, § 9.13). The rationale underlying these statutes appears to be that the potential benefit of these services, along with the fear that adolescents will not seek services if they are forced to inform their parents, outweighs any rights of the parents to control the provision of services to their children (Melton, 1978). However, the fundamental question remains as to whether children are capable of making such a weighty decision.

Melton (1980) found that seventh graders believe that they should have a right to seek medical help for mental health problems. Adelman, Kaser-Boyd, and Taylor (1984) examined the effect of children's participation in consent to psychotherapy on the outcome of therapy. Although this research suffers from some methodological flaws (e.g., a nonrandom sample), it does suggest that children's participation in the consent process has a positive effect on their adjustment to treatment and its final outcome.

Much of the research on minors' competence has focused on medical decision making. Overall, this research supports a finding that, although children age 10 and under are less competent than adults to make treatment decisions, adolescents age 14 and above are no less competent than adults in this context (Crosby & Reppucci, 1990). However, the research examining minors' ability to give informed consent is limited by two difficulties: 1) the lack of a clear definition of legal competence, and 2) the difficulty in confirming the null hypothesis (i.e., that there is no difference between the ability of minors and that of adults to make treatment decisions) (Crosby & Reppucci, 1990). More specifically, researchers have been limited to comparing the competence of minors to that of adults when this standard is obviously not the equivalent of that applied as a matter of law (i.e., if the standard were the level of competence of the average adult, then all adults below the mean would be incompetent).

Weithorn and Campbell (1982) concluded that minors of age 14 demonstrated a level of competence equivalent to that of adults when presented with four hypothetical treatment dilemmas (diabetes, epilepsy, depression, and enuresis) measured by four standards of competence (evidence of choice, reasonable outcome, rational reasons, and understanding). However, 9-year-old subjects appeared to be less competent than adults when standards of competency requiring understanding and a rational reasonable process were applied.

The decision-making process was examined by Lewis (1980) in the context of women awaiting the outcome of pregnancy tests. She found few age-related differences between minors ages 13–17 and adults ages 18–25 in regard to their knowledge of the law, the number and type of individuals consulted, and decision reasoning as measured by a semi-structured interview. More recent studies (Ambuel & Rappaport, 1989; Rowe, 1989) also provide no evidence to suggest that minors over age 13 are less competent than adults to consent to treatment in the pregnancy context.

Some concern as to minors' ability to consent to medical and/or mental health treatment has focused on their susceptibility to outside influences. Research by Scherer and Reppucci (1988) supports the notion that parents have a strong influence over their children's decision-making process. Parental influence significantly affected the level of confidence of subjects ages 14 and 15 in their treatment decisions; the more coercive the parental influence, the more adolescents' confidence was diminished. However, confidence was less susceptible to parental influence when the decisions were more serious (e.g., donating a kidney) and involved more significant consequences.

Many advocates for children's rights would contend that this research demonstrates that, by mid-adolescence, minors are indistinguishable from adults in decision-making capacity, and thus legal restrictions based on this assumption should be removed. Scott (1992a, 1992b) cautioned against this conclusion, noting that these studies are few in number and are limited by having been conducted in a laboratory setting under highly structured circumstances. Moreover, tests of competence under the informed consent doctrine have focused on only two aspects of cognitive functioning: the capacities for understanding and reasoning (Scott, 1992a, 1992b). Scott (1992a, 1992b) and Scott and Reppucci (1992) have proposed that a different framework, one incorporating the element of judgment, is required. However, to date, the research remains limited by this constraint.

Involuntary Commitment

Involuntary commitment of minors is "voluntary" commitment by the child's parents when he or she objects or is unable to express a competent decision regarding commitment (Crosby & Reppucci, 1990). The constitutionality of involuntary commitment of minors by parents and guardians was specifically addressed by the Supreme Court in *Parham v. J.R.* (1979). *Parham* presented the issue of what process the constitution requires be afforded to a minor when his or her parents or guardian attempt to commit the child to institutional mental health care. The majority held that an adversary proceeding was not required either before or after commitment.

The Court's language in *Parham* once again reflects the delicate balance between the interests of child, family, and state, and the Court's adherence to "the traditional presumption that the parents act in the best interests of their child" (442 U.S. at 604). The Court noted that, in challenging Georgia's procedure for the voluntary commitment of a minor to a state mental health institution, the plaintiffs placed in issue the matter in which the state had chosen to balance, both procedurally and substantively, the individual, family, and social interests involved.

In examining whether the challenged procedure violated constitutional safeguards, the Court declined to focus solely on the rights of the child, instead reasoning that the interests of the child are "inextricably linked" with the parents' interest in and obligation for the health and welfare of their child. The Court expressly rejected the plaintiffs' contention that the rights of the child are so compelling and the potential for parental abuse so great that the traditional view of the judiciary, which emphasizes the rights of the parents, should be abandoned, at least to the extent that children would be entitled to a formal adversary hearing before commitment:

> Our jurisprudence historically has reflected Western civilization concepts of the family as a unit with broad parental authority over minor children. Our cases have consistently followed that course . . . . The law's concept of the family rests on a presumption that parents possess what a child lacks in maturity, experience, and capacity for judgment required for making life's difficult decisions. More important, historically it has recognized that natural bonds of affection lead parents to act in the best interests of their children. (442 U.S. at 602)

The Court went on to note that allowing minors the right to a hearing prior to commitment raised special problems with pitting parent and child against one another in an adversarial proceeding and thus intruding into the family relationship. In addition, although a finding by a neutral factfinder is required by constitutional due process mandates, the Court deemed a staff physician to be an appropriate factfinder. Moreover, the Court reasoned that trained mental health personnel could easily assess the motivations of family members and thus detect potential abuses or "dumping." As a final justification for its decision, the Court stated that most children and adolescents are incapable of making sound judgments, particularly when the need for medical care or treatment is at issue—a finding that, at least for adolescents age 14 and older, is in direct contradiction with the research evidence previously discussed in this chapter.

Legal commentary subsequent to the Court's decision in *Parham* has strongly criticized the majority on two main grounds: 1) several of the psychological assumptions on which the Court bases its decision are questionable, and 2) the Court's decision is inconsistent with other recent holdings in the area of adolescent abortion that limited parental authority (Crosby & Reppucci, 1992). Melton (1984) set out 14 assumptions on which the majority based its opinion and noted that they were inconsistent with both the facts of the case and current psychological knowledge. Weithorn (1988) also criticized certain assumptions, such as the potential harm of adversary proceedings and the neutrality of the hospital staff. Despite these criticisms, *Parham* remains the authority. Nonetheless, some states have gone beyond these restrictions to require a formal judicial proceeding to evaluate the propriety of involuntary admission.

Because Supreme Court decisions restricting the power of the state to commit adults involuntarily have not been extended to minors, procedures in this area are governed largely by state statute. As Weithorn (1988) stated, state legislation in this area differs in:

> the extent to which [the states] require *any* type of review prior to admission of a minor beyond that performed by admitting staff; the timing of such review; whether such review is mandatory or triggered by petition; the form and process of such review and the concomitant rights of prospective patients (such as right to counsel); the substantive standards applied in such review; the role, if any, minors of various ages are given in choosing or refusing admission and in triggering any review process; and the extent to which admissions to private facilities are governed by statute. (pp. 781–782)

In simply defining mental illness, the states have adopted diverse and often inconsistent terminology. Typically, these definitions are set forth in the general mental health provisions rather than appearing as a special consideration in juvenile proceedings. Representative of these laws is the Alabama statute, Code of Alabama § 13A-6-60, which classifies an individual as "mentally defective" when he or she "suffers from a mental disease or defect which renders him [or her] incapable of appraising the nature of his [or her] conduct." Notably, the Alabama code does not include a definition for "mental disease or defect." A number of states specifically distinguish mental illness from mental retardation and substance abuse. For example, the Arizona statutes, § 8.242.01 define mental illness as a "substantial disorder of emotional processes, thought, cognition, or memory" that is not characterized as substance abuse. Other states, such as Virginia, expressly include substance abuse within the definition of mental illness, contributing further to the inconsistencies between the states' procedures.

Although the specific criteria for involuntary commitment differ from state to state, most courts require some showing that the mental illness results in the minor's posing a real and present threat of substantial harm to himself or herself or to others. However, there are many noted limitations on "dangerousness" as a criterion, such as differences in definition, discrepancies in timing and measurement source, and the court's reliance on testimony and witness demeanor (Hiday, 1981). Some states go on to require that this threat be evidenced by a recent, overt act—without, however, indicating what constitutes a "recent" act.

Parental Custody

A final area within the context of residential mental health treatment for children that merits more attention involves the practice of requiring parents to relinquish custody of their children before they can receive services. Cohen et al. (1993) found that many states continue to adhere to the practice of transferring custody to the state as a prerequisite for receiving financial aid. This practice may arise from erroneous beliefs that federal reimbursement for mental health services is available only to wards of the state or that the states' legal liability is reduced if it has legal custody of children in its care, as well as the desires of certain residential treatment providers to eliminate the necessity of involving or consulting with parents (McManus & Friesen, 1989). Cohen et al. (1993) concluded that the use of custody transfer appears to be attributable primarily to the lack of an appropriate system to provide services for minors suffering from serious emotional disorders; in the current system, scarce resources may be allocated first to children who are wards of the state.

Summary

When examining children's placement outside the home as a result of mental illness, both voluntary and involuntary commitment must be considered. Although there is no binding authority, the Supreme Court's opinions on minors' rights in regard to abortion and contraception suggest that adolescents may have a qualified right to seek psychological counseling without parental consent. Whether this proposition can be extended to minors' ability to consent to inpatient treatment is open to question. Although there are limitations, the research generally supports the position that, whereas children age 10 do not have the competence to make such treatment decisions, adolescents age 14 and above are as well equipped as adults to act in this context.

In contrast to voluntary commitment, situations in which the child is committed by his or her parents over the child's objections are governed by Supreme Court precedent. In addressing the process to be afforded a minor in this situation, *Parham v. J.R.* (1979) provides that an adversary proceeding is not required either before or after commitment, again reflecting the courts' deference to the right of family autonomy while seeking to serve the best interests of the child. Although widely criticized, *Parham* remains the law.

JUVENILE DELINQUENCY

Court intervention in child placement may be prompted by the acts of the child rather than those of the parents. The juvenile justice system is aimed at dispensing "justice" to children on a more individualized basis than its adult counterpart. Whereas adult offenders typically are incarcerated, juveniles may be incarcerated or instead subjected to a number of less restrictive placements.

The first juvenile court was created in Illinois in 1899, and was based on a philosophy of individualized justice that encompassed five fundamental notions:

1. A special court was needed for neglected, dependent, or delinquent children under the age of 16.
2. This court's purpose was to rehabilitate, not to punish, children.
3. All records and proceedings were to be confidential, in order to ensure that no stigma would result from a court appearance.
4. When incarcerated, children had to be separated from the corrupting influence of adult criminals.
5. All proceedings were to be informal (Crosby & Reppucci, 1992).

Although this policy, along with the relevant policies enunciated by the Supreme Court, may constitute the ideal rather than the actual operation of any individual court, these basic premises continue to underlie today's juvenile justice system.

In contrast with the view that adult offenders should be punished, society has chosen to apply a less stringent adjudication to minors, reasoning that they are less responsible for their "criminal" behavior.

Rather than subjecting children to the harshness of the adult criminal justice system, it was initially believed that the more informal, nonadversarial nature of juvenile "civil" proceedings was more consistent with the system's underlying purpose. As a result, during the first 60 years following their inception, juvenile courts were afforded almost unlimited discretion in making decisions concerning delinquent youth, with only the broad standard of "the best interests of the child" as a guideline. Through legislation, many states recognized that this guideline, along with the goals of rehabilitation and treatment, might require that children be diverted from the juvenile justice system to alternative programs; however, the legislatures and the courts offered little guidance as to the exact nature of the treatment contemplated and its implementation.

In *In re Gault* (1967), the Supreme Court recognized that children's constitutional rights had been sacrificed in favor of the theoretically beneficial treatment that they supposedly received within the juvenile justice system. *Gault* provided juveniles with many of the due process safeguards previously guaranteed to adult criminal defendants, including notice of charges, the right to counsel, the right to confront and cross-examine witnesses, and the privilege against self-incrimination. Three years later, the Court determined that application of the adult criminal standard of proof beyond a reasonable doubt, rather than the less stringent civil standard of proof by a preponderance of the evidence, applied to juveniles (*In re Winship*, 1970). Notably, the Court declined to guarantee to juveniles the right to trial by jury, apparently based on a concern that a jury trial would disturb the informal and confidential nature of juvenile proceedings (*McKeiver v. Pennsylvania*, 1971). Currently, the debate persists as to whether further expansion of juveniles' rights is warranted. More generally, many commentators continue to question the very nature of the system, contending that the juvenile courts' original purposes of rehabilitation and treatment have given way to a more punitive system. Such concerns regarding the effectiveness of the system are critical because many states allow a child adjudicated as delinquent to be committed to an institution for an "indefinite" period of time, which, in some jurisdictions, may exceed the mandatory sentence for an adult convicted of the same offense.

Intake and Pretrial Proceedings

The extreme variability among local jurisdictions as to the manner in which juveniles are processed on being taken into police custody makes any general statement of the factors affecting prosecution or diversion to alternative programs impossible. However, the first assessment of the culpability of the child is inevitably made by the police. Although the officer may defer to the courts, he or she still must make the initial decision of whether the child should be arrested and where the child should be taken. Once a juvenile is taken into custody, police may return the child to his or her home, a relative, or a guardian; place the child in temporary custody in an authorized facility, secure or nonsecure; detain the child in the adult jail; or, when the juvenile's demeanor suggests that he or she has mental problems, place the child in a psychiatric facility. Assuming that the officer decides to detain the child, certain minimum requirements apply to all states.

When detained for interrogation, juvenile suspects typically are treated like their adult counterparts (Crosby & Reppucci, 1992). Under *Miranda v. Arizona* (1966), defendants must be informed of their Fifth Amendment privilege against self-incrimination and their Sixth Amendment right to counsel because of the coercion inherent in the interrogation process. Despite its pronouncement in *In re Gault* (1967) that juveniles require special care when they are interrogated after arrest, the Supreme Court held in *Fare v. Michael C.* (1979) that Michael C., a 16-year-old, had made a valid waiver after having been informed of his *Miranda* rights. Using data gathered prior to the *Fare v. Michael C.* decision, Grisso (1980) examined minors' capacity to waive *Miranda* rights using three groups of juveniles, ages 10–16, all of whom were in some form of detention, and two groups of adults. Juveniles ages 15 and younger were unable to comprehend either the function or the significance of the rights when measured against both an absolute and an adult standard. Grisso concluded that juveniles should be afforded a nonwaivable right to counsel given their inadequate understanding of their rights.

All cases involving juveniles typically are initiated by filing a petition through a special juvenile justice agency. In most states, the intake officer has discretion as to whether the petition should be filed in delinquency or some alternative disposition, such as "child in need of services." It is also within the intake officer's discretion to dispose of the action informally. The complaint can be kept on file and the child's family simply notified of the incident or referred to other social service agencies. An intake officer may refuse to file a petition if there is no probable cause, the filing would not serve the best interests of the child, or some agency other than the court could deal with the matter more effectively. At this juncture, the juvenile court judge also may be consulted on a more informal basis.

When the child is noticeably suffering from some mental disturbance, the judge or other agency representatives may urge the child or parents to institute commitment proceedings. The majority of the states provide that questions concerning the mental capacity of a minor may be raised by a variety of individuals, including persons who are not connected to the court, such as social service agency representatives and parents. For example, the Alabama statutes provide that a petition for the involuntary commitment of a child to the custody of the state department of mental health as being mentally ill or having mental retardation may be made by the state, any county or municipality, any other governmental agency, or "any person," including "a parent, legal guardian or other person standing in loco parentis." In certain instances, if the parents are not willing to approve the proposed commitment, the court may issue orders compelling their cooperation. Conversely, court personnel may fail to advise parents who recognize that their child's problems extend beyond delinquency that this option is available to them. In addition, if the court itself does not make this election, it is difficult for other already overworked agencies to intervene when the court makes no provision for their compensation.

When the child has not been diverted to alternative treatment before delinquency proceedings are instituted, he or she will follow a much different route to final disposition. Although police or other detention personnel typically may impose emergency detention for 1–3 days, a judicial hearing is required for extended detention.

In *Schall v. Martin* (1984), the Supreme Court upheld the constitutionality of a New York statute that allowed the state to hold a juvenile in a detention center for up to 72 hours prior to a hearing, reasoning that, although the juvenile's interest in freedom from institutional restraint is significant, it is "qualified by the recognition that juveniles, unlike adults, are always in some form of custody" (467 U.S. at 265). Although this view has been dissected as faulty (Worrell, 1985), it remains a legal fact.

Only Alabama, Nevada, and Rhode Island have not adopted decision standards to be applied by the juvenile courts in exercising their discretion regarding continued pretrial detention. The standards adopted by the majority of the remaining states comprise three categories: detention for the protection of the juvenile, detention if the juvenile is likely to flee the jurisdiction while charges are pending, and detention if the juvenile poses a danger to the community. Continuing detention also may be deemed appropriate when adequate supervision is otherwise unavailable or the juvenile requests protection. Some states direct the court to consider the nature of the alleged offense and the child's character, reputation, prior record, community ties, and mental condition in making a detention determination.

Adjudication

At the adjudication phase, the sole question presented for determination by the court is whether the juvenile is "guilty" of the act charged. The juvenile is represented by counsel and evidence relevant to the alleged offense is presented. As in adult criminal proceedings, the traditional burden of proof in a delinquency case is reasonable doubt (*In re Winship*, 1970).

Before adjudication in the juvenile court, the prosecutor may request an investigation of whether a particular juvenile case meets the standards for transfer to the adult criminal system. Juveniles have a constitutional right to a hearing when being transferred to adult court (*Kent v. United States*, 1966). Waiver criteria include both threshold criteria (e.g., age of the offender, seriousness of the offense) and status criteria specific to the case (e.g., the juvenile's expected future dangerousness and amenability to treatment). Predominant decision standards for waiver include: 1) a finding that the juvenile is unamenable to treatment, and 2) a finding that prosecution in adult court is necessary for the protection of the community (Grisso, Tompkins, & Casey, 1988). Many states also require a finding that the juvenile is not insane and does not have mental retardation (Grisso & Conlin, 1984). Although state statutes may list a variety of factors to be considered in determining whether a juvenile may be transferred to adult court, little guidance is provided on how to evaluate these criteria. The waiver decision is still an individualized determination made by the judge.

Disposition

Assuming that a child is retained in the juvenile system and adjudicated delinquent, his or her case next proceeds to the disposition phase. At disposition, the judge must make a decision regarding a treatment plan, once again balancing the protection of society and rehabilitation of the youth. Although there are again no clear guidelines, 31 states require the judge to choose the "least detrimental alternative" when making a disposition determination (Grisso et al., 1988).

As indicated, juvenile justice relies heavily on judges' discretion. In determining the best interests of the child, judges are free to use almost any information available to reach their decisions; however, much of this information is sought from mental health professionals, who contribute their opinions as to the juvenile's needs, character, and treatment (Grisso et al., 1988). In addition to psychiatric evaluations, social workers and other agency personnel may make evaluations prior to placement. The judge eventually reviews this input and makes a final dispositive judgment.

Studies investigating discretion in juvenile justice decision making have focused on the standards used by juvenile justice personnel (Crosby & Reppucci, 1992). Grisso and colleagues (1988) identified nine factors that affect these decisions: 1) motivation to accept intervention, 2) self-reliance, 3) prior contacts with the juvenile justice system,

4) presence of serious mental disorder, 5) family's caring and resource capability, 6) opportunity for delinquent peer influence, 7) unsocialized family, 8) degree of behavioral compliance with legal settings, and 9) functioning in academic or work settings. In addition, one of the most investigated variables examined in connection with judicial decisions is race (Crosby & Reppucci, 1992). Studies by Arnold (1971) and Westendorp, Brink, Roberson, and Ortiz (1986) indicate that race may have an effect on the likelihood of a juvenile remaining in the juvenile justice system.

Most often, clinicians are called on to make determinations regarding a juvenile's amenability to treatment or likelihood of rehabilitation (Mulvey, 1984). Psychiatric evaluations are common in many jurisdictions—especially for more serious offenses and when incarceration is likely. The expertise needed to make this decision is all too often lacking. More research and evidence are needed in this area to improve the validity of amenability determinations. At present, there is a dearth of empirical evidence in regard to matching of juvenile offenders and appropriate treatment alternatives. The research on amenability has focused more on the process of decision making rather than its content (i.e., linking up outcomes and case characteristics).

Although the provision of treatment is one of the motivating principles behind the juvenile justice system, the Supreme Court has not held that juveniles have a right to treatment through the juvenile justice system. The issue of a right to treatment for juveniles involuntarily committed to state institutions through the juvenile justice system was raised in a well-known case, *Willie M. v. Hunt* (1980); however, the parties entered into a settlement and the court was not required to rule on this question. More recently, Woolard, Gross, Mulvey, and Reppucci (1992) have argued that the right to treatment for juvenile offenders with mental disorders in the least restrictive, most appropriate setting should be made explicit in case and statutory law.

Monitoring of Placement and Service Provision

Once the court has developed a treatment plan for a juvenile and put it into place in the dispositional hearing, the issue remains as to what role the court should assume after its order has been entered. Historically, the juvenile court's role has been that of *parens patriae*. Many commentators suggest that the court should continue to prescribe interventions after disposition as an all-knowing parent substitute; others urge that the court should revert to a more administrative function, acting to ensure that other agencies are meeting prescribed standards of care.

The ultimate issue is the extent of judicial authority to control how an agency treats children and families after disposition. If the court does not retain the power of review or the ability to change placement, the court's only alternative may be to terminate the grant of custody to a particular agency. To address the issue of whether a prescribed treatment has "failed," some states require continued judicial review of juvenile court placements. For example, Arizona requires review by the court every 60 days after a child is committed. In an intriguing case, *In the Matter of A.A.I.* (1984), an appellate court for the District of Columbia determined that, when the Department of Human Services fails to execute a treatment plan mandated by the court, the juvenile court has the authority to change the original placement order. Only when the original order is met by the designated department does the court relinquish authority to make a new disposition. Thus, some courts have recognized not only a right, but a duty to continue to monitor the course of juveniles' treatment.

Summary

Children entering the juvenile justice system may follow several alternative routes. Some may be diverted to treatment outside the juvenile justice system, whereas others are transferred to adult criminal court. Those children who remain within the system will move through the adjudication and disposition phases, which afford a wide range of discretion to the individual judge. The limited existing research indicates that there are different orientations toward the juvenile justice system that may influence discretionary decisions; race may have an effect on the probability of a juvenile's remaining in the juvenile justice system; and the relationship between the complaining party and the juvenile may affect the outcome of the case (Crosby & Reppucci, 1992).

CONCLUSIONS AND RECOMMENDATIONS

The issue of placement of children may arise in a number of legal contexts, including proceedings that arise from abuse and neglect, divorce and custody determination, mental health and commitment, and juvenile delinquency. In each of these contexts, the courts strive to balance the rights of the state, parents, and children while serving the best interests of the child. The success that the legal system has achieved in this regard remains the subject of debate.

An advocacy movement—fueled largely by mental health professionals—has begun to challenge the power of parents and the state over the lives of children, especially adolescents (Scott & Reppucci, 1992). The receptivity of the legal system to psychology's efforts at empirical validation of the many assumptions on which legal precedents are based has become an important and controversial issue (Reppucci & Crosby, 1993).

Although the courts continue to voice their commitment to serving the best interests of children, the lack of scientific knowledge regarding child development and family functioning makes it difficult to determine with 100% accuracy what is in the best interests of children in general and virtually impossible to determine what is in the best interest of any individual child. A determination of best interests may differ depending on whether best interests are measured from a short- or long-term perspective (Mnookin, 1978). To the extent that the laws that affect minors are based on erroneous assumptions about the nature of childhood and adolescence or reflect the judiciary's view of how children should fit into the social order, researchers can assist in exposing errors and formulating more appropriate policies (Melton, 1987a; Scott, 1992a). Arguably, however, a child's best interests are not susceptible to scientific proof because they are a matter of values rather than empirical fact (Mnookin, 1978).

Overall, actions by the courts in the past decade are suggestive of a move toward increasing consideration of children's rights. Nonetheless, there is little, if any, indication that the Supreme Court is willing to abandon more traditional views that afford great deference to the rights of parents to autonomy in raising their children. Although courts are prepared to intervene in exceptional circumstances, the basic legal assumption remains: The best place for a child is with his or her parents.

REFERENCES

Aber, M., & Reppucci, N.D. (1992). Child abuse prevention and the legal system. In D. Willis, E.W. Holden, & M. Rosenberg (Eds.), *Prevention of child maltreatment: Developmental and ecological perspectives* (pp. 249–266). New York: John Wiley & Sons.

Adelman, H.S., Kaser-Boyd, N., & Taylor, L. (1984). Children's participation in consent for psychotherapy and their subsequent response to treatment. *Journal of Clinical Child Psychology, 13,* 170–178.

Ambuel, B., & Rappaport, J. (1989, August). *Developmental change in adolescents' psychological and legal competence to consent to abortion.* Paper presented at the 97th Annual Convention of the American Psychological Association, New Orleans.

Arizona Statutes, § 8.242.01 (1993).

Arnold, W.R. (1971). Race and ethnicity relative to other factors in juvenile court dispositions. *American Journal of Sociology, 72,* 211–227.

Atteberry-Bennett, J. (1987). *Child sexual abuse: Definitions and interventions of parents and professionals.* Unpublished doctoral dissertation, University of Virginia, Charlottesville.

Barnard, C.P., & Jensen, G. (1985). Wisconsin judges and child custody criteria. *Conciliation Courts Review, 23,* 69–73.

Benedek, R.S., & Benedek, E.P. (1979). The child's preference in Michigan custody disputes. *American Journal of Family Therapy, 7,* 37–43.

Bulkley, J. (Ed.). (1988). *Child sexual abuse and the law.* Washington, DC: American Bar Association.

Ceci, S.J., & Bruck, M. (1993). The suggestibility of the child witness: A historical review and synthesis. *Psychological Bulletin, 113,* 403–439.

Children's Defense Fund. (1991). *An opinion maker's guide to children in election year 1992: Leave no child behind.* Washington, DC: Author.

Code of Alabama, § 13A-6-60 (1993).

Cohen, R., Preiser, L., Gottlieb, S., Harris, R., Baker, J., & Sonenklar, N. (1993). Relinquishing custody as a requisite for receiving services for children with serious emotional disorders: A review. *Law and Human Behavior, 17,* 121–134.

Colorado Revised Statutes, § 27-10-103 (1993).

Coy v. Iowa, 108 S.Ct. 2798, 487 U.S. 1012, 101 L.Ed.2d 857 (1989).

Crosby, C.A., & Reppucci, N.D. (1990). *Children, families and the state: Psychological research and legal policy.* Child/Adolescent Mental Health Research Review Series (No. 4). Monograph prepared for the Virginia Treatment Center for Children, 515 N. 10th Street, Richmond, VA 23201.

Crosby, C.A., & Reppucci, N.D. (1992). The legal system and adolescents. In P. Tolan & B. Cohler (Eds.), *Handbook of clinical research and practice with adolescents.* New York: John Wiley & Sons.

Derdeyn, A.P. (1976). Child custody contests in historical perspective. *American Journal of Psychiatry, 133,* 1369–1376.

DeShaney v. Winnebago County Department of Social Services, 489 U.S. 189 (1989).

Doris, J. (Ed.). (1991). *The suggestibility of children's recollections: Implications for eyewitness testimony.* Washington, DC: American Psychological Association.

Emery, R. (1988). *Marriage, divorce, and children's adjustment.* Newbury Park, CA: Sage Publications.

Fare v. Michael C., 442 U.S. 797 (1979).

Franklin, R., & Hibbs, B. (1980). Child custody in transition. *Journal of Marital and Family Therapy, 6,* 285–291.

Freed, D.J., & Walker, T.B. (1988). Family law in the fifty states. *Family Law Quarterly, 21,* 501–523.

Garbarino, J., Guttman, E., & Seely, J.W. (1986). *The psychologically battered child: Strategies for identification, assessment, and intervention.* San Francisco: Jossey-Bass.

Garrison, E.G. (1991). Children's competence to participate in divorce custody decisionmaking. *Journal of Clinical Child Psychology, 20,* 78–87.

Gendon, J.K. (1975). Separate legal representation for children: Protecting the rights and interests of minors in judicial proceedings. *Harvard Civil Rights–Civil Liberties Law Review, 11,* 565–595.

Goldstein, J., Freud, A., & Solnit, A. (1973). *Beyond the best interest of the child.* New York: Free Press.

Goodman, G., & Bottoms, B. (Eds.). (1993). *Child victims, child witnesses: Understanding and improving testimony.* New York: Guilford Press.

Grisso, T. (1980). Juveniles' capacities to waive *Miranda* rights: An empirical analysis. *California Law Review, 68,* 1134–1166.

Grisso, T., & Conlin, M. (1984). Procedural issues in the juvenile justice system. In N.D. Reppucci, L.A. Weithorn, E.P. Mulvery, & J. Monahan (Eds.), *Children, mental health and the law* (pp. 171–193). Beverly Hills, CA: Sage Publications.

Grisso, T., Tomkins, A., & Casey, P. (1988). Psychosocial concepts in juvenile law. *Law and Human Behavior, 12,* 403–436.

Haugaard, J., & Reppucci, N.D. (1988). *The sexual abuse of children: A comprehensive guide to current knowledge and intervention strategies.* San Francisco: Jossey-Bass.

Hiday, V.A. (1981). Court discretion: Application of the dangerousness standard in civil commitment. *Law and Human Behavior, 5,* 275–289.

In re Gault, 387 U.S. 1 (1967).

In re Gregory K., (1992).

In re Winship, 397 U.S. 358 (1970).

In the Matter of A.A.I., 483 A.2d 1205 (D.C. App. 1984).

Inker, M.L., & Peretta, C.A. (1971). A child's right to counsel in custody cases. *Family Law Quarterly, 5,* 108–120.

Kent v. United States, 383 U.S. 541 (1966).

Lassiter v. Department of Social Services, 452 U.S. 18 (1981).

Lewis, C. (1980). A comparison of minors' and adults' pregnancy decisions. *American Journal of Orthopsychiatry, 50,* 446–453.

Lowery, C.R. (1981). Child custody decisions in divorce proceedings: A survey of judges. *Professional Psychology, 12,* 492–498.

Lowery, C.R. (1984). The wisdom of Solomon: Criteria for child custody from the legal and clinical points of view. *Law and Human Behavior, 8,* 371–380.

Maryland v. Craig, 110 S.Ct. 3157, 497 U.S. 836, 111 L.Ed.2d 666 (1990), *on remand,* 588 A.2d 328.

Massachusetts General Laws Ann., Ch. 123.10 (1994).

Mathews v. Eldridge, 424 U.S. 319 (1976).

McKeiver v. Pennsylvania, 403 U.S. 528 (1971).

McManus, M., & Friesen, B.J. (1989). Relinquishing custody as a means of obtaining services for children who have serious mental or emotional problems. *Testimony before the United States House Ways and Means Committee.*

Melton, G.B. (1978). Children's right to treatment. *Journal of Clinical Child Psychology, 7,* 200–202.

Melton, G.B. (1980). Children's concepts of their rights. *Journal of Clinical Child Psychology, 9,* 186–190.

Melton, G.B. (1984). Developmental psychology and the law: The state of the art. *Journal of Family Law, 22,* 445–482.

Melton, G.B. (1985). Sexually abused children and the legal system: Some policy recommendations. *American Journal of Family Therapy, 13,* 61–67.

Melton, G. (1987a). *Reforming the law: Impact of child development research.* New York: Guilford Press.

Melton, G.B. (1987b). The clashing of symbols: Prelude to child and family policy. *American Psychologist, 42,* 345–354.

Meyer v. Nebraska, 262 U.S. 390 (1923).

Miller, B., Shireman, J., Burke, P., & Brown, H.F. (1982). System responses to initial reports of child abuse and neglect cases. *Journal of Social Service Research, 5,* 95–111.

Miranda v. Arizona, 384 U.S. 436 (1966).

Mnookin, R. (1978). Children's rights: Beyond kiddie libbers and child savers. *Journal of Clinical Child Psychology, 7,* 163–167.

Model Rules of Professional Conduct, Sec. 1.6 (1992).
Mulvey, E.P. (1984). Judging amenability to treatment in juvenile offenders: Theory and practice. In N.D. Reppucci, L.A. Weithorn, E.P. Mulvey, & J. Monahan (Eds.), *Children, mental health, and the law* (pp. 195–210). Beverly Hills, CA: Sage Publications.
Myers v. Morris, 810 F.2d 1437 (8th Cir. 1987), *cert. denied,* 108 S.Ct. 97, 484 U.S. 828, 98 L.Ed.2d 58.
New York Mental Hygiene Law, § 9.13 (1992).
Ohio v. Roberts, 448 U.S. 56 (1980).
Parham v. J.R., 442 U.S. 584 (1979).
Pennsylvania Statutes Ann., § 6303 (1991).
Perry, N.W., & Wrightsman, L.S. (1991). *The child witness: Legal issues and dilemmas.* Newbury Park, CA: Sage Publications.
Pierce v. Society of Sisters, 268 U.S. 510 (1925).
Podell, R.J. (1973). The "why" behind appointing guardians ad litem for children in divorce proceedings. *Marquette Law Review, 57,* 103–110.
Polier, J. (1973). Note. In A. E. Wilkerson (Ed.), *The rights of children: Emergent concepts in law and society* (pp. xiii). Philadelphia: Temple University Press.
Prince v. Massachusetts, 321 U.S. 158 (1944).
Reppucci, N.D. (1984). The wisdom of Solomon: Issues in child custody determination. In N.D. Reppucci, L.A. Weithorn, E.P. Mulvey, & J. Monahan (Eds.), *Children, mental health, and the law* (pp. 59–78). Beverly Hills, CA: Sage Publications.
Reppucci, N.D., & Crosby, C.A. (1993). Law, psychology and children: Overarching issues. *Law and Human Behavior, 17,* 1–10.
Reppucci, N.D., Weithorn, L.A., Mulvey, E.P., & Monahan, J. (Eds.). (1984). *Children, mental health, and the law.* Beverly Hills, CA: Sage Publications.
Rosenberg, M.S., & Hunt, R.D. (1984). Child maltreatment: Legal and mental health issues. In N.D. Reppucci, L.A. Weithorn, E.P. Mulvey, & J. Monahan (Eds.), *Children, mental health, and the law* (pp. 79–101). Beverly Hills, CA: Sage Publications.
Rowe, K. (1989). *The competence of minors and adults to make reasoned decisions about abortion: An empirical investigation with legal policy implications.* Unpublished doctoral dissertation, University of Virginia, Charlottesville.
Santosky v. Kramer, 455 U.S. 745 (1982).
Schall v. Martin, 467 U.S. 253 (1984).
Scherer, D.G., & Reppucci, N.D. (1988). Adolescents' capacities to provide voluntary informed consent. *Law and Human Behavior, 12,* 123–141.
Scott, E.S. (1990). Rational decision-making about marriage and divorce. *Virginia Law Review, 76,* 9–94.
Scott, E.S. (1992a). Judgment and reasoning in adolescent decision making. *Vanderbilt Law Journal, 37,* 1701–1763.
Scott, E.S. (1992b). Judgment and reasoning in adolescent decision making. *Villanova Law Review, 37,* 1607–1669.
Scott, E.S., & Reppucci, N.D. (1992, September 24). *Evaluating adolescent decisionmaking in legal contexts.* Paper presented to the MacArthur Foundation Research Network on Mental Health and the Law, Cambridge, MA.
Scott, E.S., Reppucci, N.D., & Aber, M. (1988). Children's preference in adjudicated custody decisions. *Georgia Law Review, 22,* 1035–1078.

Siegel, D.M., & Hurley, S. (1977). The role of the child's preference in custody proceedings. *Family Law Quarterly, 11,* 1–58.
Speca, J.M. (1980). Representation for children in custody disputes: Its time has come. *UMKC Law Review, 48,* 328–341.
Stanley v. Illinois, 405 U.S. 645 (1972).
Texas Family Code, § 34.02 (1994).
Uniform Marriage and Divorce Act of 1970, § 402 (1973).
Virginia Code, §§ 63.1-248.13:1, 13:2, and 13:3, (1992).
Wadlington, W., Whitebread, C.H., & Davis, S.M. (1983). *Children in the legal system: Cases and materials.* Mineola, NY: Foundation Press.
Weithorn, L.A. (1984). Children's capacities in legal contexts. In N.D. Reppucci, L.A. Weithorn, E.P. Mulvey, & J. Monahan (Eds.), *Children, mental health and the law* (pp. 25–55). Beverly Hills, CA: Sage Publications.
Weithorn, L.A. (Ed.). (1987). *Psychology and child custody determinations: Knowledge, roles, and expertise.* Lincoln: University of Nebraska Press.
Weithorn, L.A. (1988). Mental hospitalization of troublesome youth: An analysis of skyrocketing admission rates. *Stanford Law Review, 40,* 773–838.
Weithorn, L.A., & Campbell, S.B. (1982). The competency of children and adolescents to make informed treatment decisions. *Child Development, 53,* 1589–1599.
Westendorp, F., Brink, K.L., Roberson, M.K., & Ortiz, I.E. (1986). Variables which differentiate placement of adolescents into juvenile justice or mental health systems. *Adolescence, 21,* 23–37.
Willie M. v. Hunt, Civil No. C-C-79-294-M (W.D. N.C. 1980).
Wisconsin v. Yoder, 406 U.S. 205 (1972).
Wolfe, D.A. (1987). *Child abuse.* Beverly Hills, CA: Sage Publications, Inc.
Wolman, R., & Taylor, K. (1991). Psychological effects of custody disputes on children. *Behavioral Sciences and the Law, 9,* 399–417.
Woolard, J.L., Gross, S.L., Mulvey, E.P., & Reppucci, N.D. (1992). Legal issues affecting mentally disordered youth in the juvenile justice system. In J.J. Cocozza (Ed.), *Responding to the mental health needs of youth in the juvenile justice system* (pp. 91–106). Seattle: The National Coalition for the Mentally Ill in the Criminal Justice System.
Worrell, C. (1985). Pretrial detention of juveniles: Denial of equal protection masked by the *parens patriae* doctrine. *Yale Law Journal, 95,* 174–193.
Zimring, F. (1982). *The changing legal world of adolescence.* New York: Free Press.

2

The Plight of Homeless Children

Ellen L. Bassuk and Linda Weinreb

Families, composed primarily of women and children, have changed the face of homelessness in this country. Not since the Great Depression of the 1930s have large numbers of families lived on the streets and in shelters. Reflecting the increase in numbers of Americans who are extremely poor, mothers and children are the fastest growing segment among the homeless (Bassuk, 1991a). Homeless families now constitute approximately one third of the overall homeless population, according to a 30-city survey conducted by the U.S. Conference of Mayors (1990).

For most families, the origins of homelessness are complex and multidimensional. Although the routes onto the streets are as numerous as the families involved, extreme poverty combined with the lack of decent, affordable, low-income housing is the final common pathway. The widening gap between income and housing costs has left many families precariously housed (Bassuk, 1991a; Hartman & Zigas, 1991; Wright & Lam, 1987). Because female-headed families tend to be poorer than other families, they are particularly at risk in this housing market. The marked discrepancy between median rents and income or benefit levels means many families spend far more on rent and utilities than the 30% allotment that is considered feasible, and hence have little left for other essential expenditures. Any rise in expenses or fall in income may push a family onto the streets (Bassuk, 1984).

Once on the streets, the journey is perilous. In many communities, affordable housing is largely unavailable, already fragmented support

---

Portions of this chapter are adapted from Bassuk, E.L., & Gallagher, E. (1990). The impact of homelessness on children. *Child and Youth Services, 14,* 19–34.

networks are further attenuated, and shelter living is generally overcrowded, unsafe, and overwhelming—especially for mothers with young children. Daily life is unpredictable and focused largely on survival needs. The lack of routine, structure, and rules in some shelters and most welfare hotels increases the stress and chaos within the family. Even the most resilient children are traumatized by these circumstances.

It is not only the stresses related to living on the streets and in shelters that adversely affect children, but also the mere fact of losing one's home. Even though homeless children are not necessarily separated from their parents, they are living, along with their parents, "out of home." The severity of the impact on the child depends on the nature of the events leading to homelessness, the stresses related to the condition of homelessness per se, the age of the child, and the relationships among family members. Whatever the configuration of events and relationships, however, the lack of a home may influence children's development significantly, leading "to problems of alienation, rootlessness, and depression" (Garbarino & Kostleny, 1991, p. 6). "Home" implies secure shelter, permanence, safety, and connection to a community of supports (Bassuk, 1991b; Garbarino & Kostleny, 1991). "For a child to have a home is for that child to have a family that lives somewhere, that belongs somewhere" (Garbarino & Kostleny, 1991, p. 8).

Some homeless children, already traumatized by having no home, also suffer the trauma of additional separations, particularly foster care placement. Although there are few systematic data describing the relationship between homelessness and foster care, the two are entwined. Homeless mothers live in dread of losing their children to foster care because some officials view the inability to provide a child with a home as neglectful and requiring involuntary foster care placement (Solarz, 1992). Once without children, parents lose their welfare benefits and are far less likely to secure adequate housing, often the prerequisite for regaining custody of their children.

Foster care also affects homeless mothers in other pernicious ways. Although this chapter describes homeless families as those consisting of a parent or parents with child(ren) in tow, this categorization is artificial because many women in shelters for adult individuals have children who have been placed in foster care or are living with relatives—often because the mothers suffer from mental illness or substance use disorders (Bassuk, in press; Buckner, Bassuk, & Zima, 1993). Furthermore, families are sometimes forced to split up in order to receive shelter, particularly if they have adolescent boys, who are often excluded from family shelters. In other instances, parents may elect to place their children with relatives or in foster care while they cope with the stress of homelessness, search for housing (Solarz, 1992), or participate in a drug rehabilitation program.

This chapter describes the plight of homeless children, with particular emphasis on the impact of losing one's home. It outlines the serious consequences of homelessness for children and the range of coping strategies homeless children adopt to weather the stress. It also gives some examples of the complex relationship between homelessness and alternative placements, particularly foster care. The chapter concludes with a discussion of programs and policies that successfully meet the needs of these vulnerable children.

EXTENT OF THE PROBLEM

The numbers of families on the streets have grown dramatically since the early 1980s. In only 5 years, from 1985 to 1990, families increased from 27% to 34% of the overall homeless population (Bassuk, 1991a). Their numbers continue to climb. Reflecting the escalating rates of extreme poverty in our country, most homeless families are female headed. The number of poor families run by women grew 25.5% between 1970 and 1979 and another 15% between 1980 and 1989 (Bassuk, 1991a).

Homeless children comprise a significantly larger percentage of the family population than do mothers. Most families consist of two to three youngsters, most of whom are preschoolers. Approximately 100,000 homeless children sleep each night in emergency shelters, welfare hotels, abandoned buildings, or cars (Institute of Medicine, 1988).

HOMELESS CHILDREN: LOSING ONE'S HOME AND ENDURING OTHER OUT OF HOME PLACEMENTS

Losing one's home and moving repeatedly is traumatic for most children. The uncertainty and lack of routine engendered by moving activates many children's concerns about abandonment, safety, and adequate protection. Some children regress and manifest various behaviors that are attempts to cope with the stress of homelessness. The child's response is largely determined by the parent's capacity to buffer the stress, and the child's age and resilience. According to Garbarino and Kostleny (1991), "researchers have shown that young children (ages 6 and less) can cope with the stress of social disasters, such as war, if they retain strong positive attachments to their families, and if parents can continue to project a sense of stability and competence to their children" (p. 6). A preschooler's distress about becoming homeless, for example, may mirror his or her mother's anxiety and depression rather than his or her feelings about housing. Ideally, if a parent is able to buffer the child's stress, the impact on a young child may be less. However, this may be a heroic task given the cascading set of negative events leading to homelessness, the chaos of a homeless existence, the constant demands of young children, and the stress of being a single parent.

In contrast to young children whose experience of homelessness is mediated by their parent(s), older children tend to be more tied to their houses, and consequently their reaction to losing their home may be less determined by family relationships and their concept of family (Bassuk, 1991b; Garbarino & Kostleny, 1991). School-age children often express a deep sense of embarrassment and shame about their lack of a home—frequently remaining secretive with their peers in school about where they live.

Although shelters offer refuge to many families, the stresses of shelter life are many (Bassuk & Gallagher, 1990). The quality of the sheltering facilities varies by region and type of facility, from small neighborhood-based family shelters open 24 hours a day to barracks-type shelters where families must leave after breakfast and may return again for dinner (Bassuk, Rubin, & Lauriat, 1986; Boxill & Beaty, 1990) Regardless of the type of facility, quarters generally are cramped and families have little privacy. Both physical and emotional space is lacking. Guests are subjected to the various stresses, problems, and behavioral patterns of each family. Boxill and Beaty (1990) described how all aspects of the mother–child relationship, which were formerly private, are now "conducted in full public view," a situation that may contribute to the "unraveling of the mother role." The atmosphere in the shelter is generally volatile, and it is not uncommon for mothers to discharge tension by arguing with each other, most often about their children's behaviors. Mealtime, in particular, is very stressful because mothers must prepare and feed their children in communal kitchen and dining areas.

The stresses of hotel living are somewhat different, and perhaps more harmful to children. Families often are isolated from other families and, because of the lack of accessible transportation, from a network of services. "Whereas shelters offer regular contacts with other families, staff persons and various resources, such as laundry facilities, telephone, meals and transportation, hotels provide a room and little else. Families live 'behind closed doors,' usually without access to common areas for recreation and communication" (Gallagher, 1986, p. 61). The lack of structure, routine, and rules frustrates an already difficult living situation; hotel managers often disparage welfare families and fail to provide necessary services. Furthermore, it is not uncommon for illicit drug traffic and prostitution to occur in the hotel setting (Gallagher, 1986).

Because homeless children's experiences are mediated partly by their mothers' experiences, we also must appreciate the nature and extent of the mothers' struggles. Most mothers are concerned about the survival of their families and overwhelmed by the task of providing for their children and trying to make "ends meet." Many worry about functioning effectively as single parents and are understandably anxious and depressed about being homeless and extremely poor.

Homeless mothers suffer from every problem specific to their gender and race. The difficulties they experience mirror those of low-income women, but with greater intensity and frequency. Many homeless women have inadequate earning power, poor education, and overwhelming childcare responsibilities. While in shelters, mothers often spend 24 hours a day with their children, sleeping in the same room with the whole family. An alarming number of homeless mothers have other difficulties as well. Research reveals that as many as 89% of homeless women have been physically or sexually abused at some point in their lives (Browne, 1993; Goodman, 1991). Some homeless mothers also have psychiatric and substance abuse problems (Bassuk, in press). Combined with the stresses they face on the streets, "homeless women are quintessentially stressed women" (Hammen, 1991, p. 32).

At best, life for a homeless family is fraught with peril. Mothers frequently have little energy left to respond adequately to their children's distress and increased neediness. In turn, the children must muster any resources they have and, to a greater degree than usual, fend for themselves. This pattern often sets up a cycle that is harmful both to the individuals and to the mother–child interaction (Bassuk & Gallagher, 1990; Boxill & Beaty, 1990).

Unfortunately, many homeless children have had other traumatic experiences with separation and loss, in addition to becoming homeless. Because some shelters cannot accommodate large families or adolescent boys, such families must be broken up to obtain emergency housing (Weinreb & Buckner, 1993). These children may fend for themselves on the streets or may be placed in foster care or with relatives. Homeless children whose mothers decide to participate in a drug treatment program often must face the hard reality of being temporarily placed in foster care because so few treatment resources enable women to remain with their children. The shelter stay itself may bring into full view patterns of child abuse or neglect that went unseen while the family was in housing. Whether the shelter staff and associated caregivers elect to assist a mother while preserving family integrity or decide to precipitate an evaluation by the child welfare system, and possible foster care placement of the children, depends on the extent of the abuse, shelter ideologies, staff skills, and available local resources.

In some states, the mere fact of homelessness is cause to investigate the mother for neglect and to place the children in foster care; the parents are told that, once they have found decent housing, their children will be returned (Bussiere, 1990). According to a 1988 Children's Defense Fund report, "housing problems and homelessness are the reason for placement of about 40% of the foster care cases examined." Once a mother has lost her child to foster care, she may become ineligible for welfare benefits and food stamps, further decreasing her chances of reuniting her family (Robertson, 1991). This creates an all too often insurmountable situation in which mothers do not have the income to secure housing unless they get their children back, and cannot regain custody of their children until housing is found. Even though the primary reason for losing their children is related to inadequate housing, mothers now not only must cope with serious economic constraints but also are expected to comply with additional requirements established by the child welfare system, such as participation in parenting classes and counseling (Bussiere, 1990). Many mothers never regain custody of their children.

In general, separating children from their parents to languish in foster care placements, many of which are inadequate, inflicts excessive harm and compounds the trauma of homelessness—even in families in which the mother is having difficulty parenting effectively (Hanrahan, 1990). Children suffer from feelings of terror, desolation, helplessness, and sorrow, and sometimes develop long-term emotional problems. There are times, however, when placement in foster care is necessary for homeless children. The guidelines for placing them are not significantly different than those for placing any child. Foster care placement is an appropriate option if homeless mothers are unable to protect their children or provide a basic level of care, or when they have no other supports to care for their children while participating in a drug treatment program. For some women, temporary foster care placement may give them the time necessary to build the life skills needed to strengthen themselves and their families. Homelessness or inadequate housing alone, however, are not sufficient reasons to separate families.

Recognizing the damaging effects of placing children in impermanent settings away from their parents, Congress passed the Adoption Assistance and Child Welfare Act in 1980. According to this legislation, states must make every effort to preserve the family and reunite families when they have been disrupted. Attorneys and advocates have used this act to obtain orders to ensure that individuals receive effective housing assistance and related services. According to Bussiere

(1990), "a body of law (is beginning to develop) that limits intervention in families if the only danger to the child is lack of housing" (p. 4). In addition to efforts on behalf of individuals, lawyers have also filed "affirmative litigation to require state and local child welfare agencies to structure their programs in a manner that will assist homeless families and families at risk of becoming homeless to stay together" (p. 4). Although the legislation is a good start, considerable work must be done to prevent additional traumatic disruptions in the lives of homeless children.

THE NEEDS OF HOMELESS CHILDREN

Increasing numbers of young children are spending critical formative years on the streets without the resources to meet their basic physical, emotional, and educational needs. Researchers have documented that homeless children more frequently suffer from an array of serious problems shared by their poor, housed counterparts, and many locales lack the essential services to respond to these difficulties (Bassuk & Rosenberg, 1990; Bassuk & Rubin, 1987; Molnar & Klein, 1990; Rafferty & Shinn, 1991). Many of these problems are longstanding, but they are exacerbated by the stresses of losing one's home and living in overcrowded shelters or on the streets. Anecdotal accounts from shelter staff and homeless mothers suggest that, in general, the pressures of shelter living intensify the children's difficulties and may even create additional ones.

Medical Problems

Homeless children suffer from increased rates of both acute and chronic medical illnesses, especially upper respiratory disorders, minor skin diseases, and ear infections (Wright, 1990, 1991). Compared to poor housed children, they tend to have higher rates of other poverty-related problems, including delayed immunizations, elevated lead levels, and iron deficiencies, which most likely are related to poor nutrition (Alperstein, Rappaport, & Flanigan, 1988). Similar to poor housed children, many homeless youngsters are hungry and do not receive nutritionally balanced meals (Wood, Valdez, Hayashi, & Shen, 1990b). According to a U.S. Conference of Mayors report in 1989, in the majority of cities surveyed, emergency food programs turned away many families because of inadequate resources.

∞

Julie, a 3-year-old child living in an emergency shelter with her two siblings and mother, was referred to the local family health clinic for routine medical care. Julie has moved many times since birth. According to Julie's mother, the family had been evicted from several apartments for being excessively noisy and failing to pay rent. In just the past year, the family moved five times. Julie is a petite and frail-looking child who weighs significantly less than expected for her age. Although she is young, Julie did not have any difficulty becoming involved with an unfamiliar adult; in fact, she seemed to enjoy the individual attention she was receiving. Understanding her speech, however, was difficult because of problems with articulation. Her excessive and unusual concern with the availability of food was a dominant theme in spontaneous play. When given a juice box during developmental screening, she became very worried that the clinician was going to take it away. Because her mother has been preoccupied with meeting day-to-day needs, taking the children to the doctor has been a low priority. Julie has an eczematous rash that has gone untreated. She and her two siblings also have significant delays in routine immunizations.

∞

Developmental Delays

Homeless preschool children ages 2–5 years suffer from serious and often multiple developmental delays. Studies from cities such as Boston (Bassuk & Gallagher, 1990; Bassuk & Rubin, 1987; Bassuk et al., 1986), Los Angeles (Wood, Valdez, Hayashi, & Shen, 1990a), Philadelphia (Rescorla, Parker, & Stolley, 1991), St. Louis (Whitman, Accardo, Boyert, & Kendagor, 1990), and New York (Fox, Barnett, Davies, & Bird, 1990; Molnar, 1988; Molnar & Klein, 1990) have documented that homeless children tend to lag in language development, gross motor skills, fine motor coordination, and personal and social development. In Bassuk and colleagues' (1986) Boston study of 156 children from 82 families sheltered in Massachusetts, almost half (47%) manifested at least one developmental lag, 33% had two or more, and 14% failed in all four areas tested. When compared to their housed counterparts, a significantly greater percentage of homeless children manifested developmental delays (Bassuk & Rosenberg, 1988, 1990).

Unfortunately, temporary placement in foster care may contribute to some of the developmental problems experienced by homeless children.

∞

Three-year-old Ann and her two siblings, Jane and Robert, joined their mother, Donna, at a transitional shelter 1 month ago; the children had been in foster care for the past 9 months. Donna, who is 35 years old, talks easily about her life. She spent most of her adolescence in residential programs, only occasionally visiting her mother and grandmother. Her mother had a serious alcohol problem, "yelled all the time," and kept sending her away. Even though Donna missed her mother terribly, she was glad to get out of the house because the father of her two middle sisters moved in after marrying her mother. He physically and sexually abused Donna for 3 years, beginning when she was 10.

Donna has been moving among many shelters, apartments, and relatives' homes for the past 17 years. She met the father of her two older children 5 years ago. His drinking and physical abuse escalated over the course of their relationship. Because Donna used drugs intermittently during this time and had trouble caring for her children, the Department of Social Services placed her children in foster care. The oldest child, Ann, was placed in one household and the two younger children were placed in another. Having lost her income from Aid to Families with Dependent Children (AFDC), Donna was unable to cover her rent and almost immediately became homeless. Donna was highly motivated to reunite her family. With the help of shelter staff, she identified a residential drug treatment program. Unfortunately, the only available program was 30 miles away, making it virtually impossible for Donna to see her children regularly during her 9-month stay.

One month ago, after Donna completed the treatment program, the family was reunited. Donna worries that her drug use during her pregnancy with Ann is responsible for some of her daughter's difficulties. Donna "hit her stomach many times a day" to make the pregnancy go away. She also thinks that Ann may be more troubled than her siblings because of the long separation. Placed in a foster home with multiple other children, Ann did not receive adequate attention.

Ann, 3 months shy of 4 years of age, is an engaging child with good social skills. Although Ann is cooperative and tries hard, she has difficulty focusing on specific tasks even when they are structured. During testing with the McCarthy Scales of Children's Abilities, she frequently punched herself, pulled on the skin of her face, and pounded on the table. These self-stimulatory behaviors seem to help Ann soothe herself and release energy so she can continue to perform the testing tasks. Ann uses very little spontaneous speech. Her expressive language is sparse and unelaborated. For example, when asked to define the word *coat,* she responded by saying "put on." Ann also has difficulty with fine motor tasks such as grasping a pencil and manipulating blocks; she is unable to count or identify any colors or shapes. Performance on the McCarthy Scales suggests that Ann is functioning significantly below age level, with delays in language development, fine motor/perceptual skills, and preschool readiness.

The foster placement, while giving Donna an opportunity to become drug free and learn additional parenting and life skills, did not support Ann's development. Ann's siblings also suffer from serious developmental delays. Eighteen-month-old John rarely vocalizes or smiles. Thirty-month-old Jane is withdrawn and reticent. Her play is listless, she refuses to eat, and she appears depressed.

∞

Emotional and Social Difficulties

Many homeless children manifest anxiety, depression, and behavioral problems. Using the Children's Depression Inventory, Bassuk and her colleagues (Bassuk & Gallagher, 1990; Bassuk & Rubin, 1987) found that more than half of the children over the age of 5 in their studies needed further psychiatric evaluation, suggesting the possible presence of serious depressive symptoms. Overall, many homeless children reported that they had had suicidal thoughts, but said they would not translate them into action. On the Children's Manifest Anxiety Scale, almost one third of homeless school-age children—compared to only a tenth of children with homes—required additional psychiatric evaluation. Masten (1990), however, found that, in a comparison study of poor housed and homeless children, there were no significant differences in the percentage of children in the clinical range. Using various instruments including the Child Behavior Checklist and the Children's Depression Inventory, she concluded that "homeless children, even those who have not been homeless for very long, are at grave risk. A significant proportion have emotional and behavioral problems" (p. 23).

∞

Joseph is an average-sized 7-year-old boy with brown hair and blue eyes. He has been living with his mother and two younger brothers in an emergency shelter for the past 2 months; this followed a 2-week placement in a welfare hotel. Joseph seems unusually sad and worried for a child of his age. He rarely smiles, and did not laugh at any point during the evaluation. He is cooperative but needs a great deal of encouragement to continue the assessment tasks. He said he is "ugly" and "no good," and frequently is teased by peers. Psychological testing demonstrated that Joseph is struggling with many sad and angry feelings. Although he is very young, he has symptoms of a clinical depression. Intellectually, he is functioning one year below age level.

Joseph appears to be very worried about his mother's difficulties in maintaining housing and taking care of herself. He has witnessed physical violence between his mother and her boyfriends. In his mother's absence, he shared his concern that she has already broken the shelter rules twice. "She didn't watch me and my brothers one time; the other time she stayed out too late with her boyfriend. If she breaks the rules one more time, we'll be on the streets again." Because he cannot solve his mother's problems, Joseph sees himself as "bad" and deserving of punishment.

∞

Several researchers have investigated children's behavior using parents' reports from Achenbach's Child Behavior Checklist. The results vary, but generally there are only marginally significant differences between homeless children and their poor housed counterparts. Most of these studies highlight the pervasive needs of homeless children, but also indicate that poor housed children have pressing problems as well (Bassuk & Gallagher, 1990; Bassuk & Rubin, 1987; Masten, 1990; Rescorla et al., 1991).

Educational Problems

Homeless children attend school erratically or not at all (Rafferty & Rollins, 1989). A 1985 U.S. Department of Education report estimated that 30% of the nation's 220,000 homeless school-age children do not attend school regularly. This estimate was contested by the National Coalition for the Homeless (1987), an advocacy group, which claims that two to three times as many school-age children are homeless and almost half do not attend school regularly.

Mothers must frequently overcome daunting obstacles in order to ensure that their children attend school regularly. Timely enrollment may be obstructed by sluggish bureaucracies that transfer essential records slowly or by delayed immunizations and poor record keeping. The frequent lack of adequate transportation and child care for other children in the family also interferes with regular attendance. The trek to and from school is particularly arduous when the whole family must travel on public transportation for hours each day—and these are the more fortunate mothers whose travel is subsidized. Some children must change schools repeatedly as their families move among multiple hotels and shelters. Each move involves losing newly made friends and missing days or weeks of school.

Once in school, the needs of homeless children often are overlooked by a public system that is underfunded, overcrowded, and resource poor. It is not surprising that many homeless children are doing below-average work or failing. In the Boston study, 43% had already repeated a grade and 25% were in special classes (Bassuk et al., 1986).

∞

Sheila is a 30-year-old woman who developed a posttraumatic stress disorder after her house burned to the ground, killing her mother and four siblings. Since then she has been abusing alcohol. She and her four children have moved frequently, sharing apartments with friends and relatives and living in shelters. They currently are living in an emergency shelter. Sheila's three school-age children have been attending school erratically, especially during the past year. Dana, the 9-year-old, is performing below average in most subjects and has already repeated a grade. She is worried that her classmates will discover that she is homeless and tells the bus driver to "drop me off at another street so nobody knows." Her two brothers, Bill and Tony, are 6 and 8; both have repeated grades and are in special classes.

Sheila is stressed by the family's homelessness and unable to offer much support to her children. Worrying about meeting basic needs and looking for an apartment "takes up all my energy." Getting into a treatment program would require placing the children in temporary foster care, something Sheila is unwilling to do. A few months ago, while still in housing, Sheila tried to arrange for her children to stay with a friend for 1 week while she enrolled in a detoxification program. Her friend backed out as the time approached and Sheila still refused to place her children in foster care. "My children are all that I have. I can't be without them. Anyway, once your kids get into foster care, lots of times, you don't get them back."

∞

HOW CHILDREN COPE WITH BEING HOMELESS

Regressive Behaviors

It is not unusual for homeless mothers to report that, after moving into the shelter, their children—especially the preschoolers—behave differently, generally "becoming more babyish." Many manifest eating and sleeping difficulties and start bed wetting again. One young mother said that, the longer her two children, ages 2 and 4 years, stayed in the shelter, the more introverted and withdrawn they became:

> "They now only speak in fragments and have lost a lot of the words they used to have before they got here." Another mother reported that her son could eat by himself before they moved into the shelter, but now "he can't even hold a cup of milk without spilling it." A recent report of four boys shooting pool in a welfare hotel described them as talking as tough as any New York pool sharks. One wore just his shorts, and another's face was smeared with sweat. With the boys as old as 12, they might have seemed wise about the streets—except that two of them were sucking their thumbs. Nearby, Jessie, a gangly 11-year-old, introduced a visitor to his stuffed puppy. "His name is Snuff," he said, clutching a doll that seemed appropriate for a child half his age. (Chavez, 1987, p. B1)

When people are overwhelmed by external stress or internal conflicts, they frequently return to an earlier developmental level. Their unconscious hope is to rework and master unresolved conflicts and obtain gratification for unmet needs. Homeless children's regressive behaviors reflect their current level of overwhelming stress as well as their real need for nurturance and protection.

Aggressive or Shy and Withdrawn Behaviors

Mothers' reports and our own observations suggest that many children change after becoming homeless, exhibiting aggressive and noncompliant or shy and withdrawn behavior. Many mothers report that their children are angry, provocative, and hard to control; many children also cry for no reason. Some mothers comment that, as their children's behavior deteriorates, the only way they can get their attention and control their aggressive behavior is to punish them physically.

∞

> A 20-year-old mother, who is now 8 months pregnant, had to leave her parents' home because of severe overcrowding. She has been living in a family shelter with her two daughters for the past 3 months. Five-year-old Heather is overweight, aggressive, and "won't listen to anything I tell her. She talks fresh like the other children and says things she never used to say. If I don't hit her now, she'll never listen or she'll just get worse." The mother also said that, since coming to the shelter, both girls have lost their appetite and will only eat if they are at their grandmother's house. In contrast to Heather, 3-year-old Patty is quiet and anxious, and often is scapegoated by other children because of severe eczema and a protruding umbilical hernia. She appears frightened, cries with little provocation, and clings to her mother.

∞

These observations were supported by the results of the Simmons Behavior Checklist, an instrument used in the Massachusetts study (Bassuk & Rubin, 1987). Mothers completed a 28-item questionnaire about the behaviors of their 3- to 5-year-old children. Each item was scored on a 5-point scale, from never to always; 11 factors were derived from the 28 items. In addition, a total behavioral score was obtained and compared to normative data. The 55 homeless children studied scored significantly higher than the mean for a sample of normal and disturbed children. Compared to emotionally disturbed children, the homeless children scored equal to or higher than the mean on the following factor scales: sleep problems, aggression, shyness, and withdrawal.

Increased aggressiveness may be a way for homeless children to express anger at their circumstances and at their parents for being unable to protect them. In some children, it may be a way of covering up sorrow and terror. At the same time, unruly, provocative, and aggressive behaviors are a "cry for help," a way to get more attention from adults who are depressed, anxious, and preoccupied with issues of survival. Some children use aggressive behavior as a way of imitating their parents:

> [T]hey are doing actively what they have experienced and continue to experience passively. In play they assume adult roles in which they yell, curse, and punish as an outlet for their poorly mastered aggressive drives. It appears that they use such identification with the aggressor as part of their repetitive efforts in play to master and assimilate hurtful, threatening aspects of their relationships with their parents.... (Pavenstedt, 1967, pp. 135–136)

Defying adults also may help children gain acceptance from peers.

Other children feel too unsafe to trust adults or to express their feelings and needs openly, and instead become shy and withdrawn. Some distrust adults, "gave up" on relationships at an early age, and feel hopeless about having their needs fulfilled; many are also despairing and fearful of expressing their wishes or feelings (e.g., hostility) directly. Homeless children who have experienced the loss of a primary caregiver (e.g., father, grandparent) often are reluctant about becoming involved in another potentially disrupted relationship.

Mothering Behaviors

Homeless children seem to be searching for adults to nurture and protect them from a dangerous, uncertain, and unreliable world. "[These children] do not have inner confidence that they will not suddenly be whacked or humiliated or deserted, or that the situation will not unexpectedly change" (Pavenstedt, 1967, p. 131). In one instance, a 5-year-old homeless boy who had been sexually abused asked a staff person to write the following message to his mother: "Please keep us company." "Us" referred to him and three younger brothers, ages 8 months to 3 years (Bassuk & Gallagher, 1990).

Sometimes siblings turn to each other for nurturance and protection.

∞

> Thirteen-year-old twins Laura and Patricia have been inseparable since they became homeless 2 years ago. They are always together and, to make up for their mother's inability to care for them, they fiercely support each other. Despite their mother's generally irresponsible behavior and the family's constant moving, they have attended school regularly and have received above-average grades. They are generally more functional than their mother and try both to nurture and to discipline her.

The sisters' concerns about survival and protection unfortunately have a basis in fact in their lives because Laura is a brittle juvenile diabetic; she has been hospitalized repeatedly because of dangerously high blood sugar levels that resulted from the mother's neglect of her medical and dietary needs. Pat has taken on the responsibility of helping to regulate her sister's diet. Three months ago Laura was rehospitalized for regulation of her diabetes. During this time, Pat noticeably regressed, began talking in a babyish manner, and missed several days of school. Although the doctors wanted to place Laura in foster care, shelter staff and the Department of Social Services intervened to keep the family together because of the sisters' interdependence. They wanted to give the mother "one more chance" to attend more closely to her daughters' needs.

∞

Another coping strategy is for children to identify with the nurturant mother and to try to replace her.

∞

Sam, a 4-year-old boy, has assumed the care of his 3-month-old brother, David, who was born 2 months prematurely. He mimics his mother's maternal behaviors and at times seems to be a better and more devoted mother. His 24-year-old mother considers Sam "a responsible adult" and gave him permission to feed the baby, carry him around, and babysit. When the mother is taking a shower, doing errands, or making phone calls, he assumes full responsibility for both David and his 2-year-old sister. One of the shelter staff commented that "he doesn't seem to be having a childhood and is instead moving directly into become a parent."

∞

Sometimes the child's identification with the nurturant parent becomes excessive.

∞

Annette, a 37-year-old single mother of four children (ages 6 months to 17 years) and cocaine user, has been homeless for 5 months. She is involved in a destructive symbiotic relationship with Susan, her 17-year-old daughter. Susan has been in various foster care placements and was sexually abused. She is overweight, very immature, and neglectful of personal hygiene. Last summer Susan worked, but her mother took Susan's earnings to buy drugs.

Recently, the mother disappeared for 3 days, leaving the younger children in Susan's care. Susan dressed up like her mother, putting on too much makeup and flamboyant clothes, and acted out sexually. She then claimed she was pregnant. When the mother returned, she insisted that Susan was infertile and that, in fact, she herself was pregnant and had to schedule an abortion. When the mother left, Susan felt hurt and talked angrily about her mother's sexual involvements, drug use, and inability to parent. After her mother returned, Susan denied any negative feelings toward her. Susan now has an option to move into a residential treatment program. She viewed the opportunity favorably only while her mother was away. Although the mother superficially supports this move, she emotionally imprisons Susan by making her feel that no one in the family can survive without her. So far, Susan has been unable to leave and continues to function as the primary caregiver in the family.

∞

Boxill and Beaty (1990) interpreted mothering behaviors such as those in the first two examples in this section as indicative of the "unraveling of the mother role." They imply that these behaviors are largely contextual and result from the necessity of mothering publicly:

> When normally it is anticipated that adults set the standards for civility, compromise, and cooperation, shelter living seemed to provoke the unraveling of that responsibility and the assumption of childlike behavior on the part of the adults. Mothers appeared to have temporarily become children along with their children. (Boxill & Beaty, 1990, p. 60)

As indicated by the Massachusetts study of sheltered homeless families (Bassuk & Rubin, 1987; Bassuk et al., 1986), for some children the disordered mother–child relationship is long standing and predates the current shelter stay. In these families, the visibility of the mother–child relationship in the shelter may provide an opportunity for intervention to help mothers parent more effectively.

WHAT CAN BE DONE? PROGRAM AND POLICY RESPONSES TO HOMELESS CHILDREN'S NEEDS

Homeless children suffer from serious medical, developmental, emotional, and educational problems. They often lack the supports and protection that would ameliorate the adverse effects of having no home. Unfortunately, many homeless children fail to receive the services necessary to promote normal development, remediate existing problems, and prevent further difficulties. Sadly, most homeless children's problems continue far beyond the family's shelter stay. Their desperate needs call for immediate programmatic action and policy change.

What will it take to meet the needs of homeless children? Both crisis-oriented strategies and long-term approaches are necessary. Short-term responses are essential: families' basic needs for shelter, food, clothing, and medical care must be met. Immediate preventive measures such as immunizing children or enrolling them in preschool programs can promote their health, development, and well-being. Efforts to stabilize children during the crisis of homelessness and that strive to keep families together despite homelessness also will minimize the damage that children suffer. Short-term responses, however, are little more than stopgap measures if they are not combined with comprehensive long-term strategies. These include increasing the availability of affordable housing, developing approaches that prevent homelessness, and implementing innovative programs that integrate services with permanent housing.

Short-Term Responses

Given that homelessness will not be eradicated in the near future, emergency and short-term responses are critical. In addition to meeting families' basic needs for shelter, food, clothing, and health care, it is imperative that specialized and developmentally appropriate services are provided for children. Furthermore, programs must address parents' needs. For the many homeless families who have been seriously isolated from supports, the shelter stay offers an opportunity to link children and families with desperately needed services. Finally, efforts must be designed to help families whose children are at risk of placement in foster care or who cannot return to their families because of homelessness or inadequate housing.

Programs and policies that ensure some measure of stability and structure during the homelessness crisis offer children the best chance of developing a sense of security and of preventing additional difficulties. Many homeless children have moved many times and have never experienced the stability of a "permanent" home. For some children, staying in a shelter may be the most secure and safe experience they have had. Emergency shelter placements should provide children and their families with as much structure and routine as possible. Allowing families to remain in a shelter 24 hours a day, reducing moves among shelters when length-of-stay requirements have been exceeded, and ensuring that families stay together regardless of their size or children's ages will add to a child's sense of stability. In addition, minimizing interruptions in schooling and changes of schools will ensure that children form consistent and stable relationships with teachers and peers. As discussed earlier, when a child lacks suitable housing, the family needs housing search assistance and supportive services, not another traumatic dislocation, such as foster care placement. Foster care placement should be reserved for those occasions when a child's safety is threatened or when a mother is unable to care for her child. Sometimes, a mother may choose to participate in a drug treatment program that will not allow children to be with her, or she requires time without the stress of parenting to build her economic self-sufficiency and life skills.

Many homeless children suffer from serious developmental lags and would benefit greatly by participating in developmentally appropriate programs. Preoccupied with issues of survival, homeless parents often cannot respond to their children's need for nurturance and stimulation. Unfortunately, many homeless children are not enrolled in programs and have been deprived of adequate stimulation long before becoming homeless. Through shelter- or community-based child care or early childhood education programs, homeless infants and preschool children can receive the support necessary to promote normal development. For example, in some communities, early intervention teams go into shelters and screen children under age 3 for developmental delays. On-site parent education and play groups may be conducted as part of this effort. Other shelters may have an on-site child specialist who supervises developmentally appropriate programs for children. When possible, shelter staff should link children with community-based programs, such as Head Start and early intervention, that can provide children with stable, ongoing relationships with adults regardless of where families move.

Special programs that provide homeless children with structure, routine, and supervised play support their development and reduce their distress. Within shelters, children should be given adequate space and developmentally appropriate toys. Recreational activities and summer camp participation offer homeless children a chance to play and be children again. Programs of this nature also will provide mothers with relief from the stress of continual child care (Bassuk & Gallagher, 1990).

"School is especially crucial for homeless children because it may instill a sense of stability that they otherwise lack" (Rafferty & Shinn, 1991, p. 1176). By providing structure and offering services, schools can play a critical role in fostering homeless children's development and academic achievement, and preventing further damage from the trauma of homelessness (Rafferty & Rollins, 1989). Nonetheless, public education for homeless school-aged children is often seriously compromised.

The Stewart B. McKinney Homeless Assistance Act, initially enacted in 1987, attempts to respond to the urgent needs of homeless school-age children by requiring that states develop educational plans that ensure that these children have access to services equal to those available to their housed peers. Parents also have the option of keeping their children in the same school district for the remainder of the year or enrolling them in the district where they are temporarily housed. Although most state boards of education have developed plans to promote the education of homeless children, barriers to enrollment and attendance still persist. Innovative programs that include remedial educational services and enrichment, such as after-school activities and tutorial efforts, can enhance a child's experience. For children suffering from serious behavioral or emotional problems, psychological services also must be provided.

In addition to meeting the complex and urgent needs of homeless children, their mothers' needs also must be met. As discussed earlier, the problems of homeless mothers are staggering. Feelings of stress and isolation often reduce a mother's capacity to respond to her child's difficulties. Many homeless mothers require parenting support and education. Furthermore, in order to become self-sufficient, many homeless mothers need help acquiring employment and problem-solving skills and building supportive relationships. Some mothers also suffer from substance abuse problems and depression or are victims of domestic violence. All of these problems, if not dealt with, may further jeopardize a child's progress. For example, a mother with a drug problem may have difficulty getting her child to school regularly. Her problem also may prolong homelessness and limit her capacity to maintain a permanent home (Weinreb & Bassuk, 1990). Although long-term continuous services are necessary to address problems such as these, failure to respond during the emergency shelter stay will miss an important opportunity to minimize the devastating impact of homelessness on children and improve their well-being.

When possible, homeless mothers should be provided with the supports necessary to keep their children with them while they are living in shelters and as they stabilize into permanent housing. In some instances, however, temporary foster care may offer a viable option. For example, in some locales, inadequate child care resources may make a mother's participation in an education or job training program impossible. For women who are determined to build their earning power and participate in such programs, and who have no relatives, foster care placement represents a possible alternative.

Sometimes, however, a woman's capacity to voluntarily place her children in foster care may be limited. Congress and some states have established restrictions on voluntary placements in an effort to encourage the child welfare system and families to resolve problems before it becomes necessary to remove children (Bussiere, 1988). Another obstacle to voluntary placement is diminishing child welfare resources, such as staff shortages and inadequate numbers of foster homes (resources are directed primarily to cases of abuse and neglect) (Children's Defense Fund, 1991).

An example of a program aimed at helping families at risk is the Family Unification Program, administered by the Department of Housing and Urban Development. This program, funded with an appropriation of $48 million in 1992, provided Section VIII housing certificates to help 1,300 households in 11 states regain custody of children or avoid placement of children as a result of homelessness or inadequate housing; during 1993, $73 million has been appropriated to help 2,200 households (G. Benoit, Operations Branch, Rental Assistance Program, U.S. Department of Housing and Urban Development, Washington, DC, personal communication, July 23, 1993). Services provided from the child welfare system are combined with housing subsidies to achieve the program goals.

Long-Term Responses

Although short-term measures are essential to ameliorating the dire consequences of homelessness for children, so too are long-term strategies. In particular, we must increase the supply of affordable housing, develop programs to prevent homelessness among vulnerable families, and stabilize homeless families in the community by integrating innovative and continuous services with permanent housing.

All children must have the security of a safe and stable home; all parents must have a stable environment in which to raise their children. So long as there is a severe housing shortage in this country, more children will become homeless. During the past decade, the government virtually ceased supporting rehabilitation or construction of low- and middle-income housing (Bassuk, 1991a). In fact, the federal government's efforts to provide affordable housing, other than in emergency or transitional facilities, have been minimal. The McKinney Homeless Assistance Act of 1987, although authorizing funds for emergency shelters and for a diverse array of programs to aid homeless persons, did not provide for either the development of low-rent housing or the distribution of adequate income supports for extremely poor families (Weinreb & Rossi, 1991). Until this country establishes a comprehensive housing policy to increase the supply of decent, affordable housing, there is little hope that our other efforts on behalf of children can be sustaining.

Policies must focus not only on rehousing homeless children and their families, but also on preventing homelessness among families at risk. "As long as there are substantial new entries into homelessness, helping only the already homeless cannot significantly reduce the size of the problem" (Lindbloom, 1991, p. 957). In the face of a scarce supply of low-income housing and inadequate income levels, many families—particularly those headed by women—are at risk of homelessness. Preventive efforts that identify families at risk for homelessness and provide them with the economic, institutional, and informal supports needed to remain housed are crucial. Once a family becomes homeless, the road back is long. Providing shelter and services to families and children after they become homeless rather than intervening before the event results in unnecessary suffering and a large expenditure of resources.

The special needs of homeless children and their mothers require that innovative and long-term services be integrated with permanent housing. Housing without appropriate support services is not enough. To ensure the well-being of children and successful family resettlement, housing must be connected to comprehensive, long-term, community-based services. Most families can maintain housing if a network of community services is available, accessible, and coordinated, usually by case management programs. Coordinating services is essential for addressing the diverse needs of homeless children, which cut across many different systems. Local coalitions that integrate service providers, the subsidized and low-income housing system, and the benefits and entitlements system optimize the distribution of local resources and the coordination of services.

Because no two communities face the same challenges and each local area offers a unique mix of state and local entitlement packages, successful programs must be individually tailored. For example, acquired immunodeficiency syndrome may pose a serious threat to newborns and children in one community, whereas, in another, improving children's access to educational entitlements in a resource-poor school system may be the most urgent need. Such variation notwithstanding, it is possible to identify particular program components that, when combined, will increase the likelihood that the needs of homeless families will be met. In an analysis of social programs for disadvantaged children, Schorr (1989) suggested that programs that improve outcomes for high-risk children differ "in fundamental ways from prevailing services" (p. 256).

> In short, the programs that succeed in helping the children and families in the shadows are intensive, comprehensive, and flexible.... Their climate is created by skilled, committed professionals who establish respectful and trusting relationships and respond to the individual needs of those they serve. The nature of their services, the terms on which they are offered, the relationships with families, the essence of the programs themselves—all take their shape from the needs of those they serve rather than from the precepts, demands, and boundaries set by professionalism and bureaucracies. (Schorr, 1989, p. 259)

The Kidstart program, established by The Better Homes Foundation in collaboration with IBM and currently being replicated in numerous sites nationally, is an example of an innovative intervention for homeless preschoolers and their families. Trained case managers, called Kidstarters, assess homeless preschoolers' social, emotional, and cognitive development, help them gain entry to Head Start and other developmentally appropriate programs, and link them with essential services. Kidstarters provide counseling and assist mothers with their parenting responsibilities. The Kidstart model is particularly effective because it ensures that homeless children, many of whom have special needs, access the educational entitlements mandated by state and federal legislation. Kidstarters work intensively with parents and their children during the homelessness episode and beyond, when families settle into permanent housing. Through a range of shelter-, agency-, and home-based approaches, Kidstart responds flexibly and continuously to the needs of homeless preschoolers and their families. By identifying children's difficulties early on, the Kidstart program helps prevent further problems.

CONCLUSION

We realize that significantly changing a child's developmental course is a formidable task that cannot be achieved with modest or short-term approaches. Even some of the long-term approaches described above may not be long enough. Growing up in isolated, single-parent families, living in neighborhoods marred by physical, economic, and social deterioration, and moving many times set the stage for developing many serious problems. How could we have thought that short-term interventions would be enough to diminish the negative effects of a child's lifetime experience of poverty or ensure that he or she would not suffer more difficulties in later years (Zigler, 1990)? The 1-year Head Start program is a good example. Although recent data investigating the sustained effects of the Head Start program into kindergarten and grade 1 demonstrated lasting effects for poor children on some measures of success, the powerful effects of Head Start for the children with the greatest cognitive disadvantages were not sustained through the early primary years (Lee, Brooks-Gunn, Schnur, & Fong-Ruey, 1990).

The reality is that poor and homeless children have significant disadvantages and problems that require long-term, intensive strategies. Optimal health and development are encouraged by providing developmentally appropriate experiences for children throughout their lives. Interventions that solely target certain age groups fall short of responding adequately to homeless children's needs.

> [T]here is no one magic period in the life of a child. Each and every period is a magical and important one ... we must commit ourselves to the principle of the continuity of human development. Each period of development grows out of each preceding period. Given this fact, we should realize the dangers of trying to provide societal supports at only one stage, as if intervention at that time would absolve us from the need to be concerned with other ages as well. Our task, therefore, is not to find the right age at which to intervene, but to find the right intervention for each age. (Zigler, 1990, p. 10)

Interventions must span the full life of a child, beginning with good prenatal care and continuing through adolescence.

Homeless children have pressing problems. It is vital that we develop immediate and long-term programs and policies to respond to their complex and diverse needs. The effects of homelessness on children during their formative years are devastating and long lasting. Without attention to eliminating homelessness, many more children and their families will be caught in the tragedy of homelessness and its intergenerational devastation.

REFERENCES

Alperstein, G., Rappaport, C., & Flanigan, J.M. (1988). Health problems of homeless children in New York City. *American Journal of Public Health, 78,* 1232–1233.
Bassuk, E.L. (1984). The homelessness problem. *Scientific American, 251,* 40–44.
Bassuk, E.L. (1991a). Homeless families. *Scientific American, 265,* 66–74.
Bassuk, E.L. (Ed.). (1991b). *Homeless families with children: Research perspectives.* Rockville, MD: National Institute on Alcohol Abuse and Alcoholism.
Bassuk, E.L. (in press). Lives in jeopardy. The plight of homeless women. In C. Willie & P. Rieker (Eds.), *Racism, sexism and mental health.* Pittsburgh: University of Pittsburgh Press.
Bassuk, E.L., & Gallagher, E. (1990). The impact of homelessness on children. *Child and Youth Services, 14,* 19–34.
Bassuk, E.L., & Rosenberg, L. (1988). Why does family homelessness occur? A case-control study. *American Journal of Public Health, 78,* 783–788.
Bassuk, E.L., & Rosenberg, L. (1990). Psychosocial characteristics of homeless children and children with homes. *Pediatrics, 85,* 257–261.
Bassuk, E.L., & Rubin, L. (1987). Homeless children: A neglected population. *American Journal of Orthopsychiatry, 57,* 279–286.
Bassuk, E.L., Rubin, L., & Lauriat, A. (1986). The characteristics of sheltered homeless families. *American Journal of Public Health, 76,* 1097–1101.
Boxill, N., & Beaty, A. (1990). Mother/child interaction among homeless wom-

en and their children in a public shelter in Atlanta, Georgia. *Child and Youth Services, 14,* 49–64.

Browne, A. (1993). Family violence and homelessness. The effect of trauma on the lives of homeless women. *American Journal of Orthopsychiatry, 63,* 370–384.

Buckner, J., Bassuk, E.L., & Zima, B. (1993). Mental health issues affecting homeless women: Implications for interventions. *American Journal of Orthopsychiatry, 63,* 385–399.

Bussierre, A. (1988). Children in foster care. *Youth Law News, 9,* 5–9.

Bussiere, A. (1990). Homeless families and the child welfare system. *Children's Legal Rights Journal, 11,* 2–7.

Chavez, L. (1987, July 16). Welfare hotel children: Tomorrow's poor. *New York Times,* pp. B1, B5.

Children's Defense Fund. (1988). *A Children's Defense Fund budget, FY 1989.* Washington, DC: Author.

Children's Defense Fund. (1991). *The state of America's children.* Washington, DC: Author.

Fox, S., Barnett, J., Davies, M., & Bird, H. (1990). Psychopathology and developmental delay in homeless children. *Journal of the American Academy of Child and Adolescent Psychiatry, 5,* 732–735.

Gallagher, E. (1986). *No place like home: A report on the tragedy of homeless children and their families in Massachusetts.* Boston: Massachusetts Committee for Children and Youth.

Garbarino, J., & Kostleny, K. (1991). *What does it mean for a child to be without a home? A review of issues in studying family homelessness.* Unpublished manuscript.

Goodman, L. (1991). The prevalence of abuse in the lives of homeless and housed poor mothers: A comparison study. *American Journal of Orthopsychiatry, 61,* 489–500.

Hammen, C. (1991). Parenting. In E.L. Bassuk. (Ed.), *Homeless families with children: Research perspectives* (pp. 30–32). Rockville, MD: National Institute on Alcohol Abuse and Alcoholism.

Hanrahan, P.M. (1990). *In Re: Homeless Children.* Generic Reasonable Efforts Brief on 42 U.S.C. §§ 620 and 670.

Hartman, C., & Zigas, B. (1991). What is wrong with the housing market? In J.H. Kryder Coe, L.M. Salmon, & J.M. Molnar (Eds.), *Homeless children and youth: A new American dilemma* (pp. 71–103). New Brunswick, NJ: Transaction.

Institute of Medicine. (1988). *Homelessness, health and human needs.* Washington, DC: National Academy Press.

Lee, V., Brooks-Gunn, J., Schnur, E., & Fong-Ruey, L. (1990). Are Head Start effects sustained? A longitudinal follow-up comparison of disadvantaged children attending Head Start, no preschool, and other preschool programs. *Child Development, 61,* 495–507.

Lindbloom, E.N. (1991). Toward a comprehensive homelessness prevention strategy. *Housing Policy Debate, 2,* 957–1025.

Masten, A. (1990, August). *Homeless children: Risk, trauma and adjustment.* Paper presented at the annual meeting of the American Psychological Association, Boston.

Molnar, J. (1988). *Home is where the heart is: The crisis of homelessness in*

children and families in New York City. New York: Bank St. College of Education.
Molnar, J., & Klein, T. (1990). Constantly compromised: The impact of homelessness on children. *Journal of Social Issues, 46,* 109–124.
National Coalition for the Homeless. (1987). *Broken lives: Denial of education to homeless children.* Washington DC: Author.
Pavenstedt, E. (Ed.). (1967). *The drifters: Children of disorganized lower-class families.* Boston: Little, Brown.
Rafferty, Y., & Rollins, N. (1989). *Learning in limbo: The educational deprivation of homeless children.* New York: Advocates for Children of New York, Inc.
Rafferty, Y., & Shinn, M. (1991). The impact of homelessness on children. *American Psychologist, 46,* 1170–1179.
Rescorla, L., Parker, R., & Stolley, P. (1991). Ability, achievement and adjustment in homeless children. *American Journal of Orthopsychiatry, 61,* 210–220.
Robertson, M. (1991). Homeless women with children: The role of alcohol and other drug abuse. *American Psychologist, 46,* 1198–1204.
Schorr, L., with Schorr, D. (1989). *Within our reach: Breaking the cycle of disadvantage.* New York: Anchor Books.
Solarz, A. (1992). To be young and homeless: Implications of homelessness for children. In M. Robertson & M. Greenblatt (Eds.), *Homelessness: A national perspective* (pp. 275–286). New York: Plenum Press.
U.S. Conference of Mayors. (1989). *A status report on hunger and homelessness in America's cities: 1989. A 27-city survey.* Washington, DC: Author.
U.S. Conference of Mayors. (1990). *A status report on hunger and homelessness in America's cities: 1990. A 30-city survey.* Washington, DC: Author.
U.S. Department of Education. (1985, February 15). *Report to Congress: State interim report on the education of homeless children.* Washington, DC: Author.
Weinreb, L., & Bassuk, E. (1990). Substance abuse: A growing problem among homeless families. *Family and Community Health, 13,* 55–64.
Weinreb, L., & Buckner, J. (1993). Homeless families: Program responses and public policies. *American Journal of Orthopsychiatry, 63,* 400–409.
Weinreb, L., & Rossi, P. (1991). Homeless families: Public policies, program responses and evaluation strategies. In E. L. Bassuk (Ed.), *Homeless families with children: Research perspectives* (pp. 53–58). Rockville, MD: National Institute on Alcohol Abuse and Alcoholism.
Whitman, B., Accardo, P., Boyert, M., & Kendagor, R. (1990). Homelessness and cognitive performance in children: A possible link. *Social Work, 35,* 516–519.
Wood, D., Valdez, B., Hayashi, T., & Shen, A. (1990a). Homeless and housed families in Los Angeles: A study comparing demographic, economic and family function characteristics. *American Journal of Public Health, 80,* 1049–1052.
Wood, D., Valdez, B., Hayashi, T., & Shen, A. (1990b). The health of homeless children: A comparison study. *Pediatrics, 86,* 858–866.
Wright, J. (1990). Homelessness is not healthy for children and other living things. *Child and Youth Services, 14,* 65–88.
Wright, J. (1991). Poverty, homelessness, health, nutrition, and children. In

J.H. Kryder-Coe, L.M. Salmon, & J.M. Molnar (Eds.), *Homeless children and youth: A new American dilemma* (pp. 71–103). New Brunswick, NJ: Transaction.

Wright, J., & Lam, J. (1987, Spring). Homelessness and the low-income housing supply. *Social Policy,* pp. 48–53.

Zigler, E. (1990). Foreword. In S. Meisels & J. Shonkoff (Eds.), *Handbook of early childhood education.* Cambridge, England: Cambridge University Press.

―――――――――――――― 3 ――

Consequences of Placement for Children Who Are Abused

Virginia G. Weisz

Child abuse, including neglect, is not a recent phenomenon in the United States, or indeed in any country. History books, literature, and scriptures tell stories of ancient cities being founded by abandoned twins raised by wolves, or children being crippled from working in clothing mills and as chimney sweeps (DeMause, 1974). Child labor laws can keep children out of factories, but child abuse laws cannot protect them initially in the home from uncaring, overstressed, or cruel parents. In the last century, waifs were removed from the streets of large cities and farmed out to families in rural areas; today they are placed in foster care for months and years, sometimes drifting from one home to another with crisis stops at emergency shelters or residential treatment centers. In 1992, 2.9 million child abuse and neglect reports were made (McCurdy & Daro, 1993). As reporting statistics steadily rise, the incidence of fatalities from child abuse follows the same chilling trend. Every day, there are heartwrenching newspaper stories and television accounts of abusive acts toward children. Sometimes the parents are the accused; sometimes it is temporary or long-term caregivers. In either instance, what happens to those children?

Many children are left in their abusive family homes without protective services or are placed in temporary foster care because of a crisis situation that protective services might earlier have been able to prevent. When parental abuse is substantiated, the parents can be required to cope with the bureaucratic complexities of the legal and social services system or risk having the child removed from their care and possibly never returned. This forceful intervention is allowed on the premise that only in that way can the child be protected; in reality, the child may go from the home of the neglecting or abusing parent to an unpredictable series of subsidized homes that neglect the child's most basic needs for continuity and loving, individualized care. Unfortunately, the meaning of the familiar saying "Home is where the heart is" can elude the child who remains with harmful or neglectful parents, as well as the child shunted from one temporary foster home to another, or the child left in limbo for years in a foster home while awaiting adoption.

Should a child be allowed to remain in a home where he or she does not get enough food, or where there is no heat, or, worse, where he or she is physically mistreated? In considering the effect of abuse on children and families, two critical factors must be evaluated:

1. Does the neglect or abuse result from poverty, cultural practices, or a lack of education or resources that could be remedied better by family support services than by removal of the child?
2. How will the child be affected by either removal from the family or remaining in the home?

This chapter details the nature of child abuse and neglect and the consequences of placement. Case studies are used to examine how children come to be abused or neglected and what public agencies and courts are doing to help these young victims. Definitions of abuse and neglect are reviewed and mandated reporting of abuse is discussed before describing the development and mechanics of the social and legal framework that governs the options for children suddenly threatened with placement out of the home because of the harmful behavior of their traditional protectors.

DEFINING CHILD ABUSE AND NEGLECT

Child abuse and neglect are complex problems, and formal definitions are required to ensure that instances of abuse and neglect are recognized and appropriate action is taken. As a social, legal, medical, and psychological phenomenon, child abuse is described as an intentional action by a parent or caregiver that causes injury to the child or failure of a parent or caregiver to provide protection and care for the child. Child abuse also has been called "endangerment" or "maltreatment." The Federal Child Abuse Prevention and Treatment Act of 1974 defined maltreatment as "the physical or mental injury, sexual abuse, negligent treatment or maltreatment of a child under the age of 18." Each state has its own definition for use by the courts and by public and private agencies. Child abuse and neglect take the following forms: physical abuse, sexual abuse, neglect, emotional abuse or neglect, and prenatal substance abuse.

Physical Abuse

Dr. C. Henry Kempe and his colleagues, in their groundbreaking article, "The Battered Child Syndrome," defined child abuse as a condition with diagnosable medical and physical symptoms in children who have been deliberately injured by a physical assault (Kempe, Silverman, Steele, Droegemueller, & Silver, 1962). Since publication of this article, the medical profession has developed research and literature that describes symptoms indicative of different types of physical child abuse. These symptoms include bruises, burns, fractures, head, eye, and mouth injuries, abdominal injuries, poisoning, and parent-induced or fabricated symptoms. Careful medical diagnosis is needed to determine whether the injuries were accidental or intentional. Medical personnel obtain a detailed, concise history from the parent as to how and when the injury occurred and compare that history with the medical evidence of trauma before making a determination as to whether physical abuse has occurred.

Various theories have been proposed to explain the causative factors of physical abuse of children. The medical model of abuse focuses on abnormal emotional characteristics of the parent, who needs clinical diagnosis and treatment. In contrast, a sociocultural model focuses on variables external to the individual, such as poverty, social isolation, pornography, and social violence against poor families (Giovannoni & Becerra, 1979). An ecological model adds the elements of dysfunctional patterns of family interaction, abuse-promoting cultural values, and the quality of social networks and supports (Belsky, 1980). In a fourth theory, an individual–environmental model finds physical abuse to contain three main factors: special parent, special child, and a crisis (Schneider, Pollock, & Helfer, 1972).

Sexual Abuse

A child is sexually abused when the child suffers from rape or incest, is exploited for pornographic reasons, or is molested by any act that can be reasonably expected to disturb, irritate, trouble, or offend the child victim (California Penal Code). Child abuse expert David Finkelhor analyzes the experience of sexual abuse in four traumagenic dynamics: traumatic sexualization, stigmatization, betrayal, and powerlessness. That is, the child is rewarded for sexual behavior, has a distorted sense of self-worth, learns someone he or she loved has harmed him or her, and has a distorted sense of personal ability to control life (Finkelhor & Browne, 1986).

The National Center on Child Abuse manual on Child Sexual Abuse suggests two causal factors in sexual abuse: prerequisites and contributors. Prerequisite factors include sexual arousal to children and the propensity to act on arousal. Contributing factors emanate from the culture, the family, the marriage, and the perpetrator's personality, life history, or current situation. Alcohol or drug abuse may increase the risk of sexual abuse as would unsupervised access to children (Faller, 1993).

Many children who are sexually abused do not exhibit any physical symptoms of the abuse. Proving the case may depend on the child's statements and any corroborative evidence that can be collected to support the child. Physical signs of sexual abuse can include bruises, scratches, bites, sexually transmitted diseases, pregnancy, blood stains on underwear, injury to labia, pain in anal, genital, gastrointestinal, and urinary areas, grasp marks, enuresis, or head trauma caused by wedging against a hard surface. Some behaviors of children can signal that the child may have been sexually abused. Evidence of detailed and age-inappropriate sexually related knowledge or activity, especially by young children, is a strong indicator. Inappropriate, unusual, or aggressive sexual behavior with peers or toys can be another indicator. For the preteen and young teenager, unusually seductive behavior, promiscuity, and pregnancy are indicators for girls, whereas boys may show an exceptional depth of concern about homosexuality. The significance of other behavior changes is related to the child's age and the ruling out of other causes of the atypical behavior.

Neglect

Neglect is the failure to provide proper care, control, and supervision to the child. The neglected child may be consistently dirty, hungry, inappropriately dressed for the weather, sickly, tired, or listless. A child may be medically neglected when a parent or caregiver fails to provide the child with necessary medical or remedial care. Parents who do not provide adequate food, clothing, and shelter to their children when they possess the resources to do so are considered neglectful parents. Parents who fail to send their children to school can be charged with educational neglect. Neglect may be caused inadvertently by a parent who has a developmental disability or by a parent's abandonment of the child. Some parents are charged with neglect for disciplining their children with such force as to cause injury to the child.

Neglect is more common than abuse. In a 1990 study of children in foster care in California, 67% of all children were removed from their homes for neglect, abandonment, and caregiver incapacity; 17% for physical abuse; and 11% for sexual abuse (Watahara & Lobdell, 1990). In addition, the study found that the long-term effects of neglect on the child can be much more debilitating than those of abuse.

Emotional Abuse and Neglect

The National Center on Child Abuse and Neglect (NCCAN) defines emotional abuse as a verbal or emotional assault, close confinement, or threatened harm; emotional neglect is defined as inadequate nurturance or affection, allowance of maladaptive behavior (delinquency), and any other refusal to provide essential care (NCCAN, 1978). Psychologist James Garbarino defines emotional maltreatment as "assault on the psyche," which can include such actions as terrorizing, isolating, ignoring, rejecting, or corrupting (Garbarino, Guttman, & Seeley, 1986).

Determining the incidence of emotional abuse and neglect is difficult because, although emotional maltreatment may be present, physical or sexual abuse or neglect is reported more often. Emotional abuse often is undetected until a child reaches adolescence. Rarely does an incident of sexual abuse or physical abuse or neglect occur without accompanying emotional maltreatment. Conversely, emotional abuse and neglect can occur without physical or sexual abuse. The emotional effects of child maltreatment often are more damaging and longer lasting than those of physical or sexual abuse. Unfortunately, the child placed in multiple foster homes or institutions also may suffer emotional neglect at the hands of the very system given the power to protect the child from harm.

States must mandate reporting of "mental injury" in their child abuse statutes in order to receive federal funds from the Child Abuse Prevention and Treatment Act of 1988. However, the inclusion of emotional abuse and neglect in juvenile codes is difficult because the terms defining cause, treatment, and consequences are vague. Some scholars urge avoidance of the inexact emotional abuse and neglect concept in writing regulations and social services policies because the so-called objectively observable symptoms, such as depression or withdrawal, could result from a multitude of other factors (Goldstein, Freud, & Solnit, 1973). Other professionals argue that parental behavior can have such devastating effects on the psychologically battered child that a finely drawn definition must be included in the law and in service mandates of public and private agencies (Helfer & Kempe, 1987).

Prenatal Substance Abuse

In recent years the use of drugs has had a profound effect on the newborn. The National Association for Perinatal Addiction Research and Education estimates that 375,000 infants, or 1 in every 10 newborns in the United States, has been prenatally exposed to drugs (Toufexis, 1991). Marijuana, cocaine, and alcohol, as well as some prescription medications, tobacco products, and caffeine, can present serious threats to the pregnancy or to fetal development. Distinguishing the effects of one drug from another is complicated by the widespread concomitant use of a variety of drugs. Polydrug use is, in fact, more common than single-drug use. To further complicate etiology, alcohol often is used to counteract the down side of the drug cycle. The American Medical Association, former Surgeon General Koop, and numerous other experts have concluded that total abstinence is the only way to ensure an absence of ill effects from alcohol consumption during pregnancy (American Academy of Pediatrics, 1993; Council on Scientific Affairs, 1989).

A positive toxicology screen of the newborn provides direct evidence of drugs in the body only within the 72 hours prior to birth. Therefore, although positive toxicology tests do not prove the child has been harmed, a negative screen does not prove the child has escaped harm. The cluster of evidence that may indicate harm to the child includes: 1) premature birth at less than 37 weeks, 2) low birth weight, 3) small head circumference, and 4) abnormal neurobehavioral development.

REPORTING CHILD ABUSE

Statutory reporting laws clarify the duty of the professional to report reasonable suspicion of abuse. With passage of the 1974 Child Abuse Prevention and Treatment Act, the comprehensive system of child protection that was created contained the requirement that states receiving those funds must mandate reporting of child abuse and neglect (42 U.S.C.A. 5103). This has been further refined to make certain that reasonable suspicion of abuse or neglect is included as part of universal mandatory reporting laws. As an added effort to protect children, those reporting laws abrogate the statutory professional–client privilege.

Although it is a difficult challenge to define abuse and neglect precisely, and although specialists in child service professions vary greatly in their standards for reporting and treatment, each of the 50 states has now adopted a definition of physical, sexual, and emotional abuse and neglect and has mandated reporting. In most states, mandatory reporters include licensed mental health professionals as well as physicians, teachers, day care workers, and others who have professional contact with children. In some states, all persons, professional or not, have a mandatory duty to report any reasonable suspicion of abuse or neglect. By understanding how abuse is defined, the signs to look for before making a report, and the choice society has made to give child protection preference over patient confidentiality, the person making a report can feel assured of contributing to both the protection of innocent children and support for quality care and treatment for child victims and their families.

Some states have dealt with the prenatal drug exposure issue by mandating that prenatal drug exposure and parental drug use be reported. As of 1991, 21 states required the reporting of drug-exposed babies and three mandated reporting pregnant substance abusers (McCurdy & Daro, 1993). The condition of an infant that triggers mandatory reporting laws varies from state to state. Some require only a positive toxicology screen; other states require physical signs of addiction or dependence.

SOCIAL AND LEGAL PROCESSES IN CASES OF ABUSE

Several significant events in the first half of this century have helped to bring national recognition and response to the problems and treatment of child abuse and neglect. At the height of the Great Depression, the first large-scale federal intervention to prevent neglect—the creation of the Aid to Families with Dependent Children (AFDC) program —was an integral part of the 1935 Social Security Act. This major federal program sought to provide basic income to single mothers who could not otherwise provide the minimum necessities of life for their children. Three decades later, in 1962, Henry Kempe and his medical colleagues identified the battered child as a child who needs protection from an abusive parent. By 1974, the federal government heeded the resulting national outcry by allotting funds to each state that statutorily mandated the reporting of child abuse and established Child Protective Services units to respond to those reports (42 U.S.C. 620 et seq. and 670 et seq.).

By the end of the 1970s, thousands of abused children had been placed in foster care and left there to drift until they aged out of the system. Then, in 1980, the landmark Adoption Assistance and Child Welfare Act was passed. This federal act was designed to prevent unnecessary placement of children in foster care by mandating that reasonable efforts be made to prevent out-of-home placement and, if placement does become necessary, that reasonable efforts be made to reunify the family as quickly as possible. Keeping families together was the motto for child protection agencies of the 1980s. Although the foster care population dropped at the beginning of the decade, plans to provide more than lip service to this new agenda of family-oriented intervention were washed away with the decade's devastating budget cuts to children's services and to such related public services as housing and mental health. Families simply did not receive the support they needed while struggling through a prolonged recession, and children became the most deprived victims of our society.

As child abuse reports continued to come in to investigative agencies, the responses often were more punitive than supportive. By the mid-1980s a surge in numbers of infants born with drug exposure and the renewal of budgetary cuts caused an increase not just in reports, but in foster care placements. With child abuse fatalities rising in the 1990s, policy makers are taking a renewed interest in funding in-home protective services as well as such neglect and abuse prevention programs as Head Start, Women, Infants and Children (WIC), drug rehabilitation (especially for pregnant women,) child support enforcement, and improved health screening, diagnosis, and treatment. These services work hand in hand in the effort to keep families safely together.

Too often, however, parents may slip into stressful situations that bring about an urgent need for public services they do not know how to find or how to utilize. Mindy and her children are a typical example:

∞

Mindy came to the attention of the child protective services (CPS) unit when she went to a hospital emergency room in her fifth month of pregnancy. The fetus had stopped moving and Mindy was afraid the baby was dead. Hospital personnel assured her the fetus was fine. Mindy admitted to smoking crack cocaine the night before. She had tried to stay away from drugs since learning she was pregnant, but her boyfriend Jim was a dealer and when he got high he wanted Mindy to join him. Besides, she explained, caring for three young children was very stressful, and drugs offered an escape.

The hospital social worker offered to find a drug rehabilitation program for Mindy immediately. Mindy agreed she needed intensive inpatient treatment but was worried about her children. She had left her two preschool children with a friend. An older child was at school. Jim was in no condition to care for the children. The social worker called the CPS unit to see if they could find a safe place for the children while Mindy participated in the drug treatment program.

The investigative CPS worker asked Mindy to sign a voluntary agreement to place the children in foster care. Mindy did not want her children in foster care. She said she thought her mother might be willing to take care of them for a few months, but would not have the energy to care for them day and night. Also, her social security income could not support so many people. The CPS worker explained that the first placement they seek is always with relatives so the children will feel at home. She also told Mindy that foster care funds may be paid to relative caregivers who qualify as foster parents. The foster home investigation normally takes a few days, but she offered to expedite it so the children would not have to go to an emergency shelter.

Although Mindy was still worried, she consented to foster placement, voicing the feeling she had no other choice. Mindy's mother had been avoiding her because of her drug habit and her child care practices. The last time her mother saw the children and the mess the apartment was in, she threatened to report Mindy for neglecting the children. Mindy's mother had made it clear that she wanted Mindy to get off drugs, and Mindy said she trusted her mother with the care of her children. The older child needed to be in an after-school program and the younger two in day care, but they would have their grandmother to come home to. Mindy expressed worry about losing her apartment because, without the children, she would not have AFDC or her low-cost housing voucher. The social worker agreed to help Mindy get back her AFDC benefits and find adequate housing as soon as she finished her rehabilitation program. By this time, Mindy had begun to feel comfortable with voluntarily placing her children in foster care until she could break her drug habit. With the day care and after-school care in place, she could look forward to taking better care of all her children after the birth of the baby.

∞

Perhaps this picture seems unreasonably bleak, but it is reality for many families. Prenatal care, drug rehabilitation, AFDC, food stamps, day care, after-school care, and low-cost housing are services someone in Mindy's shoes needs but, commonly, has difficulty accessing on his or her own. The range of services urgently needed by most at-risk families are not located within the same agency, if they exist at all. Although Mindy was resourceful enough to seek help in an emergency, her children easily could have become separated from her for months or even years had her community's configuration of human resources been less integrated or had there been insufficient support funds because of governmental budget limitations. This would present her children with another, and possibly worse, set of environmental and emotional challenges: the risk of separation from each other, perhaps in farflung foster homes, in addition to the time and distance barriers to visitation by their mother, with the resultant loss of attachment.

The legal and social services system that has developed in response to the problem of child abuse and neglect is complex, and even a well-organized parent without the complications of pregnancy or drug addiction will find it difficult to mobilize the initiative and expertise needed to gain access to basic family services. Every state has established a CPS unit to respond to reports of child abuse 24 hours a day. Unfortunately, although the response reflects community concern about identifying children who need protection, it sometimes stops there. The wide-ranging services and agency coordination these children require to be able to remain safely in the home are far more challenging to develop than are reporting hotlines and investigative units. Agencies are bureaucracies with budget allocations often restricted to a specific area of service: mental health therapy, education, drug rehabilitation, housing, nursing, child support, medical care, child care, welfare, job training, recreation. For these agencies to work together effectively to enable a family to stay together, it is essential to have well-coordinated and precise budgetary and staff planning.

A careful investigative process follows the report to ensure the validity of the charge and to protect persons named who may be innocent of the charges. This investigation is equally concerned with the family's potential for utilizing protective services with the alternative being out-of-home placement and separation of the children from family members. The child's best interests are paramount in the decisions made to work toward preserving the family unit by marshalling a broad spectrum of community services or to remove the children from the care and control of their parents.

Investigating Child Abuse Reports

Reports to the Department of Children's Services or to the police are screened to determine whether they warrant investigation. Some reports involve children who have been harmed by noncaregiver adults outside the home. These cases, which do not come under the legal definition of child abuse, are referred to the police because the child does not need to be protected from a parent or caregiver. In family/caregiver abuse cases, the intake worker determines whether the report involves children in an already active case and refers this report to the CPS worker handling the case. New cases are assigned a CPS worker at this time.

In 1991, out of a total of 2.7 million child abuse reports in the United States, over 700,000 were unsubstantiated. The term *unsubstantiated* does not necessarily mean the reported abuse or neglect did not occur, but it does indicate that some reports arise from spiteful child custody battles or interpersonal hostilities, or are made by well-meaning reporters whose standards for parental behavior are higher than the minimum acceptable in the community (Besharov, 1990). In general, substantiated cases are more critical and more complex. These families usually have needs that involve multiple community service systems, such as health, drug treatment, mental health, nutrition, and housing. As money for publicly funded protective services is diminishing, the threshold for substantiation is rising. Children in need of services must be at higher risk before services will be provided.

The most serious reports of abuse and neglect must be investigated immediately. Thorough investigation involves gathering information from a parent or caregiver, medical personnel, mental health professional, police, school or day care personnel, relative, or neighbor, and/or personal observation by the CPS worker. All valid reports must result in a face-to-face investigation of the child. A child's behavior or condition may suggest that further psychological or physical evaluation is needed in order to determine what, if any, harm the child has suffered and how the child was harmed. All data are recorded carefully so that the information may be used later in court if necessary.

The CPS worker who makes the investigation assesses the danger to the child along with the family's strengths and weaknesses and then determines whether the family has the potential to be helped sufficiently by protective services to forestall placement of the child out of the home. The CPS worker looks for family strengths to build on so the child can remain in the home, with protective services provided if needed. Sometimes other family members or close friends can stay with the children until the parent's condition stabilizes. Concrete services such as housing, emergency aid, or food stamps can keep a child in the home if made available before family needs reach a crisis level and threaten the children's safety. Some decisions regarding removal must be made quickly because of the late hour or the seriousness of the situation. Determining whether to place children out of the home after a report is investigated is a complex process.

∞

> The report came from the police station, where charges of sexual abuse of the 15-year-old daughter had been made against the father. When the investigative CPS worker arrived at the station, she learned that charges of spousal abuse and physical child abuse also were being filed. The mother, daughter, and son described what the father had done and left no doubt about whether the case could be substantiated. The major responsibility for the CPS worker was the decision as to whether the children could remain in the mother's care.
>
> Because the girl had told her mother about the abuse over a year earlier and the mother had taken few steps to protect her, the mother's ability to protect the children was questioned. She had taken her children out of town to live with relatives, but later forgave the father and returned. Because the father was likely to be released on bail, the initial CPS recommendation was for the family to go to a shelter. The mother did not want this because of her religious practices, which required food and prayer restrictions impossible to maintain at a public shelter. Instead, she wanted to stay with friends. Afraid the mother would return to the father again, the CPS worker said she could go

with her friends but the children would have to go to the emergency children's shelter. On hearing that, the mother agreed to go to the shelter.

When the mother's friends arrived at the police station, the CPS worker discussed the situation with them. She determined that these friends could offer the children and their mother a safe placement with a religious and cultural setting that would make them feel at home. The mother's fear and anxiety changed to relief when she realized that she and her children could remain together as a family and stay with their friends. The decision had not been an easy one. The CPS worker had to weigh the emotional well-being and attachment of the children to their nonabusing parent against their physical and psychological danger from the abusing parent. Psychological, cultural, and religious factors all had to be considered in determining where to place the children. Follow-up services will be provided so the mother and children can remain together as the father goes through the criminal process and all members of the family receive the counseling and support services they need.

∞

In most substantiated cases of child abuse, the children can avoid the need for placement during the period of the family crisis that precipitated the abuse or neglect. If the investigating worker substantiates abuse or neglect, in-home services can be offered to the family in an effort to protect the children and keep the family together. The CPS worker prepares a written service contract or a verbal agreement that usually is negotiated in an early session between the CPS unit and the parents. The contract spells out the target problem(s), goals and objectives, plan of action by parents and social services agency, and time limits. The parents can cooperate with the plan by agreeing to the services and entering into the contract to fulfill the parental obligations specified as a condition of keeping custody of the children. If the parents refuse to accept the services and the children remain in danger, the CPS worker may petition the court for custody of the children so they can be placed immediately with relatives or in foster care.

Intervening to Preserve the Family Unit

In a nonemergency situation, before a child is removed from the home for either abuse or neglect, the CPS unit is mandated by federal funding laws to provide services to keep the family together. Prior to 1980, the federal foster care program provided unlimited federal reimbursement to states to cover their foster care costs. To put a stop to inappropriate, prolonged, and multiplacement foster care, the Adoption Assistance and Child Welfare Act (PL 96-272) was passed in 1980. The goal of PL 96-272 is to provide services to prevent the placement of children in foster care, to reunite children with their families as soon as possible after placement, and to maximize adoption opportunities for children for whom adoption is an appropriate plan. Eligibility for federal foster care funding requires that children receiving or eligible for AFDC may not be placed in foster care unless: 1) reasonable efforts are made prior to placement to prevent or eliminate the need for removal of the children from their home, and 2) if they must be placed, to provide reunification services to make it possible for them to return home (42 U.S.C.A. 671 [a] [15]).

The Indian Child Welfare Act of 1978 (PL 95-608) gives American Indian tribes jurisdiction over custody procedures involving their children and authority to provide services that address the needs of Native American children. The act was designed to halt practices that threatened Native American families and cultures. This act requires that "active efforts" be made to provide remedial services and rehabilitative programs and that these be proven unsuccessful before a child may be removed from the home (Northwest Resource Associates, 1986). These distinctions must be remembered when working with Native American families in the context of abuse and neglect, because legal requirements for in-home services and removal of the child differ in such cases.

Making reasonable efforts to prevent placement requires more than referral to other agencies. The reasonable efforts mandate was designed to encourage counties to provide such in-home services as:

1. Parenting training
2. Out-of-home respite care
3. Day care or after-school care
4. Temporary or emergency in-home caregivers
5. Persons to teach or demonstrate homemaking skills
6. Welfare services such as AFDC, food stamps, the WIC program, Medicaid, cash assistance, or emergency shelter
7. Counseling services, including assessment, diagnosis, testing, and short-term therapy
8. Transportation
9. Health support services, including family planning
10. Housing and home improvement services

It has been suggested that some families should be excluded from the reasonable efforts mandate, including those with infants who have been seriously injured or malnourished or those in which the parents are not amenable to treatment because of mental illness or debilitation by drug or alcohol abuse and are unable to provide minimal child care (Crittenden, 1992). However, many parents neglect their children only because they cannot cover minimum family expenses or fulfill their children's other basic needs in some way. In-home services such as homemaker services, parenting skills training, family counseling, or financial aid can be of significant help. Multifaceted problems, which are becoming more common with the increases in substance abuse and poverty, need more than one-stop-shopping solutions. The CPS worker may be limited by the availability of services. Although PL 96-272 requires that reasonable efforts be made to provide services less restrictive than foster care, federal dollars did not fund sufficient services but continued to fund foster care, thus defying the basic purpose of the act.

The CPS worker may not have access to many of the services a parent must have to prevent neglect or to decrease the stress that may lead to abuse. However, to make reasonable efforts, the CPS worker must endeavor to find services that meet the specific needs of the family. In response to the reasonable efforts mandate, special family-focused programs have developed that aim to keep families together. Two of the most useful types are family preservation programs and programs for children with disabilities.

Family Preservation Programs Family preservation is a type of crisis intervention that focuses on providing in-home services by a social worker or mental health professional who is responsible for only one or two cases. All energy centers on making the crisis a catalyst for positive, long-term change. Because this short-term intervention is aimed at preventing foster care placement, only families on the verge of having a child removed from the home are accepted. The caseworker responds to the family around the clock, maintaining flexible hours 7 days a week. He or she deals with each family as a unit, rather than focusing on individual parents or children as problematic individuals. The caseworker sees families at home rather than in the office, making frequent visits convenient to a family's schedule. The first-hand experience in the home gives the caseworker the opportunity to observe the family dynamics and offer help on the spot. An understanding of how the particular family functions as a system forms the basis for teaching family members skills needed to obtain necessary resources, services, and counseling. If a family needs a service not normally provided at public agencies, the caseworker makes every effort to find those services. The in-home assessment of the family helps the family build on its strengths and gives the caseworker and the court crucial information needed in making permanent placement decisions about the children (Edna McConnell Clark Foundation, 1985; "Tennesee's Home Ties," 1993).

∞

Kristi is referred to CPS by her doctor when he sees her baby for a third ear infection. She has not given the infant the prescribed penicillin. His fever spiked and he had two convulsions before she brought him to the emergency room. The doctor has placed the baby on a hospital hold pending an investigation. The CPS worker meets Kristi in the hospital waiting room to discuss the baby's condition. Kristi is afraid her three children will be taken away. She explains that she does not have a job or enough income to pay the rent. She used up her annual emergency assistance allotment, which meant that, when the baby got another ear infection near the end of the month, she could not afford to buy the penicillin. Her husband has not returned since he beat her up a month ago, but she is afraid he will show up when she gets her next AFDC check in the mail. He is using methamphetamines, which trigger his violent behavior.

With the children now at high risk for foster care placement, family preservation services are the next step. The CPS worker spends the morning at Kristi's home, scheduling house calls by a visiting public health nurse and looking into specialized day care for the toddler. She contacts the teacher and school counselor to inquire about the oldest child's situation and arranges after-school care for him. Medicaid pays for the penicillin, and the WIC program and food stamps help Kristi obtain food for her family. A nearby church has an emergency fund to help pay for utilities so the AFDC check can be used for rent. The CPS worker also used this home visit with Kristi to help identify her positive parenting and homemaking skills and to observe family dynamics. The CPS worker plans to show Kristi ways to budget her time as well as her money, but she goes slowly so Kristi will not be overwhelmed with too many changes and new responsibilities. Kristi is referred to the local women's center, where she can join a support group and learn how to obtain a temporary restraining order against her husband.

The CPS worker remains involved with Kristi and her children for 6 weeks, working with her through another end-of-the-month cycle to make certain she can survive both the stress of stretching her meager income to pay basic bills and her fear of her husband's return. The first week, the CPS worker arrives at 7 A.M. to help Kristi organize her morning routine so she can get all the children dressed, fed, and off to school and child care. By the second week, Kristi feels she can handle the morning schedule by herself. The CPS worker then reduces the time she spends with Kristi to late afternoon and early evening until the fourth week. After accompanying Kristi on a well-baby visit to the doctor and helping her enroll in a job training class, the social worker leaves her to manage on her own, feeling that family preservation averted unnecessary foster care placement. Kristi is now attached to support systems in the community, and she knows she can call the social worker when she needs help.

∞

Existing family preservation programs have been developed and funded at the state and local levels. The success of many of these programs in keeping families together finally led to the passage in 1993 of Family Preservation and Support provisions on the federal level. One billion dollars over 5 years will provide specific services to keep children with their parents and keep agencies from using foster care as a first rather than last resort for protecting children. Keeping families together with in-home services costs less than foster care and helps preserve the family unit. A study in Tennessee found that the average cost of a family preservation program was $2,255 per child, as compared with the $10,000 needed to maintain the child in foster care for a year ("Tennessee's Home Ties," 1993). In addition, investing money at the beginning of intervention is seen by many professionals as the surest, most cost-effective way of protecting abused and neglected children. The delay of federal legislation and its accompanying funding represented a continuing social disaster in which many families were denied public services to prevent abuse and neglect until the children had already suffered.

The overall effectiveness of family preservation programs has been the subject of several recent studies, in which they have received mixed reviews. In one study of 530 families, the majority of the children avoided out-of-home placement. Children from neglectful families were almost twice as likely to be placed as children from abusive families, and those suffering both abuse and neglect were at highest risk of placement (Bath & Haapala, 1993). In another study, family preservation was found to keep families together during the short period in which in-home services were provided. However, many of the families surfaced again in the abuse/neglect system, usually within a year after services were discontinued, indicating that treatment effects faded over time (Feldman, 1991). Children in poverty, or those who are homeless or have parents with emotional, mental, and addictive difficulties, need a longer intervention period for success, with recommendations ranging from 9 months (Gaudin, Wodarski, Arkinson, & Avery, 1990–1991) to 18 months (Daro, 1988). If support services are continued by the agency after family preservation efforts, lasting success is more likely, especially when concrete services such as housing, food stamps, or emergency assistance are provided.

Programs for Children with Disabilities Two federal programs have recently made it easier for services to be provided for the child with disabilities who may be abused or neglected. The first of these, the Federal Infant–Toddler Program of early intervention (Part H of PL 99-457, the Education of the Handicapped Act Amendments of 1986), encourages states to establish comprehensive, multidisciplinary systems of early intervention services for children with disabilities from birth to the third birthday who meet state-established eligibility criteria. Amendments added in 1991 clarify the requirement of this program to include both an eligible child and the child's family in an assessment as follows:

(1) a multidisciplinary assessment of the unique strengths and needs of the infant or toddler and the identification of services appropriate to meet such needs, and

(2) a family-directed assessment or identification of the supports and services necessary to enhance the family's capacity to meet the developmental needs of an infant or toddler with a disability. (20 U.S.C. Sec. 1477 [a])

Services available through this federal program may provide just the support the parent at high risk for abuse needs to keep the child with disabilities safely in the home. Family training, counseling, and home-based consultation are available, as are nursing, psychological, nutritional, and social services. As a critical facilitator, transportation is provided, when necessary, to enable the child and family to receive early intervention services (20 U.S.C. Sec. 1472 [2] [E]). This family program is intended to strengthen the parent's role in the care of the child rather than subject the parent to the guilty, dependent role of one whose children have been removed for abuse or neglect.

Children with disabilities who are victims of child abuse and neglect also are finding needed services through educational and social benefit programs. Many children at risk for foster care placement have special education needs that can be met if they are identified early and treated in the public school. In a study of children entering foster care in Cook County, Illinois, a third of the children eligible for school either had not yet been enrolled or were identified as needing special education. Of the children 3 years of age and under, 52% needed an infant stimulation program; 57% of those over 3 years of age needed psychological intervention (Hochstadt, Jaudes, Zimo, & Schachter, 1987). The Individuals with Disabilities Education Act mandates evaluations for children recommended for special education and individualized education plans for each child identified as needing these special educational services. A guiding principle is to provide children who have physical, mental, or learning disabilities with appropriate education services in the least restrictive environment suited to meet their individual needs. Toward that goal, children with disabilities are mainstreamed with other children for as much of the day as possible. Children who have serious emotional disturbances may spend most of the day in a special classroom or, if the disability is quite serious, may be schooled at a special day or residential treatment center.

The liberalized Supplemental Security Income (SSI) program has become another contributor to family stability. Within income limitations, the parent may be eligible for SSI funds for any child with a condition or illness that results in a substantial disability. Family income eligibility levels for receipt of the monthly SSI check are more liberal than those for some public assistance programs, such as general relief or AFDC. In 1990, the Supreme Court decision in *Sullivan v. Zebley* became a potentially strong force for prevention by broadening the eligibility for moderate-income parents whose children have chronic and severe disabilities to receive monthly SSI payments of over $400. Along with the monthly income, the parent will receive automatic Medicaid coverage for the child (20 C.F.R. 416.924).

Parents with children who have disabilities have an added chronic dimension of stress that puts them at higher risk for abuse or neglect. Because these public support programs are relatively new, many parents who need them are not aware of how much help is available. A caseworker sensitive to the special needs of the parent of a child with developmental delays or other disabilities will make certain the parent knows how to connect with programs that provide supplemental income, health care coverage, and supportive services. Having the double security of a regular source of income and medical care can make all the difference for some parents between being able to care for their children with disabilities at home and being forced to place them in institutions or special foster homes.

∞

Sheri is positive for human immunodeficiency virus (HIV). Her 8-year-old son Lee learned to read the *TV Guide* when he was 3 years old; he is in a magnet school for gifted children. Her 6-year-old twins were prenatally exposed to drugs and alcohol. Cary has cerebral palsy, limited vision, and extreme developmental delays and is still not toilet trained. Justin has learning disabilities but has made great strides his last year in special kindergarten. His attention deficit hyperactivity disorder makes him difficult to watch when he is not in a small, tightly structured classroom. Sheri has more trouble parenting Justin than Cary. The stress of caring for all three boys wears her down physically and emotionally.

The twins received substantial services from infancy through age 3 in an extensive daytime intervention program. Cary receives SSI payments that allow $114 per month for respite care. This gives Sheri time for doctor's appointments and grocery shopping without all three boys in tow. Sheri receives AFDC for Justin and Lee. All three boys have medical, dental, and mental health coverage through the federal Early Periodic Screening, Diagnosis, and Treatment Program (EPSDT) for children living in poverty. Sheri relies heavily on federal and state assistance and is determined to keep her family intact. In order to avoid foster care placement when her health deteriorates, Sheri has joined a support group for mothers with HIV or acquired immunodeficiency syndrome who want to find potential guardians and adoptive parents to take their children when they are no longer able to care for them.

∞

Removing the Child from the Home

Countless parents do not have the community social supports in place that help them withstand the stress of poverty, disability, or addiction. New federal programs can provide needed services and health coverage to qualified children, but basic services for parents, such as housing, job training, or drug rehabilitation, are underfunded or nonexistent. The absence of preventive services leaves some parents with no help for the stresses that result in their unloading negative feelings and frustration on their children by way of neglect or abuse. Those children must be protected.

The CPS worker must consider several factors in determining whether to remove such children from the home. Is the child seriously injured or seriously ill? Did the parent's action or inaction cause the child's condition? Are the parents able or motivated to make the changes necessary to make the home safe for the child? Have services been provided that match the specific needs of the family? If these services failed, should others be tried before removing the child? Will the child suffer more harm in the long run if removed and placed in the uncertainty of foster care?

Petitioning for Emergency Removal Before removing the child from the parent's home, the caseworker must file a petition with the court requesting emergency removal and must specify the acts of abuse or neglect and the futility of making reasonable efforts to keep the family together. The child then may be removed and placed in a temporary foster home or emergency shelter. An immediate detention hearing is held for the judge to determine whether there are good reasons to keep the child in foster care pending the adjudication.

∞

Renee was on crutches when she came to the detention hearing for her children. The judge needed to determine if there was good reason to allow Renee's baby and 3-year-old son to remain in emergency foster care until the adjudication hearing in 3 weeks. The social worker briefly told the court that she had gone to pick up the children at the police station the night before after police had been called to the mother's home because of gunshots. The mother was holding the baby when she was hit in the foot by rifle fire. Renee had been reported twice before. The CPS worker had been working with her for months, but was having little success in weaning her away from her violent boyfriend, who was involved in a drug gang. A previous court order, finding neglect, had ordered Renee to cooperate in in-home services, parenting training, and drug rehabilitation. At the detention hearing, the judge determined that the children would be safer in foster care than with their mother. He did order the social worker to provide transportation to Renee so that she could visit with her children at least twice each week prior to the next hearing.

∞

In a study of abuse and neglect cases in Denver, Los Angeles, and Newcastle, Delaware (Tjaden & Thoennes, 1992), chronic maltreatment, abandonment, and sexual abuse cases were more likely to result in a dependency court filing. Hearings for cases of physical abuse, neglect, and emotional abuse were more likely to begin with settlements voluntarily produced by caseworkers and parents. In half the cases opened for services, the child was placed out of the home at least temporarily either by parental agreement or by court order. The frequency and severity of maltreatment and prior CPS reports, rather than type of maltreatment, were case variables significantly and positively related to the decision to remove the child from the home. Even so, 44% of the children who were removed did not suffer severe maltreatment, 33% had experienced only a single episode, and 44% had no prior CPS report (Tjaden & Thoennes, 1992).

Adjudication Court approval is necessary for continued placement of a child in foster care, and can be given only after the court has determined that the child suffered abuse or neglect within the statutory definition of those terms. This determination is made at a hearing called an adjudication, which usually is scheduled within a month from the date of removal of the child from the home. The juvenile court judge determines whether the child has been harmed or threatened with harm and to what extent the parent is responsible. The purpose of the juvenile court hearing is to provide protection to the child if it is found necessary.

During the time the juvenile court is providing protection to the child, another proceeding may be occurring in criminal court to prove guilt and inflict punishment. Usually, only the most egregious cases are also heard in criminal court. In the Tjaden and Thoennes (1992) study, only 4% of the sample cases had associated criminal proceedings. Criminal prosecution was much more likely in cases of sexual abuse, especially those involving elementary school–age girls. If the victims were too young, they were not viewed as credible witnesses; if they were adolescents, the prosecutors feared they might be viewed as promiscuous or angry, thus casting doubt on their testimony. Criminal prosecution was found not to be related to the frequency of maltreatment (Tjaden & Thoennes, 1992).

The juvenile court judge also will need to determine whether the agency made reasonable efforts to provide services needed to keep the family together or if this is an emergency situation in which the child cannot be protected without removal (Dodson, 1983). The court will consider the family services made available before the child was removed, why the efforts made to provide family services did not prevent removal of the child, and whether the efforts made to prevent removal of the child were reasonable.

∞

A mother suffering mental illness had a 4-year-old child who was placed out of the home after a finding of neglect. The mother attended biweekly visits with her son for about 6 months, then lost contact with the agency. The CPS worker had discussed psychotherapy with the mother on several occasions but never reviewed the mother's psychiatric hospital record. The CPS worker failed to discuss the mother with the agency psychiatrist, or make any appointments for the mother to meet with the psychiatrist. Despite her absence, the New York Appellate Court refused to allow termination of the mother's parental rights because the agency failed to make reasonable efforts to remedy the mother's mental illness, which was the problem preventing the child's return. (*In re Shantelle,* 1992)

∞

To aid in the adjudication process, the National Council of Juvenile and Family Court Judges (1992) released a Protocol for making reasonable efforts determinations in cases involving drug-dependent mothers. The guidelines provide a comprehensive list of suggested questions for the judge:

Does the social service agency report include information on resources available to the family?
Has there been adequate interagency or intraagency coordination to ensure that concrete services have been made available in a timely manner so that the child is not removed as a result of delays in processing approval or beginning delivery of such services?
How has the social service agency helped the substance-abusing parent obtain treatment?
Has there been an assessment by substance abuse professionals of the mother's substance abuse problems, with recommendations for appropriate treatment?

Has the agency identified appropriate programs that are experienced and qualified in treating women with the mother's particular addiction and problems with small children?

Are the programs accessible to the mother financially as well as in other ways?

Did the agency provide or help the mother obtain transportation and day care so that she could attend treatment?

Have appropriate and frequent visitation opportunities been facilitated for all family members to promote reunification of those children who have been placed?

Have appropriate, family-focused services been provided to promote reunification?

Are active family strengthening services being continued after reunification has occurred?

Has the availability/eligibility of the following service programs been examined: family-centered drug treatment services, other family-centered services, intensive family preservation services, counseling, emergency housing, in-home caregiver, out-of-home respite care, teaching and demonstrating homemakers, parent skills training, transportation, emergency cash assistance, and government aid programs such as WIC food supplement program, food stamps, AFDC, Medicaid, SSI, disability payments, and Head Start or age-appropriate infant/child care programs?

After determining the issues of abuse or neglect and reasonable efforts, the court considers whether the child should remain in the home or be placed in foster care.

Disposition Hearing The judge determines where the child will be placed and what services should be ordered at the disposition hearing. Questions are asked about the parent's ability and motivation to make changes rapidly so the child can remain in the home or be returned to the home from emergency foster care placement. The special needs of the child also are considered, including what harm the child may be expected to suffer if separated from the parents. The court has a number of choices. The judge may decide to allow the child to remain in the home or return to the care of the parents with in-home protective services ordered. The child may be placed in the home of relatives, with certain restrictions placed on the parent's interaction with and responsibilities to the child. If children are placed in foster care, all efforts will be made to place siblings together and near enough to parents to facilitate frequent visitation. The parents may be ordered to comply with a visitation schedule, and to participate in drug treatment or parenting education programs.

The decision to place may be based more on local placement policies, placement availability, or publicity over a recent child homicide than any actual changes in family dynamics that may have occurred during family preservation efforts. The court may order CPS to provide counseling, transportation, child care, or other specific services for the parent or child. Every service ordered must meet a child or parental need that has been entered into evidence. One study of family preservation programs found that the services most successful for neglectful families are parent education and problem solving, specific skills development with concrete demonstrations, personal counseling, and efforts to strengthen and expand the social support network of the parents (Bath & Haapala, 1993).

Six-Month Review Hearing At the disposition hearing, the judge will schedule a court review within 6 months. Prior to this review hearing, the CPS worker will ensure ongoing assessment of progress toward reunification. The family's strengths will be balanced against their problems in areas including medical, nutritional, social, psychological, environmental, educational, developmental, financial, and housing needs. At the 6-month review hearing, if custody is not returned to the parents, the court will consider whether other services should be provided and will continue to look for alternative placements for the child among the extended family or with a nonabusing, noncustodial parent. Another review usually is required within the year. At each hearing, the court will make a finding as to whether the CPS has made reasonable efforts to reunify the family. Unless this determination is made, costs for the foster care placement will not be paid out of federal funds (Dodson, 1983).

The court reviews the progress the parents have made at each review hearing. The child will be returned to the parents if they have followed the court order and progressed enough for the safe return of the children. Often the judge will allow frequency of visits to increase prior to the return of the children in order to provide supervision prior to permanent reunification.

∞

> Sandy was only 17 when she was reported for child abuse. When her baby Crystal began teething, Sandy's frustration with her incessant crying led the young mother to throw Crystal against the wall. The baby sustained broken ribs, but was able to be placed from the hospital into foster care 3 days after the incident. Sandy needed to learn basic parenting skills. The court ordered her to participate in Crystal's child care. Each day Sandy went to the specialized child care center where Crystal had been enrolled and, under the tutelage of the caregivers at the center, Sandy learned to provide care for her. After

2 months in the supervised setting, Sandy was permitted to take Crystal home overnight. By the time of her first 6-month review hearing, the social worker could recommend that Crystal be returned to Sandy.

∞

Reunification with the Family Under federal funding statutes, when a child is placed in foster care, the caseworker must file a case plan with the court that provides a timeline for reunification services. Visitations with the parents must be scheduled, with transportation provided by the social services agency if necessary. When parents cooperate with the service plan and court order, the child usually is returned to them. The time frame for parental compliance may range from 1 day to 2 years. If special precautions must be taken, the child will be allowed only supervised visits with the parents. If all goes well, unsupervised day visits and then weekend visits will be allowed before the child is finally returned home. However, in spite of all efforts in some cases, reunification with the parent does not work because of severely disturbed dynamics between the parent and child.

∞

Bunny's mother was brought to the attention of CPS when she gave birth to a prenatally drug-exposed baby boy. Sixteen-year-old Bunny and her four brothers and sisters were allowed to remain in the home under voluntary CPS supervision until the mother had three consecutive negative drug tests. When the mother failed to achieve this goal, the children were removed from the home; Bunny was placed separately from her siblings in a group home. She was later allowed to leave the group home to live with an aunt until she and her siblings could be reunified with their mother.

In spite of the mother's continued drug use, the court was convinced the mother was capable of providing adequate care for her children. The children were released to her care on the condition that she enroll in an extensive drug treatment program in the community. Bunny did not want to return to her mother's care because of their "love–hate" relationship. Her mother told the CPS worker that she could not control Bunny and did not want her living in the home. Bunny and her mother were in counseling for 2 months after Bunny made a suicidal gesture. When Bunny refused to return to her mother's care, CPS asked the court to order her to a emergency youth facility. Instead, the court considered the individual emotional needs of the child and, on the recommendation of Bunny's attorney, allowed her to remain in the care of her aunt.

∞

The American Academy of Pediatrics recommends that a child's sense of time should guide the pace of decision making regarding reunification efforts (American Academy of Pediatrics, 1993). However, any time a child spends in temporary care may be harmful because of interruption in the child's continuity of care. Repeated moves back to the parents or from one foster home to another only compound the problem. Children may be returned to foster care several times before the parents are able to assume complete custody. Caseworkers who observe legal time frames for reunification must make permanent plans for children whose parents are not working toward reunification goals.

∞

> Lamont and Shawna were placed in foster care with their grandmother after a finding of chronic parental neglect. Their parents were addicted to drugs. The court ordered the parents to participate in parenting education and drug rehabilitation and provide the court with six clean drug samples before overnight visits would be considered. Over the course of 2 years, the parents participated in drug treatment sporadically, usually just before a court hearing. They attended parenting classes but showed little improvement in parenting skills when they visited Lamont and Shawna. Their home was unstable. During the 2-year period they lived in eight different places. Neither had been able to keep a job.
>
> A new social worker, assigned just before the 18-month review hearing, was influenced by a current methadone clinic report to allow the parents to increase visitation to overnight visits. Before the second overnight visit, the parents asked the grandmother to keep the children because the friends they were living with said the children were too much trouble during the night. The parents quit the methadone treatment after the court hearing and were soon looking for another place to live. By the time of the 2-year hearing, the grandmother asked the court to appoint her guardian for the children so they would not have to continue to be involved in reunification efforts. The children's behavior had deteriorated after each contact with their parents. The new social worker was in the reunification unit and hated to give up on the parents. In spite of her recommendation to give the parents another chance, the judge ordered that the case be transferred to the permanency planning unit, and that the grandmother be awarded guardianship of Lamont and Shawna.

∞

Reunification efforts do not always work. Family members are not always available or willing to provide homes for children of parents who cannot be responsible for their care. Foster parents become frustrated with caring for children who grow anxious and then sad each time their parents fail to come for an allowed visit or do not communicate with them at holidays or birthdays. If the parent does not comply with the court order within the statutory timeframe (usually 1–2 years), or if the original abuse or neglect was extremely severe, most states allow a petition to be filed to terminate parental rights so the child can be placed in a permanent home.

Termination of Parental Rights Seeking termination of parental rights is the natural and legal outcome of parental failure to respond positively to the rehabilitative and reunification services the caseworker offers. Parenthood carries responsibilities for the child that, at a minimum, include the duties to provide necessary food, clothing, shelter, education, and medical care, and a safe environment. These general parental duties are the avenues by which a parent supports and expresses personal concern and love for a child. Only when parents have failed to function adequately as caregivers for the child, despite the efforts of CPS to strengthen the parent–child relationship, should proceedings begin for termination of parental rights. The termination of parental rights is the most serious decision a judge must make in any juvenile proceeding. The result is permanent severing of all ties between the natural parents and their child. Not only do the parents permanently lose custody, they forfeit the right to correspond, visit, or have any communication with the child.

Termination proceedings are initiated with the filing of a petition in juvenile court. The Department of Social Services and, in some states, the child may file the petition. The highly publicized 1992 Florida case of the boy who "divorced" his parents is a well-known example of a termination of parental rights case. Factors alleged in the petition that generally are considered sufficient to terminate parental rights include: abandonment, willful nonsupport, severe or chronic physical abuse, chronic parental mental or physical illness rendering the parent incapable of caring for the child, willfully leaving the child in foster care for an extended period of time without responding to a social service agency's reasonable efforts for reunification, and severe alcohol or drug dependency that endangers the child's welfare.

∞

> A termination of parental rights petition was filed against a mother and father who were schizophrenic and suffered delusions and hallucinations. When their baby Sara was born, CPS was granted custody and placed Sara in foster care. For the next 3 years the parents had supervised visits with their daughter. CPS provided the parents 30 hours of in-home parenting classes but discontinued them because the parents showed no improvement in parenting skills. Although the court believed the parents truly wanted to care for Sara, the court concluded they were not capable of meeting her needs because of their

chronically severe psychiatric problems, which the reunification efforts could not remedy. (*In re Sara K.*, 1992)

∞

In the hearing on the merits of the termination case, the judge must hear evidence, find facts, and decide whether grounds for termination exist. The burden of proof is higher than for an adjudication of abuse or neglect, but not as high as for a finding of guilt in a criminal trial. Once a determination is made that at least one of the grounds exists for termination, the court determines whether it is in the best interest of the child to terminate parental rights. In some states, such as California, a termination petition cannot be considered until an adoptive placement has been found for the child. In other states, the first order of business following the termination is to begin looking for an appropriate adoptive placement.

Interest in finding an alternative permanent home for the child arises only when it is clear that the natural parent cannot or will not provide a minimally adequate family home. Too often, the decision to terminate is not made until the passage of months or even years of attempts to keep the family together. When the alternative is the transiency and security-shattering movement of children in and out of foster care or from one foster home to another, and recurrent wrenchings from parents and siblings, a timely termination decision must be made to allow a permanent home to be established.

PLACEMENT ALTERNATIVES FOR CHILDREN WHO ARE ABUSED

When conditions of abuse or neglect necessitate the removal of a child from his or her home, alternative living arrangements must be made. These alternatives can range from emergency shelters to permanent adoption, depending on the child's situation and his or her parents' ability to change the conditions leading to abuse. Children removed from their homes are first placed temporarily with relatives, in a foster home, or in a variety of institutions such as group homes, halfway houses, or emergency shelters. A study of children in foster care concluded that children's developmental and psychological needs cannot be met well in institutional settings (Simms, 1991). Simms suggested that placement plans should not fall back on institutions simply because poor planning and management do not provide needed foster homes. Until a permanent home can be found for the child, Simms recommended that the foster home be the preferred option for out-of-home care. However, extraordinary physical or emotional needs of the child may require his or her placement in specialized foster homes, group homes, or residential treatment centers.

When the home situation improves, the child may be returned from foster care to his or her family. Because the length of time required for return of a child to his or her natural home can vary greatly depending on the home situation, many children spend prolonged periods of time in foster care, and some are shifted from one foster care placement to another when circumstances do not permit them to remain in the first placement indefinitely. Foster parents may request the child's removal because of physical or emotional problems of the child or for other reasons such as frustration over difficulties resulting from parent visitations. If the home situation does not improve, the courts and social services must petition to terminate parental rights in order to allow the child to be placed for adoption, thus enabling the child to find a new permanent home. However, adoptive homes may be more difficult to find than foster homes, and the legal procedures needed for adoptive placements may discourage adoption as a preferred placement. In addition, the longer a child remains in foster care, the more difficult it becomes to find him or her an adoptive home. Timely application for termination of parental rights is therefore in the best interests of the child.

When adoption is not feasible, alternate legal placements include guardianship and long-term foster care. Unlike adoption, these alternatives do not require termination of parental rights. Unfortunately, when a social services agency does not have sufficient evidence to warrant termination of parental rights, long-term foster placement is often used by the custodial agency as a convenient solution. Although the intent of the Adoption Assistance and Child Welfare Act of 1980 was to place children with adoptive parents if reunification efforts failed, children are still retained in foster care in what becomes an unintended permanent plan.

Temporary Foster Care

Some children do not survive chronic neglect or abuse in the home. Differentiating between those children and the ones who would be at great risk from losing the continuing love and affection of their parents is more complex than it may seem. A psychologist evaluating the indications of harm that would come from separation will look for signs of bonding and attachment. When removal from the home is necessary to protect the child, adequate parental contact should be maintained in most cases, especially for the young, already bonded child. Because foster care presents the possibility of multiple placements, a child who goes from caregiver to caregiver may lose or never gain the ability to bond and form trusting relationships. Therapy can help the at-risk child maintain important family ties while family resources are being shored up.

If the child must be placed outside the home, close proximity to the home of the natural parents is desirable both to promote visitation and to keep the child closer to the familiar school, neighborhood, and peers. If siblings are removed, every effort should be made to place them together. Most states list an order of preference for placement—first with relatives, then in a foster home with the same racial or ethnic identification as the child. The child's religious background also may be considered. The National Commission on Family Foster Care (1991) cautioned that, although kinship care can affirm the value of family, the assessment process used to determine the best placement option should include "unique family strengths and needs, cultural and ethnic identification, necessary financial and service supports, continuity of care, and permanency goals" (p. 104).

Enforced separation of the child from the extended family, friends, and school—which is so detrimental to the child's basic attachments—should be an option to consider with much caution because it is fraught with problems and complications. In a study of children in Michigan's child welfare system, newborns only had a 61% chance of being placed in a permanent family within 4 years of foster placement. This compares to the 10-year-old's 69% likelihood of finding a permanent family. Seventy-three percent of the newborns experienced multiple placements, which threaten the infants' learning and attachment processes (Schwartz & Ortega, 1992). Furthermore, dependent children whose first placement is an institution are 59% less likely to be in a permanent home 4 years after entering out-of-home care than are children from all other placement settings (Schwartz & Ortega, 1992). Of greater concern, a Michigan study of private youth service providers showed that, among children in out-of-home placement under the custody of a child welfare agency and delinquent youth released from the agency's group homes or large institutions in 1987, one in four were in prison within 3 years (Kapp & Schwartz, in press).

Ironically, children in out-of-home care under the custody of child welfare agencies also are particularly unlikely to get appropriate mental health care when they need it (Knitzer, 1982). Although the most frequently identified disorder of children in foster care is emotional illness, services for the foster child's emotional problems have been found to be the least available (Halfon & Klee, 1986). Abused and neglected children are at extreme risk for long-term clinical dysfunction. They evince such symptoms as depression, inappropriate aggression, slow and deficient cognitive and interpersonal development, dissociative reactions, and poor academic functioning (Institute of Medicine, 1989).

Finally, an increasing number of studies show that children in foster care have a disproportionate incidence of acute, chronic, or disabling medical problems (Simms, 1991; Watahara & Lobdell, 1990). Foster parents need specialized training on how to care for medically fragile infants and children. The federal EPSDT program provides screening services at regular intervals for infants and children that include a comprehensive health and developmental history, immunizations, laboratory tests, vision services, dental services, and hearing services, as well as mental health screening, diagnosis, and treatment. Children in foster care should qualify for these services as well as Medicaid. Several states have devised a medical "passport" system for children in out-of-home care. Health passports provide the child's caregiver with a full record of health history and immunizations as well as the birth parents' medical history. This record is especially important as infants go on to experience multiple placements.

In an attempt to improve the outlook for abused children, the state of New Jersey has enacted a "Bill of Rights" for children who are placed out of the home. The new law explicitly defines the child's rights as independent and separate from his or her parents' rights once placement occurs. The law defines a broad range of rights for these children, including the right to adequate food, clothing, and housing, and appropriate medical, educational, and other services. The child's right to permanency is stressed. Regular visitation with parents and siblings is required, as well as involvement of the child in the case plan whenever possible. The child has the right to be free from physical or psychological abuse and from repeated changes in placement before permanent placement or return home (New Jersey Department of Youth and Family Services, 1991). Such laws are increasingly necessary because, for many children, foster care involves a series of placements away from the family, none of which are "home" to the child. Multiple placements can lead to severe problems for some of these children.

∞

> Thirteen-year-old Larry had been removed from his parents when he was 18 months old. At that time, he and his infant sister were left with a neighbor by the parents, who had a long history of drug abuse, child neglect, and antisocial behavior. Larry's parents did not return for their children. By age 7, Larry's behavior grew increasingly out of control. In his most recent foster care placement, Larry cracked tiles in the bathroom, punched holes in the wall, and pulled doors off the hinges. After being in and out of the emergency foster care shelter, he spent 9 months in the adolescent ward of a state mental hospital.

The psychologist evaluating Larry believes he suffers from suicidal ideation, oppositional behavior, poor self-esteem, poor impulse control, aggressive and physically assaultive behavior, and attention deficit hyperactivity disorder. He is classified by his school as severely emotionally disturbed. The psychologist believes Larry's maladaptive behavior results from feelings of desperation and neediness. During his 11 years in foster care, Larry went through 25 changes of placement, including state hospitals, group homes, the county emergency foster care shelter, and two failed adoptive placements. He and his sister were finally freed for adoption. His sister, who was placed separately in foster homes, is still waiting to be adopted at age 12.

Ideally, Larry and his sister would have been placed together in a preadoptive home as soon as they entered the foster care system. When the parents failed to respond to reunification efforts, their rights to the children would have been terminated and the children adopted immediately by their foster parents. Instead, they continued in separate long-term foster care as Larry's emotional condition deteriorated.

∞

As this case study and that of Lamont and Shawna illustrate, the court is extremely reluctant to terminate parental rights even when it is clearly shown that the parents take no responsibility for their children and the condition of the children is deteriorating. The National Commission on Children, in its 1991 report, encouraged child welfare agencies to move more quickly to terminate parental rights so infants abandoned at birth and other children who need the support of a stable, committed caregiver, but who cannot be safely returned to their biological parents, can be successfully adopted.

Adoption

Adoption is the legal procedure that establishes a new parent–child relationship for the child who has been abused and whose parents' rights have been terminated. The child's interests are advanced by permanently settling the question of where the child belongs in relation to the biological parents and to the new adoptive family. Adoptive parents assume all the rights and responsibilities of natural parents.

One judge looked at the future for many children in state custody who have had their parental rights terminated and stated:

> It is an unfortunate truth that not all children who are "freed" from their legal relationship with their parents, find the stable and permanent situation that is desired even though this is the implicit promise made by the state when it seeks to terminate the parent–child relationship. Multiple placements and impermanent situations sometimes mark the state's guardianship of a child. This unstable situation is frequently detrimental

to a child. Indeed, the detriment may be greater than keeping the parent–child relationship intact since the child's psychological and emotional bond to the parent may have been broken with nothing substituted in its place. (*In re Angelia P.,* 1981)

A decade after the *Angelia P.* case, too many children continue to remain in foster care without a permanent home. Of the children living in foster care each year, fewer than 8% are adopted. This contrasts with the official plan for selected children in foster care. In 1991, New Jersey reported that over 30% of its children in foster care had a formalized goal of adoption. Of these adoptable children, almost 50% had been in foster care for over 4 years in multiple placements (New Jersey Department of Youth and Family Services, 1991). A Michigan study found that only 33% of children eligible for adoption in Michigan are adopted within 3 years after termination of parental rights (Binsfield Commission on Adoption, 1992).

The Department of Social Services controls the process of adoption for abused and neglected children in their custody after termination of parental rights. In many communities, adoption services are under contract with private agencies. The adoption agency gives preferential consideration to relatives or foster parents to provide the child the emotionally beneficial continuity of relationship. If neither of these alternatives is available, the agency seeks other parents for the child.

Many children will need to begin therapy to prepare for the move from foster care into an adoptive home. After placement, continuity of therapy with the same professional is ideal for the troubled child, but often unfeasible because children can be placed in distant counties or states. However, the high rate of disrupted adoptions makes a strong case for continuing therapy. *Disruption* is a term used to describe the interruption of an adoptive placement before the court enters its final order of adoption. Especially during the first year of placement, supportive services to the adoptive family may reduce the possibility of a disruption.

∞

Just after she was born, Jeannie was removed from her mother on the basis of neglect. She lived in foster care until she was returned home at age 7 months. Her mother had completed parenting classes but left most of the child care to Missy, her 6-year-old daughter. Before her first birthday, Jeannie again was removed for neglect. She lived in three different foster homes before the age of 4. Jeannie told her foster mother how her own mother tied her to the bed or punished her by putting rocks in her ears. Her nightmares were so fearful that Jeannie needed therapeutic treatment. In therapy, she talked about sexual abuse by her mother's boyfriend. By the age of 4 Jeannie was an emotionally traumatized child. Her therapist saw her for several months prior to the hearing for termination of parental rights to prepare her for separation from her foster family as well as from her biological family. She concentrated on helping Jeannie develop the potential to form positive attachments in a new family environment that could give her love and security. As soon as parental rights were terminated, Jeannie was placed in an adoptive home. The court ordered that she continue in therapy for at least 6 months to help her transition into her new family.

∞

Special Needs Adoptions A large number of abused and neglected children whose parents' rights have been terminated may be hard to place for adoption because of one or more historic or intrinsic factors: age; race; the presence of a sibling group; medical problems; physical or developmental disability; emotional instability; genetic history; or multiple foster care placements. In some instances, abused or neglected children who have been in foster care during 18 months of reunification efforts will qualify for a special needs adoption subsidy. Some states designate by statute which factors qualify the child as a "hard-to-place" or "special needs" child, thus making the child eligible for the special adoption assistance funds.

Some prospective adoptive parents, whether they be relatives, foster parents, or strangers to the child, may need a special subsidy to enable them to provide an adequate home for a child who has been abused or neglected, especially if the child has special needs. Foster parents who want to adopt may experience economic difficulties surviving the cutoff of foster care funds or the loss of federal health insurance. To encourage adoption of these children by either foster parents or others, the state and federal governments provide monthly supplements and Medicaid coverage for special needs children. The supplement is never higher than the payment for foster care. The health coverage is especially significant for children with preexisting disabilities, who might not qualify for coverage under their new parents' insurance (LeMay, 1989).

Guardianship

Legal guardianship provides adult protection to children who are deprived of the natural guardianship of their parents. Foster parents may want to take this step toward stabilizing their relationship with foster children who have been in their homes for some time. Children may need a guardian because the parent has left them in the proposed guardian's care or because the person who has been caring for the children wants to protect them from parents who are unable to care for them. The guardian has the right to custody, the right to make decisions for the child, and the right to represent the child in legal action. The guardian is not responsible for support and education of the child. The parents remain responsible for child support, although the guardian may receive assistance from tax-supported programs such as AFDC or SSI. In many states, guardianship is an alternative way to establish a legal relationship with a child without going through the dependency court system requiring proof of parental abuse and reunification efforts.

∞

> Alicia's father was in jail; her mother had kicked her out of the home four times in the past year. The last time Alicia left home, her mother changed the locks on the door and then went to the high school and withdrew her daughter. Alicia lived with a neighbor for a few months, but was unable to attend school because her mother refused to sign admission papers. Her glasses broke and she developed a serious eye condition. When her grandparents located Alicia, she moved in with them. They bought her new glasses but, on their limited retirement pensions, could not afford needed eye treatment. Alicia found a children's attorney in town who would help her file a petition in Probate Court for her grandparents to be appointed her guardians. Once the grandparents became guardians, they could begin receiving AFDC and Medicaid for Alicia and could enroll her in the high school in their neighborhood. With the grandparents willing to assume legal guardianship, there was no need for protective services to become involved with Alicia or her mother or grandparents.

∞

Long-Term Foster Care

Long-term foster care is an option that keeps the child living in foster homes in the custody of the county. Long-term foster care can provide the child continuity in the relationship with the natural parent if that is what the child desires and if it is safe for the relationship to continue. Although long-term foster care is the least desirable arrangement for the child seeking permanence and the most expensive of the permanent options available, it is the most widely used type of permanent placement. In Los Angeles, 57% of all children in foster care are in long-term foster placements (Commission for Children's Services, 1992). Even very young children are placed in long-term foster care. In California the number of preschool children in long-term foster care without an adoption goal increased from 1,860 in 1987 to 4,889 in 1990 (Barth, Berrick, Courtney, & Pizzini, 1990).

To prevent prolonged foster care placement after termination of parental rights, the Adoption Assistance and Child Welfare Act requires that a judicial review of the child's placement must occur 6 months after the termination proceeding and at regular intervals thereafter. This time frame should encourage the agency to find the child an appropriate permanent home, both for the child's benefit and to eliminate further court reviews. Thus, to the high cost of foster care must be added the administrative cost of social worker visits and court reviews, which are required. However, the primary problem with long-term foster care is the absence of guaranteed stability of placement, as illustrated in the earlier case study of Larry, who had 25 placements, an instance of institutional abuse. Although the foster child may be able to remain with the same foster parents in long-term care, there is no guarantee that the child will not be moved again and again. A history of multiple foster care homes makes a permanent adoptive placement even more difficult to accomplish.

Residential Treatment Centers

Some children are unable to live in adoptive or special foster homes because their emotional disturbance is acted out in severe antisocial behaviors. Most of these youths come from profoundly dysfunctional family backgrounds in which there was severe physical, sexual, or emotional abuse, abandonment, or adoption failure. Most have a history of multiple placement failures and psychiatric hospitalizations. For those with the best prognosis, a residential treatment center provides specialized services to help children and adolescents become stabilized and eventually return to less restrictive environments, such as a foster family, an adoptive family, or their own biological family. Programs include 24-hour care, individual and group therapy, family therapy, educational services, and recreational and social activities. An average stay in such a facility is approximately 12–18 months.

CONCLUSION

Theories of child abuse causation blame many factors—the parent, genetics, drugs, today's society, the economy, stress, disabilities. Yet blame has not uncovered positive solutions. Sometimes, a parent can face insurmountable obstacles in dealing with a family crisis, which can lead to acts of neglect or abuse. In the absence of strongly supportive social policies, these acts, in the most serious instances, may place the family on the pathway to intervention by Child Protective Services, foster and institutional care, termination of parental rights, and adoption.

The history of abuse and neglect cannot be rewritten. Public policy must change to make a brighter future for families in today's world. A few isolated public programs have a proven record of positive results that place this hope for a brighter future within realistic grasp (Schorr, 1988). Head Start, Family Preservation, EPSDT, and WIC are all programs that are good investments for children and for taxpayers. If stress causes parents to lose control and lash out at their children, family support services to mitigate the cause of major family stresses should be provided through community agencies. If a child with a chronic severe disability lives in an already overstressed home, the known greater possibility of abuse can be decreased through specialized medical and educational services for the child and case management with respite care for the parents.

The state should intervene only in the most severe situations or only after families receiving successful programs of support and services in the home fail to make the home a safe and caring environment for children. After children are removed from the home, if the parents fail to exercise their parental responsibilities to enable reunification to occur within the year, their parental rights should be terminated and the children speedily placed for adoption. States should no longer be allowed to keep thousands of children in places not like home: emergency shelters, residential treatment centers, and a succession of foster placements. Until these children finally become part of permanent, safe families of their own, they will not be able to say, "There's no place like home."

REFERENCES

American Academy of Pediatrics, Committee on Early Childhood, Adoption, and Dependent Care. (1993). Developmental issues in foster care for children. *Pediatrics, 91,* 1007–1009.

Barth, R., Berrick, J., Courtney, M., & Pizzini, S. (1990). *A snapshot of California's families and children pursuant to the child welfare reforms of the 1980's.* Sacramento, CA: Child Welfare Strategic Planning Commission.

Bath, H.J., & Haapala, D.A. (1993). Intensive family preservation services with abused and neglected children: An examination of group differences. *Child Abuse & Neglect, 17,* 213–225.

Belsky, J. (1980). Child maltreatment: An ecological integration. *American Psychologist, 35,* 320–335.

Besharov, D. (1990). *Recognizing child abuse.* New York: Free Press.

Binsfield Commission on Adoption. (1992). *A child is waiting.* Lansing, MI: Office of the Lieutenant Governor.

Commission for Children's Services. (1992, June). *Community plan for family preservation in Los Angeles County.* Los Angeles: Author.

Council on Scientific Affairs. (1989). *Fetal effects of maternal alcohol abuse.* Chicago: American Medical Association.

Crittenden, P.M. (1992). The social ecology of treatment: Case study of a service system for maltreated children. *American Journal of Orthopsychiatry, 62,* 22–34.

Daro, D. (1988). *Confronting child abuse.* New York: Free Press.

DeMause, L. (1974). *The history of childhood.* New York: Harper & Row.

Dodson, D. (1983). Advocating at periodic review proceedings. In M. Hardin, (Ed.), *Foster children in the courts* (pp. 86–127). Boston: Butterworth.

Edna McConnell Clark Foundation. (1985). *Keeping families together: The case for family preservation.* Author.

Faller, K.C. (1993). *Child sexual abuse: Intervention and treatment issues.* Washington, DC: US Department of Health and Human Services Administration for Children and Families; National Center on Child Abuse and Neglect.

Feldman, L. (1991). Evaluating the impact of family preservation services in New Jersey. In K. Wells & D.E. Biegel (Eds.), *Family preservation services: Research and evaluation.* Newbury Park, CA: Sage Publications.

Finkelhor, D., & Browne, A. (1986). Initial and long-term effects: A conceptual framework. In D. Finkelhor (Ed.), *Sourcebook on child sexual abuse* (pp. 143–179). Beverly Hills, CA: Sage Publications.

Garbarino, J., Guttman, E., & Seeley, J.W. (1986). *The psychologically battered child.* San Francisco: Jossey-Bass.

Gaudin, J.M., Wodarski, J.S., Arkinson, M.K., & Avery, L.S. (1990–1991). Remedying child neglect: Effectiveness of social network interventions. *The Journal of Applied Social Sciences, 15,* 97–123.

Giovannoni, J.M., & Becerra, R.M. (1979). *Defining child abuse.* New York: Free Press.

Goldstein, J., Freud, A., & Solnit, A. (1973). *Beyond the best interests of the child.* New York: Free Press.

Halfon, N., & Klee, L. (1986). *Health care for foster children in California.* Report to the David & Lucille Packard Foundation, Los Altos, CA.

Helfer, R.E., & Kempe, R.S. (1987). *The battered child* (4th ed.). Chicago: University of Chicago Press.

Hochstadt, N.J., Jaudes, P.K., Zimo, D.A., & Schachter, J. (1987). The medical and psychosocial needs of children entering foster care. *Child Abuse & Neglect, 11,* 53–62.

In re Angelia P., 28 Cal. 3d 908 (1981).

In re Sara K., 611 A.2d 71 (Me. 1992).

In re Shantelle, 587 N.Y.S. 2d 393 (App. Div. 1992).

Institute of Medicine. (1989). *Research on children and adolescents with mental, behavioral and developmental disorders: Mobilizing a national initiative.* Washington, DC: National Academy Press.

Kapp, S., & Schwartz, I.M. (in press). Following youth from residential placement to prison. *Journal of Crime and Delinquency.*

Kempe, C.H., Silverman, F.N., Steele, B.F., Droegemueller, W., & Silver, H.K. (1962). The battered child syndrome. *Journal of the American Medical Association, 181,* 17–24.

Knitzer, J. (1982). *Unclaimed children: The failure of public responsibility to children & adolescents in need of mental health services.* Washington, DC: Children's Defense Fund.

LeMay, S.K. (1989). The emergence of wrongful adoption as a cause of action. *Journal of Family Law, 27,* 475–488.

McCurdy, K., & Daro, D. (1993). *Current trends in child abuse reporting and fatalities: The results of the annual 1992 50-state survey.* Chicago: National Committee for the Prevention of Child Abuse.

National Center on Child Abuse and Neglect. (1978). *Interdisciplinary glossary on child abuse and neglect.* Washington, DC: U.S. Department of Education.

National Commission on Children. (1991). *Beyond rhetoric: A new American agenda for children and families.* Washington, DC: Author.

National Commission on Family Foster Care. (1991). *A blueprint for fostering infants, children, and youths in the 1990's.* Washington, DC: Child Welfare League of America.

National Council of Juvenile and Family Court Judges Permanency Planning for Children Project. (1992, January). *Protocol for making reasonable efforts to preserve families in drug-related dependency cases.* Reno, NV: Author.

New Jersey Department of Youth and Family Services Report. (1991, December). New Jersey Child Placement Bill of Rights Act.

Northwest Resource Associates. (1986). *Active and reasonable efforts to preserve families.* Seattle: Author.

Schneider C., Pollack, C., & Helfer, R.E. (1972). The predictive questionnaire: A preliminary report. In R.E. Helfer & H.C. Kempe (Eds.), *Helping the battered child and his family* (pp. 271–282). Philadelphia: J.B. Lippincott.

Schorr, L. (1988). *Within our reach: Breaking the cycle of disadvantage.* New York: Doubleday.

Schwartz, I.M., & Ortega, R.M. (1992). *Michigan infants in the child welfare system, preliminary tables.* Ann Arbor: University of Michigan, School of Social Work, Center for the Study of Youth Policy.

Simms, M.D. (1991). Foster children and the foster care system, Part I: History and legal structure. *Current Problems in Pediatrics, 21,* 297–322.

Sullivan v. Zebley, 110 S. Ct. 885 (1990).

Tennessee's home ties keep families together. (1993, May). *CDF Reports.*

Tjaden, P.G., & Thoennes, N. (1992). Predictors of legal intervention in child maltreatment cases. *Child Abuse & Neglect, 16,* 807–822.

Toufexis, A. (1991, May 13). Innocent victims. *Time,* pp. 56–63.

Watahara, A., & Lobdell, T. (1990). *The children nobody knows: California's foster care-dependency system.* Los Angeles: California Tomorrow.

4

Mental Health Policy and the Psychiatric Inpatient Care of Children
Implications for Families

Charles A. Kiesler

There has been a good deal of national discussion of children's mental health and treatment recently. In 1989, the Institute of Medicine published its review of research on children with mental, behavioral, and developmental disorders. In 1990, the National Institute of Mental Health (NIMH) published a national plan for research on child and adolescent mental disorders (NIMH, 1990b). Neither of these reports raises issues directly relevant to the psychiatric inpatient treatment of children and youths: Who is treated, and where? How many? At what cost? With what effects? What are the public policy implications? What are the implications for families?

This chapter takes up questions of psychiatric inpatient treatment of children and youth directly. It looks at some new data regarding treatment in general hospitals and then pieces together the national

---

Based on the Julian and Jessie Harrison Distinguished Visiting Professor Lecture on Mental Health, University of Tennessee, Memphis, Health Services Center, September 27, 1991; edited from the version published in Kiesler, C. A. (1993). Mental health policy and the psychiatric inpatient care of children. *Applied and Preventive Psychology, 2,* 91–99. Reprinted with the permission of Cambridge University Press. The Editor would like to thank Dr. Bruce L. Baker for providing case material that appears in this version.

inpatient treatment picture for the years 1980 and 1985. It then relates some of these issues and findings to other public policy issues in children's health, education, and welfare. Finally, it comments on out-of-home placement as an option for children with psychiatric disorders.

A POLICY FOCUS
ON MENTAL HEALTH CARE

A health services provider *should* regard inpatient treatment as very important because it presumably encompasses the most serious cases for both physical and mental disorders. However, a policy analyst would immediately focus on this area because the nation spends over 70% of all mental health dollars on inpatient care (Kiesler & Sibulkin, 1987). Even without any specific knowledge of mental health, the policy analyst immediately would ask if such a concentration of funds in one style or site of treatment is wise. Is the care cost-effective? Are all people needing treatment being treated? If not, could or should we redistribute the funding priorities so as to expand cost-effective treatment in the general population? Is inpatient care the best approach for the *families* involved—for example, does it allow for parent involvement in the care of the child, and is the child still "connected" to his or her family during treatment?

For nonelderly adults, the answers to some of these policy questions are reasonably clear. Consider, for example, the research base on the efficacy and cost-effectiveness of adult inpatient care (ages 18–64) for psychiatric disorders. Kiesler and Sibulkin (1987) described 14 experimental studies (with random assignment to condition) of psychiatric inpatient care compared to an organized system of care outside the hospital (Kiesler, 1982a, 1982b; Kiesler & Sibulkin, 1987). In all 14 studies, care outside the hospital was more effective, on a wide variety of dimensions, than care inside the hospital, and usually less expensive. It seems clear that a substantial majority of adults now being treated as psychiatric inpatients could be treated more effectively and less expensively in an alternative system of care outside the hospital. Probably 70%–80% of adults now treated in hospitals could be treated more cost-effectively outside the hospital.

Special Policy Issues for Children

The issues surrounding mental health care for children are more complex. First, we do not have the same data base on treatment effectiveness for children as we have for adults. Second, we cannot simply extrapolate from adult data to children. Children are different than adults; they do not have the same mental health problems, or the same responsiveness to particular forms of treatment (Inouye, 1988). Third, any consideration of residential treatment requires removal of a child from his or her family home for a period of time. It is critical that the "way back home" remains obvious in such cases.

Children's mental health policy issues also must be placed in the context of broader issues involving health and social welfare. It is commonly estimated that 12%–15% of the nation's children (18 and younger) need mental health care; an estimated population of 7.5–9.5 million children are in need (Saxe, Cross, & Silverman, 1988). However, even this number must be put into the broader context of children at risk. Of the 34 million Americans without health insurance, 11 million are children (England, 1991). Another 35 million people are without health insurance sometime during the year, probably involving another 10–11 million children. There are 300,000 children who are homeless at least sometime during the year (Institute of Medicine, 1988). Rotheram-Borus, Koopman, and Ehrhardt (1991) found that there are another 370,000 children currently in placements such as foster care and group homes, and they estimated the number will rise to 840,000 by 1995. They further estimated 1.5 million children are on the streets who are throwaways or runaways. In a national housing survey, 7 million people were found to be living in crowded conditions (meaning more than one person per room), and there are at least 2 million children among them (McChesney, 1990). These 2 million children are one step away from being homeless—a family financial crisis is all that it would take. The 11 million children (and their families) without health insurance are also one step away from being homeless. Indeed, the survey of homeless people by the Institute of Medicine (1988) found that a serious health problem occurring in anyone in the family was often the penultimate step before homelessness.

Furthermore, poverty has increased in the United States in recent years. In 1989, 12 million children under 18 were living in families with incomes below the poverty level—3 million more than in 1978, a 33% increase. The purchasing power of the least wealthy 40% of the United States has decreased substantially in the last decade or so (Blasi, 1990).

Independent Effects of Poverty and Homelessness It seems clear from the data that poverty in general, and homelessness in particular, have devastating long-term developmental effects on the nation's children. Homelessness alone has a powerful effect. Income equal, children in temporary housing do better on mental health, educational, and developmental indices than children who are homeless.

However, there are substantial residual differences. Income equal, children in temporary housing do worse on these indices than children in stable housing (Molnar, Roth, & Klein, 1990).

Of course, poverty has an effect independent of the home situation. Within each of these three levels—homelessness, temporary housing, and stable housing—poorer children have worse outcomes on mental health, educational, and developmental indices. A huge number of children in the United States are living in poor and unstable home environments, and concerns for the mental health of children must be placed in that more general context (Kiesler, 1991).

Mental Health Policy Issues

Among policy analysts of children's mental health, all seem to agree that we need to decrease inpatient psychiatric treatment for children and youths (Dougherty, 1988; Jackson-Beeck, Schwartz, & Rutherford, 1987; Kiesler, Morton, & Simpkins, 1989; Kiesler & Simpkins, 1991a; Saxe et al., 1988; Weithorn, 1988). All available data suggest that quite the opposite is happening—psychiatric inpatient treatment of children and youths is increasing (Weithorn, 1988).

Many states' uses of Medicaid funds are heavily biased toward inpatient care. The state of Oklahoma recently spent $38 million on inpatient care of children's mental disorders and $1 million on outpatient care for children under Medicaid (and other states are not dissimilar; England, 1991). Until recently, in the state of Tennessee the most frequent diagnosis for children and youths in state mental hospitals under Medicaid was a conduct disorder, and the average length of stay approached 6 months. These data, and others that I discuss later in this article, strongly suggest that a good deal of psychiatric inpatient care of children and youths may be inappropriate, indeed iatrogenic.

∞

> Keith spent his 10th birthday in the psychiatric unit of a teaching hospital. His parents' continuing concerns about Keith's hyperactivity and their journey through the referral maze (in search of "the best doctor") had led them to a hospital-based psychiatrist. He recommended a 3-week inpatient stay, for a more intensive diagnostic workup and a trial of psychostimulant medication. The financial costs would be covered largely by insurance. The emotional costs to Keith would not be determined for some time.

∞

However, Medicaid has been a leader in the past several years in developing a public sector system sufficiently flexible and comprehensive so as to enhance care while reducing inappropriate mental hospitalization of children. Managed care and utilization review are critical elements of this approach (Feldman, 1992), with somewhat different models being tested in several cities or states (e.g., South Carolina, Philadelphia, New York, and Rhode Island; see Hadley, Schinnar, & Rothbard, 1992). The expansion of rehabilitation services to include social rehabilitation and coverage of mental health clinics was important as well (Koyangi & Goldman, 1991). Medicaid is also a central component in several currently discussed schemes to broaden health insurance coverage to include the current under- and uninsured populations (Davis, Anderson, Rowland, & Steinberg, 1990).

INPATIENT CARE OF CHILDREN AND YOUTHS IN GENERAL HOSPITALS, 1980–1985

The period from 1980 through 1985 was a turbulent public policy time for both mental health and general health services. In the Omnibus Budget Reconciliation Act of 1981, the federal community mental health center system was effectively dismantled. Funds that previously had been directed by the NIMH to the nation's system of community mental health centers were decreased substantially, and made part of a block grant program to states. In 1982, the Tax Equity and Fiscal Responsibility Act was enacted, which pressured hospitals to decrease length of stay for health problems generally, and allowed some of the potential savings to be shared by hospitals. In 1983, Medicare's Prospective Payment System was begun, which organized care into diagnosis-related groups (DRGs), with a more or less set payment for each DRG. These DRGs were organized into major diagnostic categories (MDCs), of which two applied to psychiatric care: MDC-19, Mental Disorders, and MDC-20, Alcohol and Drug Disorders.

The total number of episodes of inpatient care involving children and youths (ages 0–18) increased 8% from 1980 to 1985, compared to a decrease in episodes of those over age 18 (Kiesler & Simpkins, 1991a). Treatment site changed as well: There was a substantial decrease (29%) in the number of episodes of inpatient care in general hospitals with psychiatric units, and an 87% increase in episodes in hospitals without psychiatric units. The number of episodes of inpatient care in hospitals without psychiatric units increased 26,000, whereas the episodes in all other hospital sites decreased almost 18,000.

Diagnoses for children were substantially different as well. Hospitals without psychiatric units increased the number of episodes involving DRG-431 (Childhood Mental Disorder) by over 9,000, whereas the increase in all other hospitals was a little over 4,000. Episodes of depressive neurosis (for which we found a substantial decrease overall in the total population treated in general hospitals; Kiesler & Simpkins, 1992) actually increased in hospitals without psychiatric units by almost 10,000 episodes, compared to a 7,000-episode decrease in all other general hospital sites. The increase in DRG-430 episodes (mainly schizophrenia and affective disorders), in contrast, was only about 1,000 compared to a 6,600-episode increase in all other sites.

Furthermore, these phenomena focused on two funding sources. The vast majority of the increases in episodes in hospitals without psychiatric units were funded by either Medicaid ($n = 9,175$) or commercial insurance ($n = 11,946$). Conversely, all other hospital sites had only a trivial increase in episodes funded by Medicaid (1,277), and a very substantial decrease in episodes funded by commercial insurance (11,928).

∞

> When Rosa, age 15, became more than normally depressed, it was time to get help. She was now often absent from school, sleeping away most of the day, and losing weight. Her talk about "the world being better off without me" was the last straw. The family did not have a family doctor, so Rosa's mother took her to the Forrest General Hospital's emergency room. Forrest was a small community hospital without a special psychiatric unit; however, psychiatric patients often were admitted onto the general medical ward. This practice had, in fact, helped keep beds full and had become important to the hospital's financial survival. The admitting physician explained about depression and expressed some worries about suicide. Medicaid covered the costs for the 18 days of inpatient care. At discharge, the antidepressant medication was showing some effects—Rosa was eager to return home and she talked of trying school again.

∞

The proportion of all psychiatric inpatient episodes in general hospitals accounted for by children and youths rose from 8.9% in 1980 to 10.5% in 1985. The average length of stay, ignoring case mix, increased from 16.9 to 18.9 days. The length of stay for children in hospitals without psychiatric units—which are called *scatter hospitals*—almost doubled in this time period, rising from an average of 8.55 days in 1980 to 15.64 days in 1985. Could this mean that the scatter hospitals in 1985 were treating patients they would have referred in 1980? No. The percentage of referrals for scatter hospitals in 1985 actually was larger than in 1980.

These data illustrate the necessity of looking at all inpatient sites when attempting to inspect national trends. Most discussions of psychiatric inpatient care in general hospitals do not even mention care outside a psychiatric unit. Had one focused only on the psychiatric unit, one would have concluded that between 1980 and 1985 the frequency of psychiatric inpatient treatment of children and youths had declined by 25%, and that the total days of care had decreased by 17%. Ignored would be the 87% increase in episodes and the 347% increase in days of care for child psychiatric patients in scatter hospitals and beds. Obviously what one would conclude about general hospital care would be seriously distorted if one focused only on specialized care.[1]

NATIONAL DE FACTO SYSTEM OF INPATIENT CARE

Now let us place these data in the larger context of the national de facto system of psychiatric inpatient care. Kiesler and Simpkins (1991b) looked at the changes in psychiatric inpatient treatment episodes in all sites of care (except nursing homes). They found that only three sites experienced substantially increased episodes from 1980 to 1985: residential treatment centers (RTCs) (and residential treatment outside a formal center); private psychiatric hospitals; and what Kiesler and Simpkins referred to as "quasi-units," those general hospitals with organized systems of psychiatric care but not meeting formal requirements for a psychiatric unit as defined by the Joint Commission for the Accreditation of Hospitals. In total, the number of treatment episodes in these three sites increased from 231,000 to 566,000, or 145%. Treatment episodes in all other inpatient sites in the United States actually decreased by 272,000, from 2,324,000 to 2,052,000. The 2.5% increase in the total number of inpatient episodes masks a huge difference among the treatment sites entering into the total.

From these national data on psychiatric inpatient care, let us extract the data on children and youths (ages 0–18). Of course, this requires the detailed analysis of the 1980 and 1985 Hospital Discharge Survey data from the National Center for Health Statistics. The closest comparison years for other sites of care are 1980 and 1986, from NIMH data (Redick, Witkin, Atay, Fell, & Manderscheid, 1990). Table 1 presents these data. As one can see, no site of care decreased its number of psychiatric inpatient episodes of children and youths, and the total number of children's inpatient episodes increased from 189,278 in 1980 to 368,312 in 1985 (or 1986), or 94.6%. Although RTCs dominate these

---

[1]We have completed some preliminary analyses of Hospital Discharge Survey data for subsequent years, but without going through the time-consuming task of adding information regarding specialized treatment units. The number of inpatient episodes for children and youths continued to rise through 1989, but we cannot yet say where in the hospital they were treated (Kiesler & Simpkins, 1993).

Table 1. Psychiatric inpatient episodes for children and youths: 1980–1985

Site of care	1980	1985[a]
RTCs	34,000	169,000
Private psychiatric hospitals	16,535[b]	49,237
General hospitals[c]	114,638	118,337
("quasi-unit")	(595)	(19,576)
Multiservice mental health organizations	—	8,940
State/county facilities	22,105	22,798
TOTAL	189,278	368,312

[a] All numbers but general hospitals represent 1986 data (source: NIMH, 1990a); general hospital data are original analyses.

[b] Based on NIMH statistics for additions plus average daily census.

[c] General hospital data include both MDC-19 and MDC-20, and hence are different from data in Table 2.

data, substantial changes were observed in private psychiatric hospitals and quasi-units in general hospitals, mimicking the data from adults. Note that the number of children and youths (ages 0–18) in the U.S. population actually decreased slightly during this time period (Weithorn, 1988).

Within the general hospital system, care of children and adolescents in the period from 1980 to 1985 changed dramatically from sites of specialized care to quasi-units and scatter hospitals, where the degree of specialized care is unknown. Outside the general hospital system, there were strong national trends toward increases in inpatient care involving residential treatment and private psychiatric hospitals.

These increases in psychiatric inpatient care run counter to a decrease in psychiatric inpatient beds in the United States. In 1970, there were approximately 525,000 psychiatric beds, decreasing to 275,000 in 1980 and 268,000 in 1986 (Manderscheid & Barrett, 1987; NIMH, 1990a). However, the overall national decrease in psychiatric beds masks very important differential changes within the system. In general, state hospitals dramatically reduced their psychiatric beds from 413,000 in 1970 to 119,000 in 1986. The Veterans Administration (VA) also reduced its number of psychiatric beds from 50,700 in 1970 to 27,000 in 1986. All other sites of psychiatric care showed impressive increases in the number of psychiatric beds during this time period. Overall, sites other than the state hospitals and the VA systems increased the number of psychiatric beds from 61,000 in 1970 to 122,000 in 1986.

The changes are fairly uniform across sites: private psychiatric hospitals increased beds from 14,300 to over 30,000; hospitals with psychiatric units increased beds from 22,400 to over 45,000; and RTCs increased beds from 15,000 to 24,500. All other sites went from 9,300 beds in 1970 to 21,150 in 1986. Consequently, the public sector decreased the number of its psychiatric beds by over two thirds, whereas the private sector essentially doubled the number of psychiatric beds.

Given substantial shifts in number of beds, it is interesting to note changes in bed occupancy rate. We do not have exactly the comparable years, but 1969 and 1986 are very close (NIMH, 1990a). In spite of a dramatic upheaval of number of beds in the total system of care, overall, psychiatric beds had an 88% occupancy rate in 1969 and an 85% rate in 1986. State and county hospitals, which cut their numbers of beds by two thirds, had the same occupancy rate in 1986 as in 1969. Only the VA substantially decreased its occupancy rate over this 17-year period. Residential treatment centers, which had a 50% increase in beds available during this time period, actually increased their occupancy rate as well, from 82% to over 92%. Recall further that all these changes occurred in spite of powerful hospital cost-containment pressures. The occupancy rate of all general hospitals, for all disorders, in 1981 was 71%, and had dropped to 65% by 1986 (Kiesler & Simpkins, 1993).

Inpatient care for mental disorders has become an increasingly important resource for hospital administrators to fill beds. Not only do psychiatric patients stay longer than general medical patients, but the corresponding occupancy rate is substantially higher. Kiesler and Simpkins (1993) found that the ratio of psychiatric inpatient days to general medical days in general hospitals increased fivefold from 1969 to 1986. One can only speculate about the increasing pressures of hospital administrators on psychiatric physicians to keep psychiatric beds filled, on financial grounds alone.

A PROXY FOR QUALITY OF CARE

We are putting more children and youths into inpatient sites, but with what effect? As mentioned, we do have a substantial body of evidence regarding adults indicating that an organized system of care outside a hospital is both more effective and more cost-effective than care inside a hospital. However, it is worth noting that most of the inpatient care episodes in those studies occurred in very well-known psychiatric units of general hospitals. We do not have comparable outcome studies for children and youths, but, if we did, they would not necessarily be directly relevant to the observed changes in the overall national system.

Inpatient care in psychiatric units is not what is increasing. Care in quasi-units (in scatter hospitals), in RTCs, and in private psychiatric hospitals represents the most substantial increases. I know of no studies for either adults or children and youths that compare the quality and outcome of care in psychiatric units versus other sites of inpatient care, yet it is those "other sites" of inpatient care that show the increase in episodes of care.

There are very few data regarding the outcomes or quality of care for these sites (and those few do not meet the minimum scientific criterion of random assignment). I did find, however, an interesting proxy for the quality of care. The NIMH (1990a) has recently published data on staffing patterns in different sites of care. Table 2 shows a reanalysis of these data.

Table 2 shows staffing patterns in three sites: psychiatric units in general hospitals, private psychiatric hospitals, and RTCs. Within limits, staffing patterns should be a reasonable proxy for quality of care. Staffing patterns do not indicate the quality of care directly, but substantial differences in them could certainly indicate limitations in the intensity of care and, if different enough, allow an inference of limitations in quality of care, as well. One can see from Table 2 that the differences are substantial. In psychiatric units, there are 5.7 patients

Table 2. Index of quality of care based on staffing patterns in three sites of inpatient care (for all ages)[a]

	Psychiatric units	Private psychiatric hospitals	RTCs[b]
Patients[c] per FTE[d] psychiatrist	5.7	15.1	64.8
Patients per FTE nonpsychiatric physician	51.3	166.5	472
Patients per care staff[e]	.56	.66	.91
Patients per professional staff[f]	.79	.86	1.28
Cost per stay[g]	$3,259	$10,160	$20,719
Occupancy rate[h]	75.2%	77.7%	92.3%

[a] NIMH data for 1986 (NIMH, 1990a).
[b] For children.
[c] Average daily census used to determine all numbers of patients.
[d] Full-time equivalent.
[e] Staff with bachelor's degree and above.
[f] All care staff (excludes maintenance, etc.).
[g] NIMH (1990a) expenditures ($\times$ 0.8), divided by days of care, multiplied by average length of stay (1986 dollars).
[h] Beds divided by average daily census.

per full-time equivalent (FTE) psychiatrist, whereas in private psychiatric hospitals there are over 15 patients per psychiatrist, and in RTCs there are 65 patients per psychiatrist. If one assumes that the average FTE psychiatrist spends approximately 6 hours a day in direct patient care (a liberal assumption), then the average FTE psychiatrist has almost 1 hour a day for each patient in a psychiatric unit, whereas the psychiatrist in a private psychiatric hospital has a little over 20 minutes and a psychiatrist in an RTC has about 6 minutes available per day for each patient.

These staffing differences are very substantial and clearly indicate that there are serious limitations to high-level professional care in private psychiatric hospitals and RTCs. The differences in the number of patients per FTE nonpsychiatric physician are similar to those for psychiatrists. If one focused only on the data regarding physicians, one might guess that private psychiatric hospitals and RTCs for children have a different philosophy, employing fewer psychiatrist providers and involving substantially more care by nonpsychiatrist providers. Table 2 clearly contradicts this notion. The number of patients per professional staff member (bachelor's degree and above, a category that includes psychologists) is about the same for psychiatric units and private psychiatric hospitals, but 50% higher for RTCs. For total staff, which includes all care staff, the data are similar. Psychiatric units and private psychiatric hospitals have approximately the same number of patients per professional staff, and RTCs are about 50% higher.

Table 2 also shows cost per stay; that is, the cost per day times the average length of stay. One can see that these data are very different as well. The average cost per stay in a psychiatric unit (in 1986) was $3,259; the cost in a private psychiatric hospital was over three times that; and the cost in a RTC was over six times the cost of a stay in a psychiatric unit. Of course, the cost per stay is dominated by the length of stay. Cost per day in a RTC is substantially less than in a psychiatric unit, but the patient stays so much longer that the total cost for an episode is six times as much.

One could make an a priori case, absent data, that inpatient care in a private psychiatric hospital should be very similar to that in a psychiatric unit in a general hospital. However, data on staffing patterns in those two sites of care clearly indicate that the care in a private psychiatric hospital could not be as intense as that in a psychiatric unit. Assuming intensity is directly related to quality of care (and the relationship is surely imperfect), care in a private psychiatric hospital is not as good as that in a psychiatric unit.[2]

---

[2] It is noteworthy that, in medicine in general, investor-owned hospitals have fewer professional staff than not-for-profit hospitals (Weithorn, 1988).

It should not surprise us that RTCs have many fewer psychiatrists and other physicians involved in care than either psychiatric units or hospitals. However, RTCs for children show a startling absence of any staff dedicated to care, compared to other sites. Note further that these data are NIMH data and they focus on the formal RTCs surveyed by the NIMH. However, other national data suggest that residential treatment for children is increasing much more rapidly outside formal RTCs than inside. Note again that there are literally no data meeting minimum scientific standards regarding the effectiveness of treatment in sites other than psychiatric units. We do know that, for adults, care in an organized system of care outside a hospital is better than that in a psychiatric unit. The data presented here suggest that care in a psychiatric unit is much better than any other inpatient care.

CONTEXT OF OTHER POLICY ISSUES FOR CHILDREN

These empirical shifts in the de facto system of inpatient care for children and youths must be juxtaposed with other policy issues for psychiatric care for children and youths. Jackson-Beeck and colleagues (1987) have discussed the growing reliance on inpatient mental health care facilities to treat troubled juveniles with behavioral problems. They stated, "parents and children have come forward to report they are surprised to find restraints, coercion, and medication used in what they thought would be a loving, therapeutic environment" (p. 153). At the same time, health care corporations are aggressively marketing inpatient services for juveniles, stressing their ability to treat everything from mild depression to bad grades to runaway tendencies (Jackson-Beeck et al., 1987; Weithorn, 1988).

Garmezy (1978) warned against victimizing minors by labeling them as mentally ill for behaviors that are indistinguishable from those accompanying normal adolescent development. Schwartz (1989) went further, stating that children and youths are being hospitalized for problems that are not only clearly inappropriate for but not particularly amenable to psychiatric intervention. He decried the lack of legal protection for children and youths in inpatient care:

> Both federal and state courts have ruled that administrators of . . . training schools, mental health facilities, and detention centers cannot arbitrarily and capriciously put young people into solitary confinement, incarcerate juveniles with adults, censor or keep mail, or deny access to visitors and the use of a telephone. Yet, these very same practices are alive and well in the private child and adolescent psychiatric and substance abuse treatment system. (p. 477)

The violation of rights for youths and adolescents is a central issue. Children usually do not have a right to a precommitment hearing until they reach the age of 16. Indeed, most of the states that do have laws providing such a right at age 16 do not have a requirement that the adolescent be informed of that right. The youth must be aware of the right in order to request a hearing (Jackson-Beeck et al., 1987; Schwartz, 1989). Children below age 16 do not have the right to request a hearing, yet it is the 13- to 15-year-old group that shows the greatest increase in psychiatric inpatient care in general hospitals.

There is decided disagreement among responsible professionals about which specific psychiatric problems of children and youths require inpatient treatment. Scahill and Riddle (1990) attempted to give some systematic analysis to creating diagnostic groups that are clinically coherent (as opposed to DRGs, which are formed on the basis of similar resource consumption, i.e., length of stay). They divided the psychiatric disorders into three categories:

1. Neuropsychiatric disorders, consisting of mental retardation, schizophrenia, pervasive developmental disorders such as autism, bipolar affective disorder, and Tourette syndrome (see Blacher, chap. 8, and Pfeiffer & Baker, chap. 10, this volume)
2. Emotional and psychosomatic disorders, which include major depression, dysthymia, obsessive compulsive disorder, anorexia, bulimia, anxiety disorders, and "failure to thrive"
3. Behavior disorders, which include oppositional disorder, conduct disorder, attention deficit hyperactivity disorder, and adjustment disorders

In reviewing six studies of diagnostic groups of child psychiatric inpatients, they found that the behavior disorders group was consistently the largest and the neuropsychiatric group consistently the smallest. Although one might encounter legitimate expert disagreement as to whether neuropsychiatric disorders or emotional/psychosomatic disorders should be the most frequent diagnoses requiring inpatient care, most responsible diagnosticians would agree that behavior disorders should be the least frequent category of hospitalization (Weithorn, 1988). Yet consistently in the literature, behavior disorders or conduct disorders, if not the most frequent diagnoses for inpatient care of children and youths, are always among the most frequent diagnoses.[3]

---

[3]One might argue that there are many more children with behavior disorders in the population, and hence one should not be surprised to see many more as inpatients as well. Weithorn, Schwartz, and others would argue that psychiatric inpatient treatment of a behavior disorder is almost always inappropriate.

It seems clear from the literature that nonpsychiatric factors and personnel are playing important roles in the hospitalization of children. Over half of children's inpatient episodes are referred by nonpsychiatric or nonmedical personnel (Schwartz, 1989). The simple majority of referrals come from parents, teachers, and ministers.

Costello and Janiszewski (1990) studied which children with clinical disorders were treated as inpatients and which were not. They found that the treated children had more cases of conduct disorders and depressive disorders, and were more likely to be poor, male, and black. The factors that seemed to tip the balance in some youths being treated in inpatient care and others not (diagnosis equal) were problems of behavior control as perceived by teachers and/or parents. Thus, it is our troublesome children who end up in psychiatric inpatient care, rather than children with serious psychiatric problems.

∞

> Luther had been living in a RTC for 5 months now. Only 13 years old, he was dually diagnosed with conduct disorder and substance abuse. Behind these labels was the too-familiar story of a child in constant trouble with teachers for fighting and disobedience, an arrest for stealing, and some drug use. It seemed that he was selling cocaine at school, although this had not been proven. When Luther's mother was incarcerated for again driving under the influence of alcohol, Luther went in fairly quick succession to live with his aunt, to live with foster parents, and then into residential treatment.
>
> Luther took to the structure and confines of residential treatment surprisingly well; he liked to play sports and admitted that two staff members were "OK." However, the center was not really equipped to offer Luther individual psychotherapy or to work with his mother toward family reunification. No one really could say where Luther would live when the funding ran out.

∞

We hospitalize our troublesome youths, instead of our troubled youths. Their problem is not a serious mental disorder, but rather that they create problems for adults. Weithorn (1988) traces part of the increase of hospitalization of troublesome youths to "transinstitutionalization."

> Whereas in prior years, the juvenile justice system institutionalized troublemaking youth as status offenders, recent legal reforms have closed the doors of juvenile justice institutions to a sizable population of difficult children. Families and community agencies seeking intensive intervention have turned increasingly to mental hospitals: the only institutional alternative that is available, provides easy access, and is adequately funded by third-party payors. (Weithorn, 1988, p. 799)

There are significant public policy failures that facilitate the psychiatric inpatient care of children and youths without serious psychiatric disorders. The Prospective Payment System produced a dramatic increase in psychiatric beds for children, but little growth in ambulatory services (England, 1991). Organizational entrepreneurial activity has another independent effect on the incarceration of children in psychiatric facilities. Support services for families of children and youths with behavioral problems or conduct disorders are either absent or seriously underfunded. As shown elsewhere in this volume (Blacher, chap. 8, and Pfeiffer & Baker, chap. 10), family involvement with children and their programs in placements such as RTCs can enhance the treatment process.

Jackson-Beeck and colleagues (1987) found in national data that 47% of the juvenile care in psychiatric units of general hospitals represented primary diagnoses of adjustment reaction, behavior disorders, or neuroses; only 12% represented schizophrenia. Eight percent in 1980 involved alcohol or drug disorders, but the vast majority of those were alcohol or drug *use*, not alcohol or drug *dependence*. Only 27% of the referrals to psychiatric units came from psychiatrists or other physicians, and only 10% came from an outpatient psychiatric service or a community mental health center. These data are national data on psychiatric units in general hospitals. It seems reasonable to suppose that they represent substantially greater psychiatric justification than RTCs or private psychiatric hospitals.

INAPPROPRIATE VERSUS NECESSARY HOSPITALIZATION

Weithorn (1988) described the standards for inpatient treatment of the American Academy of Child and Adolescent Psychiatry (AACAP), which suggest that outpatient and/or community care must be shown to be inadequate prior to hospitalization. Hospitalization as brief as 2 weeks, according to AACAP standards, should be used only for severe problems *specifically attributable* to a psychiatric condition (e.g., disordered or bizarre behavior, danger to self or others, *and attributable* to a primary psychiatric condition; severely impaired functioning). Longer length of stay should require more substantial justification. Weithorn concluded that fewer than one third of admitted children and youths meet these conditions (compared to one half to two thirds of adults). She cited a study in Nebraska that found that 71% of juvenile state hospital admissions rested primarily on socially deviant behavior, not psychiatric need.

Some children and youths presumably are best treated as psychiatric inpatients. What the number is exactly is open to debate. The public policy analysts cited earlier (e.g., Saxe, Dougherty) argue that it is much smaller than that arising from current practice. The AACAP, through its standards, strongly implies it should be less. Medicaid, through its recent efforts to deflect children and youths from inpatient treatment, rests its policy on the assumption that less inpatient treatment is appropriate and needed.

We described earlier the substantial body of data indicating that psychiatric inpatient treatment of adults is less efficacious, on average, than alternative care. Similar studies do not exist for children. However, there are a number of reasons why inpatient treatment of children might be even less effective than that for adults. For adults, investigators have discussed possible iatrogenic effects of mental hospitalization related to undercutting a sense of self-efficacy and encouraging dependency; the potentially harmful effects of labeling oneself as crazy, which inhibit subsequent improvement; and the cutting of social support and social relationships. For each of these, one can make a strong case that, to the extent these effects exist for adults, they are much more powerful for children. The maturational process in children depends on growth in social relationships and in a sense of self-competence and independence, and in trying out self-labels. Undercutting such important developmental processes could be especially debilitating for children. Return for a moment to Keith, the 10-year-old mentioned earlier who experienced a 3-week inpatient stay.

∞

> Keith, now 16 years old, recalled his inpatient stay as if it were yesterday: "I've never forgiven my parents for putting me in there, as if I was, you know, crazy." Indeed, the diagnosis of attention deficit hyperactivity disorder had been confirmed, and Ritalin was helpful even still. Yet Keith's anger, defiance, and oppositional behavior also tracked back to that hospitalization. Perhaps this was just coincidence, but, to see Keith now, still hurting from what he perceived to be his parents' mistreatment of him, one could not but wonder whether the same diagnostic purposes could have been served in some other way.

∞

Some of the inappropriate hospitalizations are due to lack of available alternate treatment sites. For example, Gobel and Frances (1991) found that 40% of juvenile inpatients in a day hospital had (at least) one parent who was or had been incarcerated in prison (and all of the incarcerated parents were substance abusers, as well). However, a lack of alternative treatment site does not make an inappropriate hospitalization any less iatrogenic.

CONCLUSION

A wide variety of public policies have failed children and youths in the United States. The policies have failed them regarding preventive medical care, stable income, stable housing, and psychiatric care. There seems no question that, on any and all of these dimensions, the situation of American children and youths has worsened substantially since 1980 (Kiesler, 1991).

Psychiatric, psychology, and other professional groups must organize themselves to affect public policy regarding the psychiatric care of children. They must promote responsible research regarding the cost-effectiveness of care. They must act to reduce inappropriate and iatrogenic inpatient care of children and youths without serious psychiatric problems. They must promote responsible preventive and diagnostic assessments of children and youths, and adequate funding of appropriate services. They must help to facilitate a change in public policies regarding support for the family and the continued treatment of youths within the family context, and, where appropriate, they must facilitate continued contact and involvement of families with their children, once hospitalized.

These are not psychology's problems alone, nor psychiatry's, nor any mental health, educational, or medical professional group's. They are problems of the total child in American life, and substantial public policy changes are needed to give our children an opportunity to succeed as responsible, educated adults. Further attention to the assessment of the American family and its effect on its children is needed. Removal of children from family life to psychiatric inpatient care, to residential treatment care, and to foster care must be reviewed systematically and new standards developed. We probably focus too much on what often is alleged to be a middle-class evaluation of the American family in making determinations to remove children from their families, without at the same time realizing our responsibility to review, more systematically and rigorously, the other sites of care to which we are assigning these children—often for life. For example, foster care is meant to be a temporary solution, but Tuma (1989) claimed that 66% of children and 88% of adolescents reach the age of majority while in foster care. It often has been noted that children are very resilient to stress, but they are much less resilient to multiple stressors (Rafferty & Shinn, 1991). We also need to focus more attention on determining the resiliency of an appropriate family culture.

To be sure, there are a number of encouraging recent thrusts. The Medicaid efforts are the most substantial but, of course, are limited to the categorically poor. The Defense Department has funded a substantial effort, but one that is limited to military dependents (Bickman, Heflinger, Pion, & Behar, in press). The recent NIMH effort regarding children and youths is also a positive step, but the issue of inpatient care—its appropriateness and cost-effectiveness—is not a central concern (NIMH, 1990b). The development of research centers on children's mental health services by the NIMH is to be applauded (although they actively discourage the kind of secondary analyses of existing data bases reported here; NIMH, 1991).

In aggregate, these are exciting steps. However, special effort may be required to keep as a central concern the appropriateness and cost-effectiveness of psychiatric inpatient care of children and youths. Because inpatient care represents such a large share of mental health funding, its reduction could represent a substantial funding base for more precisely tuned appropriate and cost-effective care. Furthermore, the close relationship of children's mental health issues with those involving health, education, and welfare must be kept firmly in mind.

REFERENCES

American Psychiatric Association. (1980). *Diagnostic and statistical manual of mental disorders* (3rd ed.). Washington, DC: American Psychiatric Press, Inc.

American Psychiatric Association. (1987). *Diagnostic and statistical manual of mental disorders*. (3rd ed., rev.). Washington, DC: American Psychiatric Press, Inc.

Bickman, L., Heflinger, C.A., Pion, G., & Behar, L. (1992). Evaluation planning for an innovative children's mental health system. *Clinical Psychologist Review, 12*, 853–865.

Blasi, G.L. (1990). Social policy and social science research on homelessness. *Journal of Social Issues, 46*(4), 207–219.

Costello, E.J., & Janiszewski, S. (1990). Who gets treated? Factors associated with referral in children with psychiatric disorders. *Acta Psychiatry Scandinavia, 81*, 523–529.

Davis, K., Anderson, G.H., Rowland, D., & Steinberg, E.P. (1990). *Health care cost containment*. Baltimore: Johns Hopkins University Press.

Dougherty, D. (1988). Children's mental health problems and services: Current federal efforts and policy implications. *American Psychologist, 43*, 808–812.

England, M.J. (1991, September 6). *Untitled invited address presented at plenary session, "How can we preserve and expand behavioural health benefits for our children and adolescents?"* at the meeting of Behavioral Healthcare Tomorrow, Boston.

Feldman, S. (Ed.). (1992). *Managed mental health services*. Springfield, IL: Charles C Thomas.

Garmezy, N. (1978). Never mind the psychologists: Is it good for the children? *Clinical Psychologist, 31*, 4–7.

Gobel, S., & Frances, R.J. (1991). Alcohol and drug abuse: Establishing links between residential placement for youth and prisons for adults. *Hospital and Community Psychiatry, 42*(12), 1203–1204.

Hadley, T.R., Schinnar, A., & Rothbard, A. (1992). Managed mental health in the public sector. In S. Feldman (Ed.), *Managed mental health services* (pp. 45–60). Springfield, IL: Charles C Thomas.

Inouye, D.K. (1988). Children's mental health issues. *American Psychologist, 43*, 813–816.

Institute of Medicine. (1988). *Homelessness, health and human needs.* Washington, DC: National Academy Press.

Institute of Medicine. (1989). *Research on children and adolescents with mental, behavioral and developmental disorders.* Washington, DC: National Academy Press.

Jackson-Beeck, M., Schwartz, I.M., & Rutherford, A. (1987). Trends and issues in juvenile confinement for psychiatric and chemical dependency treatment. *Journal of Law and Psychiatry, 10*, 153–165.

Kiesler, C.A. (1982a). Mental hospitals and alternative care: Noninstitutionalization as potential public policy for mental patients. *American Psychologist, 37*, 349–360.

Kiesler, C.A. (1982b). Public and professional myths about mental hospitalization. *American Psychologist, 37*, 1323–1339.

Kiesler, C.A. (1991). Changes in general hospital psychiatric care, 1980–85. *American Psychologist, 46*, 416–421.

Kiesler, C.A. (1993). Mental health policy and the psychiatric inpatient care of children. *Applied and Preventive Psychology, 2*, 91–99.

Kiesler, C.A., Morton, T.L., & Simpkins, C.G. (1989). The psychiatric inpatient treatment of children and youth in general hospitals. *American Journal of Community Psychology, 17*, 821–830.

Kiesler, C.A., & Sibulkin, A.E. (1987). *Mental hospitalization: Myths and facts about a national crisis.* Beverly Hills, CA: Sage Publications.

Kiesler, C.A., & Simpkins, C.G. (1991a). Changes in psychiatric inpatient treatment of children and youth in general hospitals, 1980–85. *Hospital and Community Psychiatry, 42*(6), 601–604.

Kiesler, C.A., & Simpkins, C.G. (1991b). The de facto national system of psychiatric inpatient care: Piecing together the national puzzle. *American Psychologist, 46*, 579–584.

Kiesler, C.A., & Simpkins, C.G. (1992). Changes in diagnostic case mix in general hospitals, 1980–85. *General Hospital Psychiatry, 14*, 156–161.

Kiesler, C.A., & Simpkins, C.G. (1993). *The unnoticed majority in psychiatric inpatient care.* New York: Plenum Press.

Koyangi, C., & Goldman, H.H. (1991). The quiet success of the national plan for the chronically mentally ill. *Hospital and Community Psychiatry, 42*(9), 899–905.

Manderscheid, R.W., & Barrett, S.A. (1987). *Mental Health United States 1987* (DHHS Publication No. ADM 87-1518). Rockville, MD: National Institute of Mental Health.

McChesney, K.Y. (1990). Family homelessness: A systematic problem. *Journal of Social Issues, 46*(4), 191–206.

Molnar, J.M., Roth, W.R., & Klein, T.P. (1990). Constantly compromised: The impact of homelessness on children. *Journal of Social Issues, 46*(4), 109–124.

National Institute of Mental Health. (1990a). *Mental health, United States: 1986.* Rockville, MD: U.S. Department of Health and Human Services.

National Institute of Mental Health. (1990b). *National plan for research on child and adolescent mental disorders*. Rockville, MD: U.S. Department of Health and Human Services.

National Institute of Mental Health. (1991, November). *Centers for research on mental health services for children and adolescents*. (Program announcement PA-92-20). Rockville, MD: U.S. Department of Health and Human Services.

Rafferty, Y., & Shinn, M. (1991). The impact of homelessness on children. *American Psychologist, 46*(11), 1170–1179.

Redick, R.W., Witkin, M.J., Atay, J.E., Fell, A.S., & Manderscheid, R.W. (1990). *Specialty mental health organizations, United States, 1986* (NIMH Series CN No. 12) (DHHS Publication No. ADM 90-1700). Washington, DC: U.S. Department of Health and Human Services.

Rotheram-Borus, M.J., Koopman, C., & Ehrhardt, A.A. (1991). Homeless youths and HIV infection. *American Psychologist, 46*(11), 1188–1197.

Saxe, L., Cross, T., & Silverman, N. (1988). Children's mental health: The gap between what we know and what we do. *American Psychologist, 43*, 800–807.

Scahill, L.S., & Riddle, M.A. (1990). Psychiatrically hospitalized children: A critical review. *Yale Journal of Biology and Medicine, 63*, 301–312.

Schwartz, I.M. (1989). Hospitalization of adolescents for psychiatric and substance abuse treatment. *Journal of Adolescent Health Care, 10*, 473–478.

Tuma, J.M. (1989). Mental health services for children. *American Psychologist, 44*, 188–189.

Weithorn, L. (1988). Mental hospitalization of troublesome youth: An analysis of skyrocketing admissions rates. *Stanford Law Review, 40*(3), 773–838.

II

ALTERNATIVE FAMILIES

Part II's chapters consider child placement at a more individual level, focusing on the child's experience in our most commonly used placement: alternative families. These include short-term foster care, long-term foster care, and adoption. Differences among these approaches, and their impact on the children involved, will become apparent.

5

Temporary Foster Care
Separating and Reunifying Families

Inger P. Davis and Elissa Ellis-MacLeod

The last place for me to go is home. I wanted so badly to go home and I did try a couple of times, but it never works. I crack up each time and go straight back to the psych hospital. I don't want to try any more. Can't handle it. I hope they can find me a foster home again. That would be the best for me.
   Thirteen-year-old Robert, awaiting yet another foster home placement

This pale, tense-looking boy joined a small group of adolescents in a temporary receiving shelter to discuss with the first author the pros and cons of various placement options for children like themselves. The children were unanimous in preferring foster care over group homes and other institutional arrangements, and they also agreed that the worst part of being in any kind of out-of-home care is the feeling of not really belonging *any* place.

Temporary foster care is designed to provide 24-hour substitute care for a limited period to children whose parents are temporarily unable or unwilling to care for them. Some parents voluntarily ask to have their child placed in foster care but, in most instances, the community, through its Child Protective Services system, initiates the placement when the child's life or health is in imminent danger. Whether the placement is voluntary or court ordered, the intent of separating children from the birth family is to allow parent and child functioning and/or home conditions to be restored or developed to the point at which the child's safety is no longer at stake.

This obviously did not happen to Robert, who was transferred to foster family care after several brief psychiatric hospitalizations following unsuccessful reunifications with his hostile and abusive mother. Robert's case illustrates that the yearning for a family of one's very own, with consistent parental love and care, is fundamental to human nature. It sometimes takes repeated and painful failed attempts before a child can arrive at the tragic conclusion that "the last place for me to go is home."

As background for the current review of foster care research, this chapter first describes temporary foster care in the United States, the mandates by which society temporarily takes over the parenting role, and characteristics of foster children and their families. Selected empirical findings lead to recommendations for future research and for policy and practice changes, with special attention to the foster child's ties to the birth family during separation and reunification.

BACKGROUND, DESCRIPTION, AND SCOPE OF TEMPORARY FOSTER CARE

Historical Background

Down through history, abandoned, homeless, and orphaned children have depended on relatives or other "good people" to care for them. Until the middle of the last century, some children who were old enough to work were cared for under the Indenture System. As apprentices to craftsmen, farmers, and others, they provided their labor in exchange for life's necessities. Others grew up in almshouses, orphanages, or institutions for children with specific handicaps or needs. Concerned citizens who were convinced that a family-like setting, not an institution, fosters optimal child development instituted Children's Aid Societies. The New York Children's Aid Society, under Charles Loring Brace, is credited with starting modern foster family care. From 1883 to 1929, the Society took more than 100,000 orphaned or abandoned children from the streets of New York City on the so-called Orphan Trains to the farmlands of midwestern and southern states. At small-town stations, prospective foster families met the children and selected those they would care for.

Despite a policy of placing children from the same families together, or in homes near each other, many became separated. At a reunion of Orphan Train children in New York in 1990, some expressed the anguish felt by these separations. One former foster child, a 71-year-old woman who was later reunited with her brothers, said the separation from them was the worst time of her life: "Toots was my nickname, and when the agents took them away, the twins, who were 3 years old, cried, 'Toot-toot, please don't go away'" (Morgan, 1990, p. C19).

The movement toward providing destitute children with a family-like upbringing, coupled with a growing appreciation for preserving the child's *own* family, led to the first Mother's Pension Legislation in 1911. This law made public funds available to widows in an effort to prevent family breakdown and the subsequent removal of children from financially destitute mothers. Later, the Aid to Dependent Children provision of the Social Security Act of 1935 confirmed the philosophy that no child should be separated from his or her family for reasons of poverty alone.

The notion of foster care as a temporary status turned out to be somewhat illusory, as shown by the Maas and Engler (1959) nationwide study "Children in Need of Parents." Over half of the foster children in their sample were likely to stay in foster care until reaching the age of maturity. Only a few were expected to be adopted, and less than 25% were expected ever to be returned to their parents.

The reality that a large percentage of foster children were growing up in a "limbo" state without permanent, legal ties to a family was confirmed by later studies as reviewed by Costin, Bell, and Downs (1991), Kadushin and Martin, (1988), Wiltse (1985), and others. However, findings from several of these studies, among them the Fanshel and Shinn (1978) longitudinal follow-up study that compared children who remained in foster care with those returned to their parents, are inconclusive regarding the short- and long-term effects of foster care on child functioning.

Even so, many child welfare practitioners believe that long-term foster care is harmful to children in "that conflicting expectations and loyalties affect a child's capacity for effective relationships, and that no child can grow emotionally as long as he or she never belongs to a parent except on a temporary or ambiguous basis" (Costin, 1979, p. 271). Such sentiments are poignantly expressed by a 16-year-old girl awaiting foster care:

> Foster care is the best for us. But it is not ideal because you never really belong. I know, I have been in several foster homes. In the last one they tried really hard to be nice to me. What I hated most was when they had their birthday celebrations and stuff. I would hide in my room, but they'd come and get me. Sometimes I went along, but it was *their* party. The more they enjoyed themselves, the more I felt left out. They seemed so happy, a real family. And I don't have one, probably never will. (personal communication with I. Davis)

Studies such as the Oregon Permanency Planning Project (Emlen, Lahti, & Downs, 1978; Pike, Downs, Emlen, Downs, & Case, 1977) and the Alameda Demonstration Project (Stein, Gambrill, & Wiltse, 1978) addressed shortcomings of the foster care system and proposed new practice interventions toward assuring foster children permanent living arrangements and continuity of relationships. These and other demonstration projects, along with contributions from many child welfare specialists, led to the first major change in federal child welfare legislation since the Social Security Act of 1935: the Federal Adoption Assistance and Child Welfare Act of 1980 (PL 96-272). This important law incorporates permanency planning principles and sets stringent time limits to assure that foster children are not left in limbo in interminable out-of-home care.

The permanency planning framework has been defined as:

> The systematic process of carrying out, within a brief timelimited period, a set of goal-directed activities designed to help children live in families that offer continuity of relationships with nurturing parents or caretakers and the opportunity to establish lifetime relationships. (Maluccio & Fein, 1983, p. 197)

The *legal authority* embedded in the Federal Adoption Assistance and Child Welfare Act and related state laws requires that the drastic step of removing children from their families can be carried out only after supportive and supplementary family preservation services have failed to alleviate the risk to the child.

Description

A foster care case typically starts with a call to the Child Protective Service Child Abuse Hotline or to a law enforcement office from professionals mandated to report abuse and neglect, or from neighbors, relatives, or others concerned about the child. The subsequent investigation, a complex topic beyond the scope of this chapter, may lead to a court decision of placement of the child in a licensed foster home.

Public and private placement agencies, licensed and monitored by the state, have authority to recruit, select, train, and supervise foster parents. Some foster homes are licensed to provide up to 30-day emergency care, and others to provide regular foster family care for up to six children; specialist foster homes serve children who are medically fragile or have emotional, mental, or physical disabilities (Hudson & Galaway, 1989). Placement agencies usually are staffed by professionally trained social workers, operating in collaboration with foster parents and professionals from such disciplines as education, law, medicine, nursing, psychology, and psychiatry. In the past, the foster parents' function was limited largely to the day-to-day parenting tasks. In recent years, however, the role of the foster parent has been expanded in many instances to full-fledged membership on the foster care team, with participation in decision making and service delivery to the child and the biological parents (McFadden, 1985). Foster parents receive fixed monthly reimbursement of expenses, but no regular pay for their services. In some forms of specialist foster care, the foster parents are hired as staff and receive a salary. Relatives of a child who agree to serve as foster parents generally also are required to obtain a license. It is still debated whether kinship care justifiably can be considered foster care in a traditional sense because it offers a form of relationship continuity that regular foster homes do not.

The standard-setting organization of public and private child welfare agencies, the Child Welfare League of America (CWLA), recommends that, when removal of a child is necessary, siblings should be placed together if possible. Furthermore, the CWLA recommends that foster family care should be used for all children under age 6 as well as for the majority of children in middle childhood who are in need of substitute care "who can accept other family ties, participate in family life, attend community schools and live in the community without danger to themselves and others" (Child Welfare League of America, 1975, p. 10). For adolescents, foster family care traditionally has been seen as contraindicated because of the seeming conflict between the developmental tasks of achieving emotional independence from parents and the need for forming new relations with another set of parents. Nonetheless, a sizable percentage of foster children fall within the adolescent age range. Regular foster family care is contraindicated for children whose emotional problems and/or special needs make it difficult for them to form emotional relations and get along in a family setting. Specialist foster homes, group homes, residential care, or other institutional care may be the placement of choice for these youngsters.

∞

Robert entered foster family care at age 7 because of his mother's inability to care for him. She had custody of Robert since she divorced Robert's father 2 years earlier, at which point she also was diagnosed as having multiple sclerosis. Robert was returned to his mother after 1 year in the foster home, where he unfortunately had been abused by another, older foster child. He became withdrawn, anxious, and increasingly worried about his mother's deteriorating health. He had sporadic contacts with his 50-year-old father, who lived a secluded life in a small apartment. When Robert's mother first underwent hospitalization, his father agreed to take care of him on a temporary basis. After 1 month, however, Robert's father declared him too difficult to handle and requested his removal.

At this point Robert, at age 10, became so emotionally withdrawn that no foster family could be found for him. Instead, he was placed in a residential treatment center. After a year's time, he made sufficient progress to be transferred to a treatment foster home in the vicinity of his mother's home. The plan called for at least 6 months of specialized foster care as an intermediary step toward reunification with his mother, whose health in the meantime had shown some improvement.

Throughout the years, Robert's mother maintained a very strong dependency on her son, who felt guilty for not taking better care of her. While in the treatment foster home, Robert received therapy to help him with his feelings and help him develop better peer relationship skills.

Robert did well in the treatment foster home, where his mother, as planned, visited frequently. Although strongly attached to his mother, Robert felt ambivalent about returning to her, concerned that he might not be able to care well enough for her. Although hurt by the first foster care experience, his subsequent experience provided support and nurture to this frail preadolescent. Reunification does not seem likely to succeed, however, without ongoing mental health and other supportive services.

∞

In addition to the 24-hour care the child receives in the foster family, placing agencies also are mandated to provide health, mental health, psychological, educational, vocational, and other services as needed by the child. The child's parents receive services to help them ameliorate problems that led to the removal of their child and to facilitate visitation in order to maintain the parent–child relationship during the placement period. Finally, reunification services to birth parents, or relinquishment procedures to free the child for adoption, are required.

∞

Seven-year-old Jane and her 3-year-old half-brother Tom were placed in foster family care 11 months ago, when their 23-year-old mother Christina was arrested for driving under the influence of alcohol and drugs. On investigation, Child Protective Services (CPS) discovered that Christina's live-in boyfriend, Tom's father, was physically abusive to her and both children. The Dependency Court ordered substance abuse treatment for Christina and her boyfriend, and anger management training for the latter. Christina immediately began the drug treatment and was declared "drug free" after 7 months. Tom's father, however, refused treatment and left her shortly thereafter. Christina obtained a job as a waitress and became able to support herself.

Jane and Tom adjusted fairly well in the foster home, although Jane was troubled by nightmares and school difficulties. Psychological testing showed slight intellectual disability and delay in social development in both children. Their mother maintained the court-ordered schedule for visits with Jane and Tom in the foster home and weekly counseling sessions with the CPS worker. The foster parents took an interest in Christina and at times invited her to join the family dinner and stay beyond the scheduled 1-hour visit.

In her contacts with the social worker, Christina was at first hostile and defiant, stating that she could manage her own affairs. Eventually, she expressed feelings of inadequacy as a parent and openly cried over painful memories from her own childhood. Her father had left when she was 5, and her mother often would remind Christina that she was "no good—just like her father." At 14, Christina joined a gang and began taking drugs. Her mother, unable to control her, sent her to live with her father. He sexually molested his daughter, who ran away and started living with a boyfriend, Jane's father. The young couple married, but 1 year later, at 17, Christina returned to her hometown, where she obtained a divorce. After several more unsuccessful relationships with men, she found herself pregnant with Tom. Tom's father moved in with Christina and the children.

At the 12-month Dependency Court hearing, Christina requested the children be returned to her. Despite the progress she had made in stabilizing her life and the children's eagerness to return to their mother, the Court ordered the children to remain in foster care for an additional 3 months, during which time the children would visit with their mother in her home on a trial basis. Visits also were encouraged between the children and the maternal grandmother, with whom Christina, with the caseworker's assistance, had reestablished contact. Future reunification also was conditional on Christina's remaining off drugs.

Reunification took place as scheduled. Foster family care and intensive services by the CPS worker and from agencies providing vocational training, employment, housing, child care, medical, legal aid, and other services helped this young mother take charge of her life. (It should be noted that the rich blend of services offered and used in this case predate the budget cuts of recent years.)

∞

Permanency planning practice principles require that, at the time of placement, a reunification plan be signed by the parent(s) and CPS representatives spelling out what changes parent(s) must bring about in their own behavior or home conditions, and what reasonable services CPS must provide within a specified time period as basis for the Dependency (or Family) Court's decision to reunify the child with his or her family. Court hearings are held 6, 12, and 18 months after placement to monitor what, if any, progress has been made.

At any one of these decision-making points, but not later than at the 18-month hearing, the court must make a permanency planning decision for the child. Priority must be given first to reunification with the birth family. If evidence has accumulated that reunification is not in the child's "best interest," the next option is to terminate parental rights and place the child in an adoptive home, preferably with a relative. Adoption is not considered feasible, however, if the child would benefit from maintaining a relationship with a biological parent who has been visiting the child, if the child is 12 years of age or older and does not want to be adopted, or if the foster parents are unable to adopt but the child would suffer from being removed from them (Barth & Berry, 1987). If adoption is not a viable option, guardianship is to be awarded to a relative or other adult able and willing to take on this responsibility. The final option for the court's permanency planning decision is planned long-term foster family care until the child reaches the age of majority. Further analysis of the permanency planning legislation from a legal perspective, and the role of the courts in child placement decisions, are covered elsewhere in this book (see Portwood & Repucci, chap. 1, and Weisz, chap. 3).

Scope

The 1980s have witnessed a steady increase in the number of children living in foster care, following only a brief decline in 1982. Recent estimates show a rise from 276,000 in 1982 to 323,000 in 1988, or an increase from 4.1 to 4.8 children for every 1,000 in the general population (U.S. Senate Committee on Finance, 1990). The majority of these children are living in foster family homes[1] (U.S. Senate Committee on Finance, 1990). Looking toward the future, experts have projected as many as 553,000 children in the foster care system by 1995 (U.S. House of Representatives Select Committee on Children, Youth and Families, 1989). Increases in substantiated cases of child maltreatment, poverty, family homelessness, and substance abuse have been noted as primary reasons for the rise in placements. Since 1980, the proportion of males and females entering foster care has remained fairly constant and at roughly equal rates; however, younger children of both sexes have been entering care at an increasing rate since the mid-1980s. Estimates show that 42% of all children who entered foster care nationwide were under age 6 in 1988, compared with 37% in 1985 (U.S. House of Representatives Select Committee on Children, Youth and Families, 1989). Similarly, an increasing proportion of children in foster care are adolescents (Gershenson, Rosewater, & Massinga, 1990).

Prior to 1980, parental absence or incapacity was often the common reason for placement; however, increasingly children enter dependent care for reasons of neglect or physical or sexual abuse. Placement of children as a direct result of parental substance abuse has become widespread. Drugs have been linked to the maltreatment of children of

---

[1]Voluntary Cooperative Information System data for 1986 showed that 68.1% of the children in substitute care were living in foster family homes; 20.4% in group homes, residential treatment, and emergency shelters; 3.2% in nonfinalized adoptions; 1.1% in independent living facilities; and 7.2% in other types of substitute care arrangements (U.S. Senate Committee on Finance, 1990).

all ages but are especially responsible for the large increases in very young infants entering the foster care system as a result of drug exposure and abandonment (U.S. Senate Committee on Finance, 1990). Moreover, children in all referral categories have become increasingly likely to enter dependency with a history of prior out-of-home care. Between 1983 and 1985, the number of children entering foster care more than once nearly doubled, from 16% to 30% (U.S. House of Representatives Select Committee on Children, Youth and Families, 1989).

FOSTER CARE RESEARCH SINCE 1980

The term *foster care* generally refers to any type of substitute care, including both temporary and long-term arrangements, and various types of placement settings (e.g., family homes, residential treatment centers, institutions, independent living facilities). Unless otherwise noted, the use of the term *foster care* within this chapter has been limited to describing foster family care; that is, the temporary placement of a child within a substitute family care setting. In many instances, empirical studies have not specified the exact nature of their samples; however, it can be assumed that some of the findings presented in this section represent study populations that include children in long-term care. This is especially true for cross-sectional, large-scale studies that have relied on national data sources.

Empirical research on foster care has looked at a fairly wide range of topics, including service utilization and delivery, casework decision-making processes, foster parents (their attributes and functions), treatment homes and other specialized care settings, and risk assessment and prevention. For the most part, this review is confined to studies about the children themselves—their background characteristics, placement experience, physical and emotional well-being, and contact with family members while in care. Therefore, this section is a limited review of foster care research, providing summary findings from selected studies.

Background Characteristics

Socioeconomic Factors The foster care population comprises mostly children from poor families. Historically, these children are more likely to be reported to child welfare agencies than are children from families with adequate incomes, and, once reported, they are more likely to be placed in substitute care (Hampton & Newberger, 1985; Lindsey, 1991). Most frequently impoverished children are removed from their homes for reasons associated with their economic conditions—that is, for reasons related to social and developmental deprivation—rather than for physical or sexual abuse.

At present, over 40% of all children in foster care come from the very poorest socioeconomic households, from families that qualify for federal subsidies. Once in foster care, research has shown that the families of placed children are less likely to receive supportive or remedial services such as counseling, employment assistance, health services, family planning, and financial aid than are families with children retained at home (Lindsey, 1991). Therefore, for many parents living in poverty, any economic and social hardships that may have contributed to the removal of their children are not improved by the placement of their children in substitute care. In many instances, their children's material conditions also are not improved. In 1989, roughly 70,000 foster children lived with caregiver families whose income levels were below the poverty line (National Center for Children in Poverty, 1991).

Racial/Ethnic Characteristics Disproportionate numbers of minority children live in poverty (National Center for Children in Poverty, 1991). Consequently, minority children are more likely than others to be reported as maltreated and placed in foster care. Presently, minorities are found in foster care at more than twice their proportion in the general population (47% compared with 21%) (American Public Welfare Association, 1989). Once they are placed, however, the attention focused on these children tends to decline.

Research with national-level data has shown that service delivery for minority children in foster care is slower, more limited, and less comprehensive than that for nonminority children (Close, 1983). Young Hispanic and older African American children have been found to lack formal service plans at particularly high rates (Close, 1983). Similar oversights have been reported for children of Native American backgrounds (Olsen, 1982b). Moreover, when service plans are in effect, the recommendations tend more often to be of a clinical nature, such as mental health counseling, rather than targeted toward improving the family's social and financial conditions (Olsen, 1982b). In particular, African American children have been found to remain in care longer and to be reunified with their biological families at lower rates (Fein, Maluccio, & Kluger, 1990; Jenkins & Diamond, 1985; Jenkins et al., 1983; McMurtry & Lie, 1992; Seaberg & Tolley, 1986). Additionally, parental rights are terminated more often at younger ages for African American than for Caucasian children, even when the African American children are less emotionally disturbed (Pinderhughes, 1991). In sum, the bulk of empirical studies have shown convincingly that being a member of a racial or ethnic minority places a child at special risk for referral to the child welfare system, for removal from his or her biological parents, and for extended lengths of stay in out-of-home care.

Placement Characteristics

Length of Stay Length-of-stay studies prior to 1980 consistently report a high proportion of children in care for more than 2 years. A 1977 survey reported that more than 100,000 children had been in foster care for 6 years or more (Gershenson, 1986). In this same year, the median stay for the entire population was estimated at 31 months. By 1985, however, the median time in placement had reportedly decreased to 18 months (Ensign, 1989).

More recently, Gershenson (1986, 1987) has shown that these earlier reports used statistical methods that placed too much weight on the backlog of children in long-term care. Analysis using a more accurate measure revealed that the median duration for those leaving care in 1985 was actually only 8 months. Twenty percent of the children were in care for less than 1 month and 26% for over 2 years (Gershenson et al., 1990). It is now believed that the foster care system provides short-term care to the majority of children, although some are concerned that these figures may be on the rise (U.S. House of Representatives Select Committee on Children, Youth and Families, 1989). A number of researchers have examined the association between the length of time in placement and the characteristics of placed children and their families. Generally, studies show that children tend to stay in placement longer when their natural parents suffer from financial hardships, discordant or broken marriage relationships, poor relationships with their children, and mental illness (Lawder, Poulin, & Andrews, 1986; Milner, 1987). Additionally, children whose primary reasons for removal are neglect or abandonment, or children who exhibit behavioral problems, have been shown to experience longer lengths of stay (Lawder et al., 1986). Studies also have shown that children who are older (Olsen, 1982a) and children with a minority status, most notably African Americans, tend to have longer stays in out-of-home care (Jenkins & Diamond, 1985; Jenkins et al., 1983; McMurtry & Lie, 1992; Milner, 1987; Seaberg & Tolley, 1986). Factors associated with shorter stays are the frequency and quality of parental visits (Gibson, Tracy, & Debord, 1984; Lawder et al., 1986; Milner, 1987; Seaberg & Tolley, 1986), the provision of emergency care services, and an agency goal of strengthening the family toward the objective of lessening the need for out-of-home care (Seaberg & Tolley, 1986).

Although rarely explicit, there is a common assumption underlying most of the research examining length of stay. Shorter stays often are regarded as an indication of success. However, by itself, length of stay actually provides little in the way of evaluative meaning. Children exit foster care for many reasons, only some of which represent positive outcomes. Moreover, there is recent evidence to suggest that shorter stays may be related to higher rates of reentry regardless of the reason for discharge. In a large-sample study of foster children placed in New York State, Wulczyn (1991) reported that more than a third of the children discharged within 3 months reentered foster care, compared with 19% of the children in placement from 6 months to 1 year. Such findings underscore the need for a more comprehensive examination of length-of-stay data to include reasons for exit and reentry rates. Measures of child and family functioning at the time of discharge also would provide an empirical means for assessing the relationship between length of stay and success.

Number of Placements The length of time in placement shares a strong association with the number of placements experienced while in care (Olsen, 1982a; Pardeck, 1982, 1984). That is, longer stays are linked to higher numbers of placements. However, length of stay alone provides explanation for only a minority of cases. In addition to the amount of time spent in care, other factors associated with increased placements are the emotional and behavioral problems of the child (Cooper, Peterson, & Meier, 1987; Fein et al., 1990; Olsen, 1982a; Pardeck, 1982), having single parents (Robinson, 1982) or parents who abuse drugs or alcohol (Cooper et al., 1987; Pardeck, 1982), and minimal casework involvement from the agency (Robinson, 1982; Stone & Stone, 1983). Also, Caucasian children (Pardeck, 1982, 1984), children who are very young at removal (Cooper et al., 1987), and older children who remain in care for 3 or more years (Pardeck, 1982) tend to experience more placements.

The Voluntary Cooperative Information System (VCIS) collected data on the number of placements for children in care at the end of 1986 and for the previous 3 years. Less than half (45.5%) of the children in out-of-home care experienced only one placement. Two placements were experienced by over 22% and three to five placements by more than 22%; six or more placements were experienced by over 8% of the children. The VCIS stated that there is a general trend toward a greater number of placements from the few years previous to the study, although the data are not strictly comparable (U.S. Senate Committee on Finance, 1990).

As with the length of out-of-home stay, a mere tabulation of numbers is a poor evaluative measure. Some children may move three times during a year, with each placement lasting only 4 months, whereas others may move three times within the first month and remain 11 months in their third placement. The latter pattern suggests greater placement stability, although most studies draw no distinction between these two types of pattern. As an exception to this practice, Wald, Carlsmith, and Leiderman (1988) reported the placement patterns for a small subsample of cases from a larger longitudinal study of children in care. They noted that most children moved several times shortly after intervention and then had a stable placement. Although some children never had a long placement, the authors stated that the number of children with unstable placements is smaller than one would find if looking only at the total number of moves.

Relatively few studies have provided more than a quantitative analysis of children's out-of-home experiences. As a result, the complexity of placement characteristics often is overlooked. Needed are longitudinal studies to document the more typical patterns of movement through foster care, the relationship between these and the characteristics of children and their families, and the influence of these patterns on both short- and long-term outcome.

Child Well-Being

Physical Health Most children enter foster care as a result of some form of maltreatment. Many have been neglected, others physically or sexually abused. Nearly all have undergone the difficult experience of separation and the periodic adjustment of living with different caregivers in unfamiliar environments. As a result of these conditions, foster children have been found more likely than other children to suffer from a wide array of physical and mental health problems.

Studies report that 10%–23% of the general population of children in the United States have chronic physical health problems (Moffatt, Peddie, Stulginskas, Pless, & Steinmetz, 1985). However, for children in foster care, empirical studies have documented prevalence rates that are two to four times as high (Hochstadt, Jaudes, Zimo, & Schachter, 1987; Moffatt et al., 1985; Simms, 1989). Generally, studies using direct medical examinations have reported higher rates of chronic health conditions than have studies relying solely on case records or information from caregivers (e.g., Fein et al., 1990). Nonetheless, the prevailing belief that foster children are at high risk for physical health problems is well founded. Among the most commonly reported physical health problems are growth deficiencies (DuRousseau, Moquette-Magee, & Disbrow, 1991; Hochstadt et al., 1987; Moffatt et al., 1985; Schor, 1982; Simms, 1989; White & Benedict, 1986), sensory problems (Schor, 1982; Schor & Abel, 1985), dental abnormalities (Hochstadt et al., 1987), and developmental delay (Hochstadt et al., 1987; Simms, 1989). In addition to these, health-altering conditions such as allergies, asthma, digestive disorders, and skin problems are found more commonly among foster children than in the general population (Schor & Abel, 1985).

The Child Welfare League of America (1988) has stated that the current population of foster care children shows a marked increase in the prevalence of health problems. The frequency of these problems most often is attributed to conditions existing prior to placement, which often include a history of fragmented medical care. The most frequently identified health problems of foster children, however, are problems related to mental health.

Mental Health The conditions that contribute to children's placement in foster care contribute also to their risk for psychological disorders. Research of the past decade has shown repeatedly and convincingly that foster children exhibit a higher rate of mental health problems than children in the general population, although prevalence data vary according to study samples and assessment methods. For example, in a study by Moffatt et al. (1985), it was found that 35% of the 31 school-age children in their sample had potential emotional problems, as indicated by a standardized screening instrument. Hochstadt et al. (1987), also using a standardized instrument, reported that 57% of the 86 children in their study who were over 3 years of age needed psychological intervention. Similarly, McIntyre and Keesler (1986) found, using an instrument with empirically established norms, that nearly 49% of 158 placed children manifested clinical psychological disorders. The authors calculated that the frequency of problems in their study population was almost nine times greater than that in the general population of nonplaced children. Overall, the rates reported in these studies appear higher than rates reported by major studies prior to 1980 (e.g., Fanshel & Shinn, 1978; Swire & Kavaler, 1978), although direct comparisons are problematic.

The majority of psychologically disturbed foster children manifest multiple symptoms that encompass a wide range of emotional and behavioral problems. Frequently reported problems are low self-esteem (Gil & Bogart, 1982), impaired social relationships (Klee & Halfon, 1987; McIntyre, Lounsbury, Berntson, & Steele, 1988), daily functioning deficiencies (Hochstadt et al., 1987; Klee & Halfon, 1987; Timberlake & Verdieck, 1987), and depression (Klee & Halfon, 1987; Zimmerman, 1988). Many studies have shown increased rates of developmental delays, which in school-age children often are manifested by academic difficulties (Hochstadt et al., 1987; Moffatt et al., 1985; Schor, 1982; Simms, 1989). Foster children are also at high risk for memory and cognitive dysfunctions (Cohen, Burland, Kliman, Meers, & Lopez, 1981). Not surprisingly, feelings of rejection and abandonment have been described as the most pervasive psychological effect experienced by most foster children (Gries, 1986).

There is a growing interest among child welfare practitioners about the identification of and provision of services to children with mental health problems. For the estimated 3 million young people nationwide who are considered to have severe emotional disturbances, the attention has been especially intense. By definition, children regarded as severely emotionally disturbed manifest serious and persistent problems in many spheres of their lives, including home, school, and community (Stroul & Friedman, 1986). As a result, this population requires a broad range of long-term specialized services from multiple social agencies, including child welfare, mental health, education, health, and, frequently, juvenile justice. The manner and degree to which these separate agencies can coordinate their efforts more effectively in assisting foster children and their families has been a primary concern of recent evaluative research and policy development (Burns & Friedman, 1990; Day & Roberts, 1991; Duchnowski & Friedman, 1990; Knitzer, 1982; Tuma, 1989). Calling for a continuous system of care, numerous commentators have noted that a shortage of community-based services and coordination across agencies has left this population significantly underserved (Dougherty, 1988; Saxe, Cross, & Silverman, 1988).

Special-Risk Populations

Infants Exposed to Drugs The 1980s have witnessed a significant increase in the use of drugs among woman of childbearing age. With regard to pregnant woman in particular, some sources estimate that substance abuse has increased by as much as 30 times in the last 10 years (U.S. Senate Committee on Investigations, Taxation, and Government Operations, 1989). Since 1985, births of drug-exposed infants reportedly have increased three- to fourfold, while the overall number of annual deliveries affected nationwide is estimated at 375,000 (U.S. House of Representatives Select Committee on Children, Youth and Families, 1989; Weston, Ivins, Zuckerman, Jones, & Lopez, 1989).

What is commonly called a drug epidemic has led to large increases in the number of very young children coming to the attention of child protection agencies. Newborns are entering care for drug toxicity or related serious disabilities resulting from maternal drug or alcohol use during pregnancy. Somewhat older children frequently are placed in care shortly after birth as a result of a diagnosed failure to thrive, or parental abuse and neglect (U.S. Senate Committee on Finance, 1990). Indeed, data from various regions throughout the country have shown a strong relationship between substance abuse and child maltreatment. In New York, for example, crack cocaine use was identified in nearly 9,000 cases of child neglect in 1988. In this same year, the District of Columbia reported that more than 80% of its child maltreatment cases involved alcohol abuse and emotional problems "generally related to other forms of substance abuse." In California, it is estimated that up to 60% of drug-exposed infants have been placed in foster care, and, in one California county, 80% of all foster children under the age of 1 had a history of drug exposure (U.S. House of Representatives Select Committee on Children, Youth and Families, 1989). Studies strongly suggest that, in addition to their immediate needs, in the long term these children are likely to require specialized educational, mental health, and medical services (Ensign, 1989).

Children Infected with Human Immunodeficiency Virus One of the two major groups of women at greatest risk for human immunodeficiency virus (HIV) infection, and subsequently giving birth to an HIV-infected child, is women who use intravenous drugs (Olson, Huszti, Mason, & Seibert, 1989). Consequently, there is a substantial overlap between children born of mothers who use illegal drugs and those who are born with HIV infection. Furthermore, most estimates predict that approximately 50% of the babies of HIV-positive mothers will test positive themselves (Ensign, 1989). Health officials estimate that 25%–33% of these children will not be cared for by their natural parents (Taylor-Brown, 1991). Currently, over 1,000 infants and children who have tested positive for HIV are in the foster care system, and this number is expected to climb significantly over the next several years (Ruff, Blank, & Barnett, 1990). At present, however, there is no system for recording the exact number of infected children in care.

As with drug-exposed children, children born HIV positive require specialized care. One of the few empirical studies of foster children born to HIV-seropositive mothers found that infected children show a significantly higher rate of incidence and severity of neurological and cognitive deficits than children not infected (G. W. Diamond et al., 1990). At present, however, little is known about how these children and their families cope with the illness and its psychosocial sequelae.

In her review of the impact of acquired immunodeficiency syndrome (AIDS) on the foster care system, Taylor-Brown (1991) advocated for a family-centered approach to HIV-infected children, consonant with the intent of PL 96-272: "By viewing HIV-infected children as members of families confronting a life-threatening illness . . . services will be developed to preserve the child's chosen family" (p. 202). The author recommended ethnically sensitive family-centered assessment and assistance to the child's biological and foster families, with accessing of medical services and psychosocial support. She further suggested that caseworkers receive ongoing education about the course of HIV infection, medical management, resulting developmental disabilities, and the dynamics of substance abuse.

Currently, the rate of pediatric AIDS surpasses that of adult cases. However, an important implication for foster care administrators is that research has found that between 50% and 60% of the children who test HIV positive prior to 18 months of age will convert to HIV negative at about this same age (Rendon, Gurdin, Bassi, & Weston, 1989). This represents a group of children who are born with the maternal antibodies but not the virus itself. With regard to children in foster care, this represents a particular problem. As yet, there is no evidence that the seroconversion is definite; however, as some commentators have noted, caution must be used in designating these children as children with AIDS (Rendon et al., 1989).

Children with Developmental and Other Disabilities Children with developmental and other disabilities are at a greater risk for maltreatment (L. J. Diamond & Jaudes, 1983; Frodi, 1981; Garbarino, Brookhouser, & Authier, 1987; Jaudes & Diamond, 1985). Studies strongly suggest that any characteristics that contribute to the parent's perception of the child as "different" or "difficult" can increase the likelihood of abuse (Camblin, 1982) and subsequent placement into foster care. However, unlike children without disabilities, many children with special needs are placed voluntarily by their parents, in the absence of maltreatment. The demands of caring for a child with severe disabilities can simply prove too overwhelming for one family, making the possibility of placement "an ever-present reality" (Blacher, 1990).

Although information on the numbers of children with developmental and other disabilities in foster care is limited, estimates suggest that it is about 3% of all school-age children (Hill, Hayden, Lakin, Menke, & Amado, 1990). This includes children with mental retardation; serious emotional disturbance; specific learning disabilities; hearing, sight, and speech impairments; and other unspecified physical and health problems. Estimates of the total number of children in out-of-home care who have mental retardation or developmental disabilities alone range from 20% to 40% (Richardson, West, Day, & Stuart, 1989).

Quite obviously, children with special needs require specialized care. In addition to the usual day-to-day demands of parenting, caring for these children often requires ongoing training classes, visits to medical and mental health specialists, participation in special education programs, and a willingness to devote the time and energy required in assisting with basic daily living skills such as feeding, clothing, and toileting (Roberts & Siegel, 1988). Not surprisingly, the recruitment of foster families willing and able to care for these children commands a special effort on the part of child welfare agencies. Likewise, maintaining children with developmental and other disabilities in a stable placement setting is also often difficult.

Although empirical studies on children with disabilities in foster care are limited, these children are reported to have a higher rate of disrupted placements (Roberts & Siegel, 1988). In order to minimize placement disruption, special approaches by some agencies have been initiated to include the development of creative alternative care arrangements such as respite care and, when appropriate, co-parenting with the biological parent (Roberts & Siegel, 1988).

∞

> Four-year-old Peter lives with his mother, maternal grandmother, and sister in a small apartment. The mother brought Peter to a community mental health clinic because he was "running wild," and she did not know how to handle him. Neighbors complained about the noise coming from her apartment. Peter alternates between acts of aggression—physically attacking everybody in the household, including his 2-year-old sister—and extreme withdrawal and head-banging. His speech is inarticulate and infrequent. Psychological evaluation showed Peter to have mild mental retardation and to be significantly delayed in all areas, but especially in language development.
>
> Home visits revealed a chaotic situation. The mother and grandmother competed over controlling the children's behavior, with loud yelling and, at times, with physical punishment. After a month of unsuccessful attempts to teach the mother appropriate parenting skills, the mother agreed to voluntary placement of Peter in a specialized foster home intended to care for children with disabilities. This would give Peter's mother a needed respite and Peter an opportunity to experience a structured, reinforcing environment instead of the impoverished, chaotic, and emotionally neglectful home situation.
>
> The treatment plan included structured interventions in the foster home, in the school setting, and in the maternal home during Peter's visits twice a month. The plan also included weekly counseling sessions for the mother, who cooperated fully.
>
> Over a 3-month period, Peter made considerable progress toward reducing his noncompliance, aggressive behavior toward others, and head-banging. He also progressed rapidly toward development of appropriate speech. These improvements, however, occurred with much greater frequency in the foster home and school setting than on his visits home. The ongoing plan is to further improve in-home behaviors and parent–child interactions. Peter's reunification with his mother is the long-term goal. To succeed, however, this plan must include the

larger family structure because Peter's mother has just discovered that she is expecting another child.

∞

The difficulties and resultant stress associated with raising a child with special needs are sometimes overwhelming. Preventive measures to assist biological families with the care of these children before maltreatment occurs are strongly recommended. Garbarino et al. (1987) suggested that professionals who work with these families adopt a social systems perspective, that is, to view the risk factors associated with the likelihood of maltreatment as a result of ecological forces affecting parent and child functioning, rather than as inherent parent or family deficits. A social systems perspective has merit not only for families with children with special needs but for all families at risk for child maltreatment. The promotion of social policy and programs that address the larger environmental causes of abuse and neglect are essential if child maltreatment is ever to be averted on a large scale.

Family Contact with Child During Placement

Theoretical Background Uppermost in the minds of most children at the time of removal from their families are the questions: When can I see my parent(s) again? What is happening to my sisters and brothers? Are they going into foster care too? Will I have a chance to see them? Separating a child from his or her family ties, be they supportive, detrimental, or a mixture of both, has potentially strong consequences for all family members involved.

Several theories have contributed to the working knowledge of how children typically react to separations and the loss of daily contact with persons to whom they have formed affectional bonds. Foremost is the *attachment theory* (as formulated by Bowlby, 1988, and others), which asserts that the enduring affectional bond established between parent and child in infancy is a prerequisite for the emotional well-being of parent and child, and for the child's mastery of developmental tasks and future mental health. Three major patterns of attachment behavior formed in early years have been identified by prospective research studies (reviewed by Bowlby, 1988): the securely attached child, the anxiously attached child, and the anxious avoidant child. The securely attached child is one who is confident that his or her parents (or other parent figure[s]) will be responsive to his or her needs and encouraging of the child's exploration of the world. The anxiously attached child is uncertain that the parents will be there to give support and care, and tends to be clinging and anxious in his or her explorations. This behavior is promoted by parents who are helpful but in unpredictable ways, who separate from the child, or use threats of abandonment in order to control the child. The third behavior pattern is anxious avoidant attachment, in which the child expects to be rebuffed when seeking parental care, comfort, or protection, because that is what has been experienced in prior contact with the parents.

Although all children react to separations from their parents in predictable ways—denial, anger, grief, and depression—the unanticipated, unplanned removal of children who enter foster care may be more or less profound depending on what basic attachment pattern the child has developed and the degree of parental rejection and/or neglect.

One coping mechanism for children who have been abandoned is the creation of a fantasy parent. A follow-up study of 13 former foster children (Rest & Watson, 1984) provides examples of how children, despite efforts to help them come to grips with the reasons for being in foster care, would replace explanations with rationalizations so as to avoid facing the abandonment. One of the children, a 15-year-old boy, had been able to locate his biological mother in the hope that he could return to her. After meeting his mother, he realized that she could not even care for herself. A second similarly unsatisfactory visit to her when he was 21 was his final attempt at renewing the relationship. However, several years later, he stated that the reason for his growing up in foster care was his mother's lack of money.

It is against this background that parent–child contacts during placement take on major importance as a tool for reducing the sense of abandonment and/or maintaining or restoring attachments to parental figures. Thus, contacts are seen as a tool to reduce such child reactions as depression (Zimmerman, 1988), or to free mental and emotional energy for developmental tasks and for building nurturing relationships with foster parents or other caregivers.

Finally, child welfare practice operates within multiple interacting systems. It therefore requires a theoretical framework that goes beyond the reciprocal parent–child interaction system to include the social context of family life. That addition to the framework is the *ecological theory*, which views behavior from the standpoint of the individual's biological and psychological systems acting in combination with the family, community, and larger society. Ecological theory (Bronfenbrenner, 1977; Garbarino, Schellenbach, Sebes & Assoc., 1986; and others) and its application to foster care as voiced by Crittenden (1992), Maluccio (1985), McCartney and Galanopoulos (1988), and others is not further elaborated here.

Parent–Child Contacts Empirical findings, reviewed by Hess (1987), Maluccio and Whittaker (1989), and others, confirm the theoretical formulations sketched above. For example, study findings consistently demonstrate an association between the frequency of parental visiting and shorter lengths of stay in out-of-home care, suggesting that parent–child contacts play a role in the child's functioning and development while in care.

A correlation between parental visiting and duration of placement was firmly established in studies by Benedict and White (1991), Milner (1987), and Vega (1990). In Vega's study of 168 Puerto Rican foster children, nearly 43% did not have any contact with the former caregiver. In the 57% of the cases with contacts, office visits were the most frequent form of contact; only 16% of the children had an opportunity to visit their families in the home from which they were removed.

Information about the frequency of parent–child contacts probably is of less value to foster care practitioners than knowing how contacts are associated with other variables such as parental motivation, child and parental reactions to visits, child and parent characteristics, level of risk to the child, disability, lack of resources, conditions for visits as to location and degree of supervision, length of time in foster care, caseworker/foster parent encouragement and activities, court decisions, and agency policy. Difficulties in operationalizing many of the parent–child contact variables and suggestions for future research are made by Benedict and White (1991), Hess (1987), Maluccio and Whittaker (1989), Mech (1985), and others.

Additional topics for future research relate to what foster children themselves think, feel, and say about contacts with their close relatives. An overall impression from investigations by Festinger (1983) and M. S. White (1981) is that the youngsters would like to be consulted more about when, where, and with whom visits are conducted. Some of the children interviewed in White's (1981) study refused visits for fear of being physically harmed or out of desire to avoid painful feelings of separation and loss that would be stirred by visiting. Even so, the foster children, biological and foster parents, and social workers interviewed agreed that the benefits of visiting outweigh the problems, in the long run.

In sum, a primary purpose of parent–child contacts during placement is the preservation of family relations to meet the child's need for continuity in relationships. This is just as important in cases in which the child may not be reunified with the birth family. Other benefits of contact may be to help parents and child confront the reasons why the child cannot live at home; to reassure the child that he or she has not been forgotten or abandoned; to prevent the child from idealizing the birth parents; and to free the child from worries, thereby increasing mental and emotional energy for developmental tasks or improvement of relations with the foster family. In addition, supervised visits provide opportunity for direct observation of parent–child interactions, which is important to case planning (Hess, 1987; Hess & Proch, 1988; Maluccio & Whittaker, 1989).

Sibling Contact Separation of children in foster care from siblings has received far less attention than parent–child separation, despite the obvious value sibling relations hold for continuity in family relations beyond placement. Placement policies are clear in calling for placement of siblings together whenever feasible and possible. Difficulties in finding foster parents able to accommodate sibling groups, and other reasons, however, sometimes result in hurtful separations. Forty percent of the former foster children interviewed as young adults in Zimmerman's (1982) follow-up study wished that they had been able to visit with their siblings while in placement, regardless of how long they were in foster care.

Although there is general agreement that most placed siblings should be kept together, there are times when separation is more desirable. Hegar (1988) suggested that, when the level of conflict is destructive or stressful to both, and "if one is the consistent loser in competition for adult affection and approval, then a separate placement for that child may help develop self-esteem" (p. 462). She also suggested that, when separation is unavoidable, a plan must be developed to help the children cope with the separation and maintain optimal contact.

Research so far has contributed little in the way of knowing when separate or joint placements are in the children's best interest, or the quality of sibling relations that calls for separation. Emerging findings on the nature and effects of physical, emotional, and sexual sibling abuse (Wiehe, 1990) hold promise for contributing to such understanding in the future.

The limited research on placement characteristics of siblings in foster care has shown that siblings are placed together in anywhere from 25% to 77% of cases, depending on how shared placements are defined. Some studies have found that younger children, minority children, and children with fewer siblings in care are more likely to be placed together. Additionally, children entering care at the same time as their siblings, children without developmental disabilities, and children not placed in residential institutions have been found more likely to be jointly placed (Hegar, 1988; Staff & Fein, 1992).

Staff and Fein (1992) found, in their study of siblings in long-term foster care, that, of the 77 sibling pairs who initially were placed together, about two thirds remained together throughout their foster placement. These children also were more likely to stay in their first placement than separated siblings, offering strong support for placing siblings together in order to reduce the risk for placement disruption.

No differences, however, were found in the percentage of only children and siblings experiencing one or more placement disruptions.

Services Provided to Foster Children and Their Families

Services provided or needed during foster care placement to meet specific health, mental health, and other problems have been discussed frequently in the clinical and research literature. A full presentation of the complex picture of service delivery goes beyond the scope of this chapter. An overview of services identified as needed or delivered is presented in Table 1. Attention generally has been focused on services at the "front end" and middle periods of placement; however, recent studies emphasize the need for services to facilitate foster children's reintegration into their birth families (see especially Fein & Staff, 1991; Walton, 1991).

Discharge from Temporary Foster Care

Where do children go when discharged from foster care? As noted in the opening of this chapter, federal legislation (PL 96-272) prescribes four discharge options: 1) reunification with the birth family, 2) adoption, 3) guardianship, and 4) long-term foster care, in that order of preference. A fifth option, emancipation from the foster care system at the age of maturity, is applicable especially to long-term foster care, and thus falls outside the scope of this chapter.

Official, cross-sectional statistics on children exiting care over a given time period provide one kind of answer to the question posed. However, the difference in length of stay makes an entry cohort of foster children different from an exit cohort of children. Therefore, only longitudinal studies following an entry cohort of children over the placement period can give an accurate distribution of children among the four discharge categories.

A few such studies since 1980 have examined reunification and recidivism rates and patterns. They include studies by Fanshel, Finch, and Grundy (1989), Fein and Maluccio (1984), Fein, Maluccio, Hamilton, and Ward (1983), Fein et al. (1990), Festinger (1983), Goerge (1990), and Wulczyn (1991). It is difficult, however, to derive a composite picture from these study findings because study samples include children dissimilar in respect to demographic variables, reasons for placement, and length of stay. Nonetheless, a few findings are presented here.

The 3-year Oregon Permanency Planning Project (Emlen et al., 1978), designed to examine permanency planning outcomes and develop technology to remove barriers to reunification, was followed up about 1 year after project closure to determine stability of placements (Lahti, 1982). Findings from these studies must be seen in light of the

Table 1. Services to children and adolescents in foster care

Services[a]	Mentioned by authors of references listed[b]	Foster child/ adolescent	Parents (biological or adoptive)	Siblings	Kinship/ networks
Health related Immunizations/medications/glasses & hearing aids/physical, speech, & other therapy to cope with handicaps/health diary/dental care/sex education & family planning/drug & alcohol testing & treatment	2, 3, 4, 6, 8, 10, 11, 12, 13, 17, 18, 20, 21, 22, 23, 25, 26, 27, 31	X	X		
Mental health Psychological/psychiatric assessment & treatment, including services addressing effects of maltreatment	3, 4, 5, 6, 9, 10, 11, 14, 17, 20, 27, 29, 31, 33	X	X	X	
Counseling Individual, dyadic, group, & family treatment	1, 3, 4, 6, 9, 16, 19, 29, 31	X	X	X	X
Relationship/network maintenance Parental visiting/sibling relationships/ family & ethnic information/home visits/self-help groups (e.g., Ala-Teen, Sons/Daughters United)	1, 2, 3, 4, 6, 7, 10, 11, 15, 16, 24, 28, 33, 34	X	X	X	X
Education Special education/tutorial services/ testing/scholarships	1, 2, 6, 7, 10, 11, 15	X			
Employment/vocational testing and training	1, 2, 3, 4, 6, 7,	X	X		

Income maintenance	10, 11, 12, 16, 31				
	4, 6, 7, 10, 31	X			
Emancipation	1, 2, 3, 6, 7, 11, 12, 15, 16	X			
Life skills & independent living skills training/referrals/resource information					
Housing	1, 2, 4, 6, 12, 15, 31	X	X		
Subsidy programs/group homes/ supervised lodgings for adolescents					
In-home services/home management	4, 6, 10, 31	X	X		
Parenting skills training/day & respite care/other services					
Recreation/cultural enrichment	1, 4, 7	X		X	X
Legal services	4, 10, 17, 31	X		X	
Case management	2, 3, 5, 11, 12, 14, 16, 26, 30, 31, 32, 33	X		X	X
Assess child & family functioning/ intensive case coordination/service contracts & review/channeling of criticisms/involving volunteers, etc.					

[a]Service providers include: professionals from public and private agencies providing educational, health, mental health, and social services; the judicial system; foster parents; recreational, religious, and ethnic–cultural groups; self-help groups; vocational and youth services; and volunteers.

[b]References are: 1) Barth (1986); 2) Barth (1989); 3) Davis (1989); 4) Fanshel (1982); 5) Fanshel, Finch, and Grundy (1989); 6) Fein, Maluccio, and Kluger (1990); 7) Festinger (1983); 8) Hochstadt, Jaudes, Zimo, and Schachter (1987); 9) Klee and Halfon (1987); 10) Lawder, Poulin, and Andrews (1986); 11) Maluccio, Krieger, and Pine (1990); 12) Mech (1988); 13) Moffat, Peddie, Stulginskas, Pless, and Steinmetz (1985); 14) Molin (1988); 15) Sims (1988); 16) Timberlake, Pasztor, Sheagren, Clarren, and Lammert (1987); 17) Weinstein and LaFleur (1990); 18) Cain and Barth (1990); 19) Gil and Bogart (1982); 20) Halfon and Klee (1987); 21) Schor, Aptekar, and Scannell (1987); 22) Klee, Soman, and Halfon (1992); 23) Du Rousseau, Moquette-Magee, and Disbrow (1991); 24) McIntyre, Lounsbury, Bernston, and Steel (1988); 25) Simms (1989); 26) R. White, Benedict, and Jaffe (1987); 27) Halfon, Berkowitz, and Klee (1990); 28) Hegar (1988); 29) Katz (1991); 30) Milner (1987); 31) National Black Child Development Institute (1989); 32) Olsen (1982b); 33) Stehno (1990); and 34) Pinderhughes (1991). This list is highly selective, and services mentioned in these publications are either identified as needed and/or reported as delivered.

fact that demonstration-group children receiving intensive services, as well as control-group children receiving regular services, had at the project start been in foster care for at least 1 year, and had been judged unlikely to return home or to be adopted because of the severity of parental or child problems.

In regard to reunification rates, the two groups of children showed no difference (26% for project children and 24% for the comparison group). However, 40% of project children, compared with 21% of the control-group children, were placed in adoptive homes. The remaining 34% of project children and 55% of control-group children remained in foster care. Comparison of reunified and adopted children showed no disruption for children adopted by parents new to them, whereas 18% of children returned to biological parents had to be placed again. On measures of child well-being, little difference was found among the children who were reunited, adopted, or remained in foster care, although reunited children were more likely to be rated low on health and adjustment at the time of the follow-up interview.

Fein et al. (1983) followed 187 Connecticut children of age 14 or younger for a period of up to 16 months to establish their permanency plan at discharge. Over half (53%) returned to their parents; 31% were adopted (7% by their foster parents); and 15% went into permanent foster care (8% of these placements were with relatives). By the end of the study, 22% of all permanent home placements (not just reunifications with biological parents, but adoptive and relative homes) had disrupted.

A recent large-scale study by Goerge (1990) examined the progress of foster children over an 8-year period and expressed statistically the changing likelihood that children will return to the homes of their parents as a function of duration in care, type of placement, reasons for placement in care, age, race, and geographic location. Findings demonstrated a decreasing probability for reunification with length of time in placement, with the greatest decrease occurring for abused and neglected children.

Regarding reentry into foster care, Block and Libowitz (1983) identified a recidivism rate of 27% among children discharged from foster care at the Jewish Child Care Association of New York. Parental inability to cope with the child's problematic behavior, such as antisocial behavior and psychopathology, was the major reason for reentry into care in 80% of the cases. Females reentered care more frequently than males, and the 13–15-year age group reentered care more often than others.

In addition to the association between recidivism and the child and parent variables, some studies also have attempted to find links between recidivism and foster care system and social worker variables (Block & Libowitz, 1983; Fein et al., 1983; Hess & Folaron, 1991; Lahti, 1982; Rzepnicki, 1987; Walton, 1991). These studies generally underscore the need for supportive and other services to facilitate the children's reintegration into their families. For example, Walton's (1991) experimental study showed positive effects of an intensive, 90-day, family-based service to reunified families in two areas. More experimental-group than control-group children returned to their families (95% versus 28%), and at 6 months follow-up, a higher percentage of experimental-group children (73%) remained home than did control-group children (38%). The strongest predictor of successful reunification was parents' attitudes, especially with regard to "their belief that home was the best place for the child, their opinion that the treatment was helpful, and their feeling that their caseworker cared about them" (Walton, 1991, p. v). Failures were associated with excessive treatment time spent on difficult problems, such as the child's drug and alcohol use, depression, truancy, and runaway behavior.

Within each of the four discharge categories presented earlier, Barth and Berry (1987) reviewed study findings along four outcome dimensions: 1) reabuse after discharge, 2) placement stability, 3) developmental outcomes, and 4) child satisfaction. Their extensive review and analysis concluded that children reunited with their birth families are most poorly served, that adoption seems to meet its promise, that guardianship is little understood, and that long-term foster care appears to work well for some children. The latter conclusion also gained support from the study by Fein et al. (1990) of 779 children in long-term foster care.

Overall, post-1980 studies have added some information about how PL 96-272 has worked to assure permanency of placement and continuity of relationships to children who enter short-term foster care. Yet much further research is called for to gain a more complete picture of what permanency plans offer optimal opportunities for children who, for their own protection, must be removed temporarily from their biological families.

SUMMARY AND IMPLICATIONS

The current research review has kept a focus on the foster child's ties with his or her biological family throughout temporary foster home placements. Within that context, we have attempted to present a picture of who these children and their families are, what problems make placement necessary, what problems and unfulfilled needs the children bring into care, how long foster children remain in care, how many moves within a placement episode they experience, what ways contacts with parents and siblings are maintained while in care, what services are identified as needed and offered, and what are the discharge patterns from temporary foster care.

Even if the studies selected for review had provided full answers to these questions, temporary foster care still would not have been given an adequate description. Left out are important topics related to foster parent selection, recruitment, training, and roles in regular and specialized foster care; decision making by social workers, judges, and others involved with the foster child and his or her family; and the educational problems and needs of foster children, to mention a few.

Some of the main findings of the review are included in examples of research and policy implications that follow.

Research Implications

1. Foster care research prior to and after 1980 is impressive in quantity. Most studies use a descriptive design, which is appropriate in many cases considering the state of knowledge on the highly complex phenomenon of foster family care. The 1980s brought several studies utilizing experimental designs, large-sample computerized techniques, and sophisticated statistical analyses, which bode well for the quality of future foster care investigations. Yet comparison of findings from one study to another often remains problematic because of a general lack of standardization in operational definitions of crucial variables across samples, methods, and measures. Future research would gain from such standardization, and from increased emphasis on replication and more collaborative multisite studies. Furthermore, the strong reliance on case records as the primary data base could be eased by use of carefully selected standardized measures of family and child functioning and development. Replicated single-subject studies may be helpful in searching for measures that could serve both research and practice purposes. Such studies also could explore the relative weight of environmental, family, and individual factors as contributors to case outcomes.

2. We have learned from past studies that foster children are far more likely to suffer from physical, developmental, and emotional problems than children in the general population. However, at present we can only speculate about the degree to which such problems stem from the experiences associated with foster care as opposed to the experiences that led to removal. Needed are studies comparing both the short- and long-term outcomes of those children provided with in-home services as opposed to those placed in substitute care.

3. We know also that the vast majority of children placed in foster care are removed from families living in poverty. However, we lack a comprehensive understanding of the ways in which poverty contributes to a child's removal from the home and what, if any, influence an impoverished background has on a child's placement experience. Along with studies to examine how poverty and maltreatment are related, research is needed to examine how referral and assessment decisions are influenced by family income. How much and in what manner is poverty a factor in the decision to refer, to remove, and to reunify a child with his or her biological family? How are placement characteristics such as facility type, number of placements, length of stay, parental visiting, and worker contact affected by the socioeconomic status of the child's birth family?

4. Considering the large number of minority children in care, there have been surprisingly few studies of foster children that have focused specifically on this subgroup. Nevertheless, data from many sources consistently have suggested significant variances between minorities and others with regard to referral patterns, service use and delivery, placement characteristics, and case outcome. The efforts of child welfare agencies in promoting a more culturally sensitive system of care for these children and their families would benefit from further documentation and analysis with large-scale samples.

5. Similarly, relatively few studies have focused on siblings, yet the vast majority of children in substitute care are siblings. Needed are studies, preferably on large samples with inferential potential, to describe the placement patterns and to assess the outcomes of siblings placed together versus separately.

6. Few studies of placement characteristics have provided more than a quantitative analysis. As a result, the complexity of placement patterns often is overlooked. Needed are longitudinal studies to document the more typical patterns of movement through foster care (i.e., the sequence of facility types and lengths of stay) and the relationship between these and child characteristics and case characteristics, child and family functioning, quantity and quality of services provided, and case outcome. The Foster Care Mental Health Study, a longitudinal study of over 1,000 San Diego children in foster care, is one example of this type of research effort (Landsverk, Davis, & Ellis-MacLeod, 1992).

7. Decision making is an inexorable component of child welfare practice from the point of the hotline call to provision of services to prevent placement or not; assessment of risk of harm to the child; removal of the child; choice of placement type; the content and structure of the permanency plan, including visitation patterns; timing and conditions for discharge; and decisions about what kind of services to

offer during and after placement. The ultimate power to decide at many of these decision-making points rests with the judge in involuntary cases; in voluntary placements and in recommendations to the court, foster care practitioners, parents, and teams must decide what recommendations to make. Existing empirical findings on these processes are in need of augmentation. An ongoing study of "Reunification Risks and Successes," being conducted in San Diego County and the state of Washington, represents a small step in that direction (I. P. Davis, D. J. English, & J. A. Landsverk, unpublished preliminary report).

8. The current research review establishes that quantity and quality of services matter in promoting speedier permanency placements for children and reducing recidivism into care. Future research and development studies may expand on the development of service delivery models that can contribute to identification of indicators and contraindicators for placement services, for reunification and other discharge options, for the timing of these options, and for mental health and other interventions.

9. Follow-up studies should be conducted with a primary purpose of determining the level of satisfaction of parents, children, and all others involved with the foster care system.

10. Foster care is a process and not a series of discrete events. Cross-sectional, retrospective studies provide only "snapshot" images of the discrete events within this process. We can learn from cross-sectional methods—for instance, the age at which a child was first referred, the date a child was placed, and the duration of out-of-home care before he or she was returned home. Equally importantly, we can learn what other variables are associated with these events, and even how strong is the association. However, we cannot find out from these studies about the intricate and various ways in which these children came to be in foster care (i.e., how the course of actions, events, and decisions interacted and resulted in removal) or how these occurrences may have differed in the lives of other children, with similar problem histories, who were never removed from their natural families. Needed is prospective research that begins with the early stages of referral and follows the course of actions, events, and decisions that result in removal, reunification, and reentry.

11. Finally, a greater emphasis is needed across all areas of foster care research on uncovering the often complex psychosocial meanings of data findings—how particular conditions and events are interpreted and acted on by those involved. It is not enough, for illustrative purposes, to know merely that certain child characteristics are related to greater placement disruption, or that frequent parental visiting is

associated with earlier reunification. Particular relationships between one variable and another can and most probably will change through time, as society itself evolves and individuals change their own personal ideas and values.

Future foster care research may gain not only from building on prior child welfare research, but also by a greater inclusion of empirical foundations and research planning in such related fields as child development, family sociology, and special education. Examples are the proposals by Finkelhor, Hotaling, and Yllo (1988) for research agendas to stop family violence, and Herrenkohl's (1990) suggested directions for research on child abuse and neglect.

Practice and Policy Implications

In addition to implications for practice embedded in the above-mentioned research suggestions, several points are made here.

1. Provide sufficient resources to reduce caseloads and high turnover rates among child welfare workers serving foster children, and to supply respite care and other supports to foster parents responsible for children with special needs and difficulties.

2. Systematically experiment with practice models, expanding on efforts to involve parents, the foster children, and their siblings in maintaining contacts and participation in decision making; provide services prior to, during, and after placement; and create new services to meet the needs of the increasing number of infants, adolescents, and children with special needs who are in temporary foster care.

3. Experiment with temporary, trial reunifications with the biological family perhaps to stir the motivation for success and to soften the effect if the reunification is not successful.

4. Expand the concept and practice of family reunification to mean more than *either* complete reintegration of the foster child with the birth family *or* complete severance of the child's ties to that family. Although one of these outcomes may serve the best interest of the child in some cases (e.g., complete severance of the birth ties usually is preferred in most adoption cases), in other cases, the child's developmental and psychological needs may be better served by arranging for *some* contact with the birth family through visiting, letter writing, or phone contacts. This is especially true when longer term placement is necessitated by the biological family's inability to provide daily caregiving and a nurturing environment for the child.

A family reunification model, including specific child welfare practice competencies needed for its implementation, has been developed by Maluccio, Krieger, and Pine (1990). This model should be applied systematically and evaluated to provide a wider range of options for foster children and to help maintain optimal levels of ties to their birth parents. Such "family reconnecting" practice, under careful monitoring, may help the child to become "psychologically free" to better accept caregiving and nurturing from substitute parents.

5. With regard to foster care legislation and policy, reexamine the assumptions and practices of current federal legislation (PL 96-272). The strict rank-ordering of the four options for discharge appear too rigid to allow for sufficient individualization of services for children in foster care. How many children, for instance, whose biological parents are clearly unable or unwilling to care for them, do we allow to "wait it out" through the prescribed 18 months of out-of-home care before the parents' rights to the child are terminated? Perhaps the time has come, as Fein and Maluccio (1992) suggested, to think the unthinkable and "desentimentalize the concept of the biological family" (p. 345).

Much has been learned from past and present foster care practices about separating and reunifying families. Social, psychological, economic, moral, and ethical factors ultimately shape how we balance the rights of parents against the rights and needs of children. It would be utopian to expect that we could ever arrive at a consensus on what the ideal balance would be, yet, for the sake of the children and their futures, we must continue to try.

REFERENCES

American Public Welfare Association. (1989). *Foster care in the 101st Congress. W-Memo, 1*(5).
Barth, R. P. (1986). *Social and cognitive treatment of children and adolescents.* San Francisco: Jossey-Bass.
Barth, R. P. (1989). Programs for interdependent living. In J. Aldgate, A. Maluccio, & C. Reeves (Eds.), *Adolescents in foster care* (pp. 122–138). London: Batsford.
Barth, R. P., & Berry, M. (1987). Outcomes of child welfare services under permanency planning. *Social Service Review, 61,* 71–90.
Benedict, M. I., & White, R. B. (1991). Factors associated with foster care length of stay. *Child Welfare, 70,* 45–58.
Blacher, J. (1990). Assessing placement tendency in families with children who have severe handicaps. *Research in Developmental Disabilities, 11,* 349–359.
Block, N. M., & Libowitz, A. S. (1983). *Recidivism in foster care.* New York: Child Welfare League of America, Inc.
Bowlby, J. (1988). Developmental psychiatry comes of age. *American Journal of Psychiatry, 145,* 1–10.
Bronfenbrenner, U. (1977). Toward an experimental ecology of human development. *American Psychologist, 32,* 513–531.

Burns, J., & Friedman, R. (1990). Examining the research base for child mental health services and policy. *Journal of Mental Health Administration, 17*, 87–98.

Cain, C. E., & Barth, R. P. (1990). Health beliefs and practices of foster parents. *Social Work in Health Care, 15*(2), 49–61.

Camblin, L. (1982). A survey of state efforts in gathering information on child abuse and neglect in handicapped populations. *Child Abuse and Neglect, 6*, 465–472.

Child Welfare League of America. (1975). *Standards for foster family service*. New York: Author.

Child Welfare League of America. (1988). *Standards for health care services for children in out of home care*. Washington, DC: Author.

Close, M. M. (1983). Child welfare and people of color: Denial of equal access. *Social Work Research and Abstracts, 19*(4), 13–20.

Cohen, T. B., Burland, J. A., Kliman, G. W., Meers, D., & Lopez, T. (1981). Psychoanalytic observations of foster care. *Journal of Preventive Psychiatry, 1*, 37–45.

Cooper, C. S., Peterson, N. L., & Meier, J. H. (1987). Variables associated with disrupted placement in a select sample of abused and neglected children. *Child Abuse and Neglect, 11*, 75–86.

Costin, L. B. (1979). *Child welfare: Policies and practice* (2nd ed.). New York: McGraw-Hill.

Costin, L. B., Bell, C. J., & Downs, S. W. (1991. *Child welfare: Policies and practice* (4th ed.). New York: Longman.

Crittenden, P. M. (1992). The social ecology of treatment: Case study of a service system for maltreated children. *American Journal of Orthopsychiatry, 62*, 22–34.

Davis, I. P. (1989). Intervention with adolescents in foster family care and their families. In J. Aldgate, A. Maluccio, & C. Reeves (Eds.), *Adolescents in foster care* (pp. 88–101). London: Batsford.

Day, C., & Roberts, M. (1991). Activities of the child and adolescent service system program for improving mental health services for children and families. *Journal of Clinical Psychology, 20*, 340–350.

Diamond, G. W., Gurdin, P., Wiznia, A. A., Belman, A. L., Rubinstein, A., & Cohen, H. (1990). Effects of congenital HIV infection on neurodevelopmental status of babies in foster care. *Developmental Medicine and Child Neurology, 32*, 999–1004.

Diamond, L. J., & Jaudes, P. K. (1983). Child abuse in a cerebral-palsied population. *Developmental Medicine and Child Neurology, 25*, 169–174.

Dougherty, D. (1988). Children's mental health problems and services: Current federal efforts and policy implications. *American Psychologist, 43*, 808–812.

Duchnowski, A., & Friedman, R. (1990). Children's mental health: Challenges for the nineties. *Journal of Mental Health Administration, 17*, 3–12.

DuRousseau, P. C., Moquette-Magee, E., & Disbrow, D. (1991). Children in foster care: Are they at nutritional risk? *Journal of the American Dietetic Association, 91*, 83–84.

Emlen, A., Lahti, J., & Downs, S. W. (1978). *Overcoming barriers to planning for children in foster care*. Washington, DC: United States Government Printing Office.

Ensign, K. (1989). *The federal role in foster care: A paper on current priority issue areas*. Washington, DC: Office of the Assistant Secretary for Planning and Evaluation, U.S. Department of Health and Human Services.

Fanshel, D. (1982). *On the road to permanency: An expanded data base for service to children in foster care.* New York: Child Welfare League of America.

Fanshel, D., Finch, S. J., & Grundy, J. P. (1989). Foster children in life-course perspective: The Casey Family Program experience. *Child Welfare, 69*(5), 467–478.

Fanshel, D., & Shinn, E. B. (1978). *Children in foster care: A longitudinal investigation.* New York: Columbia University Press.

Fein, E., & Maluccio, A. (1984). Children leaving foster care: Outcomes of permanency planning. *Child Abuse and Neglect, 8,* 425–431.

Fein, E., & Maluccio, A. (1992). Permanency planning: Another remedy in jeopardy? *Social Service Review, 66,* 335–348.

Fein, E., Maluccio, A. N., Hamilton, V. J., & Ward, D. (1983). After foster care: Outcomes of permanency planning for children. *Child Welfare, 62,* 485–558.

Fein, E., Maluccio, A., & Kluger, P. (1990). *No more partings: An examination of long-term foster family care.* Washington, DC: Child Welfare League of America.

Fein, E., & Staff, I. (1991). Implementing reunification services. *Families in Society, 72,* 335–343.

Festinger, T. (1983). *No one ever asked us . . . A postscript to foster care.* New York: Columbia University Press.

Finkelhor, D., Hotaling, G. T., & Yllo, K. (1988). *Stopping family violence: Research priorities for the coming decade.* Newbury Park, CA: Sage Publications.

Frodi, A. M. (1981). Contribution of infant characteristics to child abuse. *American Journal of Mental Deficiency, 85*(4), 341–349.

Garbarino, J., Brookhouser, P., & Authier, K. (Eds.). (1987). *Special children—special risks: The maltreatment of children with disabilities.* Hawthorne, NY: Aldine de Gruyter.

Garbarino, J., Schellenbach, C. J., Sebes, M., & Assoc. (1986). *Troubled youth, troubled families: Understanding families at risk for adolescent maltreatment.* New York: Aldine.

Gershenson, C. P. (1986). A re-examination of the duration of foster care for children served by public agencies. *Child Welfare Research Notes,* No. 16.

Gershenson, C. P. (1987). An examination of the 1985 data for the duration of placement for children in foster care. *Child Welfare Research Notes,* No. 19.

Gershenson, C., Rosewater, A., & Massinga, R. (1990). *The crisis in foster care: New direction for the 1990's.* Washington, DC: Research and Education Foundation, American Association for Marriage and Family Therapy.

Gibson, T. L., Tracy, G. S., & Debord, M. S. (1984). An analysis of variables affecting length of stay in foster care. *Children and Youth Services Review, 6,* 135–145.

Gil, E., & Bogart, K. (1982). An exploratory study of self-esteem and quality of care of 100 children in foster care. *Children and Youth Services Review, 4,* 351–363.

Goerge, R. M. (1990). The reunification process in substitute care. *Social Service Review, 64,* 422–457.

Gries, L. T. (1986). The use of multiple goals in the treatment of foster children with emotional disorders. *Professional Psychology: Research and Practice, 17*(5), 381–390.

Halfon, N., Berkowitz, G., & Klee, L. (1990). *Health and mental health services utilization by children in foster care.* Berkeley: University of California, California Policy Seminar.

Halfon, N., & Klee, L. (1987). Health services for California's foster children: Current practices and policy recommendations. *Pediatrics, 80*(2), 183–191.

Hampton, R. L., & Newberger, E. H. (1985). Child abuse incidence and reporting by hospitals: Significance of severity, class, and race. *American Journal of Public Health, 75*, 56–60.

Hegar, R. L. (1988). Sibling relationships and separations: Implications for child placement. *Social Service Review, 62*(3), 446–467.

Herrenkohl, R. C. (1990). Research directions related to child abuse and neglect. In R. T. Ammerman & M. Hersen (Eds.), *Children at risk: An evaluation of factors contributing to child abuse and neglect* (pp. 85–108). New York: Plenum Press.

Hess, P. M. (1987). Parental visiting of children in foster care. *Children and Youth Services Review, 9*, 29–50.

Hess, P. M., & Folaron, G. (1991). Ambivalences: Challenge to permanency for children. *Child Welfare, 70*, 403–424.

Hess, P., & Proch, K. O. (1988). *Family visiting in out-of-home care: A guide to practice.* Washington, DC: Child Welfare League of America.

Hill, B. K., Hayden, M. F., Lakin, C. K., Menke, J., & Amado, A. R. (1990). State-by-state data on children with handicaps in foster care. *Child Welfare, 69*(5), 447–462.

Hochstadt, N. J., Jaudes, P. K., Zimo, D. A., & Schachter, J. (1987). The medical and psychosocial needs of children in entering foster care. *Child Abuse and Neglect, 11*, 53–62.

Hudson, J., & Galaway, B. (Eds.). (1989). *Specialist foster care: A normalizing experience.* New York: The Haworth Press. (Also published in *Child & Youth Services, 12*[1/2], 1989.)

Jaudes, P. K., & Diamond, L. J. (1985). The handicapped child and child abuse. *Child Abuse and Neglect, 9*(3), 341–347.

Jenkins, S., & Diamond, B. (1985). Ethnicity and foster care: Census data as predictors of placement variables. *American Journal of Orthopsychiatry, 55*(2), 267–276.

Jenkins, S., Diamond, B., Flanzraich, M., Gibson, J., Hendricks, J., & Marshood, N. (1983). Ethnic differentials in foster care placements. *Social Work Research and Abstracts, 19*(4), 41–45.

Kadushin, A., & Martin, J. (1988). *Child welfare services* (4th ed.). New York: Macmillan.

Katz, L. (1991). Foster care drift: A risk-assessment matrix. *Child Welfare, 70*(3), 347–358.

Klee, L., & Halfon, N. (1987). Communicating health information in the California foster care system: Problems and recommendations. *Children and Youth Services Review, 9*, 171–185.

Klee, L., Soman, L. A., & Halfon, N. (1992). Implementing critical health services for children in foster care. *Child Welfare, 71*(2), 99–111.

Knitzer, J. (1982). *Unclaimed children.* Washington, DC: Children's Defense Fund.

Lahti, J. (1982). A follow-up study of foster children in permanent placements. *Social Service Review, 56*, 556–571.

Landsverk, J., Davis, I., & Ellis-MacLeod, E. (1992, January). *Pathways through foster care.* Paper presented at the San Diego Conference on Responding to Child Maltreatment. San Diego, CA: Child and Family Research Group.

Lawder, E. A., Poulin, J. E., & Andrews, R. G. (1986). A study of 185 foster children 5 years after placement. *Child Welfare, 65*(3), 241–251.

Lindsey, D. (1991). Factors affecting the foster care placement decision: An analysis of national survey data. *American Journal of Orthopsychiatry, 61*(2), 272–281.

Maas, H. S., & Engler, R. E. (1959). *Children in need of parents*. New York: Columbia University Press.

Maluccio, A. N. (1985). Biological families and foster care: Initiatives and obstacles. In M. J. Cox & R. D. Cox (Eds.), *Foster care: Current issues, policies, and practices* (pp. 147–166). Norwood, NJ: Ablex Publishing Corporation.

Maluccio, A. N., & Fein, E. (1983). Permanency planning: A redefinition. *Child Welfare, 62*, 195–201.

Maluccio, A. N., Krieger, R., & Pine, B. (1990). *Reconnecting families: Family reunification competencies for social workers*. West Hartford, CN: Center for the Study of Child Welfare.

Maluccio, A. N., & Whittaker, J. K. (1989). Therapeutic foster care: Implications for parental involvement. In R. P. Hawkins & J. Breiling (Eds.), *Therapeutic foster care: Critical issues* (pp. 161–182). Washington, DC: Child Welfare League of America.

McCartney, K., & Galanopoulos, A. (1988). Child care and attachment: A new frontier the second time around. *American Journal of Orthopsychiatry, 58*, 16–24.

McFadden, E. J. (1985). Practice in foster care. In J. Laird & A. Hartman (Eds.), *A handbook of child welfare: Context, knowledge and practice* (pp. 585–616). New York: Free Press.

McIntyre, A., & Keesler, T. Y. (1986). Psychological disorders among foster children. *Journal of Clinical Child Psychiatry, 15*, 297–303.

McIntyre, A., Lounsbury, K. R., Berntson, D., & Steel, H. (1988). Psychosocial characteristics of foster children. *Journal of Applied Developmental Psychology, 9*, 125–137.

McMurtry, S. L., & Lie, G. Y. (1992). Differential exit rates of minority children in foster care. *Social Work Research & Abstracts, 28*(1), 42–48.

Mech, E. V. (1985). Parental visiting and foster placement. *Child Welfare, 64*, 67–72.

Mech, E. V. (Ed.). (1988). *Independent-living services for at-risk adolescents*. Washington, DC: Child Welfare League of America.

Milner,, J. L. (1987). An ecological perspective on duration of foster care. *Child Welfare, 66*, 113–123.

Moffatt, M. E. K., Peddie, M., Stulginskas, J. L., Pless, I. B., & Steinmetz, N. (1985). Health care delivery to foster children: A study. *Health and Social Work, 10*, 129–137.

Molin, R. (1988). Treatment of children in foster care: Issues of collaboration. *Child Abuse and Neglect, 12*, 241–250.

Morgan, T. (1990, November 20). Orphans return to city and recall a sad train. *The New York Times*, p. C19.

National Black Child Development Institute. (1989). *Who will care when parents can't?* Washington, DC: Author.

National Center for Children in Poverty. (1991). *Five million children: 1991 update*. New York: Columbia University School of Public Health.

Olsen, L. J. (1982a). Predicting the permanency status of children in foster care. *Social Work Research and Abstracts, 18*(1), 9–20.

Olsen, L. J. (1982b). Services for minority children in out-of-home care. *Social Services Review, 56*, 572–585.

Olson, R., Huszti, H., Mason, P. J., & Seibert, J. (1989). Pediatric AIDS/HIV infection: An emerging challenge to pediatric psychology. *Journal of Pediatric Psychology, 14*(1), 1–21.

Pardeck, J. T. (1982). *A study of the stability and continuity of foster care.* Lanham, MD: University Press of America.

Pardeck, J. T. (1984). An exploration of factors associated with the stability and continuity of the foster care system in the United States. *International Social Work, 27*(1), 5–9.

Pike, V., Downs, S., Emlen, A., Downs, G., & Case, D. (1977). *Permanent planning for children in foster care. A handbook for social workers.* Washington, DC: United States Government Printing Office.

Pinderhughes, E. E. (1991). The delivery of child welfare services to African-American clients. *American Journal of Orthopsychiatry, 61*(4), 599–605.

Rendon, M., Gurdin, P., Bassi,, J., & Weston, M. (1989). Foster care for children with AIDS: A psychosocial perspective. *Child Psychiatry and Human Development, 19*(4), 256–269.

Rest, E. R., & Watson, K. W. (1984). Growing up in foster care. *Child Welfare, 63*, 291–306.

Richardson, M., West, M. A., Day, P., & Stuart, S. (1989). Children with developmental disabilities in the child welfare system: A national survey. *Child Welfare, 68*(6), 605–613.

Roberts, M., & Siegel, M. (1988). Foster family care for hard-to-place disabled children. *Topics in Early Childhood Special Education, 8*(2), 73–80.

Robinson, J. L. (1982). The relationship of family background and casework involvement to placement stability. *Journal of Social Service Research, 4*(3/4), 51–68.

Ruff, H. A., Blank, S., & Barnett, H. A. (1990). Early intervention in the context of foster care. *Journal of Developmental and Behavioral Pediatrics, 7*(5), 265–268.

Rzepnicki, T. L. (1987). Recidivism of foster children returned to their own homes: A review and new directions for research. *Social Service Review, 61*(1), 56–70.

Saxe, L., Cross, T., & Silverman, N. (1988). Children's mental health: The gap between what we know and what we do. *American Psychologist, 43*, 800–807.

Schor, E. L. (1982). The foster care system and health status of foster children. *Pediatrics, 69*(5), 521–528.

Schor, E. L., & Abel, C. M. (1985, May-June). Back to basics in health care for foster children. *Children Today,* pp. 13–16.

Schor, E. L., Aptekar, R. R., & Scannell, T. (1987). *The health care of children in out-of-home care: A white paper.* Washington, DC: Child Welfare League of America.

Seaberg, J. R., & Tolley, E. S. (1986). Predictors of the length of stay in foster care. *Social Work Research and Abstracts, 22*(3), 11–17.

Sims, A. R. (1988). Independent living services for youths in foster care. *Social Work, 33*, 539–542.

Simms, M. D. (1989). The foster care clinic: A community program to identify treatment needs of children in foster care. *Journal of Developmental and Behavioral Pediatrics, 10*, 121–128.

Staff, I., & Fein, E. (1992). Together or separate: A study of siblings in foster care. *Child Welfare, 71*, 257–270.

Stehno, S. M. (1990). The elusive continuum of child welfare services: Implications for minority children and youths. *Child Welfare, 69*, 551–562.

Stein, T. J., Gambrill, E. D., & Wiltse, K. T. (1978). *Children in foster homes: Achieving continuity of care.* New York: Praeger Special Studies.

Stone, N., & Stone, S. (1983). The prediction of successful foster placement. *Social Casework: The Journal of Contemporary Social Work, 64*, 11–17.

Stroul, B., & Friedman, R. (1986). *A system of care for severely emotionally disturbed children and youth.* Washington, DC: National Institute of Mental Health, Child and Adolescent Service System Program.

Swire, M. R., & Kavaler, F. (1978). Health supervision of children in foster care. *Child Welfare, 57*(9), 563–569.

Taylor-Brown, S. (1991). The impact of AIDS on foster care: A family-centered approach to services in the United States. *Child Welfare, 70*(2), 193–209.

Timberlake, E. M., Pasztor, E., Sheagren, J., Clarren, J., & Lammert, M. (1987). Adolescent emancipation from foster care. *Child and Adolescent Social Work Journal, 4*(3/4), 116–129.

Timberlake, E. M., & Verdieck, M. (1987). Psychosocial functioning of adolescents in foster care. *Social Casework: The Journal of Contemporary Social Works, 68*(4), 214–221.

Tuma, J. (1989). Mental Health services for children: The state of the art. *American Psychologist, 44*(2), 188–199.

U.S. House of Representatives Select Committee on Children, Youth, and Families. (1989). *No place to call home: Discarded children in America.* Washington, DC: Author.

U.S. Senate Committee on Finance. (1990). *Foster care, adoption assistance, and child welfare services.* Washington, DC: Author.

U.S. Senate Committee on Investigations, Taxation, and Government Operations. (1989). *Crack babies: The shame of New York.* New York: Author.

Vega, L. A. (1990). *Factors associated with children's length of stay in foster family care.* Unpublished doctoral dissertation, Fordham University, New York.

Wald, M. S., Carlsmith, J. M., & Leiderman, P. H. (1988). *Protecting abused and neglected children.* Stanford, CA: Stanford University Press.

Walton, E. (1991). *The reunification of children with their families: A test of intensive family treatment following out-of-home placement.* Unpublished doctoral dissertation, University of Utah, Salt Lake City.

Weinstein, J., & LaFleur, J. (1990). Caring for our children: An examination of health care services for foster children. *California Western Law Review, 26*(2), 319–349.

Weston, D. R., Ivins, B., Zuckerman, B., Jones, C., & Lopez, R. (1989). Zero to three. *Bulletin of the National Center for Clinical Infant Programs, IX*(5), 1–7.

White, M. S. (1981). Promoting present-child visiting in foster care: Continuing involvement within a permanency planning framework. In P. A. Sinanoglu & A. N. Maluccio (Eds.), *Parents of children in placement: Perspectives and programs.* (pp. 461–475). New York: Child Welfare League of America.

White, R., & Benedict, M. (1986). *Health status and utilization patterns of children in foster care.* Final report of a project funded by the Department of

Health and Human Services, OHDS, Administration for Children, Youth, and Families (90 PD-86509).

White, R., Benedict, M., & Jaffe, S. (1987). Foster care health care supervision policy. *Child Welfare, 66*(5), 387–397.

Wiehe, V. R. (1990). *Sibling abuse: Hidden physical, emotional and sexual trauma.* Lexington, MA: Lexington Books.

Wiltse, K. T. (1985). Foster care: An overview. In J. Laird & A. Hartman (Eds.), *A handbook of child welfare: Context, knowledge and practice* (pp. 565–584). New York: Free Press.

Wulczyn, F. (1991). Caseload dynamics and foster care reentry. *Social Service Review, 65*(1), 134–156.

Zimmerman, R. (1982). *Foster care in retrospect.* New Orleans: Tulane University.

Zimmerman, R. (1988). Childhood depression: New theoretical formulations and implications for foster care services. *Child Welfare, 67*(1), 37–47.

6

The Casey Family Program
Factors in Effective Management of a Long-Term Foster Care Organization

Ruth Massinga and Ken Perry

Studies of program excellence in serving children often ignore the importance of organizational factors in determining success in meeting developmental goals for youths and families. The degree of success children experience in The Casey Family Program mirrors the degree of success the organization achieves in consciously creating a program environment that, through its structures and procedures, reinforces and supports good child and family functioning. This chapter discusses some of those management factors in this national long-term family foster care program.

A PROFILE OF THE PROBLEM

Recent statistics from all 52 states and two territories revealed that there were 407,000 children in out-of-home care at the *end* of fiscal year 1990. In terms of children *entering* any form of care that supplements that provided by biological parents, recent trends indicate a continuing increase, with 6.5% more children entering such care arrangements in fiscal year 1991, compared to fiscal year 1988 (Tatara, 1991).

An extensive analysis of the characteristics of children in foster care for 1988 done by Dr. Toshi Tatara, Research Director of the American Public Welfare Association, revealed that 37.2% (estimated at 123,700 youths) had been in substitute care for 2 years or more, and 11.6% (39,400) had been in care for more than 5 years (Tatara, 1992). For all youth remaining in substitute care, 12.4% (an estimated 42,160 children, based on reports from 29 states) of these children had long-term foster care as the primary placement goal (Tatara, 1992). The long-term foster care goal means that these children are expected to remain in substitute care until they reach the age of majority.

At the end of 1988, the majority of children remaining in family foster care were children of color (55.5%). More than one third of the children were African American (36.5%) and 10% were Hispanic. Caucasian children comprised 45.5% of children living out of their homes, and other races represented 4.2% of the youths in care (Tatara, 1992). The median age of children entering long-term foster care was 8.2 years, and 50.9% of the children were male (Tatara, 1992).

Thus, although placement prevention programs such as the Homebuilders family reunification program (Kinney, Haapala, & Booth, 1991) and aggressive adoption programs are reducing the numbers of children spending long periods of time in substitute care, a significant number of America's children will "grow up" in foster care. An increased percentage of these children enter care because of "parental conditions/absence" (e.g., economic hardships, substance abuse, homelessness, illness, imprisonment). In addition, there is an increased percentage (25.4%) of youths who experience more than one placement while in care (Maluccio & Sinanoglu, 1981). As for most youngsters with a lengthy history in foster care, these characteristics, along with sexual and physical abuse, are found in disproportionally high numbers, and frequently in combination with each other in youths referred to and accepted by The Casey Family Program (Fanshel, Finch, & Grundy, 1988). Because of the maltreatment that they have experienced and the trauma of lengthy separation from family members, these youths present special challenges, such as significant developmental delays, serious clinical issues of guilt and self-blame that relate to multiple experiences of separation and loss, and issues related to trust and attachment, power and control. The overarching goal of foster parents and social work staff is to help such youths resolve these issues in a reasonable fashion, leaving the youth able to be self-sufficient in the fundamentals of life—maintaining physical health and vigor; holding a job, which requires at least one developed skill; and being reasonably stable emotionally, with the ability to form reciprocally supportive relationships.

MELDING OF PERSONAL AND ORGANIZATIONAL VALUES

From its beginnings in 1966, The Casey Family Program sought to apply sound, progressive business practice to human services, deliberately transferring many of the elements of the success of the United Parcel Service (UPS) to its ongoing efforts to serve youths.

Over his long career as an executive, James E. Casey, one of the founders of UPS, observed that young men in the company who lacked a stable family life had more difficulty meeting company expectations. Comparing these men's histories and those of other young men with whom he grew up to his experience with his own tightly knit family and his view of the importance of his family to his own success, Casey began to search actively for an ideal way to help delinquent or rootless young people become "successful, self-supporting American citizens" (The Casey Family Program, 1966). After careful review of options, and working in consultation with leading child welfare experts of the era, especially Joseph Reid, then Executive Director of the Child Welfare League of America, Casey determined that he and his family would set up a long-term foster family program that would be committed to raising youngsters in caring, loving families.

The explicit goal of the program was to support the children's development over time in ways that focused on achieving educational and social advancement for each child. This individualized self-sufficiency focus was different from that of most foster care agencies of the time, which were more concerned with the process of adjustment of the children to the foster care milieu and not as focused on the nature of the adult who was expected to enter society at the end of the long stay in substitute care. Also, the program was expected to contribute to the development of new techniques of providing effective foster care by carefully matching youth with foster families who wanted to raise one or two children to adulthood.

To achieve these ends, Casey was concerned that the program be developed and managed just as any successful business would be. He believed that, when other public and private agencies saw that the program could achieve good and lasting results with the same types of children whom those agencies served, at a comparable cost, those agencies would change their direction to a more results-oriented approach, much as his company and its competitors changed the business goals and operations of the U.S. Postal Service.

In 1966, The Casey Family Program, a privately endowed operating foundation, began providing planned long-term foster care to youths in Seattle. Today, the program serves more than 1,300 children and 922 families in 23 communities in 13 states, including three Indian reservations. As of January 31, 1994, 57% of the youths in care were children of color. The average age of these youths was 13.7 years; the average length of time that children have been in the program is 3.6 years. The foster families also reflect the diversity of the children. In fact, about 27% of the children live with a relative, as compared with a range across the country from 15% to 50% (Baltimore City 20%, California 37%, Illinois 46%, and New York City 50%; Dubowitz, Feigelman, & Zuravin, 1993).

Many of the organizational values and the management views of James Casey were intentionally transferred to The Casey Family Program. These include:

- Small, direct-service units (Divisions) intentionally made up of well-trained, culturally diverse, and experienced staff, with Division caseloads averaging 15–17 per worker.
- A Division work-style that reinforces team decision making and shared responsibility for work with youths and families.
- Concentration of focus on one product (e.g., long-term foster care), with well-honed, consistent social work technology.
- Demonstrated support of staff retention and internal promotion opportunities, through personnel policies that support long-term service, attractive benefits, and a professional developmental package.
- Active youth, family, and staff roles in maintaining and improving the quality of service.

The Trustees of the program have maintained the single focus of the program on long-term family foster care, while supporting a refined and expanded range of service responses based on the evolving needs of increasingly troubled youths who need care. As the program has moved into new communities, we have carried forward a baseline set of program practices and philosophy, which shape recruitment of foster parents, staff, and the youths. At the same time, we seek to understand and incorporate the unique ethnic, cultural mores and successful child-rearing expectations of each community into our work, beginning with selection of foster families. This means, for example, that, although we hire trained, experienced social workers in every one of our 23 sites across the country, we aggressively pursue staff who reflect the cultural and ethnic mix of that community. This has extended to providing scholarships to current or prospective staff in order to expand the professional development of indigenous social workers and foster home developers in Native American, Hispanic, and African American communities, many of whom are in leadership positions with the program today. In turn, these staff are able to attract experienced foster families who form a core of culturally responsive foster families for youths. As of the end of December 1993, there were 53 professional staff of color, representing 21% of the work force; 17% of these staff were in direct service roles.

As a further means to tailor the clinical response for youths to the specific cultural, linguistic, and traditional treatment approaches that reflect the values of various communities, the Division staff actively recruit community leaders across a broad spectrum of professional disciplines and interests for Division Advisory Committees who provide continuous infusion of specific local input about needs of children and families that require localized program development. These perspectives are especially useful in shaping collaboration with organizations and individuals whose focus is on persistent, individualized efforts to connect adolescents to community work and social systems that will sustain them in ways that mimic the normal connections that extended families provide for young people who live with their own families.

One tangible result from these efforts in reservation communities are tribal resolutions by the tribal counsel with jurisdiction for administration of the Indian Child Welfare Act that invite us to work with Native American youths, as well as ongoing sanction for case management decisions by the Tribal Court with jurisdiction for child welfare issues. Having direct community sanction for our work has lifelong benefits for the Native American youths, who need to come to terms with their people and their lifeways, regardless of the choices they may make about remaining on the reservation as adults.

In a larger sense, planning with community leaders about individual children can lead to more systemic collaborations that may benefit families that the program does not serve directly. For example, on the Fort Berthold reservation in North Dakota, the Three Affiliated Tribes (Mandan, Hidatsa, and Arickara) and the program collaborated in a creative way to build both an office building for the program on leased tribal land and a child care center for children on the reservation. The program used local building suppliers and tribal construction workers, investing in broad community development as well as multiple generations of children.

Now completing our 27th year, the program's strengths and challenges can be described by an analysis of our successful combination of:

- Recruitment of children who do well in our unique environment
- Recruitment and retention of families who can tolerate and creatively respond to the evolving needs of damaged youths over time (e.g., learning difficulties, behavioral problems, difficulties in forming and developing positive relationships, and difficulties in becoming emotionally and economically responsible for oneself)
- Successful selection of staff who thrive within the program setting
- Deliberate development and use of rituals and traditions with children, families, and staff that promote cohesion and a sense of belonging to The Casey Family Program

- Continuous collaboration with other child- and family-focused community systems
- Relentless pursuit and adaptation of improved practice and technology.

In the following sections, we describe some of these elements more fully.

CHILDREN IN THE CASEY FAMILY PROGRAM

The Casey Family Program recruits children from the nation's child welfare system. Youths requiring long-term foster family care usually are referred by county or state foster care systems, with community sanction and oversight of our work usually provided by the juvenile or family court system. The basic program acceptance criteria include the following:

- Children accepted into The Casey Family Program are to be 6 through 15 years of age. Acceptance of children below and above these ages requires corporate headquarters approval.
- Long-term foster family care must be the plan of choice for the child at the time of intake. Children whose placement needs at the time of intake can be met best by any other type of care, including adoption or return to their natural parents, are not appropriate for placement with Casey.
- The child must be capable of self-sufficiency as a young adult. The program is not intended to serve children with disabilities at the time of intake that will interfere substantially with their likelihood of attaining self-sufficiency.
- Community sanction must be secured for all placements made with The Casey Family Program. Community sanction is legal recognition by the community that the program is responsible for care of a child (i.e., has the day-to-day case management authority to make a variety of decisions and plan for the welfare of the child), regardless of the agency, entity, or individual with ultimate legal responsibility. (Perry, Pecora, & Traglia, 1992, pp. 2–3)

These children have experienced many traumas by the time we see them, starting with the distress of frequent losses of place and kin, as well as the pain of extremes of family dysfunction, abuse, and the like. The key to determining whether these children are capable of sustaining a family relationship lies in a thorough assessment process.

Program Practice Guidelines and Services

No matter how well meaning and well trained staff are, an effective child care system must clarify how it sets out its goals for youths and subsequently works toward reaching those goals. This evolves into a flexible, multifaceted model of care that is critical in determining the results that the program expects to attain as well as the methodologies that are most likely to work (Daly & Dowd, 1992).

Beginning in 1990, The Casey Family Program systematically reviewed and clarified best practice and developed a manual, *Practice Guidelines for Clinical Practice and Case Management* (Perry et al., 1992). In addition to extensive internal review, the program used the knowledge of experts who were convened in a symposium focused on the changing needs of children in foster care and then identified standardized assessment instruments that were particularly helpful in gauging the needs of children. The final product, *Practice Guidelines*, laid out the principles of Casey social work practice throughout the program's Divisions.

Eight case planning factors are used to organize and guide the assessment that leads to an analysis of each child's strengths and needs for improvement: emotional health, family adjustment and other relationships, cultural identification, competence and achievement, physical health, educational development, self-sufficiency, and legal involvement. Definitions of each of these case planning factors, as well as procedures for child assessment in each category, are laid out in the practice guidelines (Perry et al., 1992). These baseline and ongoing criteria for assessment of foster children are supported by program policies and procedures. The initial and ongoing service planning is driven by semi-annual assessment of the child's functioning, using each of these case planning factors as a spur to a comprehensive analysis of the child's growth and developing competency. Case management is child specific, and a continual standardized cycle of identification of goals, design and provision of services, and measuring of outcomes across the eight case planning factors. Outcomes are determined by the use of subjective and objective measures, including normed educational and behavioral reports, provided periodically (e.g., the Achenbach Child Behavior Checklist, Children's Apperception Test, Practice Scholastic Achievement Test, Scholastic Achievement Test), *Diagnostic and Statistical Manual* (American Psychiatric Association, 1987) clinical diagnosis and assessments; and periodic child and family self-reports of behaviors and relationships.

Attention to the bottom line at Casey is defined as focused, persistent, specific goals planned with many community systems to obtain positive progress for each youth. Through the combination of community efforts and enhanced formalized financial contracts with public child welfare systems, we maintain Casey's level of financial support as a reasonable portion of total funds spent on child care. Each child receives an enriched array of normalizing child development experiences—art, music, and group activities (boys' and girls' clubs, scouting, etc.)—as well as unique therapeutic experiences that help them address and come to terms with past hurts. The latter include intensive therapeutic foster care experiences in homes directly licensed and supervised by the program staff, or set up through contractual arrangements with planned group home or residential treatment center providers, to work on issues or behaviors that cannot be addressed in community settings. If treatment and appraisals of the child's functioning indicate the child is unable to return to a foster home, the program makes arrangements to provide the child the treatment arrangement that meets his or her needs, outside of Casey.

In order to enhance significantly the life chances of children who have had multiple separations from parents and other significant adults, the Casey service plan must be both holistic (e.g., all components must be harmonized and complementary) and strong in each service component. We seek out therapists who focus on the effects of depression and loss over the developmental course, and educational consultants who understand how to help youths and parents knit together an adequate foundation of academic competencies from an all-too-frequent history of school interruptions and failures, as well as special learning disabilities that must be diagnosed and factored into the educational plan for each child. Health care must focus on solid determinations of the child's current health status, as well as his or her history and that of the biological family, filling in as many gaps in knowledge as we can.

Through continued reappraisal of the child's changing needs, The Casey Family Program teams have been able to affect positively more than 60% of children in the program, as measured by school completion, obtaining jobs or being engaged in vocational or job training, and avoidance of difficulty with the law (Fanshel et al., 1988).

Services for Young Adults

Young adulthood is a challenging developmental period for most individuals but particularly for those with foster care backgrounds. This is because of insecurities associated with the absence of effective adult caregivers in these youths' families of origin who can provide advocacy and viable intervention strategies on behalf of children, as well as greater than usual difficulties in establishing a stable home, or demonstrating consistently acceptable social and academic performance. In recognition of these tendencies, even among youths who make substantial gains over time, the program continues services to youths beyond the 18th or 21st year, depending on each youth's needs and his or her level of investment in further work to prepare for his or her future.

Indeed, providing youths with an organizational anchor has caused The Casey Family Program to extend surrogate parental involvement into young adulthood, to help youths cope with unfinished or delayed development tasks, especially in completing education. The Continuing Education and Job Training (CEJT) scholarship program is especially important to many youths.

The CEJT Program offers any past or current foster youth through age 22 who has been the recipient of Casey services for 1 year or more the opportunity to apply for scholarships and other support services to assist him or her with educational and vocational goals. The youth may apply for the program scholarship that best fits his or her particular situation. The types of scholarships offered are:

The *Jim Casey Scholarship* (for *full-time* schooling at vocational and technical schools or undergraduate schools, and for apprenticeship and/or entrepreneurial training).

The *Marguerite M. Casey Scholarship* (which applies to *full-time* graduate schooling toward a master's degree, doctoral degree, or professional certificate).

The *Henry J. Casey Scholarship* (for *part-time* vocational or undergraduate schooling; it requires a stable, long-term job, held either full-time or part-time, and it also may apply toward college classes taken while still in high school).

Requirements to gain the scholarships and maintain eligibility are flexible enough to support the obligations of youths to persevere and reach their goals. Consistent with increased or sustained success in school, youths are expected to contribute to their own earned scholarships. The CEJT Scholarship Committee of the Board of Trustees has become adept at helping this particular student population (representing 10% of all active Casey participants at any time period) craft a comprehensive plan that includes opportunities to maintain significant relationships with foster parents, social workers, and therapists where this seems needed, because some students are at risk for having serious emotional, learning, and developmental impairments during their school careers.

The following description of a young woman currently in the program illustrates our continued investment in a Casey youth as she has experienced the program over the past 8 years.

∞

In 1986, the program admitted Samantha, a 14-year-old white foster child, and placed her with an older couple. The foster child's pre-Casey history contained an extensive background of state child protection involvement. Samantha could not live safely with her birth mother because of her mother's severe intellectual and physical disabilities. As a result of these impairments and consequent dependency dilemmas, her birth mother frequently got involved with men with problems who further put her child at risk. Samantha's birth father's identity was never known, so he could not be considered as a placement resource. All attempts to shore up the family unit failed because of the birth mother's chronic poor decision making. The state child welfare agency's eventual plan of choice for Samantha was permanent long-term foster care, and she was referred to Casey. On admission to the program, Samantha had experienced approximately 4 years' accumulated time in seven different foster placements.

Samantha had several different living arrangements, including two Casey foster families, over the next 8 years. During this same time period, she also endured the death of one foster father and her birth mother. In other words, she had literally become orphaned. Despite these losses, which were further complicated by a couple of placement disruptions, she demonstrated resiliency and focused goal planning and goal attainment. Since admission to Casey, Samantha has attended several Casey youth therapy groups and many other Casey activities (raft trips, special camps, ski trips, etc.) available to her. This level of participation facilitated a close relationship between Samantha and the program staff and her consequent identification with Casey as an extended family. Her grades in high school were good to excellent, and she performed efficiently in her first job at a car wash service. In September 1990, she moved to a sorority house on the campus of a state university and continued to achieve academically. Her educational/career aspirations are to work with children as a psychologist or social worker.

Needing some time out, Samantha decided not to attend college in the fall of 1992, and she was placed in the independent living component of the program for 4 months. She returned to school for the spring semester in 1993 and is currently functioning well and age appropriately in most spheres of her life. She frequently has been engaged as an official spokesperson, locally and nationally, for the development of practice and policy for young adults in the Casey Family Program.

∞

An analysis of Samantha's case history in relationship to Casey reveals the following:

> Many children who literally lose or never have access to their birth parents require a different type of family constellation to raise them. In this case, both foster parents and professional staff at Casey became Samantha's "family."

Generalized as well as individual-specific bonding with agency staff and foster parents can and frequently will take place. Samantha is psychologically attached to several Casey staff members and she considers herself a "Casey kid," viewing the program and its staff as her surrogate family.

Such children, when very involved in an agency's social and treatment activities over time, can develop a positive image of themselves and productively self-actualize as both a participant in and leader of the program.

Consciously involving consumers of services (Samantha) to provide evaluative information and planning expertise over time strengthens the competencies of the young adult directly while adding to the program's relevance and authenticity for other consumers.

CASEY PROGRAM FOSTER FAMILIES

Core to children's success are foster families that invest in them around the clock, creating a caring milieu in which the children thrive, wrestle with past hurts, and begin to come to terms with who they are and what they want to become. In January 1994, The Casey Family Program had a total of 885 foster families. Of this number, 636 were in use (i.e., had one or more foster children in care). The program actively recruits families who are willing to embrace the values of the program. These families are assessed in the following areas:

Motivation to be a foster parent
Ability to work with The Casey Family Program
Personal history of caregivers
Family values and beliefs
Family system functioning
Parenting skills

A major focus of screening of foster parents and the functional emphasis during recruitment is placed on the ability to become part of a team and the parent's belief that raising children can be shared by several adults, acting in concert. Frequently, individual members of the foster family or the entire family, including the foster child, become engaged in short-term family sessions to address issues that will enhance and improve family coping skills. Peer support and strong emphasis on training for foster parents are critical, ongoing fundamental program elements. Public recognition for the family's success (e.g., graduations, weddings), keeps the program focused on the many developmental changes foster parents experience over time and the effects these evolutions have on the foster youth as well as the family system of the foster family. We consciously seek to avoid damage to a foster family system that has taken on the challenge of a foster child; in order to honor that intent, we must be concerned that we disclose to families essential elements of a child's background that are directly relevant to the child's successful adjustment to the home.

In the winter of 1992, we began a best practice process for family assessment and family support parallel to that which had been conducted for children in prior years. When completed, this work will enhance both theoretical and practice-level knowledge about good family functioning from a variety of perspectives, updating and enriching the program's operating assumptions about family well-being, as well as providing data to refine the selection, matching, and family support assumptions of our current work. Key informants in this process are current foster parents in the program as well as national experts in foster family training and support.

Within The Casey Family Program, social work practice supports preservation of existing kinship systems and increasing recruitment of extended family members to parent children who cannot remain with their biological families. In 1994, nearly 29% of children were in relative placements. For both kin and nonrelated foster families, our goal is to nurture and support multiple healthy caregivers to children, including respite providers, Casey aides who assist in transporting youth, tutoring, or other child-specific assignments. According to Dr. David L. Chadwick (cited in Cargal & Senechal, 1991, p. 9), these staff and foster families are expected to offer each youth what Margaret Mead described as "an ever widening circle of affection." As youth and families grow stronger, there is an implied and frequently overt obligation to use those strengths in the service of developing the organization and thus helping other youths who need it to enter the program.

CASEY PROGRAM STAFF

Casey staff, too, are generally products of the nation's public child welfare system. They combine that experience and a master's degree in social work with solid skills in case management and clinical treatment of children and families. In looking at staff success at Casey, the following qualities are typical:

- Toleration of ambiguity and imperfection (one's own, and those of others).
- A capacity to work effectively in a team, assuming various team roles at different times—leader, specialist, coach—but always active in promoting group effort toward a child's or family's growth.

Staff need the following knowledge:

- Understanding of what constitutes an integrated sense of well-being for a child.
- Appreciation of developmental issues along many dimensions—child, family, oneself, the organization—and an intellectual appreciation of the varying pace of interventions over the life course of the child.

Underlying these skills and expertise is devotion to doing whatever seems useful to help youths directly or through advocacy in the greater community.

Just as well-functioning families have the capacity to tolerate difference among family members, as well as a capacity for self-awareness, Casey staff must have an ability to tolerate closeness and self-disclosure with a small group of colleagues over a long period of time, because the issues that surface for youths and families evoke similar issues staff have experienced as parents or within their own families of origin. The program deliberately encourages these staff qualities by placing strong emphasis on teamwork and group decision making within divisions and across the program.

Vigilant, even obsessive staff focus is devoted to anticipating and planning for developmental changes in the lives of youngsters and families, as well as in the development of divisions. Our experience has supported and reinforced the view that anticipation and attention to natural life developmental changes, whether experienced by youth, foster families, or the staff, helps us interrupt potentially destructive patterns before they require more extensive remedy. Moreover, by anticipating evolving interests of staff and nurturing them, we maintain and enhance the productive worker and encourage long-term ties to the program. Retention is high, and total turnover rates are low among professional staff. Expectations for excellence in providing services are explicit, with ever-evolving efforts to articulate, measure, and sustain program quality.

RITUALS AND ATTENTION TO CULTURAL IDENTITY THAT SHAPE YOUTH DEVELOPMENT

Staff promote the development of family mythology for youth within the program by displaying pictures of youth and families on office walls, displaying photo albums of division activities with children and families prominently in reception areas, and encouraging retelling of vivid tales about children and families in Casey-sponsored gatherings that weave a rich tapestry of identity and belonging for specific children, families, and staff. Over time, each division has created various rituals and traditions (e.g., graduation luncheons, group campouts for older youths) that are designed to offer youths stability and appreciation of purpose and time in one's life and to facilitate development of a normalizing sense of order and pace to life events for youths and families.

The program emphasizes the use of food both to nourish children and families and as a means of encouraging bonding and building traditions for youths who lack consistent pleasant memories of family life. All divisions have kitchens that are stocked with beverages and snacks that are liberally offered to children and families. Many meetings with families and group work with children include some form of sustenance. Program gatherings, such as picnics, potluck dinners, and holiday parties, mimic family rituals and other communal functions that accent the social power of food as an offering of oneself and one's caring.

Great importance is placed on the principals of claiming and reciprocal support between the organization and staff, between children and the organization, between families and staff, and between families and youngsters. Youths frequently self-identify as "Casey kids" and describe feelings of belonging to the program as an institution, especially because many of them work with the same social worker and family for their entire life course while with the program (Fanshel et al., 1988).

Many of these children return to visit the agency, their foster families, and particular staff throughout their young adulthood in what best can be described as a kind of "coming home" phenomenon. Youths come back to introduce new spouses and babies to staff and foster families, to trace portions of their histories that have become hazy or with which they are now ready to cope, and to get helpful referrals or direct crisis-oriented support. Recently, some former program participants have expressed interest in organizing an alumni group that would continue peer support for "Casey kids" but might be a natural vehicle for mentoring opportunities for younger, current program participants.

Since the early 1980s, The Casey Family Program has placed major policy and program emphasis on cross-cultural work with youth, families, and staff. Each child has an explicit cultural identification and strengthening component in his or her service plan, and each Division has a staff member serving as a cross-cultural specialist. This person assures that experts representative of the child's ethnic or cultural background help determine that the case plan addresses his or her cultural needs, incorporating activities and training experiences that enhance the cultural identity of the youth naturally. Since 1991, each Division has developed a division-wide cross-cultural plan to bring discipline and focus to the overall program goal to become a culturally competent organization. The following case study of a family and a foster child describes the program's blending of several of these features over time.

∞

A middle-age Caucasian couple, Mr. and Mrs. Davis, approached a western division of The Casey Family Program in 1985 and expressed an interest in providing long-term care for a child in need of placement. They were anxious to work with an agency and shared the program's views and values on the successful raising of children. It was the second marriage for each of them and they had both reared children in their previous marriages. They currently had one child at home, and the decision to provide a home for other children and continue parenting was consensual and well articulated by both of them. They also shared strong ties to a particular religious denomination, but were clear that they would allow any child placed in their home to go to the church of his or her choice.

The couple was anxious to learn and they faithfully attended training and other agency functions. It became quite clear that they believed in use of a team approach to raise children and they continually demonstrated the ability to identify and appreciate difference in others.

Parallel to their selection into the program, Cindy, a 15-year-old girl of Asian descent, was considering entering the program because she was in need of long-term foster placement following an adoption failure in a Caucasian family. Because an Asian foster family could not be found, a match was made between this youth and foster family. The fit hinged on Cindy's shared religion with the Davises. Furthermore, she required a family that could tolerate her extraordinary preoccupation with her appearance and her self-centeredness.

Placement with the family occurred following a couple of preplacement visits, and the initial adjustment was described as good for all parties. The strong cohesive threads that facilitated a workable placement were the common religion and the unswerving, unconditional commitment the family and program made to this child. Through the foster family's continual inclusion of program staff in planning and child management, the foster placement was experienced by all parties as a joint parenting venture.

By the end of 2 years, it became apparent that Cindy had developmental needs that would require an intervention beyond the capability of this particular foster family. Her cultural identify confusion was causing her profound distress, as was her academic performance. She became very depressed and also began some relatively minor, although high-risk, acting-out. All parties, including Cindy, agreed to a transfer of placement to an ethnically mixed family in another community with a large Asian population and the use of a more nontraditional school resource. Cindy experienced success in school and she became more comfortable with her Asian descent because of a daily exposure to people who "looked like her." Although case management was assumed by another Casey social worker in the new city, she remained in contact with staff and her previous foster family from the referring Division throughout her placement.

At age 20, Cindy ended her ongoing official ties to the program. She continues to live as a young adult in her new home. Although she is still troubled in some ways and trying to sort out her values, she is economically self-sufficient. Cindy still maintains a relationship with her past caseworkers. She returned to her first Casey foster home (the Davises) in the summer of 1992 and 1993 to spend time with the family, Casey staff, and other friends. On one of her visits, she came into The Casey office and located her pictures on the wall in one of the hallways and commented on how much she had changed over the years. Cindy is the first to say that she wishes her life had been different and that she still doesn't have a "real family."

∞

This case study highlights the program staff's use of long-term developmental work with a youth whose combined cultural and interpersonal issues needed to be addressed in a changing milieu over time.

- A shared religious affiliation between Cindy and the Davises allowed Cindy to experience a sense of safety in the form of like beliefs and values following a devastating adoption disruption. The Davises also had raised many teenagers, and they did not have a lot of unrealistic expectations of their relationship to Cindy.
- The program's ability to work out an arrangement between Divisions and staff in two locations deliberately addressed Cindy's cultural identity needs at the time those issues were most critical for her.
- The Davises' comfort in raising Cindy in partnership with Casey allowed all parties to assist in Cindy's physical relocation to a place where Casey operates a Division *and* where she felt more psychologically secure and whole as a person. The opportunity for her to engage her cultural identity was in her best developmental interests. She also succeeded in securing her high school diploma in a place that felt safe to her.
- Depending on life circumstances, people make the journey home in different ways and for different purposes. Increasing numbers of young adults are "coming home" to Casey offices to get information about their past that assists them in making sense about who they

are in the drama of life. The organization cannot take the place of birth families, but it can, on occasion, for some children, youths, and adults, be the safest place to which they can relate.

Careful matching of foster children and families requires appreciation for making deliberate changes in the youth's environment over time in order to address emerging facets of development that the child must face and resolve in order to emerge as a more fully integrated personality. Foster parents must be helped to regard their planned contribution to a youth's development as critical, no matter how brief the stay in the home. Both foster parents and the youth need active permission and help from the program in nurturing connections that may become enhanced over the youth's lifetime.

CONCLUSIONS

Social service agency leaders must set up systems to assure congruence between broad goals and programs and the various client-specific methods for achieving them. These management systems must be grounded in explicitly described best practices to which all staff and foster parents are committed and that reflect the values of the program.

As the burgeoning rise in total quality management and other new management techniques indicates, complimentarity between management and child caring philosophy is the key to achieving planned outcomes with youths successfully. A caregiving system absent the values and characteristics of good business practice cannot adequately or successfully meet the developmental long-term needs of children in foster care. Conversely, a successful, developmentally focused caregiving program is permeated and influenced by business practices that extend and support the goals of child rearing.

The Casey Family Program benefits from the continued emphasis on sound business and sound program planning through the ideas of its founder, the trustees, and successive program executives. Its success warrants continued examination of program values and characteristics that best suit raising children to healthy and productive adulthood and the intentional incorporating of these values and characteristics into an organizational plan. Systematic examination of how to promote child welfare management technology without losing the cherished and demonstrably successful child- and family-oriented values and practices embedded within this organization, and others like it, is a key to future evolution of family-centered foster care.

REFERENCES

American Psychiatric Association. (1987). *Diagnostic and statistical manual of mental disorders* (3rd ed.—rev.). Washington, DC: Author.
Cargal, J., & Senechal, V. (Eds.). (1991). *Preparing for the future: The Casey Family Program symposium on children and youth in long-term out-of-home care*. Seattle: The Casey Family Program.
The Casey Family Program. (1966). Preamble. In *Articles of incorporation*. Seattle: Author.
Daly, D., & Dowd, T. (1992). Characteristics of effective, harm-free environments for children in out-of-home care. *Child Welfare, LXXI,* 487–496.
Dubowitz, H., Feigelman, S., & Zuravin, S. (1993). A profile of kinship care. *Child Welfare, LXXII,* 153–169.
Fanshel, D., Finch, S., & Grundy, J. (1988). *Foster children in life course perspective: The Casey Family Program experience*. New York: Columbia University Press.
Kinney, J., Haapala, D., & Booth, C. (1991). *Keeping families together: The homebuilder's model*. Hawthorne, NY: Aldine de Gryter.
Maluccio, A., & Sinanoglu, P. (1981). *The challenge of partnership: Working with parents of children in foster care*. New York: Child Welfare League of America.
Perry, K., Pecora, P., & Traglia, J. (1992). *Practice guidelines for clinical practice and case management*. Seattle: The Casey Family Program.
Tatara, T. (1991, May). Child substitute care flow data for FY90 and child substitute care population trends since FY86 (revised estimates). *VCIS Research Notes* (No. 3). Washington, DC: American Public Welfare Association.
Tatara, T. (1992, May). Characteristics of children in substitute and adoptive care—A statistical summary of the VCIS national child welfare data base. *VCIS Research Notes* (No. 4). Washington, DC: American Public Welfare Association.

7

Not Under My Heart, But In It
Families by Adoption

Laraine Masters Glidden

The title of this chapter is borrowed from a poem (Heyliger, 1952/1983) that is frequently reprinted on cards that families send to announce a new adoption (J. Crowley, personal communication, April 20, 1994). The phrase, *not under my heart, but in it,* captures their prevailing view that one does not have to conceive, gestate, or give birth to a child in order to form strong and enduring emotional bonds. Instead, this view holds, what is more important is what goes on in families rather than how they came to be constituted.

Regardless of whether one accepts this premise, there is no denial that, as we approach the 21st century, family constitution is not what it used to be. For example, in the United States 28.1% of children under 18 do not live with two parents, and, of those that do, 20.7% are in remarried (reconstituted) families (U.S. Bureau of the Census, 1992). Some of these reconstituted families are adoptive families in which one parent is the biological parent. These stepparent adoptions are adoptions by relatives, in contrast to nonrelative adoptions, in which the adopting parents have no biological tie to the adoptive child. It is the various kinds of *nonrelative adoptions,* and the placement decisions and outcomes that surround them, that are the primary focus of this chapter.

Although not this chapter's emphasis, relative adoptions do have an important bearing on nonrelative adoptions. Their substantial frequency is indicative of the liberalization of the definition of family, in general, with blended families and single-parent families becoming

---

This chapter was written with the support of Grant No. HD 21993 from the National Institute of Child Health and Human Development and a faculty development award from St. Mary's College of Maryland.

common and accepted. They have influenced the current greater acceptance of adoption and adoptive families, making adoption less subject to the dogmatism that appeared to drive negative attitudes toward it in earlier decades (Dembroski & Johnson, 1969).

Although the types of adoptions that are occurring today are different in some ways from those that occurred in past decades, adoption, regardless of its characteristics, is defined as a "personal, legal, and social act which provides for the transfer of the rights, responsibilities and privileges of parenting from legal parent(s) to new legal parent(s)" (Cole, 1990, p. 43). This transfer and the people involved with it have given rise to important questions about adoptive child, birth parent, and adoptive parent adjustment. The adjustment outcomes that can be expected, the variables that influence them, and the significance of these outcomes for adoption placement and practice are addressed in this chapter. Before those outcomes are examined in depth, however, it is important to describe the current practice of adoption, and how this practice has changed over time. The following brief historical review provides a perspective on contemporary practices and policy.

HISTORY OF ADOPTION

Adoption is an ancient concept and practice (Leavy, 1954) found among societies as geographically widespread and culturally diverse as Albanians, Puerto Ricans, and the Sudanese (Payne-Price, 1981). Along with these cultural differences are, not surprisingly, differences in the primary motivations for adoptions. In some societies at some points in time, adoption was a means of establishing an heir; sometimes, it was seen as adding another helper/worker to the family (see Kilbride & Kilbride, chap. 11, this volume). Especially in contemporary Western society, adoption has become a way to help a child in need, because of loss of birth parents through death (orphaning) or removal from birth parents as a result of neglect or abuse.

In the United States, formal, legislated adoption did not exist until the middle of the 19th century. By the end of that century, however, most states had adoption laws. Furthermore, "orphan trains" transported and permanently relocated into farm families many thousands of children who were abandoned and destitute in the growing urban centers of the country, giving considerable publicity to fostering and adoption (Jackson, 1986). Agencies responsible for the screening of children and potential adoptive parents arose in the 20th century, and until the 1950s saw their primary mission as providing a "perfect" child to traditional married couple parents.

There is general agreement (e.g., Cole, 1990; Glidden, 1989) that adoption practices began their transformation in the 1950s. A tangible manifestation of this transformation was demonstrated in 1955 when the Child Welfare League of America convened the National Conference on Adoption. This conference was designed to summarize the existing state of knowledge and practice with a view toward promulgating recommendations that would function as standards for the field. The conclusions were far reaching, ranging from focus on the administrative practices of adoption agencies to suggestions for emphasis in future research. An adamant view was that adoption should be child centered and that an adoptable child is any child "who is legally free and who can benefit from family life" (Schapiro, 1956, p. 52). It was also true, however, that there was considerable variability among agencies as to determining what kind of child would or would not be able to benefit from family life.

The initial impetus toward broadening the notion of what kinds of children were adoptable may have come from the large numbers of destitute children created by the ravages of World War II and the Korean War. Much more extensive social change, however, was responsible for the continuation and expansion of this notion. For example, the civil rights movement undoubtedly provided ideological underpinnings to transracial adoption, particularly the placement of black and racially mixed children into white homes. In the 1960s this kind of placement had become commonplace, but it declined in the 1970s as black leaders argued that white families could not provide the necessary cultural identity to black children.

It was not only the civil rights movement that led to changed adoption practice. The relative unavailability of healthy white infants also was a major factor (Children's Home Society of California, 1984; Glidden, 1989). More widespread contraception and liberalized abortion laws, accompanied by greater acceptance of single motherhood, meant that potential adopters frequently had to consider children with special needs. Although *special needs* does not have a uniform meaning from state to state, it typically includes children with disabilities, children from a minority group, "older" children (typically 8 years or over), and large sibling groups (typically three or more).

Furthermore, the move away from a monolithic view of family composed of a breadwinner husband/father with a homemaker wife/mother influenced the kinds of applicants that agencies placing children were willing to consider. For example, although most children are adopted into two-parent households, the number of single-parent adopters has increased over the last several decades (Windgard, 1987). In addition, middle age is no longer a barrier to adoption, particularly for older children, and gay rights activists have won some battles over their "fitness" as adoptive parents (e.g., Taylor, 1989).

ADOPTION IN THE 1990s

Prevalence and Incidence

Nonrelative adoption is not a common occurrence. In 1988 in the United States, slightly more than 2 million women (3.5% of approximately 57 million women) of reproductive age (15–44 years) had ever sought to adopt, although only 31% of them had actually adopted (Bachrach, London, & Maza, 1991). According to recent census data (U.S. Bureau of the Census, 1992), 1.4% of all married-couple family households have only adoptive children, and another 1.3% have at least one adoptive and one biological child. Annually, approximately 61,000 nonrelative adoptions are finalized (National Committee for Adoption, 1989). These adoptions are of children of all ages, nationalities, and physical, intellectual, and behavioral characteristics, and are arranged by public and private agencies as well as by private individuals, frequently with lawyers as intermediaries.

Who Adopts

Adoptive parents, like biological parents, vary greatly in their characteristics. Furthermore, their portraits differ depending on the kind of child or children that they adopt. In order to highlight these characteristics, two composite adoptive families are described here. These composites are based on real individuals and situations, but nonessential information is changed and events and facts from different cases are consolidated. Thus, the composites differ more from the originals than would a case study, but are actually more representative of a typical family.

∞

> The Greers are both 36 years old. They met in college, stimulated into a conversation one day in a sociology course on families and sex roles. They were juniors then, and began to date steadily soon thereafter. They married 3 years after college commencement, when Stephanie had completed a master's degree in personnel administration and Matt had finished law school. The next 4 years were a relatively happy mix of establishing their careers, settling into their first home, and traveling in Europe and South America. They took their first ski lessons together, quickly became devotees of cross-country treks, and discovered that they enjoyed a similar balance of adventure and relaxation in their leisure activities. They were certainly having fun, just

the two of them, but as the Greers approached their 30th birthdays, they began to discuss having a family. They both wanted at least one, and probably two, children, and even though they were mindful of the lifestyle change that would result, they made the decision to start a family and abandoned what had become their normal contraceptive routine.

A year later, with no pregnancy, the Greers began a search for fertility that was to last for the next 4 years. They progressed from sperm count and motility tests to endometrial biopsies, laparoscopy, hormonal analyses, and other sometimes painful, and always psychologically disruptive, procedures. After two in vitro fertilization attempts failed to produce a sustained pregnancy, they started to consider adoption.

It took only a few telephone calls to local adoption agencies and a conversation with one of their friends, an attorney who had handled some adoption cases, to discover that the healthy infant that they had been thinking about in their adoption discussions was in short supply. If they were willing to consider an older child with disabilities or emotional or behavioral problems, or one who was still in foster care status, their local department of social services would work with them. Otherwise, there were two realistic options: adopt internationally, or arrange a private or independent adoption.

∞

The Greers are typical of the majority of U.S. adopters, childless married couples who have experienced problems with fertility (Bachrach et al., 1991). Indeed, based on the 1982 National Survey of Family Growth, fully 40% of married women between the ages of 30 and 44 who were infertile and had no live births had adopted one or more children (Bachrach, 1986). They also reflect the findings that adopters tend to be more educated, older, and more financially comfortable than nonadoptive parents. Also, in contrast to the stereotype of the mother as homemaker, Stephanie, like the majority of adoptive mothers, works outside the home. Although the Greers are typical, the next composite case study reflects the variability that one does find among adoptive parents.

∞

The Wilsons had been married for 13 years and had three birth sons, 5, 7, and 10 years old. They wanted a larger family, and especially at least one daughter, but, after discussion, decided that they did not really want to start over again with another pregnancy, or with sleepless nights or dirty diapers. After all, Cora was 39, would be 40 in a few months, and Robert was already 42. They immediately thought about adoption, because they had heard that there was a shortage of black parents wanting to adopt, and that there were many black children to be adopted. It seemed like a perfect solution for them. They could have their daughter, maybe about 5 years old, and also help a needy child, something that was important to them, consistent with their values.

It took about 4 years for this idea to be realized, because they moved across the country temporarily, and were just too unsettled to even think about adding another child. But when they returned to the East, where it seemed as if they would stay for a long while, they came back to the idea. Cora had a part-time job as a pediatric nurse, but she felt that she could do more, especially with an older child who would be in school. Cora and Robert went to a foster care meeting, where they met a social worker from the Department of Social Services. They told her they were really interested in adoption rather than foster care because they wanted a *permanent* member of the family. The worker was quite positive about the possibilities, even when she found out that their income was only $24,000 a year, and that Robert had not even finished high school. That was all right, she said, especially if they were willing to take a child with special needs who would be eligible for an adoption subsidy. That would help considerably with expenses; they would even get a Medicaid card for a child with special needs, so that most of the health care expenses would be paid. The worker mentioned a little girl, 6 years old, who was currently with a foster family. The agency, however, was looking for an adoptive placement for her.

∞

The Wilsons are typical of a new type of adoptive parent. They already have birth children; they are less well educated and less affluent than traditional adopters. The Wilsons are a married couple, as are most adopters, but single applicants certainly are not eliminated from consideration. All these characteristics pertain especially to adopters of children with special needs. For example, a brochure published by Project STAR, a Pittsburgh program designed to facilitate the adoption of children with developmental disabilities, states the following with regard to qualifications of parents: "Parents may be married or single. They may come from any economic level or educational background" (Project STAR, undated). Furthermore, many agencies have made special attempts to recruit adoptive parents from minority groups, because there are large numbers of minority children waiting to be adopted (A.R. Silverman & Feigelman, 1977; Washington, 1987).

In sum, although these composites emphasize the variability in who adopts, it is also important to emphasize the central tendencies. It is married couples, with family incomes above poverty level, educational levels of high school or better, and sterility or subfecundity problems and no children born to them who represent most of the adoptive parents. However, as already explained and described in the composites, parents with particular characteristics are more likely to adopt children with certain characteristics. Who gets adopted, and how those placements are likely to occur, is described more completely in the next section.

Who Gets Adopted

Although national data collection on adoption ended in 1975, a number of independent efforts have provided information on adoptive children (Maza, 1990). The most recent comprehensive survey was done in 1986 by the National Committee for Adoption (NCFA, 1989). What follows is a summary primarily from that source.

According to NCFA estimates, 51,157 unrelated domestic adoptions were granted in 1986 in the United States, as were 10,019 adoptions of children from foreign countries, for a total of 61,176 unrelated adoptions. Slightly less than half of the domestic adoptions (24,589, or 48%) were of infants, and slightly more than one quarter (13,568, or 26.5%) were of children with special needs. The total number of unrelated adoptions has been relatively stable since 1975, although the number of adoptions of foreign-born children has increased steadily in that same period of time. These children come from many countries (e.g., Morocco, Mexico, Poland, Jamaica, Colombia), but the majority, approximately 6,000 per year, are from Korea.

Most of the healthy infants who are adopted are ones who are voluntarily relinquished at or very soon after birth by mothers (and sometimes fathers) who decide that they are unable to raise the child. Typically, these birth parents are unmarried and young. If they do relinquish their children, they are less likely to live subsequently in poverty, and more likely to complete their schooling than unmarried birth mothers who decide to keep their children (Bachrach, 1986).

In contrast, children with special needs, those who are older and/or have physical, intellectual, or psychological disabilities, may be available for adoption because of *involuntary* removal. These are the children of neglect and abuse, the children of parents deemed by the state to be "unfit." They are children who are likely to experience one or more foster care placements before an adoption plan is developed. In fact, for many children foster care has been a typical rearing environment, one in which they spend the majority of their growing-up years. Sometimes, these children move from one foster care home to another, adrift in the system, failing to attach and establish bonds with any significant adult or peer figures. This pattern was recognized as a serious problem, and in 1980 the Adoption Assistance and Child Welfare Reform Act (PL 96-272) encouraged, through federal monies, permanency planning for children removed from their families.

Thus, in the 1990s no child is considered unadoptable, regardless of age or physical, intellectual, or emotional characteristics. Nonetheless, the type of family likely to adopt a healthy infant is different from the type of family likely to adopt a child with retardation, a child who needs 24-hour medical care, or a child with acquired immunodeficiency syndrome. To illustrate the relationships between child and adoptive family characteristics, it will be useful to return to the Greers and the Wilsons and follow them as they progress through the adoption process.

∞

> Once the Greers learned about the current adoption situation, they carefully considered their options. Never having been parents, they were afraid of instant parenthood with an older child. They feared that they would not be able to cope with the problems that they were certain such a child would bring to a new family. In addition, neither Stephanie nor Matt wanted or intended to give up their careers, and they realized that a child with lots of difficulties might require far more intensive parenting than they would be able to provide. Besides, they admitted, they did not want to miss the experience of having a baby, of watching it grow and develop, of seeing its first steps and hearing its first words. They wanted their adoptive experience to be as similar as possible to the experiences of their friends who were birth parents.
>
> So, they decided on two strategies. They located a private adoption agency in their community that worked closely with an orphanage in Columbia. The U.S. agency would do their home study, process all the necessary paperwork, and help identify potential adoptive children. It even had a liaison with a lawyer in Bogota who took care of all the requirements of Colombian law. The Greers were excited about this possibility, and took out two of their travel books on South America to admire some of the beautiful children pictured in them.
>
> However, both, especially Stephanie, also were worried. They feared for the instability of the political situation, or that suddenly the laws might change. It seemed foolhardy to rely on only one route to their destination. So they decided to place ads in about a dozen newspapers serving local communities in their region:
>
> ADOPTION: Loving couple, unable to have children, wish to adopt an infant. Will pay medical/legal expenses. Call Stephanie & Matt.
>
> They even got an 800 number to encourage calls from young women who might have very little money. They also wrote to the health centers of more than 400 colleges and universities describing their situation, and suggesting that if any of the health workers knew of college

students who were pregnant, and considering adoption, to put these students in touch with them.

Four months passed, and during this time they had begun their home study for a Colombian adoption. They had also gone to an informational meeting conducted by the Latin American Parents Association, and met dozens of parents—some had already adopted, and others, like themselves, were just beginning the process. One evening, at 9:08 to be exact (Stephanie looked at her watch and the time was indelibly printed in her memory of this event), the telephone rang. It was a 19-year-old also named Stephanie, who was due to have a baby in just 7 weeks. She had seen their ad in her hometown paper and was struck by the coincidence of the two Stephanies. On an impulse she had decided to call and find out more about them.

The Stephanies and Matt talked that night and, first thing the next morning, the Greers called their lawyer. Two months later they were the proud adoptive parents of Stephan, a name selected by the birth and adoptive parents together. Also together, the Greers and Stephanie agreed on some continued contact in this "open" adoption. They would send pictures and information about Stephan to Stephanie at least once a year. Normally, Stephanie would not contact them, but all agreed that, if at some point she felt that she needed more involvement, they could renegotiate the arrangement.

∞

The experience of the Greers in pursuing alternatives to the long waits of agency adoptions is not uncommon. Indeed, some estimates are that close to half of the domestic infant adoptions are done privately (Sullivan, 1992). Even advertising, a controversial practice, is permitted in 32 states (NCFA, 1989). In addition, some degree of openness in adoption, even when it is filtered through an agency, is viewed by many as serving the needs of birth parents, adoptive parents, and adopted children (NCFA, 1989). A detailed account of an open adoption (Caplan, 1990) written by the adoptive father describes both the pitfalls and the rewards of this innovative approach.

The outcome for the Greers was a happy one for them, and they are similar to many parents who adopt healthy infants both in their characteristics and in the process by which they became adoptive parents. However, the Wilsons are also a prototype, as shown below.

∞

Cora and Robert didn't have to wait at all. In fact, the 6-year-old girl who was mentioned to them at their first informational meeting came to live with them only 2 weeks later, initially as a foster child but with the intent to adopt. Ashanti was a child with fetal alcohol syndrome, the result of her alcoholic mother's heavy drinking during pregnancy.

Actually Ashanti's birth mother was a polydrug user, and no one really knew which of Ashanti's difficulties were the results of what prenatal and what postnatal exposure. It was not until Ashanti was 4 years old that she came to the attention of social welfare workers because her mother was found on the street, passed out from an episode of binge drinking. Ashanti went into a foster home while rehabilitation plans for her mother were formulated and implemented, but after 2 years of no discernible progress, her birth mother's parental rights were terminated in a court action and Ashanti was freed for adoption. Her current foster family was not in a position to adopt her, but the Wilsons were. Thus, she was placed with them on a fostering basis, until their home study could be completed and they could be formally approved as adoptive parents.

When the Wilsons initially had heard about Ashanti, they were somewhat reluctant to consider her. She was described as a lovable girl, but with problems of hyperactivity and attention deficit disorder. Her tested IQ was 62, in the range of mild mental retardation, but her current foster mother was convinced that she was brighter than that. Given her history and that the IQ test had been administered almost 18 months earlier, not long after Ashanti had moved in with the foster family, the foster mother's view was given credence. Regardless, Cora and Robert were not certain that they could cope with it all.

But then they met Ashanti, and they fell in love. A small child, and very affectionate, she immediately cuddled into Cora's lap, looked up at her with large, black eyes, and smiled tentatively as she clutched a tattered, semi-stuffed monkey. She played with Cora's crystal pendant, seemingly fascinated with the lights and colors reflected from it. When Robert came over, and asked her if she wanted to read a story with him, she went to him easily and listened attentively as he read aloud. The Wilsons were immediately entranced, and could not believe that this was the same child who had been described as hyperactive and with attention problems. At any rate, they made up their minds after that first meeting, and Ashanti came to live with them.

∞

Ashanti is a child with special needs for three reasons: she is of African American ethnicity, she is older, and she has a disability. The Wilsons are quite typical of the kind of family that would adopt her. They are of the same race, are experienced child-rearers, have some experience with disability because of Cora's nursing background, and are motivated at least in part by a desire to help a child instead of, or in addition to, creating or enlarging their family. This kind of motivation has been found in several studies of special-needs adoptive families. For example, Nelson (1985) listed altruism as a reason that parents give for adopting a child with special needs. She provided excerpts from interviews with adoptive parents that exemplify this altruism.

Statements such as "we wanted to give a child a chance" (p. 24), and "I didn't want them to go back into the violence that they came out of" (p. 25) are typical.

I have also addressed this motivation in my research with parents who adopt children with developmental disabilities (Glidden, 1989, 1990, 1992). In an intensive study of 42 families who had adopted 56 children with mental retardation, 52% mentioned that the chance to help a child who needed help was an important factor in their decision to adopt. Sometimes this motive was expressed in a religious context, and sometimes in secular humanitarian terms. Nonetheless, this empathy with a child who needed them was frequently powerful. As one mother said, "I've got this great need in me to save a life" (Glidden, 1989, p. 81).

The Wilsons are also typical of the model family that adopts via a public rather than a private agency or independently. For example, data from California (Windgard, 1987) showed that 45% of the adoptive parents from public agencies were nonwhite, in contrast to 28% and 24% for private agency and independent adoptions, respectively. Furthermore, their lower income is again characteristic of public agency adoptions. In 1981–1982, the median income for parents adopting via public agencies in California was $25,802; in contrast, it was above $32,000 for both private agency and independent adoptions. Finally, 40% of public agency adoptions were subsidized, in comparison to only 7% for private agency and none for independent adoptions.

Many issues are raised by these two composite cases, one of them a healthy infant adoption, and the other a special-needs adoption. Some of them are explicit, such as the decision to adopt privately, to advertise for a child, and to pursue an international adoption. Others are more implicit, such as neither of the adoptions being transracial. The next two sections examine these two types of adoptions in more detail, with a focus on the impact for the individuals involved in the adoption. Moreover, current public policies are reviewed with an emphasis on how they might be changed or maintained for the benefit of those directly affected by the adoption as well as society at large.

ADOPTION OF HEALTHY INFANTS

Adoption involves adoptees, adoptive parents, and birth parents. These three components frequently are referred to as the adoption triangle. This section reviews the evidence for the impact of adoption on each of these components. Included in this review is an examination of some of the different forms of adoption (e.g., open adoptions) and how they influence different members of the adoption triangle. A set of recommendations at the end of the chapter highlights the complexity of the adoption issue and the need for maintaining a variety of options and flexibility in choosing among them.

Impact of Adoption on Adoptee

Socioeconomic Circumstances As already described, domestically, most healthy infants are adopted because their birth parents, frequently just the mother, have decided to relinquish the child as a result of the circumstances surrounding the pregnancy and birth. The birth mother is typically young, unmarried, and relatively unable to care adequately for a child at that point in her life. In contrast, the adoptive home that the child will enter is likely to be one in which the parents are older, more affluent, more well educated, and highly motivated to be parents. For example, Bachrach (1983) reported that, for the year 1976, about 84% of biological children, but 96% of adopted children, lived in a two-parent household. Furthermore, for the same year the percentage of children living in poverty was only 2.1% for adopted children but 14.4% for biological children. Data for 1982 were similar, with 2.3% of adoptive children and 18.8% of biological children living in poverty (Bachrach, 1986).

Even more compelling is the comparison between adopted families and never-married birth mothers, the likely circumstance for children if they had not been adopted. Most children (62% in 1982) living with never-married birth mothers were living below the poverty level. These never-married birth mothers also had very low educational levels—10.7 completed years of school in contrast to the 13.4 years for mothers of adopted children (Bachrach, 1986). Thus, in terms of socioeconomic resources, the healthy infant adoptee appears to be advantaged.

Psychosocial Resources and Issues Some earlier concerns about increased adoptee psychological vulnerability have not been validated by recent empirical research. For example, claims that adoptees are less likely to be securely attached were not supported by the results from a study of mother–infant attachment in adoptive families (Singer, Brodzinsky, Ramsay, Steir, & Waters, 1985). The data indicated no differences between same-race adopted and nonadopted 13- to 18-month-olds. All of the children had been adopted by 10 months of age, with a mean placement age of 1 month, 9 days.

In addition, some writers have argued that adoptee problems are related to difficulties in the transition to parenthood for adoptive mothers and fathers. Kirk (1964, 1984), writing from a sociological perspective, has emphasized the societally imposed stigma associated with infertility. He has argued that, because it is normative to give birth, anyone who does not or cannot is viewed as different and deficient, stigmatized by society. A more psychological orientation stresses the failure experience of not being able to bear children, and a utilitarian approach emphasizes the practical difficulties of infertility treatment and the adoption process. Treatment for fertility problems may take years, involve invasive procedures, and be very expensive. Furthermore, the adoption process is also lengthy, involves a kind of psychological invasion in the form of the home study, and also can be expensive, especially if done privately. Thus, it is not uncommon for adoptive parents of healthy infants to have been involved in trying to have a baby for more than a decade, to have spent tens of thousands of dollars, and to be exhausted from this process.

All these analyses, then, predict a more difficult transition to parenthood for the adoptive parents. Nonetheless, recent research with 52 adoptive (all adoptees were 2 weeks or younger) and 52 birth parent couples found differences in favor of an *easier* transition for adoptive parents. Adoptive couples had more positive expectations before the child's placement, and more satisfying experiences about 4 months after placement (Levy-Shiff, Goldshmidt, & Har-Even, 1991).

Clinical Sample Outcomes Although adoptive children live in very positive socioeconomic and psychological environments, there nevertheless has been a longstanding belief that they are more vulnerable to a variety of negative developmental outcomes than are birth children. Many studies have addressed this issue, examining children throughout their childhood and, in some cases, even young adult years. Typically, these studies involve the use of *clinical* samples. The prototype of a clinical-sample study is one in which an investigator uses a sample of subjects referred for some type of treatment or service (e.g., behavior disorder) and collects information on the proportion of adopted children in this sample. If the proportion is significantly higher than the base rate in the general population, adoptive children would seem to be at higher risk.

Hersov (1990) provided a succinct but comprehensive review of the literature relating to the belief of increased vulnerability for adoptees. He concluded that, although there is some evidence that adopted children are overrepresented in clinical samples, the rate found in recent investigations is not nearly as high as that found in early studies. Nonetheless, data from clinical studies do suggest that adoptive children are at least *twice* as likely to be represented in clinical samples as nonadopted children. These data are from studies of learning disabilities (e.g., D.M. Brodzinsky & Steiger, 1991; Silver, 1989), mental health and behavior (e.g., Zill, 1985), psychiatric inpatient treatment (e.g., Kim, Davenport, Joseph, Zrull, & Woolford, 1988), and other areas.

Nonclinical Samples Most of the studies finding overrepresentation did not use any control groups, nor did they separate infant adoptions from older child adoptions. There are other studies with more sophisticated methodologies that have incorporated both of these features. Zill (1985), for example, examined the relationship between adoptive status and behavioral and learning outcomes for children adopted in infancy or later, and compared adoptive children with children living with both biological parents as well as children born out of wedlock and reared by their birth mother. He utilized the 1981 Child Health Supplement to the National Health Interview Survey, and thus had a very large data set with a total sample size of over 15,000 children and an adoptive sample size of 358.

Zill's findings show that children adopted later than infancy had poorer developmental outcomes than either children adopted in infancy or nonadopted children. For example, for adolescents, ages 12–17, only 13% of children adopted in infancy had ever been seen by a psychologist or psychiatrist, in contrast to 42% of those adopted after infancy. Even that 13% is significantly higher that the 5% of children raised by both biological parents, although not higher than the 15% of children reared by only their birth mother. The pattern is similar for whether the child had ever repeated a grade, although the outcomes are relatively better for infant adoptees, only 7% of whom had ever repeated a grade, in contrast to 12% of children raised by both biological parents, 26% of children raised by biological mothers, and 30% of children adopted after infancy.

Results from a project conducted by the Search Institute in Minneapolis also found relatively good outcomes for adolescents who had been adopted as infants (Offen, 1992). For example, in comparison to nonadoptees, 19% versus 13% had attempted suicide, 12% versus 9% had engaged in vandalism, and 16% versus 12% had engaged in driving under the influence of alcohol at least twice in the previous year. These data indicate a slightly elevated incidence of risk behaviors for infant adoptees, but are obviously discrepant with the results from clinical populations.

A study of psychological and academic functioning in adopted and nonadopted children (mean age at placement was 3.2 months) reached a similar conclusion (D.M. Brodzinsky, Schechter, Braff, & Singer, 1984). Although nonadopted children showed slightly better adjustment than did adopted children, the differences were small. The authors emphasized that the adopted children were, for the most part, well within the normal range and functioning quite well.

Caution about drawing conclusions too early on in the developmental life span is a lesson of at least one longitudinal adoption study. Bohman and Sigvardsson (1985) reported on 22 years of data in a prospective longitudinal study of over 600 children either placed in adoptive homes, kept by their birth mothers, or put in foster care. At age 11, the children were compared with classmate controls on social adjustment. Scores for all three groups indicated more maladjustment than for the controls. By age 15, however, the adopted children were as well adjusted as controls, but the fostered and birth mother–reared children remained more maladjusted. Additional measures at ages 18 and 22 supported the relatively good outcomes for adopted children.

Explanations and Conclusions Various explanations have been offered for these sometimes contradictory findings (Hersov, 1990). Clearly, children who are adopted after infancy are more at risk than those adopted early in life. The experiences of those children before their entry into a stable adoptive home may account for this risk. Children adopted at a later age frequently have a history of family instability, including neglect and abuse and multiple placements, which can interfere with the normal attachments currently viewed as being essential to later psychological health. However, even children adopted in infancy show, at least in some studies, somewhat elevated risk over comparable nonadopted children reared in two-parent homes.

It is possible that children of unwed mothers have had adverse prenatal experiences associated with poor prenatal care, or that they are genetically vulnerable. Pregnant teens frequently have poor diets and tend not to seek medical care early in their pregnancy. Furthermore, accidentally becoming pregnant may indicate impulsiveness, immaturity, and lack of foresight, which could be characteristics for which a genetic predisposition is transmitted. Research using adoptive samples by Loehlin and his colleagues (Loehlin, Willerman, & Horn, 1982, 1985) suggests small genetic contributions to some personality traits. Their results, however, are not consistent across different ages of adoptive children.

It is always possible, of course, that *being adopted* affects development in a negative way. Certainly, the search for birth parents (Kowal & Schilling, 1985; Lifton, 1975, 1979; Sachdev, 1989; Taylor, 1989) suggests that finding one's roots is desirable for complete identity formation. Anecdotally, at least, this aspect of being adopted would appear to be related to psychological health, particularly during adolescence and early adulthood, when identity issues may be critical to developmental progress (Erikson, 1968). Other psychodynamic and ethological theorists have emphasized the salience of loss, which may be important as a primary experience as well as cognitively, as the child begins to understand the meaning of adoption and associate it with abandonment (D.M. Brodzinsky, 1990).

There is a final set of explanations for the finding of adoptive child vulnerability centers on the likelihood that adoptive children will come to the attention of professionals and, thus, be counted in studies estimating their incidence or prevalence. Adoptive parents' familiarity with social service systems, availability of postadoption support services, and openness to seeking help beyond the family all may be explanations for the overrepresentation of adoptive children in some samples. This set of explanations says, then, that adoptees are not really more likely to be at risk, but merely more likely to be identified as such.

In conclusion, infant adoptees may have more problems than children reared with both their birth parents. Nonetheless, they are likely to be placed in an adoptive home that will have more economic and problem-solving resources than the one that their birth mother could have provided. Furthermore, there is growing evidence that their psychological environment is healthy. Certainly, there is nothing in the research literature to suggest that we should advocate a policy different from promoting the adoption option for birth parents, who are likely to consider and even welcome it.

Impact of Adoption on Birth Parents

Birth parents have been a frequently neglected corner of the adoption triangle. In traditional, or closed, adoptions, they were encouraged to relinquish the child and then forget about it. Adoption agencies tended to ignore their grief and psychological pain, or to counsel them that it would soon disappear. Increasingly, however, there has been recognition that the difficulties that birth parents have in surrendering the child are enduring, and that reactions of depression, guilt, shame, uneasiness around children, and so forth are experienced by some throughout the life span (Evans, 1994; P.R. Silverman, Campbell, Patti, & Style, 1988; Stiffler, 1991). The largely invisible birth father also is coming under closer scrutiny (e.g., Sachdev, 1991) and there is evidence that the image of him as uncaring about the birth mother and child is inaccurate (Deykin, Patti, & Ryan, 1988).

A case that received a great deal of media attention in 1993 illustrates birth father involvement as well as birth parent pain in the surrendering process. Jessica, born in 1991, was surrendered by her birth mother, Cara Clausen, and the then-alleged birth father, a man to whom Cara was engaged. The couple selected to adopt her, the DeBoers, quickly filed an adoption petition. It was only 3 weeks later, however, that the real father was told of his paternity and that both birth parents went to court to try to overturn the petition and get their baby back. After more than 2 years of rulings and appeals, during which Jessica lived with her adoptive parents, she was returned to her now married birth parents in a highly controversial court decision (Whose Daughter is Jessica?, 1993). Although cases like this one are rare, when they occur they inevitably lead to criticism about adoption laws and practices and the need to ensure protection of birth parent rights.

Despite the pathos generated by this highly publicized case, however, it is still safe to say that what we know about birth parents does not allow us to decide with certainty whether the overall impact of their surrendering a child has been good or bad for their subsequent lives. Most of the writing on this issue either is anecdotal, or, when empirical, relies on birth parents involved in adoption and parental rights organizations, or on clinical samples. These individuals may be a very nonrepresentative sample of all surrendering birth parents, because they either have decided to involve themselves in these organizations or have adjustment problems. Furthermore, other methodological flaws abound (see A.M. Brodzinsky, 1990, for a detailed treatment). Nonetheless, it is important to acknowledge the legitimacy of birth parent concerns, to respond to their needs with pre- and post-surrender counseling, and to recognize the life-span duration of these needs, working to establish mechanisms for delivery of services beyond the time of relinquishment.

Impact of Adoption on Adoptive Parents

Usually, the adoption of a healthy infant is viewed as a joyous event. It signals the end of a long period of, first, physician and, second, social worker intrusion into the privacy of the family. "At last," parents may think with relief. Their feelings of disappointment, differentness, incompleteness, and inadequacy are over. This generally shared, but romantic, view of how an adoption affects adoptive parents is somewhat naive. Certainly it neglects the theoretical stance that parents by adoption are different and, therefore, suffer from what sociologists call "role handicap." This handicap is created, in part, by societal attitudes that adoption is second best and unnatural (Kirk, 1984; Levy-Shiff et al., 1991).

Despite these widespread and competing views of adoptive parents, there has been a lack of research attention to their adjustment. As described earlier in this chapter, the few studies that have examined transition to parenthood do not indicate that it is more difficult for adoptive than for birth parents (Levy-Shiff et al., 1991; Singer et al., 1985). Other studies that have tried to measure longer term adjustment in adoptive parents generally have found that they seem to be satisfied with their adoptions (e.g., Jaffee & Fanshel, 1970; Levy-Shiff et al., 1991). Rarely does this research include control or comparison groups, and, when such groups are included, they are birth parent groups, differing in many characteristics from the adoptive groups. Thus, no convincing research-based conclusion regarding the adjustment of adoptive parents can be reached at this time.

Summary of the Impact of Adoption

The adoption of healthy infants has some advantages for the adoptee and, possibly, for the adoptive parents. The impact on the birth parents is less clear and needs more thorough investigation. Certainly, it must be recognized that surrendering a child can be a traumatic event, with lifelong impact, and techniques for ameliorating that impact must be developed and implemented. Options such as open adoption should be considered, but with the recognition that these techniques may have their own hazards (McRoy, Grotevant, & White, 1988). Conversely, *not* surrendering the child also may have deleterious consequences, and these should not be ignored in preadoption counseling services.

ADOPTION OF CHILDREN WITH SPECIAL NEEDS

Special needs, in adoption terminology, refers to children who are older, are members of a minority, have disabilities, and/or need to be placed as a sibling group of more than two. These kinds of adoptions represent between 25% and 30% of all domestic adoptions, and even more of foreign adoptions, because many of those children are of minority cultures in this country. This section does not attempt to focus separately on the issues and outcomes relevant to all these kinds of special-needs adoptions. Rather, brief summaries of the current state of research and practice that are most important for public policy initiatives are provided. These summaries revolve around three questions of current interest:

1. Can older children with histories of abuse, neglect, and "foster care drift" be successfully placed in adoptive homes?
2. Do adoptions of children with disabilities, particularly those with developmental disabilities, result in satisfactory outcomes for adoptive families?
3. Is the current practice against placement of children with parents of a different race, so-called transracial placement, justified?

Adopting Older Children

There is a growing body of evidence that more risks are involved in adopting older children (Barth & Berry, 1988; Festinger, 1990; Nelson, 1985; Rosenthal & Groze, 1992). Almost always, these are children who have had histories that are markedly different from what is regarded as psychologically healthy. They frequently have been abused and/or neglected, have lived in many different environments, and have failed to develop the kinds of trusting and secure relationships with others that we know to be the essential foundation of good mental health. Most of the research on adoption of older children uses the probability of a disruption (the child leaving the adoptive home before legalization) or a dissolution (terminating the adoption after legalization) as the indicant of failure. For this chapter, I do not distinguish between these two outcomes, and I use the term *disruption* for either one.

Many research studies (e.g., Barth & Berry, 1988; Berry & Barth, 1990; Groze, 1986; Nelson, 1985; Rosenthal, Schmidt, & Conner, 1988) indicate a higher probability of adoption disruption as a function of increasing child age at placement. Specific data and estimates vary from under 10% to close to 50%, with such variability being due, no doubt, to differences in the samples and studies themselves. Barth and Berry (1988) have one of the most thorough treatments of this issue in their analysis of 1,156 adoptive placements of children 3 years or older in California between January 1, 1980 and June 30, 1984. Even in this sample of older child adoptions, increasing age was a strong predictor of disruptions. Although the disruption rate for the sample as a whole was only 10%, at the youngest age level (3–5 years) 4.7% of the adoptions had disrupted, whereas at the oldest age level (15–18 years) 26.1% of the adoptions had disrupted.

Characteristics other than age also were predictors of disruption. With respect to child characteristics, boys, children with multiple problems, and children who had had previous adoptive placements all were likely to encounter disruptions. In addition, two placement characteristics differentiated the disrupted and nondisrupted adoptions: disrupted adoptions were *less* likely to be foster parent adoptions, and *more* likely to have more highly educated adoptive parents. Many characteristics, such as family income, ethnicity, parental age, number of other children in the home, and whether the mother worked outside the home, did not differentiate disrupted from nondisrupted placements.

Disruption is an important, but not the only, measure of the success or failure of an adoptive placement. Even when an adoption does not disrupt, it may still be problematic. This kind of outcome is illustrated in Reid, Kagan, Kaminsky, and Helmer's (1987) study of adoptions of older, previously institutionalized youth. These children were at risk in the extreme. Most of them had histories of abuse and/or neglect in their birth families. They had been in foster care for an average of 4 years, and about one third had at least one previous adoption disruption. They were, on average, 11 years old when they entered the current placement.

Although these were supposedly intact placements, at the time of interview 7 of the 26 adoptees either were in residential or correctional treatment or had run away. Furthermore, only 9 of the 26 adopting couples thought that the child's problems had lessened since placement, and 15 of the 26 couples expressed substantial reservations about the adoptions, with some indicating clearly that they would not do it again, if they had a second chance.

Despite these findings, and even though older child adoptions are more risky than those of infants, there is still a reasonable chance that they will be successful even with the children most likely to have difficulties (Barth, 1988). Regardless, society has few feasible alternatives available. A reasoned public policy would recognize the difficulties with increasing age and other problems, attempt to place children as early as possible, and provide a spectrum of pre- and postadoption services to safeguard against disruption (Groze & Gruenewald, 1991).

Adoption of Children with Disabilities

As the placement of children with disabilities has increased, so have the data indicating that these adoptions are, for the most part, resoundingly successful. Many research projects have examined outcomes in terms of family satisfaction (e.g, Coyne & Brown , 1985; Glidden, 1989, 1991; Glidden & Pursley, 1989; Marx, 1990; Nelson, 1985; Todis & Singer, 1991). In all of these studies, although parents admitted that the placements were not problem free, they also cited many examples of benefit and reward as a result of the adoption. For example, in the study by Glidden, Valliere, and Herbert (1988), 62% of mothers felt that they had become better people as a result of the adoption. As one mother of two adopted preschoolers with disabilities said, "We just feel we know more what life is all about because of them . . . life is about living and not about just getting and consuming and trying to reach something in a material way" (Glidden, 1989, p. 123).

Parents also focused particularly on the feelings of pride and pleasure that they take in the child's accomplishments. Perhaps the best summary of these outcomes comes from the words of a mother who adopted a 2½-year-old boy with moderate mental retardation. After describing her experiences with her adopted son, Michael, and expressing the joy that other family members felt as he progressed, overcoming one obstacle after another, she ends, "But most of all, I want to thank Michael for sharing his life and lesson with us" (Kravik, 1975).

Despite this generally rosy picture, neither professionals nor parents should be complacent about guaranteed success. Many of these adoptions need extensive resources, both financial and psychological. Most adoptions of children with disabilities are subsidized. These subsidies, which may include payment of adoption expenses, medical assistance, monthly cash payments, various educational services and therapies, and other benefits depending on the state of residence and the degree of disability of the child, are absolutely necessary for some families. Indeed, financial strain still may be a problem. My interviews with parents confirm that there are frequently extraordinary expenses as well as lost work time and money that are never compensated by subsidies.

In addition to financial strain, families, despite their overall satisfaction, report considerable difficulty with other sources of acute and chronic stress. Todis and Singer (1991) reported that advocacy for the child with school and other professionals, medical crises, and adoptive child behavior problems were all sources of stress for adoptive parents. Moreover, other research suggests that some families may be more predisposed to difficulty than others. My own work, for example, shows that parents who were depressed or had reservations at the time of placement, who were not married, who had little experience with disabilities, and for whom religion was not an important part of life had more adjustment problems approximately 5 years after placement (Glidden, 1991). The recognition of these individual differences is critical in making placement decisions, and in providing services before, during, and after placement.

Transracial Adoptions

Transracial adoptions are more controversial today than are any other kind of adoption. Opponents claim that a child's identity cannot be adequately formed in a family of a different race. Both Native American and African American spokespersons have been especially vocal in this regard. Advocates, in contrast, usually argue that, whereas same-race or inracial placements are optimal, if the choice is between a transracial placement or delayed or no placement, it is in the best interests of the child to be placed rather than languish in foster care.

Most of the evidence seems to support the less extreme position. That is, research on transracial and transethnic placement generally has found positive outcomes for children (A.R. Silverman & Feigelman, 1990; Tizard, 1991). For example, Simon and Altstein (1987, 1992) concluded that, with the exception of a few families with problems, their sample of more than 100 transracially adopted children were quite well adjusted as adolescents or young adults. A similar conclusion was reached by Gill and Jackson (1983), after studying British transracial adoptions. At adolescence, their sample of black children adopted into white families appeared to differ little from nonadoptive children on measures of family and peer relationships or self-esteem. Interestingly, both of these sets of investigators advocated, despite their findings, for the primacy of inracial placements. They were concerned with the issue of racial identity and whether it can be properly formed when the family is of a different racial group than the child. Similarly, Johnson, Shireman, and Watson (1987), despite no indication of identity or adjustment problems in transracially adopted 8-year-olds, also argued that "an all-black home is preferable for a black child" (p. 53).

Andujo (1988) took a comparable position for transethnic placements. She interviewed Hispanic adoptees raised in Hispanic families and others raised in non-Hispanic families. These children (average age 14 years at time of interview) had comparable levels of self-esteem, but the transethnically raised children indicated less identification with Hispanic culture. They were likely to describe themselves as American rather than Hispanic American. The author is somewhat cautious in interpreting these data, but does recommend that, if at all possible, children be placed with families of their own ethnicity. The maintenance of cultural identity is seen as an important goal, independent of the overall mental health of the individual.

Sometimes policy positions, even though they benefit society as a whole, interfere with individual rights of both adoptive and birth parents. For example, a 1978 law, the Indian Child Welfare Act, established guidelines for the placement of Native American children. It was designed to prevent the typical adoption of these children by white families. In 1988, a young pregnant Navajo woman selected a non-Indian couple to adopt her to-be-born child. In a planned open adoption, she lived with them for 3 months, before and after her daughter was born. Before the adoption could be finalized, however, the Navajo Tribal courts intervened to protect the child's Indian heritage. After negotiation, a compromise was reached to provide for permanent guardianship by the white couple, and extensive visitation rights by the Navajo mother and other family members ("Accord Reached," 1988).

In conclusion, most adoption specialists agree with the importance of inracial and inethnic adoptive placements. Certainly, agencies have a responsibility to reach out to minority families and reduce the large numbers of minority children who are waiting for permanent placement. However, reason and balance should win out over unthinking and rigid adherence to policy. As the Interagency Task Force on Adoption, created in 1987 by then-President Ronald Reagan, wrote in its 1988 report:

... it is preferable to place a child in a family of his own racial background. However, racial considerations alone should not determine the selection of a family for a child. Therefore, transracial adoption should be permissible to provide a child with a loving, permanent home. (p. 30)

If this policy recommendation were universally practiced, it might have prevented the absurdities experienced by the Haases, two special education teachers who wanted to adopt Robby, a black 3-year-old with mental retardation, cerebral palsy, and hearing and vision losses. They were ideal adoptive parents for a number of reasons. They knew and were attached to him, as he was to them. In addition, they had the professional skills that could help him progress. However, because they were white and the state had a policy against transracial adoptions, this placement was opposed, and the Haases were forced to end their weekend visits with Robby (Erlandson, 1984).

It was only because of their persistence that the Haases' view prevailed and, as a result of a court case, they were approved to be Robby's adoptive parents (Saperstein, 1984). Reason tells us, however, that they should not have had to fight. Certainly cultural identity is important, but should it have been primary in this case, when Robby had been waiting for a home for 3 years before the Haases expressed interest? This story, then, should be an important illustration of the potential for damage when policy runs amok, enforced without regard to the good in the individual situation.

SUMMARY, CONCLUSIONS, AND RECOMMENDATIONS

Adoption, despite its relatively low incidence, is an important option for all members of the adoption triangle. In the case of healthy infant adoptees, it provides a secure, loving environment with a stable financial situation and mature, highly motivated parents. Although these adoptees have a slightly greater risk for negative developmental outcomes than do nonadopted children, alternatives such as pregnancy termination, foster care, or rearing by a young, unmarried, and frequently poor and uneducated mother are not necessarily better.

Surrendering birth parents, regardless of the long-term consequences of their decision, obviously view placement of their child as a reasonable alternative to either termination of the pregnancy or rearing the child under adverse circumstances. Even the long-term negative consequences for some birth parents may be more a function of traditional, closed adoptions and societal attitudes toward illegitimacy, sin, and punishment.

Adoptive parents, of course, are major beneficiaries of the adoption option. We are in an era when there may be as many as 20 potential adoptive parents for every adoptable infant, and finding a child can approximate the search for the holy grail. Thus, as a group, potential adopters strongly benefit from any policy that encourages more adoptions, and makes them easier.

In the case of children with special needs, adoption is an alternative that offers the best chance for a healthy childhood and the foundation for a stable adulthood. We know enough now about the outcomes of these adoptions to realize that virtually every child is adoptable, but that a variety of supports must be available to facilitate these placements. Despite the higher probability of disruption and other negative outcomes, the ultimate conclusion is that many children and adoptive families do benefit greatly, and the system should operate to increase this occurrence.

Despite the currently recognized benefits of adoption for all involved, society could be doing more to maximize these benefits. The following recommendations are based on an analysis of the public policies that are important to maintain or implement in order to ensure that no child who can benefit from an adoptive home will go without one.

Recommendations to Optimize the Adoption Option

1. We should continue to publicize the kinds of children who are waiting for homes, emphasizing that even children with the most significant disabilities are adoptable. Children who are positive for human immunodeficiency virus, for example, are adoptable, as are those whose life expectancy is short for other reasons (Skinner, 1989).

2. Outreach for parents for children with special needs must continue and increase. This outreach should target parents who are known to be successful with certain types of children, as well as parents who are members of minority groups from which there are many children available for adoption.

3. Although inracial and inethnic adoptive placement is an important goal, it should not be more important than ensuring that a child has a stable, nurturing environment as early as possible. Given that we have evidence for good outcomes in transracial adoptions, such placements should be considered when the alternative is no placement or significantly delayed placement.

4. Adoption subsidies have been an important component of special-needs adoptions. They must be guaranteed so that no family who would provide a good rearing environment is prevented from adopting because of financial reasons.

5. Additional resources must be devoted to adoption units in many regions, so that children do not languish in institutional care, or await

permanent placement in temporary foster homes. A recent story about the Washington, D.C., system (Castaneda, 1992) highlighted one adoptive applicant couple's experience of a yearlong series of delays resulting, in large measure, from inadequate staffing. While 115 children were waiting for almost a year for adoptive homes, only 17 children had been placed in a 3-month period.

6. Flexibility in the processes of adoption is important. Open adoption, for example, although anathema to some, is favored by others (McRoy et al., 1988). Policy makers and implementers need to be sensitive to new initiatives that keep pace with an ever-changing climate. In the end, all component members of the adoption triangle must be effectively served, because they are each essential to the mission of healthy and happy children and families.

REFERENCES

Accord reached in custody of Navajo baby. (1988, April 24). *The Washington Post,* p. A5.
Andujo, E. (1988). Ethnic identity of transethnically adopted Hispanic adolescents. *Social Work, 33,* 531–535.
Bachrach, C. (1983). Children in families: Characteristics of biological, step-, and adopted children. *Journal of Marriage and the Family, 45,* 171–179.
Bachrach, C. (1986). Adoption plans, adopted children, and adoptive mothers. *Journal of Marriage and the Family, 48,* 243–253.
Bachrach, C.A., London, K.A., & Maza, P.L. (1991). Adoption seeking in the United States, 1988. *Journal of Marriage and the Family, 53,* 705–718.
Barth, R.P. (1988). Disruption in older child adoptions: We now know enough to develop a profile of children whose placements are in greatest jeopardy. *Public Welfare, 46,* 23–29.
Barth, R.P., & Berry, M. (1988). *Adoption and disruption: Rates, risks, and responses.* Hawthorne, NY: Aldine de Gruyter.
Berry, M., & Barth, R.P. (1990). A study of disrupted adoptive placements of adolescents. *Child Welfare, 69,* 209–225.
Bohman, M., & Sigvardsson, S. (1985). A prospective longitudinal study of adoption. In A.R. Nicol (Ed.), *Longitudinal studies in child psychology and psychiatry* (pp. 137–155). New York: John Wiley & Sons.
Brodzinsky, A.M. (1990). Surrendering an infant for adoption: The birthmother experience. In D.M. Brodzinsky & M.D. Schechter (Eds.), *The psychology of adoption* (pp. 295–315). New York: Oxford University Press.
Brodzinsky, D.M. (1990). A stress and coping model of adoption adjustment. In D.M. Brodzinsky & M.D. Schechter (Eds.), *The psychology of adoption* (pp. 3–24). New York: Oxford University Press.
Brodzinsky, D.M., Schecter, D.E., Braff, A.M., & Singer, L.M. (1984). Psychological and academic adjustment in adopted children. *Journal of Consulting and Clinical Psychology, 52,* 582–590.
Brodzinsky, D.M., & Steiger, C. (1991). Prevalence of adoptees among special education populations. *Journal of Learning Disabilities, 24,* 484–489.
Caplan, L. (1990). *An open adoption.* New York: Farrar, Straus, & Giroux.

Castaneda, R. (1992, October 4). Couple caught on D.C. adoption treadmill. *The Washington Post,* pp. D1, D6.
Children's Home Society of California. (1984). *The changing picture of adoption.* Los Angeles: Author.
Cole, E. (1990). A history of the adoption of children with handicaps. In L.M. Glidden (Ed.), *Formed families: Adoption of children with handicaps* (pp. 43–62). New York: The Haworth Press.
Coyne, A., & Brown, M.E. (1985). Developmentally disabled children can be adopted. *Child Welfare, 64,* 607–615.
Dembroski, D.G., & Johnson, D.L. (1969). Dogmatism and attitudes toward adoption. *Journal of Marriage and the Family, 313,* 788–792.
Deykin, E.Y., Patti, P., & Ryan, J. (1988). Fathers of adopted children: A study of the impact of child surrender on birthfathers. *American Journal of Orthopsychiatry, 58,* 240–248.
Erikson, E. (1968). *Identity: Youth and crisis.* New York: Norton.
Erlandson, R.A. (1984, July 11). Md. interracial policy impedes adoption attempt. *The Baltimore Sun,* pp. A1, A9.
Evans, S. (1994, January 18). The other side of adoption. *The Washington Post,* pp. Health 10–13.
Festinger (1990). Adoption disruption: Rates and correlates. In D.M. Brodzinsky & M.D. Schechter (Eds.), *The psychology of adoption* (pp. 201–218). New York: Oxford University Press.
Gill, O., & Jackson, B. (1983). *Adoption and race.* London: Batsford.
Glidden, L.M. (1989). *Parents for children, children for parents: The adoption alternative.* Washington, DC: American Association on Mental Retardation.
Glidden, L.M. (1990). The wanted ones: Families adopting children with mental retardation. *Journal of Children in Contemporary Society, 21*(3,4), 177–206.
Glidden, L.M. (1991). Adopted children with developmental disabilities: Postplacement family functioning. *Children and Youth Services Review, 13,* 363–377.
Glidden, L.M. (1992). Chosen ones: Adopted children with disabilities. In T. Thompson & S.C. Hupp (Eds.), *Saving children at risk: Poverty and disabilities* (pp. 116–140). Newbury Park, CA: Sage Publications.
Glidden, L.M., & Pursley, J.T. (1989). Longitudinal comparisons of families who have adopted children with mental retardation. *American Journal on Mental Retardation, 94,* 272–277.
Glidden, L.M., Valliere, V.N., & Herbert, S.L. (1988). Adopted children with mental retardation: Positive family impact. *Mental Retardation, 26,* 119–125.
Groze, V. (1986). Special-needs adoption. *Children and Youth Services Review, 8,* 363–373.
Groze, V., & Gruenewald, A. (1991). PARTNERS: A model program for special-needs adoptive families in stress. *Child Welfare, 70,* 581–589.
Hersov, L. (1990). The seventh Jack Tizard Memorial Lecture: Aspects of adoption. *Journal of Child Psychology and Psychiatry, 31,* 493–510.
Heyliger, F. C. (1983). Not flesh of my flesh. Collected in P. E. Johnston (Ed.), *Perspectives on a grafted tree.* Indianapolis, IN: Perspectives Press. (Original work published 1952)
Interagency Task Force on Adoption. (1988). *America's waiting children.* Washington, DC: Author.

Jackson, D.D. (1986, August). It took trains to put street kids on the right track out of the slums. *Smithsonian*, pp. 95–102.
Jaffee, B., & Fanshel, D. (1970). *How they fared in adoption: A follow-up study.* New York: Columbia University Press.
Johnson, P.R., Shireman, J.F., & Watson, K.W. (1987). Transracial adoption and the development of black identity at age eight. *Child Welfare, 66*, 45–55.
Kim, W.J., Davenport, C., Joseph, J., Zrull, J., & Woolford, E. (1988). Psychiatric disorder and juvenile delinquency in adopted children and adolescents. *Child and Adolescent Psychiatry, 27*, 111–115.
Kirk, H.D. (1964). *Shared fate: A theory of adoption and mental health.* New York: Free Press.
Kirk, H.D. (1984). *Shared fate: A theory and method of adoptive relationships.* Port Angeles, WA: Ben-Simon.
Kowal, K.A., & Schilling, K.M. (1985). Adoption through the eyes of adult adoptees. *American Journal of Orthopsychiatry, 55*, 354–362.
Kravik, P.J. (1975, September–October). Adopting a retarded child: One family's experience. *Children Today*, pp. 17–21.
Leavy, M.L. (1954). *The law of adoption* (2nd ed.). New York: Oceana.
Levy-Shiff, R., Goldshmidt, I., & Har-Even, D. (1991). Transition to parenthood in adoptive families. *Developmental Psychology, 27*, 131–140.
Lifton, B.J. (1975). *Twice born: Memories of an adopted daughter.* New York: McGraw-Hill.
Lifton, B.J. (1979). *Lost and found: The adoption experience.* New York: Dial Press.
Loehlin, J.C., Willerman, L., & Horn, J.M. (1982). Personality resemblances between unwed mothers and their adopted-away offspring. *Journal of Personality and Social Psychology, 42*, 1089–1099.
Loehlin, J.C., Willerman, L., & Horn, J.M. (1985). Personality resemblances in adoptive families when the children are late-adolescent or adult. *Journal of Personality and Social Psychology, 48*, 376–392.
Marx, J. (1990). Better me than somebody else: Families reflect on their adoption of children with developmental disabilities. In L.M. Glidden (Ed.), *Formed families: Adoption of children with handicaps* (pp. 141–174). New York: The Haworth Press.
Maza, P. (1990). Trends in national data on the adoption of children with handicaps. In L.M. Glidden (Ed.), *Formed families: Adoption of children with handicaps* (pp. 119–138). New York: The Haworth Press.
McRoy, R.G., Grotevant, H.D., & White, K.L. (1988). *Openness in adoption: New practices, new issues.* New York: Praeger.
National Committee for Adoption. (1989). *Adoption factbook.* Washington, DC: Author.
Nelson, K.A. (1985). *On the frontier of adoption: A study of special needs adoptive families.* New York: Child Welfare League of America.
Offen, C. (1992). Teens adopted in infancy: Risk and families. *APS Observer, 5*(2), 18.
Payne-Price, A.C. (1981). Ethnic variations on fosterage and adoption. *Anthropological Quarterly, 54*(3), 134–145.
Project STAR. (undated). *Questions and answers for parents.* Pittsburgh, PA: The Rehabilitation Institute for Pittsburgh.
Reid, W.J., Kagan, R.M., Kaminsky, A., & Helmer, K. (1987). Adoptions of older institutionalized youth. *Social Casework: The Journal of Contemporary Social Work, 68*, 140–149.

Rosenthal, J.A., & Groze, V.K. (1992). *Special-needs adoption: A study of intact families.* New York: Praeger Publishers.

Rosenthal, J.A., Schmidt, D., & Conner, J. (1988). Predictors of special needs adoption disruption: An exploratory study. *Children and Youth Services Review, 10,* 101–117.

Sachdev, P. (1989). The triangle of fears: Fallacies and facts. *Child Welfare, 68,* 491–503.

Sachdev, P. (1991). The birth father: A neglected element in the adoption equation. *Families in Society: The Journal of Contemporary Human Services, 72,* 131–138.

Saperstein, S. (1984, August 4). White couple wins fight to adopt black child. *The Washington Post,* pp. B1, B3.

Schapiro, M. (1956). *A study of adoption practice.* New York: Child Welfare League of America.

Silver, L.B. (1989). Frequency of adoption of children and adolescents with learning disabilities. *Journal of Learning Disabilities, 22,* 325–328.

Silverman, A.R., & Feigelman, W. (1977). Some factors affecting the adoption of minority children. *Social Casework, 58,* 554–561.

Silverman, A.R., & Feigelman, W. (1990). Adjustment in interracial adoptees: An overview. In D.M. Brodzinsky & M.D. Schechter (Eds.), *The psychology of adoption* (pp. 187–200). New York: Oxford University Press.

Silverman, P.R., Campbell, L., Patti, P., & Style, C.B. (1988). Reunions between adoptees and birth parents: The birth parents' experience. *Social Work, 33,* 523–528.

Simon, R.J., & Altstein, H. (1987). *Transracial adoptees and their families.* New York: Praeger.

Simon, R.J., & Altstein, H. (1992). *Adoption, race, and identity.* New York: Praeger.

Singer, L.M., Brodzinsky, D.M., Ramsay, D., Steir, M., & Waters, E. (1985). Mother-infant attachment in adoptive families. *Child Development, 56,* 1543–1551.

Skinner, K. (1989). Counselling issues in the fostering and adoption of children at risk of HIV infection. *Counselling Psychology Quarterly, 2,* 89–92.

Stiffler, L.H. (1991). Adoption's impact on birthmothers: "Can a mother forget her child?" *Journal of Psychology and Christianity, 10,* 249–259.

Sullivan, K. (1992, October, 5). Wanted: baby for loving home. *The Washington Post,* pp. A1, A10.

Taylor, E. (1989, October 9). Are you my mother? *Time,* p. 90.

Tizard, B. (1991). Intercountry adoption: A review of the evidence. *Journal of Child Psychology and Psychiatry, 32,* 743–756.

Todis, B., & Singer, G. (1991). Stress and stress management in families with adopted children who have severe disabilities. *Journal of The Association for Persons with Severe Handicaps, 16,* 3–13.

U.S. Bureau of the Census. (1992). *Marriage, divorce and remarriage in the 1990's* (Current Population Reports, pp. 23–180). Washington, DC: Author.

Walsh, E. (1993, June 4). Two parents too many for a little girl: Michigan supreme court hears emotional adoption case. *The Washington Post,* pp. C1, C9.

Washington, V. (1987). Community involvement in recruiting adoptive homes for black children. *Child Welfare, 66,* 57–68.

Whose daughter is Jessica? (1993, July 31). *The Washington Post,* p. A20.

Windgard, D. (1987). Trends and characteristics of California adoptions: 1964–1982. *Child Welfare, 66,* 303–315.

Zill, N. (1985, April). *Behavior and learning problems among adopted children: Findings from a U.S. national survey of child health.* Paper presented at the biennial meeting of the Society for Research in Child Development, Toronto, Canada.

III

RESIDENTIAL PLACEMENT

Part III's chapters describe placements for children who have special needs. For them, placements tend to be riskier and more likely to become permanent. We convey the general theme that existing policies regarding placement may not provide the best outcome. Changes should be implemented to provide support in the natural home when permanent out-of-home placement is undesirable. When placement is found to be the best option, however, continued involvement of the family in the child's life must be facilitated.

8

Placement and Its Consequences for Families with Children Who Have Mental Retardation

Jan Blacher

∞

Sam's parents placed him in a residential facility when he was 16. Two events were the deciding factors. First, Sam had begun molesting his 4-year-old younger brother. Second, he became more defiant and engaged in somewhat self-destructive behaviors. For example, one morning he went for a bicycle ride down the middle of a local freeway and he was picked up 30 miles away. Thus, Sam's retardation, coupled with his aggressive and oftentimes defiant behaviors, required his parents to be vigilant at all times. They constantly tried to avoid having confrontations with Sam or provoking his aggressive outbursts. "Home" may have been comfortable and secure for Sam, but it was stressful and worrisome for his parents and siblings.

Sam's parents completed the difficult process of selecting an appropriate residential facility, one nearby that they could visit often. Although they realize that placement is no panacea, they no longer consider home life a viable option for Sam. Now that he is placed, his parents and family experience a sense of rest and relief. However, Sam's parents are not uniformly happy with the facility, worrying about inadequate care and possible abuse. They work hard to remain in close contact with Sam and his residential care providers.

∞

Although there is "no place like home," families of children with significant disabilities must consider *which* home environment is most appropriate for their child. Only under the rarest circumstances would parents of a healthy child, one without physical or mental disabilities, consider placing that child into another residence to live. For parents of children like Sam, the possibility of placement is an option that at once raises anxiety and hope. However, for Sam's family, and for other families like them, placement out of the home does not have to mean placement out of the family.

Which children with mental retardation are at highest risk for placement? They usually have what has been referred to as severe or profound retardation, with IQs of 40 or less. (Tests of intelligence, or IQ, are normed such that the average score is 100 and 94% of people fall between 70 and 130. Approximately 2–3 individuals of every 1,000 will have severe or profound mental retardation, according to figures derived from Grossman [1983] and Hallahan & Kauffman [1991].[1]) Severe or profound retardation often brings with it a range of physical disabilities such as seizure disorder and visual and/or hearing impairment. In addition, such children may not walk or talk, and may need assistance in feeding, washing, dressing, and toileting. Severe behavioral problems are also likely (Abramowicz & Richardson, 1970; Moroney, 1986). Some children with severe mental retardation may have good motor skills along with behavior disorders, like Sam. Thus, as Moroney pointed out (1986), mental retardation is not just a measure of intellectual level; in its severe form, it also implies a level of daily caregiving that is much beyond what "typical" children require.

Although most children with mental retardation and severe disabilities will spend their childhoods in their own family homes (Meyers & Blacher, 1987a), many will not. Recent statistics are not readily available, but Meyers, Borthwick, and Eyman (1985) provided data indicting that, by the end of adolescence, up to 40% of children with severe or profound retardation may no longer be living at home. Today, parents continue to struggle with making the placement decision, a struggle perhaps exacerbated by the current zeitgeist that disparages the decision to place (Taylor & Bogdan, 1992). This chapter is about the decision-making process families engage in as they struggle with the

---

[1]New terminology adopted in 1992 by the American Association on Mental Retardation (AAMR) (Luckasson, Coulter, Polloway, Reiss, Schalock, Snell, Spitalnik, & Stark, 1992) does not utilize the classification scheme of mild, moderate, severe, and profound retardation. Because the utility of this new definition is under debate, and the forthcoming edition of the psychiatric classification system continues to diagnose levels of mental retardation (APA, 1994), we have used AAMR's earlier terminology (Grossman, 1983) here.

ever-present question of where, and with whom, their child with mental retardation shall live.

Today's community residences and group homes for persons with mental retardation were born of yesterday's institutions. Thus, I begin with a brief historical perspective on institutional placement, followed by research findings on who makes the decision to place, and why. Some current efforts to delay or prevent placement have paradoxical effects, and these are considered along with some of the consequences of placement for families. Finally, research on placement has implications for public policy affecting families, the children placed, and the children remaining at home. I end with a consideration of policies and research that affect placement practices and quality of life for families with children with significant disabilities.

HISTORICAL PERSPECTIVE

Readers unfamiliar with the field of mental retardation and developmental disabilities would have no reason to encounter or even know about the array of residential options now available for persons with mental retardation. The likely assumption is that they live either at home or in an institution of some sort. The second part of this assumption was never really true. Even at its height, around 1967, the number of people with retardation living in institutions in the United States only reached about 200,000. This was a small number of the total population of persons with mental retardation—less than 5% (Amado, Lakin, & Menke, 1990).

It is much less true today. Large-scale institutions that each served hundreds, even thousands, of persons with mental retardation dominated the service delivery scene during the earlier part of this century. Fortunately, institutional populations have decreased steadily each year since the late 1960s (Braddock & Fujiura, 1991), as this model has been replaced with smaller, presumably more humane residential alternatives, typically located right in our communities. Nevertheless, the image of an "institution" looms as a reminder to today's parents of what life in an out-of-home placement might be like.

Institutional Placement as the Only Alternative

During the earlier part of this century, institutionalization of children with mental retardation was the only alternative available to parents who looked for an out-of-home placement. Physicians, in particular, were known to advise new mothers to place their child early on, before becoming attached. Indeed, data on family involvement with individuals placed in institutions are nearly nonexistent; the implication is that families were discouraged from such involvement. Many families who did place their child readily admitted to having no plans to bring the child back home (Lei, Nihira, Sheehy, & Meyers, 1981). All too often the limited family involvement observed was attributed to factors within the family, a sentiment perhaps driven by some careprovider antifamily bias, or a belief that parents simply should not get involved (Blacher & Baker, 1992; Willer & Intagliata, 1984). In reality, it may have been due more to the lack of involvement opportunities provided by the placements (Baker & Blacher, 1993), or to the fact that the institutions were, simply, depressing to visit.

The only alternative to institutionalization that most parents had was to provide care at home, often without the assistance of the public schools. Many school systems excluded children functioning at lower levels, especially those with medical or self-care needs. Fortunately, after the social and political changes of the late 1960s and the 1970s, views changed dramatically concerning both the location and quality of services provided to persons with mental retardation.

The Normalization Movement

Whereas institutionalization of persons with mental retardation was the predominant form of service delivery during much of the 20th century, the growth of community-based alternative residences has characterized the last 25 years. One of the biggest influences on locating services in the community was the articulation of what has become the normalization principle—"making available to the mentally retarded patterns and conditions of everyday life which are as close as possible to the norms and patterns of mainstream society" (Nirje, 1969, p. 181). This principle was backed by practice in Denmark and Sweden, where personalized, modern, and comprehensive community-based services for persons with retardation were considered a right, not a privilege (Baker, Seltzer, & Seltzer, 1977). Indeed, N.E. Bank-Mikkelson aptly stated that "the mentally retarded are human beings who are more like other people than they differ from them, no matter the degree of retardation. Their happiness—exactly as that of other people—depends greatly on the houses they live in" (Baker et al., 1977, p. 3). Thus, the physical location and setting of "home" for persons with retardation became an important consideration.

The application of the normalization principle in the United States also provided a foundation for some of the court decisions to follow—for example, those establishing a constitutional "right to treatment" and placement in the "least restrictive alternative." Decisions and court decrees that established the "right to treatment" spelled out what institutional treatment must entail, in terms of physical surroundings, staffing, habilitation, and services. Treatment in the "least restrictive alternative" most often was interpreted to mean the provision of community-based alternatives to institutions (Baker et al., 1977). Court actions, in turn, led to widespread deinstitutionalization, or depopulating of large institutions. The deinstitutionalization movement, and its support from humanitarians and anti-institution professionals and advocates, had vast implications for families. Having already gone through the often agonizing decision to place their child, many parents were very conflicted about the news that their son or daughter might return home, or live in a nearby community. It was difficult for them to now accept that institutions were "bad," having at one time found them good enough for their child.

On the educational front, the passage of PL 94-142, the Education for All Handicapped Children Act, in 1975 (subsequently known as the Individuals with Disabilities Education Act [IDEA] of 1990) further supported less restrictive, in-home care for children with mental retardation. Among other things, this law provided free, appropriate public education for all children, no matter how severe or debilitating their behavior or disability. Furthermore, children were now to be educated in the "least restrictive environment," meaning that they should be educated with children who do not have disabilities to the maximum extent appropriate.

Much has been written to clarify the meaning and implementation of "least restrictive environment" (Smith & Luckasson, 1992). As pointed out by Seltzer and Krauss (1984b), philosophy in the field of mental retardation advocates maintaining children *in the home* with their families, and returning children *to the home* from institutional environments. Yet A.P. Turnbull, Brotherson, and Summers (1982) cautioned:

> ... the right to live in the least restrictive environment should apply to family members as well as to handicapped individuals. Thus [the] concept of least restriction should be considered in light of the needs of each family member. Placing many severely handicapped children and youth in the least restrictive environment of their families results in their family being required to live in a highly restrictive manner. (p. 63)

Sam's parents, in the case that opens this chapter, did indeed feel like their family was being forced to live in a highly restrictive manner. Yet families like Sam's now find themselves pushing against the antiplacement zeitgeist.

Full-Scale Inclusion and the Natural Home as "Better"

With the current emphasis on home placement as best for children with mental retardation, many parents are facing difficulties in finding placements. Those who appear to be "proinstitution" may merely be worried about the lack of community alternatives. Fern Kupfer (1982b), parent and author, took her turn in *Newsweek* to say the following:

> Most retarded people do not belong in institutions any more than most people over age 65 belong in nursing homes. What we need are options and alternatives for a heterogeneous population. We need group homes and halfway houses and government subsidies to families who choose to care for dependent members at home. We need accessible housing for independent handicapped people; we need to pay enough to foster-care families to show that a good home is worth paying for. We need institutions. And it shouldn't have to be dirty word. (p. 36)

Without a doubt, families who are desperately seeking placements do not easily find them. Coupled with this is the pressure emanating from social service delivery systems for "permanency planning" (Pecora, Fraser, & Haapala, 1992; Plumer, 1992). This philosophy first began with the foster care system and children without disabilities. The current premise of permanency planning is that all children, regardless of disability, belong in families, primarily because "a stable family life and enduring relationships with adults are essential to the development and well-being of children" (Taylor, Lakin, & Hill, 1989, p. 542). There are several implications of this philosophy. First, families should be supported to keep their children at home. Second, in the event of placement, agencies should work toward reunifying families. Third, if neither of the above options is possible, agencies should either maintain high levels of family involvement with the child or pursue adoption or some other permanent relationship (Taylor et al., 1989).

Thus, one can see that the pendulum does swing—from recommending removal of children with mental retardation or developmental disabilities from the home, to supporting such children and their families in order to prevent placement. Today, the majority of children with mental retardation still live as they did in the past, with their own families (Meyers & Blacher, 1987a). Indeed, there are both state and federal programs that allocate financial subsidies to families so that they may provide services for their child at home. Even though families are encouraged to keep children at home until they reach late adolescence or early adulthood (ages 19–22 or so), some families opt to place their children. When they do, postplacement family involvement is one mechanism for ensuring that the child is not placed out of the family (Baker & Blacher, 1988; Blacher & Baker, 1992). Postplacement involvement, and the other consequences of placement for families, are discussed further later in this chapter.

WHO PLACES, AND WHY

Let us return to the scenario at the beginning of this chapter, to Sam and his family:

∞

Although his parents admitted there were times when they "want[ed] to pin him against the wall," young Sam fit comfortably in his family with a minimum of daily stress until he was 12. Originally diagnosed as having moderate to severe mental retardation with delayed language acquisition and good motor skills, Sam displayed behaviors that his parents found unpleasant but tolerable: finger biting and picking, nighttime bedwetting, and tooth grinding. While Sam's parents worked steadily to build his self-help skills by engaging in home parent teaching (to improve dressing and toileting skills), they accepted his limitations (in intellectual ability and social behavior), lived patiently with his inappropriate behaviors, took pride in his accomplishments and small successes, and never even considered placing their son outside of the family home.

By the time Sam turned 14, however, his repertoire of behaviors had grown to include repeated aggressive outbursts at school, physical assaults on his younger brother at home, and persistent self-injury through biting his wrists and nails. His family received funding only for emergency respite care, repeatedly lost work time (and money) dealing with Sam's medical needs and his behavioral difficulties at school, and struggled increasingly with financial hardships. The younger brother's social needs went largely unmet as a result of Sam's demands on parental energy and the family lifestyle, while Sam's increasing physical size created behavior and care management problems for both his parents. When Sam's father suffered two major heart attacks, a condition exacerbated by the combined stresses of dealing with his son, Sam's parents finally discussed placement for Sam. Before actually researching specific facilities, however, they first reached out to recreation resources in the community, becoming very active in a boys' outdoor activities organization. Breaking their self-sufficiency and isolation of previous years, they also developed a support system with their extended family. These two changes, together with the father's return to health, bought them time—but only a limited amount. Sam's parents placed him in a residential facility when he was 16.

∞

The case of Sam and his family contains many factors that ultimately influence placement. Let us examine the key features of this case before considering the broader literature on who places, and why.

Sam's retardation is in the moderate to severe range (American Psychiatric Association, 1994). However, his very low level of self-help skills, nearly absent language, penchant for bizarre or annoying behaviors (excessive finger picking, bedwetting), and aggressive outbursts coinciding with adolescence certainly created stress for his parents. The scenario also shows how parental attitudes toward placement evolve over time. This process, which in Sam's and most other cases does not happen overnight, is the subject of ongoing research (Blacher & Hanneman, 1993). In the sections following, I briefly discuss the placement decision-making process and characteristics of children who are placed.

Placement as a Decision-Making Process

Sam's parents did not sit down one day and abruptly decide to place their child. Placement is not a discrete event; rather, it is the result of a protracted process that can take as long as 2 years or more to complete (Blacher, 1990a; Kobe, Rojahn, & Schroeder, 1991). Parents demonstrate a kind of "placement tendency," or movement toward placement, that has behavioral as well as cognitive components. In two studies, we (Blacher, 1990a; Blacher & Hanneman, 1993) assessed parents' placement tendency using a six-point scale. What is significant is that parents usually progress through stages of thinking about placement before taking any action; once parents actually begin to look at placement options (behaviorally defined as visiting a facility), placement is almost inevitable. One explanation for this phenomenon is that parents' attitudes toward or intentions regarding placement change in advance of their behavior, which is consistent with theories of reasoned action (Blacher & Hanneman, 1993).

Another explanation for the length of the placement process is that placement of children constitutes a nonnormative event, or premature launching of one's offspring; launching of typical children takes place in late adolescence or young adulthood (Seltzer & Ryff, 1994). Thus, parents may find the placement process itself traumatic and are more likely to delay it by continuing to look for other options or solutions. This is illustrated in our case study of Sam, whose parents made great efforts to find social support and community activities for Sam. For some parents, long committed to keeping the family together, moving toward placement initially may be experienced as defeat (although it subsequently is viewed more positively, as shown below).

Transitions that occur out of sequence with the normal course of events in the family life cycle tend to produce additional stress, whether the events are earlier or later than usual. As shown in the literature on parenting across the life span (Seltzer & Ryff, 1994), parents of adolescents developing normally experience a loosening of bonds with their children as preparation for "launching" them as young adults. Whereas placement of children with mental retardation often constitutes premature launching, placement of an adult son or daughter with retardation could be called postmature or delayed launching. In their longitudinal study of aging mothers, Seltzer and Krauss have shown how continued caregiving for adult offspring with retardation who still reside at home contributes positively to the mothers' overall sense of well-being (Seltzer & Krauss, 1989). For these mothers, who have experienced lifelong caregiving, placement occurs later than usual and may be accompanied by health-related rather than stress-related concerns —for example, death or severe illness or incapacity of the caregiving parent.

To say that placement of *children* with severe retardation is a traumatic event does not mean that it is a negative act or symptom of some kind of family dysfunction. A theoretical model developed by Cole (1986) addresses family adaptation to a child with severe disabilities and the relationship of such adaptation to placement. Cole specifically noted that family adaptation at any point in the life course can range from "bonadaptation" to "maladaptation." For some families, bonadaptation may result from deciding to place their child; for others, bonadaptation is better achieved with the child at home. This article was one of the first to highlight that placement of children with mental retardation may be a positive act.

Characteristics of Children Who Are Placed

Many studies relate age to placement and suggest that, as the child with severe disabilities grows older, the likelihood of placement increases (Borthwick-Duffy, Eyman, & White, 1987; Eyman & Call, 1977; Meyers et al., 1985, Stone, 1967). Many of these studies have compared populations of children currently living in institutions or elsewhere to children still living at home. An obvious confound is that, once placed, few children move back home; movements from one placement to another are rarely documented. Nevertheless, even more recent studies (Blacher, Hanneman, & Rousey, 1992; Rousey, Blacher, & Hanneman, 1990) indicate that, as children grow older, they are more likely to be placed.

Other child characteristics that heighten the risk of placement include: behavior problems or severe maladaptive behaviors (Allen, 1972; Borthwick-Duffy et al., 1987; Eyman & Call, 1977; Sherman, 1988; Tausig, 1985); medical difficulties (Seltzer & Krauss, 1984a, 1984b); severe or profound retardation or the diagnosis of autism (Anderson, Thibadeau, & Christian, chap. 9, this volume; Birenbaum &

Cohen, 1993); and being male (Farber, 1959; Stone, 1967; Wolf & Whitehead, 1975). Some also have hypothesized that lack of attachment behavior emitted by the child, or lack of mutual attachment development between mother and child, may increase the likelihood of placement (Blacher & Meyers, 1983).

Until recently, researchers assumed that the greater the disability of a child with mental retardation was, the more likely he or she was to be placed. However, some investigators report cases in which children with very significant disabilities remain at home with their parents, and others in which children with less severe impairments are placed (Birenbaum & Cohen, 1993). Thus, researchers need to look within the sample of children with severe disabilities at factors beyond child characteristics to really determine who places and why.

Characteristics of Families that Place

A number of studies have identified family structural characteristics as correlates of placement. It is important to note that one major difference between studies conducted prior to about 1975 and more recently is that the definition of *placement* may be different. Earlier studies more often dealt with large-scale facilities such as institutions. Later studies pertained more to community residences, which are likely to be smaller and located closer to the family home.

Several studies examined parental age and well-being, finding that placement is more likely if parents are elderly or report their health as poor (Allen, 1972; Suelzle & Keenan, 1981; Tausig, 1985). Other studies have suggested that single parents may place more frequently than married ones (German & Maisto, 1982). Also, separation or divorce is more prevalent in families who have placed their child, in comparison to families who still have their child at home (Birenbaum & Cohen, 1993; Sherman, 1988). However, without a longitudinal analysis of marital adjustment, we cannot determine whether marital problems made it more difficult for parents to care for the child at home, or whether the stress of caring for a child with significant disabilities directly led to marital dissolution.

Large-scale studies that have examined ethnicity, primarily those conducted in the state of California, routinely indicated that Anglo families have proportionately more children in placement than non-Anglo (Hispanic, African American, Asian) groups (Borthwick-Duffy et al., 1987; Meyers et al., 1985). Ethnicity findings are no doubt confounded by socioeconomic status (SES), a proxy for income, and possibly also by acculturation. Research findings on SES, for example, are equivocal on the placement issue, with some studies indicating a greater frequency of institutionalization among lower SES families (Appell

& Tisdall, 1968; Shellhaas & Nihira, 1969; Stone, 1967), and other studies indicating that families who placed their children in institutions had higher incomes than those who did not (Eyman, O'Connor, Tarjan, & Justice, 1972). These older studies did not control for parents' knowledge about placement alternatives or access to services.

Although the above-mentioned family factors may indeed influence placement, it is important to keep in mind an additional factor: One reason that parents of children with very significant disabilities place is that "they can." It is the availability of placement options for such families that enables families to consider this alternative. Families of children with ostensibly milder disabilities (e.g., learning disabilities, mild mental retardation) could not find residential settings for their children even if they sought them.

PREVENTING PLACEMENT

Although substantial research has been conducted to determine why parents place children with mental retardation and other disabilities (Blacher & Bromley, 1990a; Cole & Meyer, 1989; Farber, 1959; Seltzer & Krauss, 1984b; Tausig, 1985), few studies have examined factors that delay or prevent placement. Predictors and preventors of placement are not necessarily opposites. Although family stress correlates with placement as an outcome, families who do not place hardly feel unstressed. Rather, there appears to be a complex relationship between family stress, family resources, and the family's placement plans (Cole & Meyer, 1989).

Most families with children without disabilities feel stress at one time or another, but the majority of writers in the disability and retardation fields attest to the increased stressors that a child with mental retardation can produce. Examples of such stress can include difficulties in managing the child's behavior, increased impact on family time, social stigma or rejection, or demands of other children without disabilities. Some families undergo additional strain as a result of lifelong caregiving or financial responsibilities. In most cases, families adapt and learn to appreciate both the trials and triumphs of having such a child. One of the major ways in which these families buffer stress is through the use of formal and informal supports.

Resources Intended to Prevent Placement

Many families who decline to consider placement for their child have access to informal sources of support as well as more formal services for their child (Sherman, 1988; Singer & Irvin, 1989).

Informal Support The role of informal support in helping families cope with a child with significant disabilities, and implicitly avoid placement, has been rather elusive. Informal support networks, sometimes referred to as social support, may consist of friends, immediate family, other relatives, or even professionals. *Emotional support* can include giving advice, providing companionship, sharing confidences, or counseling (Wikler, 1981). *Instrumental support* refers to activities such as helping with driving, teaching, or caregiving functions (Waisbren, 1980). Informal support networks have been touted as important in promoting the well-being of families and young children (Zigler & Black, 1989).

Research findings suggest that one of the most important aspects of informal support is the mother's satisfaction with such support (Blacher & Steinback, 1992; Seltzer & Krauss, 1989). In other words, the actual number of individuals assisting the mother with a variety of tasks is not as crucial as the satisfaction the mother feels with her available help. Some mothers feel perfectly satisfied with their support network if they have one person they can count on at all times; in two-parent families that is most often the spouse.

Formal Support Formal support services include schooling, parent training, respite care, homemaker services, or financial aid supplements of some kind (Birenbaum & Cohen, 1993). One of the most widely used and effective types of formal support for families who have children with severe disabilities is called *respite care*. Respite care commonly is viewed as a temporary relief service for families who have children with disabilities living at home. Some also believe that it is an essential element in preventing placement (Townsend & Flanagan, 1976; Upshur, 1983). However, the rationale for respite should go beyond preventing or even delaying placement to simply reducing stress and helping families to live a fuller life day to day. The concept of respite care has been developing over the last 3 decades or so, but it is now considered a crucial and necessary service for families.

There is no one form of respite care. It can consist of care for a few hours a day, overnight, for a weekend, or longer. Respite care may be provided in the home or in a separate facility, often one that also provides more permanent residential care. Some families use it routinely (weekly, monthly); others avail themselves of the service only for special occasions or emergencies. Many states offer respite care free, and others might charge according to a sliding scale of some sort. Finally, some private agencies also train and provide respite workers to families, usually for a fee. Parents seem to express general satisfaction with the provision of respite care (Ptacek et al., 1982).

There are some assumptions about the use of formal supports. Respite is presumed to improve the quality of family life and to alleviate strains related to caregiving, especially in families with younger children (Halpern, 1985; Joyce, Singer, & Isralowitz, 1983). Only recently have investigators focused on how the receipt of other formal services, such as public schooling, also might provide respite, moderating the child's impact on the family and/or the decision to place. For example, one anticipated effect of PL 94-142 was that the availability of schooling and related services would provide respite and relief to families (Blacher & Prado, 1986), possibly even preventing or delaying placement.

Cole and Meyer (1989) more directly assessed the impact of resources on family plans to seek placement. However, they defined resources more broadly than respite, and included aspects of family strengths or functioning. They found that, over and above child-related stressors, family resources related negatively to immediate plans for placement; families who had more resources (in the form of better adjustment, daily functioning, higher income, and various forms of assistance and respite care) were the ones who planned to *keep their child at home* indefinitely or at least until age 21.

Emotional Resources Early literature on attachment between children with severe disabilities and their mothers clearly indicated that attachment was delayed, dulled, or even absent in these dyads (Blacher & Meyers, 1983). This led to the supposition that parents who were less attached to their children would be more likely to place them out of the home (Blacher & Meyers, 1983). However, there are data suggesting that this is not the case. In one study, parents who had recently placed their children were asked why they did not do so sooner; these parents identified their attachment to their child as the most important reason (Bromley & Blacher, 1989). This reason was given by both mothers and fathers, interviewed independently (Blacher & Bromley, 1990b). Thus, there are emotional factors, such as attachment, that may help prevent or delay placement.

The attachment finding has important theoretical implications for both the development of parent–child relations and the understanding of future parent–child interactions once a child is placed out of the home. For example, recent findings suggest that "detachment"—the loosening of ties or greatly reduced feelings of attachment—was not in evidence in the early years after a family placed a child with significant disabilities out of the home (Blacher & Baker, 1994a). Blacher and Baker (in press) found that intense emotional bonds seemed to persist for at least the initial 2 years after placement. Whereas about a third of parents reported that feelings of attachment had weakened after placement ("Out of sight, out of mind"), a surprising 21% of parents said that attachment had become stronger ("Absence makes the heart grow fonder").

Paradoxical Findings

The issue of what prevents or precipitates placement is not always clear. We have discovered that, contrary to what often appears in the literature, the more respite care and other formal supports (e.g., financial aid) that parents of children with severe disabilities receive, the more likely they are to consider placement (Blacher & Hanneman, 1993; Blacher & Steinback, 1992). There are two interpretations of this paradoxical finding. The first is that this is an artifact of the severity of the child's disability. The number of respite care hours received by many families correlates negatively with level of child functioning, with more respite care received by families with children who have the lowest functioning. The children who function at a very low level typically have other medical impairments and needs that would require additional support and, as we have noted, are at heightened risk for placement. Thus, it may be that the families who receive many types of support have children at very high risk of placement to begin with, or they have already begun to give placement some thought.

A second interpretation of this counterintuitive finding is that, once parents obtain relief, whether it is through daily babysitting or overnight respite, they cannot go back to the "old way." As parents and the family system adapt to the child's temporary absence, they are gradually shaped toward longer and ultimately more complete placement. In other words, the more formal and informal support that parents have, the more they "need." The following case demonstrates the paradoxical role of respite care.

∞

> "It looked real hopeless. I'd look into the future and think . . . I can't bear the idea of institutionalizing him but I can't have my life go on like this." These words reflect one mother's struggle during the first 3 year's of her son's life, when she could find no satisfactory child care situation, no school, and no other form of respite care. Her child had severe mental retardation with hydrocephaly; he frequently screamed, rarely slept through a night, and was nonambulatory, nonverbal, and not toilet trained. This mother was both physically and emotionally overwhelmed.
>
> Thoughts of placement receded, however, during the first 2 years that her son attended public school: "I don't think I would ever institutionalize him . . . I can't really imagine doing it." This mother was

encouraged not only by the progress her son was making in school, but by her own freedom to work outside the home and the relief from constant caregiving. The public school clearly provided her with a form of respite. Her relationship with her son dramatically improved from her previous exhaustion and resentment to, "He comes home from school and I'm glad to see him." Even this early, however, this mother found that the respite provided by the school was more than a relief—it was a necessity. "I can't imagine going back to having him home all the time . . . it would really be devastating."

Over the next few years, as the amount of respite increased—formal respite, in the form of school and state-funded day babysitters, and informal respite through friends and family—so did this mother's need for and reliance on the other careproviders. She reacted to the thought of the loss of school with, "I think we would really consider a residential placement. Sometimes we still contemplate it . . . if he's going through a bad time or we are." Her reluctance to contemplate a loss of all caregiving assistance grew into a firm refusal to consider going back to living a life in which her son was the center of everything in her family. When her funding for babysitters decreased, this mother, in fact, did search for a permanent residential placement for her 9-year-old son.

∞

The solution to this situation is not, of course, to withhold respite care and other formal support services such as financial aid. Rather, the problem appears to be one of timing (Blacher & Steinback, 1992; Mink, 1993), and begs for earlier distribution of support services, *before* crises arise. The types of personal and professional support networks needed by parents likely change over the life cycle of their child with mental retardation (Suelzle & Keenan, 1981). Formal services often arrive too late to families—if they arrive at all—long after these families have endured an overload of stress, adjustment difficulties, and perhaps even financial hardships. Furthermore, some of these parents already may have experienced some "detachment" from their child and have mentally imagined what it would be like to place him or her (Blacher & Baker, 1994a). Simply having more resources, at this point, may not facilitate further accommodations to the child.

Pressure to Prevent Placement Altogether

A prevailing professional presumption of the 1980s and 1990s is that placement for children with mental retardation and severe disabilities is to be avoided at all costs. Two policies bolster this belief. One, noted previously, is the concept of permanency planning, which has as its central belief that all children, regardless of disability, belong in families. The implications of this philosophy are that the family must be supported in every way to keep the child at home. If there is a placement, however, the most important goal is to facilitate reunification with the natural family or placement with another family (Taylor et al., 1989).

A second policy perspective is that of "helping families," or family support (Birenbaum & Cohen, 1993). Birenbaum and Cohen (1993) made an ardent plea for defining health care needs more broadly for families of children with disabilities, so that expenses such as babysitting for a child with spina bifida, for example, would be viewed as a medical habilitative service. They further argued that there are serious, significant nonmedical expenditures and opportunity costs for families trying to maintain a child with severe disabilities at home. Their policy proposal contains a plea for flexibility in the provision and administration of support services to parents. As they stated: "The natural desire of parents to nurture their children during their growing years should be especially encouraged for children whose progress is measured in centimeters" (p. 72).

For families who may be struggling to cope with their child at home, but who are dead set against placement, these policies may be welcome. For them, increased levels of in-home support and guidance in planning their son's or daughter's financial, social, and residential future truly may prevent placement (H. R. Turnbull, Turnbull, Bronicki, Summers, & Roeder-Gordon, 1989). However, these same policies may create conflict or guilt in other families by not giving them the license to explore placement.

Perhaps it is appropriate for professionals to ask: At what costs do we attempt to preserve the family–child bond? What do parents and other family members give up, in terms of opportunity costs, when they provide in-home care under difficult circumstances? Even Birenbaum and Cohen (1993) recognized that the answers to these questions may lead to no other option than placement itself, because they further stated: "Whenever families decide that they can no longer bear the burden of care, the transition to a residential placement should be facilitated" (p. 72).

Thus, some families do come to the conclusion that placement is right for them, even after they have received an array of formal and informal services. As noted by Pecora and colleagues (1992), "In spite of the burgeoning of intensive family preservation and other family-based services, there will always be a need for high quality substitute care services for certain families" (p. 186). Furthermore, some children may be better off, receiving more appropriate and targeted services, in a formal placement other than at home. Placement considerations must include the child, as well as what is best for the family members at home. At this point, it behooves professionals and the service system to empower parents with the next level of formal services—placement options—and to endow them with decision-making responsibilities.

SELECTING A PLACEMENT SETTING

Parents who make the decision to place their child with significant disabilities are faced with yet more decisions to make, foremost among them being selection of a placement setting. Conceptually, a placement may be considered any residence for the child with disabilities that is not the same as that of the natural family. Specific definitions of placements vary, but there are some general placement types that are well known (Baker et al., 1977). Placements can be arranged along a continuum based on the degree to which the setting resembles a normalized home environment. With the exception of adoption, the placement considered most like the natural home is the foster care setting, where approximately one to four individuals live in a family home. Group homes comprise the next level of the continuum and consist of a larger group of individuals (anywhere from 5 to 40) who are supervised by a paid staff of houseparents and assistants. Medium-sized placements would include intermediate care facilities and convalescent care homes, which could house as many as 100 individuals. Large, institutional-type settings comprise the least normalized residence, usually providing for over 100 individuals. Community residences for children with disabilities are most common and most desirable.

Unfortunately, there are no popular books on the "how to's" of selecting placements, but we are learning more about family decision making and satisfaction with placement. All too often placement becomes a daunting task, one that many parents dread. Indeed, fears about selection or the unavailability of placements actually may impede the placement process. In conjunction with the Eastern Los Angeles Regional Center, I have developed a workshop series called "Placement Decision-Making: There Are No Right's and Wrong's" (Blacher, 1990b). Disseminated to 6 of California's 21 Regional Centers that serve all persons with developmental disabilities, this four-meeting workshop deals with the specifics of selecting a placement setting. Several key themes can be derived from these workshops.

First, placement is a very "individual" decision, implying that unique factors will likely influence each parent or family. Second, parents and professionals need to acknowledge that placement need not be a permanent decision; placements can be changed or moved. However, it is important to recognize that the better the placement or the more positive parents feel about it, the less likely it is that they will initiate a change. Third, parents should never rule in or out any particular placement setting until they themselves have researched or visited it. One mother told us, during a time that she was not considering placement: "I could never put my child in one of *those* places!" Yet 2 years later she did place—in the very setting that did not seem acceptable to her when she had not seen it. Fourth, parents should give prior thought to the kind of relationship or involvement the family would like with their child after placement, and then look for a setting that will provide opportunities for such involvement.

In the University of California, Riverside, Families Project, we have examined parental decision making about placement and actions taken to secure placements (Blacher & Baker, 1994b). We learned about how parents select a placement setting from interviews with 62 families who had placed their children with mental retardation from 1 to 22 months previously. At the time of our interview, the target children ranged in age from 2 1/2 to 17 years. Most of the families were intact and had other children living at home; the parents were generally well educated, with three quarters having attended college. Over half of the placement facilities were small, with seven or fewer residents, although there was a range in size to more than 50 residents. About half of the facilities were more than 30 miles away from the family home. Interviews with parents revealed insight regarding the following three aspects of the placement process: 1) initiating placement, 2) choosing a placement facility, and 3) satisfaction with the placement.

Initiating Placement For most families, the current placement was the first one. Most families had not done anything to inquire about facilities, to visit, or in other ways to initiate the process a year before placement (77%) or even 6 months before placement (55%). Although parents may have thought about placement for a long while, once they began to act, the placement followed in a matter of months. For most of these families, placement did not follow any specific precipitating event but, rather, was the result of a gradual accumulation of child-related stressors.

Choosing a Placement Facility This depended heavily on the assistance of the Regional Center caseworker, who for 82% of the sample was the person named as most helpful in securing the placement. Only a few respondents indicated help from facility staff, friends, the child's teacher, or others. It is interesting that no respondent reported receiving primary help from his or her spouse, physician, or clergy member. More than half of the families did not visit any facility other than the one they chose, and only 30% visited two or three facilities.

When asked about factors influencing the choice of facility, parents most often cited competent staff, followed by a homey environment, good programs, a clean facility, and their own familiarity with the facility. Only 15% of the families noted proximity to their home as a factor in selection.

Satisfaction Once the child had been placed, the parents' expressed satisfaction with the placement was, by several indicators, quite high. Eighty-four percent of the families expressed much or perfect satisfaction, and parents typically viewed specific services for the child as better in the placement than they had been at home. High satisfaction with placement facilities has been noted by other researchers, almost independently of the characteristics of the facility (Baker & Blacher, 1988). Satisfaction was somewhat less as the area of focus became more specific. When parents were asked about specific problems with the placement, dissatisfaction often was expressed, especially about the staff—their competency, numbers, turnover, or communication.

In addition, earlier studies examining parental satisfaction with placement indicated that parents were happy with whatever placement the child had, just so, apparently, that it was not in the natural home (Rudie & Riedl, 1984). For example, in a large study of foster children with mental retardation, the natural parents indicated a general satisfaction with their child's placement, and nearly 90% indicated that they had no plans to take their child back home (Lei et al., 1981).

Having once found a placement, then, parents tend overall to be satisfied with it. To some extent, following the placement with high satisfaction fits with the theory of cognitive dissonance (Festinger, 1957), which posits that people reconcile their attitudes with their actions so as not to experience discomfort over contradictions. It certainly would be disconcerting to parents to leave their child in any placement where they were not satisfied. Therefore, some parents might come to adopt unrealistically positive views in order to live with their decision—and not have to revisit it. We would hope that professionals assisting these families would recognize this possibility, and work to assure that the facility really does have quality aspects worthy of the parents' satisfaction.

CONSEQUENCES OF PLACEMENT

As one parent noted, tearfully, in a discussion about placing her profoundly retarded daughter: "You don't place them in one chunk; it takes a long time" (Stanfield, 1983). Indeed, we have shown that the placement decision-making process itself is a long and, in most cases today, a deliberative one. Yet once families place a child, they rarely are studied; it is as if placement is a final act that leaves no consequences. As we examine existing data, both empirical and anecdotal, we quickly learn that this is hardly the case. There are both immediate and long-lasting postplacement consequences for families. Some of these are apparent in the following case study.

∞

> Mrs. Small's 14-year-old daughter had severe mental retardation and severe behavior problems. The decision to place her in a residential facility arose from Mrs. Small's overwhelming exhaustion and depression. However, even though she felt relief at the freedom she enjoyed on her daughter's placement, she exhibited grief at her child's absence. In response to a questionnaire about her reactions to the placement, Mrs. Small strongly disagreed with one statement describing the actual placement process as a "positive experience." Her reactions were complicated by the fact that her husband strongly agreed that the family was better off with their child placed. This mother could find no solace in sharing her confusing emotions with her spouse.
>
> Guilt also troubled Mrs. Small, guilt not only at the relief she felt when home visits were over, but at the dread she experienced prior to each visit: "I can't even take [her] home without some incident . . . can't let down my guard . . . she knows when to strike." She described the thought of bringing her daughter back home to live as "very scary," and clearly held two strong sources of consolation for the decision to place her daughter. One was the change in their relationship from a "negative attachment" to "positive attachment," and the other was her own knowledge that no other decision was realistic. Over time, Mrs. Small did readily acknowledge the positive impact placement had on her family life.

∞

The impact of placement on parents is often striking. Two critical questions about the aftermath of placement are addressed here. First, do families stay involved after placement and, if so, what are the patterns of postplacement involvement? Second, how do families themselves think and feel after placement, and how do they think and feel about the child, once placed?

Postplacement Family Involvement

Once parents place a child, their role as primary caregivers is altered dramatically. Conroy and Feinstein (1985) wrote about the lack of attention given to families in policy making regarding placement. They noted that:

in a formal sense, our service structures generally relegate families to the role of permission-giver. Service programs do not regularly contact families unless some form of consent is needed, e.g., for medical treatment. Conversely, the family rarely makes contact with program officials (other than direct care staff seen during visits) unless they perceive a problem. (p. 3)

Satisfaction with a placement is one dimension of family involvement; a more commonly studied one is visitation. Visitation is a behavioral aspect of involvement; other aspects of involvement that are more emotional or cognitive are considered in the next section. Studies with placed adults consistently have found that families maintained little contact with their son or daughter once placed (Baker & Blacher, 1988). This near isolation has been characteristic of newer community residential placements as well as institutional settings (Anderson, Lakin, Hill, & Chen, 1992; Grimes & Vitello, 1990; Stoneman & Crapps, 1990).

We have argued elsewhere that family involvement with a placed son or daughter reaps positive benefits for the parents, the child with mental retardation, and even the careprovider (Blacher & Baker, 1992). Furthermore, we suggested that the postplacement involvement experience might be very different for families raising a child with retardation after the passage of PL 94-142, the law that afforded— even mandated—provisions for parent involvement in their child's education. These post–PL 94-142 parents have been primed for higher rates of involvement with their child than, say, parents who raised their child in the previous decades, when services and roles for parents were nearly nonexistent (Meyers & Blacher, 1987b).

What do we know about current levels of postplacement family involvement? A recent cross-sectional study involving interviews with 62 families who had placed their child within the previous 2 years examined behavioral components of involvement, including visits to the facility, visits of the child home, phone calls, and parent involvement in the child's individualized habilitation plan (Baker & Blacher, 1993). Most of the families had at least a monthly visit with the child, half called weekly, and three quarters had attended the most recent educational planning meeting. When these same parents were interviewed almost 1 year later, they indicated continued high involvement (Blacher & Baker, 1994a). Four in five families had at least a monthly visit with their child, and two in three families called weekly. Visitation, to the facility or at home, remained highly stable, and phone calls increased significantly. These findings stand in striking contrast to those from families who raised their children with mental retardation in previous generations.

There was a trend for parents to feel less welcome to visit smaller facilities. Parents of children in larger facilities saw more opportunities to be involved at the facility; for example, the facility was more likely to offer a parent group and to invite parents' participation in activities. Parents, indeed, visited more frequently at larger facilities. In view of the strong philosophical support in the mental retardation field for small, family-like residences, it is notable that we could not find any dimensions along which the parents' experience was more positive with smaller facilities.

In attempting to determine what predicts levels of family involvement, Baker and Blacher (1993) found that the single greatest predictor of postplacement involvement appeared to be opportunities available at the facility for involvement. The "opportunities" variable was a stronger predictor than any child (e.g., level of behavior problems) or family (e.g., income, distance of family home from the facility) variable. This suggests that the placement facilities themselves can play a crucial role in fostering positive consequences for families.

Adjustment: Families' Thoughts and Feelings about Placement

Everything is not carefree after parents place a child, however. Negative emotions, such as sadness or guilt, are likely chronic and never far from the surface (Blacher, 1984b; Olshansky, 1962). Seventy-three percent of the parents in the Baker and Blacher study (1993) reported some feelings of guilt after placement; about half of them felt guilt "constantly or everyday."

> Recalling the night she and her husband returned home after placing Bobby, Mrs. Smith says, "I never remembered crying that hard. It was uncontrollable. It felt like somebody had ripped out my heart. Then, in the middle of the night, I got up and went down to check on him and he wasn't there. There was this unbelievably helpless, sick feeling." (Muckenfuss, 1993, p. E5)

These feelings reported by parents no doubt are engendered, in part, by societal and professional opposition to placement. They also are due to strong feelings of attachment that parents do have for their children (Blacher, 1984a).

Nevertheless, although most parents experience some negative emotions following placement, the predominant picture is one of decreased stress, positive feelings, and positive outlooks for themselves and their families.

> I know that it is really better for Zach to be out of the everyday pattern of our lives, but I really have trouble letting him go. And even as I say this, I know that I am looking forward to it. (Kupfer, 1982a, p. 171)

Feelings of relief and freedom following placement are common. Said a mother who placed her 15-year-old child who had significant mental retardation: "With fewer ties to homebound responsibilities, our other girls had a chance to test their wings and do some things of their own."

In one study that asked parents about the positive impact of placement on their lives, respondents reported almost exclusively less stress and greater freedom to pursue personal interests (Blacher & Baker, 1994a): "I don't miss the stresses without her here. Now we're able to do things we weren't able to do before." Virtually all of the respondents noted advantages to themselves of placement, and the majority also noted improvements in family relationships and overall positive impact of the placement decision on their lives. In that same study, all but one of the 55 respondents reported having thought about what life would be like if they were to bring the child back home to stay. Fully 85% of the parents indicated that life would be worse if that were to happen.

Few investigators have asked *other* family members their thoughts and feelings about placement. However, Eisenberg (1993) recently studied adolescents with a sibling who had severe mental retardation living at home, versus adolescents with a sibling who had been placed out of the home. In the former group, she asked what they perceived would be the consequences of placement. In the placed group, she asked what the consequences had in fact been. In every category where there were differences, the home group of siblings foresaw changes for the worse following placement, whereas the placed group reported actually experiencing changes for the better. The overall conclusion was that, for the majority of siblings, placement had, in balance, positive effects. However, although positive postplacement adjustment is an asset for the family at home, it ultimately may be a liability for the placed child if family reunification is a goal. These families clearly are not eager for the child to return home.

To summarize, the consequences of placing a child with mental retardation into another home or residence to live tend to be positive for the family members involved. Families raising children in the post–PL 94-142 era are highly involved with their children before placement, and the data available today suggest high postplacement levels of involvement as well. Indeed, out-of-home placement in the 1990s need not be placement out of the family.

IMPLICATIONS FOR PUBLIC POLICY

Should there be a single policy statement about placement of children with mental retardation? No. What we have learned over the decades, and what the most recent research tells us, is that families need *options* when faced with decisions about where their child shall live. In this concluding section four policy recommendations are highlighted that derive from the research on placement and its consequences for families with retardation.

(1) Ensure that Placement Out of the Home Need Not Be Placement Out of the Family

This chapter, indeed this entire book, is built on this premise. Any viable scenario in which a child leaves home should involve family members, be they the child's natural family, foster family, or adoptive family. In this country, parents raising their children with mental retardation in recent generations want to remain involved with them. In fact, they show fairly high and consistent levels of postplacement involvement. Placement programming and policy decisions must consider roles for parents in the aftermath of placement (Plumer, 1992).

Family reunification is not typically the main goal of placement of children with mental retardation. Yet some parents seek postplacement involvement opportunities in order to expedite such restoration (Lindsey, 1991). Also, if any placement setting does not work out, both professionals and family members must remember that the child *can* go home again.

(2) Supporting Research that Gains a Broader Perspective on Family Impact

Nearly all primary respondents in studies reported are mothers. It seems reasonable to assume that fathers may have a different perspective on amounts and types of involvement that are appropriate for themselves and their families. Siblings, too, often are ignored in studies of both the process and aftermath of placement, despite a strong rationale for including them (Blacher, 1993). Research on aging parents with adult sons or daughters with mental retardation highlights the important role that siblings without disabilities play. For example, they may provide emotional and instrumental support to the individual living in the placement setting (Seltzer, Begun, Magan, & Luchterhand, 1993; Zetlin, 1986), and their involvement has been shown to contribute to the well-being of their aging parents (Seltzer, Begun, Seltzer, & Krauss, 1991). Thus, placement—from the initial decision making through stages of postplacement involvement and adjustment—should be viewed as a family affair.

Another issue of importance in consideration of broader family impact is that of placement and postplacement family involvement nested in the current life cycle stage of the family. Families seem to experience age-related changes in stress (Orr, Cameron, Dobson, & Day, 1993) and may have different placement needs depending on the age of the child. For example, parents who have placed a very young child may feel the need to remain intricately involved, with the level and form of their involvement waning as the child gradually learns adaptive skills leading to independence. Aging parents of sons or daughters with mental retardation also show some unique concerns. For example, researchers have noted an intricate interplay of social support—given to and received from the placed son or daughter—that underscores the depth of feeling experienced by aging parents who have placed their child (Seltzer et al., 1993).

(3) Identify Correlates and Consequences of Placement for Other Populations

A family's cultural or subcultural identity is likely to influence all family interactions with a child who has disabilities (Crnic, Friedrich, & Greenberg, 1983; Mink, 1993). To date, research on placement has focused almost exclusively on Anglo populations. The meaning and relevance of placement and its aftermath begs further examination in non-European cultural groups (e.g., Hispanic, African American, Asian, and Native American). The Hispanic population is projected as the fastest growing minority in the United States (Children's Defense Fund, 1989; Hanson, 1992). Consideration of the roles of culture and disability will be needed in the study of placement and postplacement involvement in Hispanic families (Lopez, Blacher, & Shapiro, in press).

(4) Consider Alternatives: Ensure a Home-Like Setting for Every Child

The philosophy of permanency planning promotes the family home as the best place for children with mental retardation to live (Taylor et al., 1989). Intensive and increased in-home support services may provide immediate relief for families who are not ready or willing to consider placement options (Birenbaum & Cohen, 1993). Yet, in the mental retardation field, as in the foster care arena (from whence comes the concept of permanency planning), family preservation services are no panacea. For families with very difficult children, there always will be a need for high-quality substitute care services (Pecora et al., 1992).

Strong adherence to the philosophies of both permanency planning and normalization by professionals can be very guilt-inducing for parents. When placement is deemed the right choice for a given family, emphasis should be placed on finding the best available alternative living arrangement—or, to put it simply, to find a home away from home.

REFERENCES

Abramowicz, H.K., & Richardson, S.A. (1970). Epidemiology of severe mental retardation in children: Community studies. *American Journal of Mental Deficiency, 80,* 18–39.

Allen, M.K. (1972). Persistent factors leading to application for admission to a residential institution. *Mental Retardation, 10,* 25–28.

Amado, A.N., Lakin, K.C., & Menke, J.M. (1990). *1190 Chartbook on services for people with developmental disabilities.* Minneapolis: University of Minnesota, Center for Residential and Community Services.

American Psychiatric Association. (1994). *Diagnostic and statistical manual of mental disorders* (4th ed.). Washington, DC: Author.

Anderson, D.J., Lakin, K.C., Hill, B.K., & Chen, T. (1992). Social integration of older persons with mental retardation in residential facilities. *American Journal on Mental Retardation, 96,* 488–501.

Appell, M.J., & Tisdall, W.J. (1968). Factors differentiating institutionalized from noninstitutionalized referred retardates. *American Journal of Mental Deficiency, 73,* 424–432.

Baker, B.L., & Blacher, J. (1988). Family involvement with community residential programs. In M.P. Janicki, M.W. Krauss, & M.M. Seltzer (Eds.), *Community residences for persons with developmental disabilities: Here to stay* (pp. 173–188). Baltimore: Paul H. Brookes Publishing Co.

Baker, B.L., & Blacher, J.B. (1993). Out-of-home placement for children with mental retardation: Dimensions of family involvement. *American Journal on Mental Retardation, 3,* 368–377.

Baker, B.L., Seltzer, G.B., & Seltzer, M.M. (1977). *As close as possible: Community residences for retarded adults.* Boston: Little, Brown.

Birenbaum, A., & Cohen, H.J. (1993). On the importance of helping families: Policy implications from a national study. *Mental Retardation, 31,* 67–74.

Blacher, J. (1984a). A dynamic perspective on the impact of a severely handicapped child on the family. In J. Blacher (Ed.), *Severely handicapped young children and their families: Research in review* (pp. 3–50). Orlando, FL: Academic Press.

Blacher, J. (1984b). Sequential stages of parental adjustment to the birth of a handicapped child: Fact or artifact? *Mental Retardation, 22*(2), 55–68.

Blacher, J. (1990a). Assessing placement tendency in families with children who have severe handicaps. *Research in Developmental Disabilities, 11,* 341–351.

Blacher, J. (1990b). *The workshop on placement decision-making: There are no right's and wrong's.* Workshop developed for Eastern Los Angeles Regional Center, Los Angeles.

Blacher, J. (1993). Siblings and out-of-home placement. In Z. Stoneman & P.W. Berman (Eds.), *The effects of mental retardation, disability, and illness on sibling relationships: Research issues and challenges* (pp. 117–141). Baltimore: Paul H. Brookes Publishing Co.

Blacher, J., & Baker, B.L. (1992). Toward meaningful family involvement. *Mental Retardation, 30,* 35–43.

Blacher, J., & Baker, B.L. (1994a). Family involvement in residential treatment of children with retardation: Is there evidence of detachment? *The Journal of Child Psychology and Psychiatry, 35,* 505–520.

Blacher, J., & Baker, B.L. (1994b). Out-of-home placement for children with

retardation: Family decision making and satisfaction. *Family Relations, 3,* 10–15.
Blacher, J., & Bromley, B. (1990a). Correlates of out-of-home placement of handicapped children: Who places and why? In L.M. Glidden (Ed.), *Formed families: Adoption of children with handicaps* (pp. 3–40). New York: Haworth Press.
Blacher, J., & Bromley, B. (1990b). Factors influencing and factors preventing placement of severely handicapped children: Perspectives from mothers and fathers. In W.I. Fraser (Ed.), *Key issues in mental retardation research* (pp. 222–235). London: Routledge.
Blacher, J., & Hanneman, R. (1993). Out-of-home placement of children and adolescents with severe handicaps: Behavioral intentions and behavior. *Research in Developmental Disabilities, 14,* 145–160.
Blacher, J., Hanneman, R., & Rousey, A.M. (1992). Out-of-home placement of children with severe handicaps: A comparison of approaches. *American Journal on Mental Retardation, 96,* 607–616.
Blacher, J., & Meyers, C.E. (1983). A review of attachment formation and disorder of handicapped children. *American Journal of Mental Deficiency, 87,* 359–371.
Blacher, J., & Prado, P. (1986). The school as respite for parents of children with severe handicaps. In C.L. Salisbury & J. Intagliata (Eds.), *Respite care: Support for persons with developmental disabilities and their families* (pp. 217–234). Baltimore: Paul H. Brookes Publishing Co.
Blacher, J., & Steinback, R. (1992, May). The role of informal and formal support in families of school-aged children with retardation. In M.W. Krauss (Chair), *The influence of support on families across the life course: Unanticipated findings.* Invited symposium conducted at a meeting of the Academy on Mental Retardation, New Orleans.
Borthwick-Duffy, S.A., Eyman, R.K., & White, J.F. (1987). Client characteristics and residential placement patterns. *American Journal of Mental Deficiency, 92,* 24–30.
Braddock, D., & Fujiura, G. (1991). Politics, public policy, and the development of community mental retardation services in the United States. *American Journal on Mental Retardation, 95,* 369–387.
Bromley, B., & Blacher, J. (1989). Out-of-home placement of children with severe handicaps: Factors delaying placement. *American Journal on Mental Retardation, 94,* 284–291.
Children's Defense Fund. (1989). *A vision for America's future.* Washington, DC: Author.
Cole, D.A. (1986). Out-of-home child placement and family adaptation: A theoretical framework. *American Journal of Mental Deficiency, 91,* 226–236.
Cole, D.A., & Meyer, L.H. (1989). Impact of needs and resources on family plans to seek out-of-home placement. *American Journal on Mental Retardation, 93,* 380–387.
Conroy, J.W., & Feinstein, C.S. (1985). *Attitudes of families of CARC v. Thorne Classmakers* (interim report No. 2, Connecticut Applied Research Project). Philadelphia: Conroy & Feinstein Associates.
Crnic, K., Friedrich, W.N., & Greenberg, M.T. (1983). Adaptation of families with mentally retarded children: A model of stress, coping and family ecology. *American Journal of Mental Deficiency, 88,* 125–138.
Eisenberg, L.H. (1993). *The psychological adjustment of siblings of placed and*

nonplaced severely handicapped children. Unpublished doctoral dissertation, University of California, Los Angeles.
Eyman, R.K., & Call, T. (1977). Maladaptive behavior and community placement of mentally retarded persons. *American Journal of Mental Deficiency, 82,* 137–144.
Eyman, R.K., O'Connor, G., Tarjan, G., & Justice, R.S. (1972). Factors determining residential placement of mentally retarded children. *American Journal of Mental Deficiency, 76,* 692–698.
Farber, B. (1959). Effects of a severely mentally retarded child on family integration. *Monographs of the Society for Research in Child Development, 24,* (2, Serial No. 71).
Festinger, L. (1957). *A theory of cognitive dissonance.* Stanford, CA: Stanford University Press.
German, M.L., & Maisto, A.A. (1982). The relationships of a perceived family support system to the institutional placement of mentally retarded children. *Education and Training of the Mentally Retarded, 17,* 17–23.
Grimes, S.K., & Vitello, S.J. (1990). Follow-up study of family attitudes toward deinstitutionalization: Three to seven years later. *Mental Retardation, 28,* 219–225.
Grossman, H.J. (Ed.). (1983). *Classification in mental retardation.* Washington, DC: American Association of Mental Deficiency.
Hallahan, D.P., & Kauffman, J.M. (1991). *Exceptional children: Introduction to special education* (5th ed.). Englewood Cliffs, NJ: Prentice Hall.
Halpern, P.L. (1985). Respite care and family functioning in families with retarded children. *Health and Social Work, 10,* 138–150.
Hanson, M.J. (1992). Ethnic, cultural, and language diversity in intervention settings. In E.W. Lynch & M.J. Hansen (Eds.), *Developing cross-cultural competence. A guide for working with young children and their families* (pp. 3–18). Baltimore: Paul H. Brookes Publishing Co.
Joyce, K., Singer, M., & Isralowitz, R. (1983). Impact of respite care on parents' perceptions of quality of life. *Mental Retardation, 21,* 153–156.
Kobe, F.H., Rojahn, J., & Schroeder, S.R. (1991). Predictors of urgency of out-of-home placement needs. *Mental Retardation, 29,* 323–328.
Kupfer, F. (1982a). *Before & after Zachariah.* Chicago: Academy Chicago Publishers.
Kupfer, F. (1982b, December 13). Institution is not a dirty word. *Newsweek,* p. 36.
Lei, T., Nihira, L., Sheehy, N., & Meyers, C.E. (1981). A study of small family care for mentally retarded people. In R.H. Bruininks, C.E. Meyers, B.B. Sigford, & K.C. Lakin (Eds.), *Deinstitutionalization and community adjustment of mentally retarded people* (pp. 265–281). Monograph No. 4. Washington, DC: American Association of Mental Deficiency.
Lindsey, D.L. (1991). Factors affecting the foster care placement decision: An analysis of national survey data. *American Journal of Orthopsychiatry, 61,* 272–281.
Lopez, S.R., Blacher, J., & Shapiro, J. (in press). The interplay of culture and disability in Latino families. In I.T. Mink, M.L. Siantz, & P. Berman (Eds.), *Childhood disability and ethnically diverse families.* Baltimore: Paul H. Brookes Publishing Co.
Luckasson, R., Coulter, D.L., Polloway, E.A., Reiss, S., Schalock, R.L., Snell,

M.E., Spitalnik, D.M., & Stark, J.A. (1992). *Mental retardation: Definition, classification, and systems of supports.* Washington, DC: American Association on Mental Retardation.

Meyers, C.E., & Blacher, J. (1987a). Historical determinants of residential care for mentally retarded people. In S. Landesman & P.M. Vietze (Eds.), *Living environments and mental retardation* (pp. 3–16). Washington, DC: American Association on Mental Deficiency.

Meyers, C.E., & Blacher, J. (1987b). Parents' perceptions of schooling for their severely handicapped child: Relationships with home and family variables. *Exceptional Children, 53,* 441–449.

Meyers, C.E., Borthwick, S.A., & Eyman, R.K. (1985). Place of residence by age, ethnicity, and level of retardation of the mentally retarded/developmentally disabled population of California. *American Journal of Mental Deficiency, 90,* 266–270.

Mink, I.T. (1993). In the best interests of the family: Some comments on Birenbaum and Cohen's recommendations. *Mental Retardation, 31,* 80–82.

Moroney, R.M. (1986). Family care: Toward a responsive society. In P.R. Dokecki & R.M. Zaner (Eds.), *Ethics of dealing with persons with severe handicaps* (pp. 217–232). Baltimore: Paul H. Brookes Publishing Co.

Muckenfuss, M. (1993, March 14). Sad separations: A decision that can tear a family apart. *The San Bernardino Sun,* pp. E1, E5.

Nirje, B. (1969). The normalization principle and its human management implications. In R. Kugel & W. Wolfensberger (Eds.), *Changing patterns in residential services for the mentally retarded* (pp. 181–194). Washington, DC: President's Committee on Mental Retardation.

Olshansky, S. (1962). Chronic sorrow: A response to having a mentally defective child. *Social Casework, 43,* 191–194.

Orr, R.R., Cameron, S.J., Dobson, L.A., & Day, D.M. (1993). Age-related changes in stress experienced by families with a child who has developmental delays. *Mental Retardation, 31,* 171–176.

Pecora, P.J., Fraser, M.W., & Haapala, D.A. (1992). Intensive home-based family preservation services: An update from the FIT Project. *Child Welfare, 71,* 177–188.

Plumer, E.H. (1992). *When you place a child...* Springfield, IL: Charles C Thomas.

Ptacek, L.J. Sommers, P.A., Graves, J., Lukowicz, P., Keena, E., Haglund, J., & Nycz, G.R. (1982). Respite care for families of children with severe handicaps: An evaluation study of parent satisfaction. *Journal of Community Psychology, 10,* 222–227.

Rousey, A.M., Blacher, J., & Hanneman, R. (1990). Predictors of out-of-home placement of children with severe handicaps: A cross-sectional analysis. *American Journal on Mental Retardation, 94,* 522–531.

Rudie, F., & Riedl, G. (1984). Attitudes of parents/guardians of mentally retarded former state hospital residents toward current community placement. *American Journal of Mental Deficiency, 89,* 295–297.

Seltzer, G.B., Begun, A., Magan, R., & Luchterhand, C.M. (1993). Social supports and expectations of family involvement in out-of-home placement. In E. Sutton, A.R. Factor, B.A. Hawkins, T. Heller, & G.B. Seltzer (Eds.), *Older adults with developmental disabilities. Optimizing choice and change* (pp. 123–140). Baltimore: Paul H. Brookes Publishing Co.

Seltzer, G.B., Begun, A., Seltzer, M.M., & Krauss, M.W. (1991). Adults with mental retardation and their aging mothers: Impacts of siblings. *Family Relations, 40,* 310–317.

Seltzer, M.M., & Krauss, M.W. (1984a). Family, community residence, and institutional placements of a sample of mentally retarded children. *American Journal of Mental Deficiency, 89,* 257–266.

Seltzer, M.M., & Krauss, M.W. (1984b). Placement alternatives for mentally retarded children and their families. In J. Blacher (Ed.), *Severely handicapped young children and their families: Research in review* (pp. 143–175). Orlando, FL: Academic Press.

Seltzer, M.M., & Krauss, M.W. (1989). Aging parents with adult mentally retarded children: Family risk factors and sources of support. *American Journal on Mental Retardation, 94,* 303–312.

Seltzer, M.M., & Ryff, C.D. (1994). Parenting across the lifespan: The normative and nonnormative cases. In D.L. Featherman, R. Lerner, & M. Perlmutter (Eds.), *Life-span development and behavior* (Vol. 12, pp. 1–40). Hillsdale, NJ: Lawrence Erlbaum Associates.

Shellhaas, M.D., & Nihira, K. (1969). Factor analysis of reasons retardates are referred to an institution. *American Journal of Mental Deficiency, 74,* 171–179.

Sherman, B.R. (1988). Predictors of the decision to place developmentally disabled family members in residential care. *American Journal on Mental Retardation, 92,* 344–351.

Singer, G.H.S., & Irvin, L.K. (Eds.). (1989). *Support for caregiving families. Enabling positive adaptation to disability.* Baltimore: Paul H. Brookes Publishing Co.

Smith, D.D., & Luckasson, R. (1992). *Introduction to special education: Teaching in an age of challenge.* Boston: Allyn & Bacon.

Stanfield, J. (1983). *What was I supposed to do?* [Film]. Santa Barbara, CA: James Stanfield Company.

Stone, N.D. (1967). Family factors in willingness to place the mongoloid child. *American Journal of Mental Deficiency, 72,* 16–20.

Stoneman, Z., & Crapps, J.M. (1990). Mentally retarded individuals in family care homes: Relationships with the family-of-origin. *American Journal on Mental Retardation, 94,* 420–430.

Suelzle, M., & Keenan, V. (1981). Changes in family support networks over the life cycle of mentally retarded persons. *American Journal of Mental Deficiency, 86,* 267–274.

Tausig, M. (1985). Factors in family decision-making about placement for developmentally disabled individuals. *American Journal of Mental Deficiency, 89,* 352–361.

Taylor, S.J., & Bogdan, R. (1992). Defending illusions: The institution's struggle for survival. In P.M. Ferguson, D.L. Ferguson, & S.J. Taylor (Eds.), *Interpreting disability* (pp. 78–98). New York: Teachers' College, Columbia University.

Taylor, S.J., Lakin, K.C., & Hill, B.K. (1989). Permanency planning for children and youth: Out-of-home placement decisions. *Exceptional Children, 55,* 541–549.

Townsend, P.W., & Flanagan, J.J. (1976). Experimental preadmission program to encourage home care for severely and profoundly retarded children. *American Journal of Mental Deficiency, 80,* 562–569.

Turnbull, A.P., Brotherson, M.J., & Summers, J.A. (1982, November). *The impact of deinstitutionalization on families: A family systems approach*. Paper presented at the Working Conference on Deinstitutionalization and the Education of Handicapped Children, Minneapolis.

Turnbull, H.R., Turnbull, A.P., Bronicki, G.J., Summers, J.A., & Roeder-Gordon, C. (1989). *Disability and the family: A guide to decisions for adulthood*. Baltimore: Paul H. Brookes Publishing Co.

Upshur, C.C. (1983). Developing respite care: A support service for families with disabled members. *Family Relations, 32,* 13–20.

Waisbren, S.E. (1980). Parent's reaction after the birth of a developmentally disabled child. *American Journal of Mental Deficiency, 84,* 345–351.

Wikler, L. (1981). Periodic stress of families of mentally retarded children. *Family Relations, 30,* 281–288.

Willer, B., & Intagliata, J. (1984). *Promises and realities for mentally retarded citizens: Life in the community*. Baltimore: University Park Press.

Wolf, L.C., & Whitehead, P.C. (1975). The decision to institutionalize retarded children. Comparison of individually matched groups. *Mental Retardation, 13,* 3–7.

Zetlin, A.G. (1986). Mentally retarded adults and their siblings. *American Journal of Mental Deficiency, 91,* 217–225.

Zigler, E., & Black, K.B. (1989). America's family support movement: Strengths and limitations. *American Journal of Orthopsychiatry, 59,* 315.

9

Comprehensive Service Programming for Children with Autism and Their Families

Stephen R. Anderson, Susan F. Thibadeau, and Walter P. Christian

∞

As he and his mother approach, Jerry seems like any other 6-year-old child who will be playing on the playground today. But as they enter the area something seems different about Jerry. He adroitly climbs to the very top of the jungle gym and walks precariously along its highest point while making a loud, high-pitched noise. After a few minutes, he jumps to the ground, picks up a handful of rocks and watches them as they fall slowly between his fingers. He repeats this action over and over again, seemingly unaware of the activities of others. Unlike many other children who are there with their parents, Jerry does not ask his mother for assistance, show her a new trick that he has learned on the trapeze, or run to her for comfort when he falls. He does not approach or observe other children who play near him and, in the 3 years that they have been coming to this playground, he has made no friends. It is as if no one else exists.

∞

The parents of a young child newly diagnosed as having autism often are unprepared to deal with the formidable challenges that lie ahead. Until recently, a diagnosis of autism often was a prescription for institutional placement. Fortunately, societal attitudes have changed to regard placement as less desirable for children with autism. Clearly PL 94-142 (the Education for All Handicapped Children Act of 1975, reenacted as the Individuals with Disabilities Education Act of 1990), with its mandate for education in the least restrictive environment, has had an impact of major proportions. Less than 20 years ago, we were asking whether children with autism could even be educated. Now many professionals and parents are advocating for full inclusion in regular neighborhood schools (Fox & Williams, 1991). Nevertheless, placement remains a reality for thousands of children with autism. Sherman (1988) compared a group of children with developmental disabilities living at home with a group of children in out-of-home placements. One striking finding was that autism was three times as prevalent in the out-of-home group than in the at-home group. Although living with a child who has autism provides many positive experiences, autism remains a devastating disability for everyone involved.

This chapter discusses the unique issues and concerns about placement that are faced by families of children with autism. For the purposes of this chapter, *placement* is defined broadly to include both educational and residential considerations, although our discussion will emphasize out-of-home placement. Multiple factors appear to influence placement decisions for children with autism (Figure 1). Child and family characteristics, the impact of the child on the family, the specific service needs of the child and his or her family, and the range of options available all interact to affect the final choice of placement.

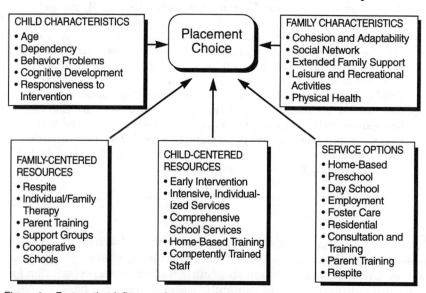

Figure 1. Factors that influence placement choice.

This chapter discusses each of these factors, advocates for the development of a broad network of service options for children and families, and discusses the general implications for families, service providers, and policy makers.

The information in this chapter is drawn both from the professional literature on autism and families in general, and from the May Institute's work with the families of children with autism. The May Institute is a private, not-for-profit service program created to deliver educational and habilitative services, conduct and disseminate research, and provide training and consultation. A chronological description of the Institute's reorganization efforts that began in 1978 has been provided by Christian (1983a) and Luce, Christian, Anderson, Troy, and Larsson (1992). Detailed descriptions of methods and procedures, such as goals, forms, and guidelines, and evaluation strategies, have been described previously as well (Christian & Hannah, 1983; Christian & Reitz, 1986). The May Institute provides a broad network of educational, residential, and habilitative placement options for individuals who have autism, behavior disorders, and traumatic head injury (see Table 1).

As we discuss later, autism can be manifested intellectually in many different ways, ranging from mental retardation to normal intelligence (Rapin, 1991). Although we discuss the entire range of children having features characteristic of autism, many of our examples describe the more severely involved children who, because of their behavior problems and deficits in adaptive functioning, present more difficult placement challenges.

Table 1. The May Institute network of services to children and adults with autism

- Early identification and referral
- Home-based early intervention
- Parent training and support
- Respite
- Specialized foster care
- Early childhood education (inclusive child care, toddler, and preschool programs)
- Day-school programming for children and youth
- Vocational education, employment training, and job placement for adolescents and adults
- Community living (e.g., group homes, supervised apartments) for adolescents and adults
- Outreach consultation to families, schools, practitioners, human services agencies, and state service systems
- Training and supervision for interns and practicum students from affiliated universities

CHILD AND FAMILY FACTORS THAT INFLUENCE PLACEMENT

Characteristics of Children

Autism is a subtype of the pervasive developmental disorders (PDDs), according to the *Diagnostic and Statistical Manual of Mental Disorders* (3rd ed., rev.) of the American Psychiatric Association (1987). Primary features of the disorder include: 1) qualitative impairment in reciprocal social interaction, 2) qualitative impairment of verbal and nonverbal communication and imaginative activity, and 3) a markedly restricted repertoire of activities and interests. In addition to the primary features involving social relatedness, communication, and interests, many children display secondary features such as a short attention span, insomnia, feeding and eating problems, and enuresis and encopresis. Hyperactivity is a common behavior problem in young children with autism. Aggressiveness and temper tantrums often are present, typically in response to a change in routines or demands. The use of the more general classification of PDD has been on the increase because many parents and professionals prefer it to the label *autism*, which they perceive as highly stigmatizing. The estimated incidence of autism is approximately 4–5 in 10,000 children, whereas the incidence of PDD is 12–15 in 10,000 children.

Most researchers and clinicians agree that children with autism demonstrate a wide range of intellectual abilities, ranging from mental retardation to above-average intelligence (Rapin, 1991). Based on the traditional definition of mental retardation, about 50% have moderate, severe, or profound retardation; about 25% have mild retardation; and 25% have IQs of 70 or more (Campbell & Green, 1985). Standardized test scores are likely to be misleading for many children having significant language delays, inasmuch as many tests rely on the child's verbal responses.[1]

Although no known cause exists, most researchers believe that autism results from some abnormality in the child's neurophysiology (Ornitz, 1985). As stated by Schreibman, Koegel, Charlop, and Egel (1990), there are many theories, but none has gained consistent support. In fact, several variables may be involved in the etiology of au-

---

[1] New terminology adopted in 1992 by the American Association on Mental Retardation (AAMR) (Luckasson, Coulter, Polloway, Reiss, Schalock, Snell, Spitalnik, & Stark, 1992) does not utilize the classification scheme of mild, moderate, severe, and profound retardation. Because the utility of this new definition is under debate, and the recently published edition of the psychiatric classification system continues to diagnose levels of mental retardation (American Pychiatric Association, 1994), we have used AAMR's earlier terminology (Grossman, 1983) here.

tism. The fact that many more boys have autism than girls, and that it occurs with a higher prevalence in siblings, may suggest a genetic influence in some proportion of the cases (Folstein & Priven, 1991).

Autism can be manifested in many different ways. Its most severe form is that of a demanding child who exhibits little or no social attachment. The child may appear socially aloof and unaware of the presence of others, exhibiting a flat or neutral affect even when presented with preferred activities or greeted by a familiar person. Appropriate communication skills may be absent entirely, although the child may use tantrums, aggression, or self-injury to gain access to desired objects and to avoid undesired activities. The child may need constant supervision to prevent exposure to dangerous situations. The parents often describe their child as having an intense fascination with specific objects and/or engaging in repetitive and bizarre mannerisms. Some examples include rocking or hand flapping, gazing at bright lights, repetitive vocalizations, and rubbing the edges of objects. More complex examples involve obsessions with dates, letters, or numbers. Appropriate play and leisure skills may be absent entirely or be dependent on structure provided by parents and siblings. Although a few children with autism may develop some independence in the completion of daily self-help skills, many children require continuous care throughout their lives.

It is reasonable to conclude that behavior problems, social deficits, and dependency issues combine to influence placement for children with autism. Rousey, Blacher, and Hanneman (1990) identified child age, level of mental retardation, maladaptive behavior, and adaptive behavior as predictor variables for placement for children with disabilities in general. That is, individuals placed in residential settings typically are older, demonstrate significantly lower adaptive behavior skills, and exhibit a greater prevalence of maladaptive behavior than individuals living at home. This finding is consistent with the research results of DeMyer and Goldberg (1983), who reported that, in their sample of children with autism, 67% of those over 14 years old were in institutional placements. In those situations in which a child under 11 years of age was placed, the parents identified an unusual family problem (e.g., parents' divorce) or behavior problems as variables that made the child's residence in the home unmanageable for the family.

Although children with autism clearly can benefit from instruction when it is intensive and systematic (Anderson, Avery, DiPietro, Edwards, & Christian, 1987; Lovaas, 1987), most will require help and protection throughout their lifetime. As many authors have indicated (e.g., Bristol, 1984; Harris, 1988), the prospect of a lifetime of dependency may be overwhelming for many parents. Consider the following case study.

∞

Keri is a 9-year-old child with autism who functions approximately at the age of a 2½- to 3-year-old child. Because of a sleeping disorder, she has difficulty falling asleep at night and she awakes at 4:00 A.M. or earlier each morning. The house has been childproofed to prevent destruction and to minimize dangers to Keri. The doors to the house are always locked, latches have been placed on all cabinets, and breakable items have been removed. Being unable to keep herself appropriately occupied with toys or activities, Keri spends much of her time unproductively engaged in stereotypic behaviors (e.g., hand flapping and pacing). Keri's mother has to prepare every meal for her, sit with her to ensure that she remains at the table, and prompt her to use her eating utensils. On days when school is not in session, her mother devotes her entire day to supervising Keri and attempting to keep her occupied. Keri rarely initiates interactions with her mother or her siblings. If weather permits, they will spend most of the day outside, because that is where Keri seems the happiest. Most days, her mother will not attempt to complete household chores or accomplish daily errands such as going to the grocery store without receiving help with Keri.

∞

This example is typical of the situation of many parents. Parents are asked to divide their time into pieces given to each other, their other children, and their extended family while providing nearly constant attention (frequently on demand) to their child with autism. In their opinion, they may never foresee a time when all their children will be self-sufficient. Parents often adapt their parenting style to stave off behavior problems and to reduce difficult and sometimes embarrassing moments in public. As the child gets older, this incongruence between normal family life and what actually occurs grows even wider. Each stage of the child's life may present a series of new challenges. Although an emotional bond develops between the child and his or her parents, it is certainly limited by the boundaries of the child's affective, cognitive, and behavioral development.

Impact on the Family

Early attempts to explain autism erroneously emphasized the effect of the parent on the child's development (Bettelheim, 1967). Parents were reported to be detached, cold, and overly intellectual. They often were separated from the child rather than accepted as active participants in intervention efforts. More recently, clinicians and researchers have begun to consider and examine the psychological impact of the child on the family (Harris, 1988; Koegel et al., 1992). As Harris (1988) pointed out, "Living in a family is not easy. Living in a family with a handicapped child, especially a child with a disability as serious as autism, is even tougher" (p. 199).

Evidence increasingly suggests that the family of a child with autism may be at risk of greater stress and adjustment difficulties than other families having a child with a disability. The characteristic behavior problems and skill deficits associated with autism often have a significant impact on families. A study by Holroyd and McArthur (1976) indicated that the parents of children with autism reported fewer leisure activities and poorer prospects for independent living than the families of children with Down syndrome or children treated at an outpatient psychiatric clinic. Two other studies (DeMyer & Goldberg, 1983; Koegel et al., 1992) suggest a characteristic profile of stress for the parents of children with autism related to the child's dependence, the level of their cognitive impairment, and the restricted range of recreational and leisure activities. Because of the child's behavior problems and skill deficits, parents often reported that community trips were limited in frequency and restricted to a few settings. DeMyer and Goldberg (1983) concluded that other aspects of family life were affected as well, including family finances, emotional and physical health of the parents, housekeeping, personal development of family members, and relationships among family members, friends, and neighbors.

Bristol (1984) suggested that, because the child with autism appears physically normal, the disability creates a great deal of ambiguity for parents and professionals. She reported that children who appeared to have a more significant disability had a less adverse effect on their families than children who exhibited milder characteristics of autism and behavior disorders. Apparently, the ambiguity between the children's measured abilities and their ability to relate to other people creates additional stress as to the nature of the disability and the proper course of intervention.

Characteristics of Families

Obviously, not all problems that occur within a family result from the presence of a child with autism. It is reasonable to expect that families including a child with autism are influenced by the same factors that affect all families with children (e.g., financial resources, physical and mental health of individual members, social support network). These family system factors interact with the characteristics of the child with varying outcomes (Figure 1).

Harris and Powers (1984) have presented the notion of the life cycle of the family as a framework for understanding normal stress and coping in families having a child with autism. That is, there are typical transitional events that occur in all families, including the child's starting school, transition into adolescence, and the death of the parents. When these events occur out of sequence or in unpredictable ways, greater stress may occur at each transition point. Families that help and support each other at these moments appear to cope and adjust more effectively. When the stress is extremely great (such as in the death of a family member), parents may seek support from extended family, friends, neighbors and the community at large (e.g., support groups, individual and family counseling). However, insular families who lack an extended support network may not adjust to and cope with a crisis. Instead, they may conclude that the child with autism is the primary source of their stress and that an out-of-home placement must be considered.

SERVICE ISSUES THAT AFFECT PLACEMENT

When effective community-based options are available for families, it is our opinion that placement can be delayed or avoided for many children with autism. Unfortunately, a gap continues to exist between our desire for progressive outcomes and the availability of a full range of community-based placement options, including both day and residential services. If society is truly committed to preventing out-of-home placement, we must provide a comprehensive set of placement options that begins at an early age. Furthermore, those options must incorporate our current best understanding of autism, provide the level of intervention needed to effect and maintain change, emphasize the important role of parents, and continuously address the acquisition of skills that will enable the individual to live more normally.

Effective Early Intervention

If we identify children with autism at an early age and begin intensive intervention, we can impact directly on the occurrence of out-of-home placement. Although there is no unassailable evidence that early intervention works, it makes good sense along a number of dimensions (Dunlap & Robbins, 1991):

1. Young children often are more responsive to intervention efforts than older children (particularly important for remediating social and language deficits).

2. Younger children have a shorter learning history; thus problem behaviors that interfere with learning may be addressed more easily.
3. The child is still very small and can be managed physically if need be.
4. The parents of young children often have greater energy and motivation.

Fenske, Zalenski, Krantz, and McClannahan (1985) reported that children with autism made greater progress when they entered an intervention program before age 5. Two other studies (Anderson et al., 1987; Lovaas, 1987) have reported substantial gains for children who were identified early and participated in an intensive program of home-based training (to be discussed later in this chapter).

It is unlikely that educational intervention—regardless of how early it is begun or how intensive it is—will eliminate completely the primary features of autism. However, we should not try to justify programming efforts purely on the basis of significant developmental outcomes for the child (e.g., higher IQ scores). As Johnson-Martin (1990) argued, studies also should examine quality-of-life issues for the child and family, focusing on "the extent to which early intervention provides parents with coping skills to allow them to keep children at home for longer periods of time, provides a better life for that child, promotes greater feelings of competence for parents, and results in greater savings to taxpayers" (p. 254). Fortunately, a number of states have already mandated free, appropriate education for children with disabilities from birth to 6 years of age. Under PL 99-457 (the Education of the Handicapped Act Amendments of 1986), 3- to 5-year-olds with developmental disabilities are entitled to educational services, and the federal government offers significant incentives to states to provide services to children under 3 years old.

Home-Based Intervention and Parent Training

One approach to early intervention is to deliver intensive home-based training that provides: 1) direct one-on-one instruction to remediate specific skills deficits and behavior problems of the child, and 2) intensive parent training. Home-based training offers an alternative to the traditional center-based intervention model that often results in gains that fail to generalize to the child's home. One example of a home-based training model was described by Lovaas (1987). He assigned preschool-age children with autism to one of two groups: an Intensive Treatment Group that received more than 40 hours of one-on-one treatment per week or a Minimal-Treatment Control Group that received 10 hours or less of one-on-one treatment per week. Each child was assigned a team of well-trained therapists to work with the child in his or her home. Posttreatment data indicated that 9 of 19 children (47%) in the experimental group "recovered." These 9 children were reported to have achieved normal intellectual and educational functioning in the first grade. In contrast, none of 19 children in the control group met this criterion. A follow-up study (McEachin, Smith, & Lovaas, 1993) that occurred years later showed that 8 of the 9 experimental subjects were still indistinguishable from average children on tests of intelligence and adaptive behavior.

These results have been replicated in part by the May Institute (Anderson et al., 1987). Like the Lovaas study, critical features of the program included: 1) early identification and treatment, 2) intensive application of behavioral teaching techniques and treatment procedures, 3) training conducted in the child's natural home and community, and 4) extensive parent training, allowing the parents eventually to serve as primary teachers for their child with autism. Most of the children demonstrated significant gains in their language, self-care, social, and academic development, as evidenced by the results of standardized assessments and individual treatment data.

Since the 1970s, a considerable body of evidence has emerged demonstrating that parent training in behavioral methods generally leads to improved teaching and management skills for the participants (Baker, 1989). These skills often enable parents to reduce associated features of their child's disability (e.g., tantrums, aggression, sleeping and eating problems) and increase the child's independence (e.g., dressing and bathing skills). Two studies provide support for the important role that parents play in the education/treatment of their child, as well as the prevention of placement. Lovaas, Koegel, Simmons, and Long (1973) obtained measures for two groups of children with autism who had received 1 year of intensive behavior therapy. One group received training without parent involvement, and subsequently were placed in residential institutions. Follow-up measures showed that none of the children had maintained treatment gains originally achieved. In contrast, the second group, whose parents participated in a training program, continued to show improvement at follow-up. In a second study, Schreibman and Britten (1984) assigned families of autistic children to either a parent-training or a no-parent-training group. All children received clinic-based instruction provided by professionals. Although both groups of children improved, the children in the parent-training group were more likely to generalize newly acquired skills to their mothers in the clinic and at home. Those who participated in the parent training also expressed improvement in their quality of life. The authors concluded that training the parents had the potential for alleviating some of the negative impact of the child on the families' everyday lives.

It has been argued by some authors (Turnbull & Turnbull, 1982) that parent training programs often make excessive demands and may increase stress and exacerbate individual and family adjustment problems. Although additional research is needed, one initial study by Baker, Landen, and Kashima (1991) appears to indicate that parent and family adjustment measures (e.g., depression, family stress, family adaptability) generally show positive changes as a result of parent training.

Although the effects of home-based training and parent training have been well documented, they are not commonly provided. Most intervention efforts continue to occur within center-based programs (e.g., public schools and hospitals) and involve groups of students in which the focus is not on the needs of an individual child. The failure to change from center-based to home-based programs may have financial as well as historical roots. That is, providing services to children within traditional school and clinic settings may be viewed as less expensive. This reasoning may prove myopic, however, resulting in short-term savings initially yet leading to significantly greater costs later if the child must be institutionalized.

Comprehensive School-Based Services

The public schools serve a multifaceted role in reducing the risk of placement: 1) they help the child to develop functional skills and behaviors leading to greater independence, 2) they provide extended-day and full-year programming, and 3) they make parent training and other family supports available. Although public schools have been mandated by law to educate children with autism, many schools continue to have difficulty meeting the needs of this unique population. Typically the reasons for their failure include inadequately trained staff, poorly designed curricula, and insufficient allocation of time. A reexamination of our approach to education is sorely needed in order to determine what constitutes appropriate education for students with autism. The following situation reflects what repeats itself in many school programs.

∞

Janice is a 12-year-old child with autism who demonstrates significant social and language delays as well as a variety of behavior problems (tantrums, screaming, aggression). She was placed in the classroom of

Ms. Arnold, a teacher trained to work with young children with moderate special needs. The classroom has seven children, including Janice. The other children present mild to moderate developmental disabilities and range in age from 8 to 12 years. The classroom materials and activities are primarily preschool level, consistent with a developmental approach to instruction. There is little or no individualized programming, and instructional goals do not include programs to address self-care and social development.

Ms. Arnold's training did not adequately prepare her to work with a child with autism, so the school system added two classroom aides, believing that more help would compensate for her lack of training. During a typical day, Janice remains unengaged in appropriate classroom activities, choosing instead to wander around the room engaging in a variety of repetitive activities such as opening and closing cabinets and doors. If the aides try to guide her toward an activity (e.g., circle time), she screams and begins to tantrum. The aides immediately terminate the interaction in order to avoid a scene. Although Janice exhibits few behavior problems (because demands are minimal), she also does not engage in very many meaningful instructional activities. Like many school programs, the day is only 5 hours long and the academic year is only 10 months, with no summer program.

∞

This case illustrates the problems often associated with the public and private education systems for children with autism. The program is not individually designed to meet the needs of the child, staff are inadequately trained, and the academic day and year are too short. Furthermore, the curriculum fails to address the development of functional skills (e.g., dressing, toileting) and the reduction of behavior problems (tantrums) likely to prevent or delay placement. What is needed is a reexamination of what constitutes appropriate education.

∞

Greg was 15 years old when he was referred by his school district to the May Center for Education and Vocational Training, a day program of the May Institute. At the time of his referral, his mother expressed her feeling that Greg needed residential placement because she could no longer manage his behavior problems and he lacked many independent skills (e.g., leisure and self-care). A single parent, with three other grown children who now lived on their own, Greg's mother currently worked outside the home. However, she complained that the shortness of Greg's school day and academic year made it very difficult for her to maintain a job. Eventually his mother and the school district agreed to place Greg at the May Center and to review the question of residential placement 6 months later.

The Center's program provided Greg with a 7-hour school day, 6 days a week, without extended vacations. This extensive schedule allowed his mother to work and provided her with respite from the many demands of daily care for him. The development of Greg's independent leisure, self-care, and domestic skills were identified as priorities over traditional academic skills. Greg's educational program increasingly emphasized providing instruction outside the classroom in inclusive settings. Vocational instruction began on campus with paid, contract work and quickly moved to employment at a local business with a member of our staff serving as a job coach. His mother also received in-home training to improve her teaching and management skills. Now, 5 years later, Greg remains at the school, continues to live with his mother, and works successfully in the community.

Family Support Services

Two other important areas of service delivery for the families of children with autism are the provision of support and empowerment. As we have discussed, a child with autism, particularly a child with significant skill deficits and behavior problems, frequently causes confusion and disruption to the family. Thus, families also will need respite from the child. The need for respite and the type of respite can vary significantly for families. Consider two families who have children with autism and behavior disorders. Both children require nearly continuous supervision and both families are committed to keeping their children at home. Nevertheless, their need for professional respite may differ significantly depending on many factors. One factor again has to do with the strategies these families use to cope with having a child with developmental disabilities and their tolerance of the child's atypical social and behavioral development. Another factor may be the availability of volunteers and a social support network. In one case, the parents may be able to turn to extended family members or friends who volunteer to provide respite and other support. In the other case, no extended family may live nearby, or they may be unable or unwilling to help. Although both families have the same commitment to their children, the needs are very different. There is very little question that both families will need some time away from their demanding child, but their need for private or publicly funded respite is very different. Where one family (or a family member) may refrain from ever asking for outside help, another may seek as much professional support as possible. Bronicki and Turnbull (1987) have suggested that professionals can best help by forming partnerships with parents and helping them to recognize what personal and professional resources are available to them.

In the last 10 years, the field's view of the role of the child's parents has changed considerably, and now parents have increasing opportunities and responsibilities. Parents should be empowered as partners (Turnbull & Turnbull, 1990) in the design and implementation of their child's program. As partners, they should have the opportunity to be full participants in the development of specific goals and objectives, the design of instructional programs, programming for generalization to the home and community, and so on. Likewise, parents must be informed of all possible placement options, the factors that should (or could) influence their decision making (e.g., Figure 1), and the possible impact of their decision on the child's development. In short, it is the professional's job to provide them with significant information and participation to empower them in the decision-making process.

TRANSITIONAL RESIDENTIAL PROGRAMMING

In spite of the best-laid plans, placement will continue to be a choice for many parents of children with autism. In our experience, parents chose residential placement for one or more of the following reasons: 1) inadequate community-based services (e.g., schools do not meet child and family needs); 2) unpredicted change in the family's life cycle (e.g., illness of one of the parents); or 3) serious risk of injury to the child or others as a result of the child's problem behavior (e.g., self-injurious behavior or aggression).

Most families who make the painful decision to place their child (particularly children under 14 years old) are not looking for permanent residential care. Instead, they seek intensive intervention to remediate specific deficits and to reduce the frequency of behavior problems (e.g., a sleeping disorder) so that the child can return to live with them. Parents may view the placement as an opportunity for them to regain emotional and physical strength as well.

In our view, progressive residential placement should be transitional (Anderson, Christian, & Luce, 1986; Luce, 1986); that is, it should provide effective intervention that facilitates the child's transition back to live with his or her family or in an alternative community-based option. Unfortunately, it appears that most agencies that provide residential services are limited to this one service option. In contrast, the May Institute has developed a broad network of services designed to impact directly, and indirectly, on the problem of placement (e.g., outreach parent training; consultation to public schools; transitional, community-based residential options; day-school programs that meet the need for extended-day and full school year programming; and home-based training). The program also has extended the philosophy of transitional residential programming to services for adults with autism, by providing an array of community-based living and employment options.

In our experience, each program addition has supplemented and enhanced our ability to meet the needs of children with autism by delaying or preventing placement for some children (e.g., early intervention, home-based services, public school consulting), transitioning children to less restrictive community-based options, and providing a graduated approach to community transition (e.g., moving along a continuum from group residential care to specialized foster care).

Although current trends to deinstitutionalize have resulted in increased scrutiny of residential programs serving children with developmental disabilities, many programs still fail to provide services that meet fundamental standards of progressive residential care, including: 1) services appropriate and responsive to individual child and family needs, 2) treatment interventions based on methods having documented evidence of effectiveness, 3) systematic planning for each child's return to live with his or her family after a period of intervention, 4) competency-based training and supervision of staff, 5) ongoing, reliable assessment of each child's progress, and 6) a network of services designed to meet the unique needs of individual children, their families, and local schools (Anderson et al., 1986).

What is sorely needed is greater emphasis on the methodology for careful, systematic transition of children to less restrictive community-based options. This system should include: 1) systematic assessment and ameiloration of the specific deficits and behavioral excesses that resulted in residential placement, 2) a detailed education and treatment plan based on a consideration of the individual's future environment (typically the child's natural home and public school), 3) a plan for systematically promoting generalization and maintenance of treatment gains, 4) preparation and training of parents and teachers in the child's future environment, and 5) follow-up support and training as needed to ensure continued community placement.

As with any child identified as in need of special education, treatment planning must begin with assessing the needs of the individual. However, in the case of children in residential placement, the onus is to identify specifically those behavior problems and skill deficits that resulted in the child's placement outside of the home. After all, these must be the target of any intervention if the child is to return to live with his or her family and attend a local school program. Although standardized instruments may be administered to provide a profile of general areas of strength and weakness, the results will be of little value in developing specific goals and objectives for intervention. Instead, goals should be delineated based on a knowledge of the environment in which the individual eventually will live and go to school. Therefore, interviews of the parents and teachers, direct observations in future environments, and assessment of other individuals who are judged to be competent in those future environments will be needed.

In an earlier paper (Anderson & Schwartz, 1986), we presented a Parent Priorities Worksheet that may be used to sample the opinions of parents regarding important goals for intervention. The worksheet asks parents to indicate which of the behavior problems and skill deficits listed very seriously disrupts the family and prevents the child from living at home. The form then asks the parent to narrow the list of behaviors and skills to five and to indicate the frequency of the behavior or the nature of the deficiency. This information, together with the results of other assessments (e.g., direct observations), is used to develop five or six goals for transition (i.e., goals that will be addressed and achieved prior to discharge from the residential program).

It should not be expected that every deficit of the child will be remediated prior to a return to in-home placement. Rather, the residential treatment team and each child's parents should focus on identifying and delineating a small set of reasonable goals that must be obtained in order for the child to return successfully to live with his or her family. Movement toward transition can be evaluated continuously by examining progress on these transitional objectives. In our experience, the areas often identified by families as preventing the child from living at home include aberrant behaviors such as aggression, noncompliance, and tantrums, as well as the absence of basic adaptive skills such as independent play, self-care, and functional communication (Anderson, Luce, Newsom, Gruber, & Kennedy-Butler, 1983). Once these behaviors are identified and operationally defined, they should serve as the primary targets of the training curriculum.

As children learn skills, programs must apply strategies for ensuring the generalization and maintenance of these skills. Students should continue to practice their newly acquired skills in a variety of settings (including future environments), in the presence of different adults, and in response to different materials. Specific strategies employed to ensure generalization are described elsewhere and will not be repeated here. The reader is referred to Anderson and Schwartz (1986), Horner, Dunlap, and Koegel (1988), and Stokes and Baer (1977) for a review of issues relevant to generalization and maintenance.

One essential part of transitional planning is to train adequately significant persons in the child's future environment, particularly the child's parents. Although the professional literature is replete with materials designed for the parents of children without handicaps (e.g., Patterson & Gullion, 1976) or children with mild behavior disorders and mental retardation (e.g., Baker, 1989), few programs (Anderson, 1989; Harris, 1983; Schreibman & Britten, 1984) address the severe behavior disorders and pervasive delays often characteristic of children with autism. Furthermore, none deals with the very unique problem of training parents when the child is not living at home.

One exception is provided in a chapter by staff of The May Institute (Czyzewski, Christian, & Norris, 1984), in which they provide a model of parent training for the families of autistic children in residential placement. In this model, parent training staff traveled to the homes of each family to complete home training sessions. The parent educators also conducted courses on several topics (e.g., teaching adaptive skills, managing problem behaviors) at sites throughout their state. This model proved to be successful in training parents to apply basic behavior management procedures and training techniques as well as increasing the parents' involvement in the residential treatment programming their child received.

In a follow-up description of parent training at the same May Institute facility, Thibadeau, Murray, and Byrne (1992) also emphasized the importance of maintaining parent involvement through observation/participation visits to the residential program. Parents visited the program for approximately 2 hours every 3 months. Each visit enabled the parents to observe their child's home and school program and to work with their child while receiving feedback from senior staff. The authors also stressed the importance of regularly scheduled home visits and vacation periods for the children. At those times, the parent educators provided direct instruction on critical competencies. Home visits by the parent educators often were scheduled to coincide with particularly stressful events, enabling the parent trainers to model and provide feedback at the most relevant times. This level of involvement with parents may be necessary both to encourage continued active participation with their child's program and to assess continuously the child's readiness to transition home to live.

As students meet the criteria established for their transitional priorities and develop greater independence in all activities of daily life, planning should begin for their return to a less restrictive environment. Although ideally children with autism will return to live with their parents, a variety of child and family variables may impact on the final decision, as the following case illustrates.

∞

> David was 6 years old when he was admitted to The May Institute's residential treatment program in Chatham, Massachusetts (our most restrictive placement option). Unemployed and single, with two children, David's mother was referred to us by a state social service agen-

cy. At the time of his referral, she described David as extremely aggressive and noncompliant. She also indicated that he often ran or wandered away from home and that he was disruptive in public. She felt that she could no longer keep him at home because of these behavior problems as well as his limited expressive language and independent self-care skills.

Based on an interview with his mother and the results of other assessments, we developed six transitional goals. An individualized curriculum was developed with 15–25 objectives targeting the major skills areas (i.e., language, social, self-care, academic, play–leisure). Behavioral procedures were employed to teach new skills (Schreibman et al., 1990), with considerable one-to-one instruction initially, gradually increasing the amount of instruction provided within groups. At first, David resisted our efforts and exhibited increased levels of aggression, tantrums, and other avoidance behaviors. However, with the systematic and consistent use of behavioral treatment methods (Luce & Christian, 1981), his behavior improved enough that he could be transitioned into our community-based group home, a single-family dwelling located in a typical residential neighborhood. At the home, David's program focused on the development of the community and cooperative living skills needed to return to live with his mother. Within 16 months, David had successfully met all of the objectives identified at placement.

While intervention was occurring with David, his mother participated in our outreach parent training program. As part of her training, she attended formal classes to introduce her to basic strategies for managing his behavior problems and teaching him adaptive skills. She also received home-based training to enable her to apply what she had learned in the classes in actual situations with David. Although she eventually received over 50 hours of home and classroom instruction, she continued to have difficulties managing David's behavior at home. As a single parent, she also voiced concern for her ability to care for him financially and to supervise him while she worked.

Eventually the team, including David's mother, agreed that an alternative plan was necessary and appropriate. David was referred to our community transition program (specialized foster care). The foster couple had received extensive training and were highly qualified to continue specialized training for David, to coordinate the development of his school program, and to serve as case managers. Two years after placement, David continued to reside in his foster home and attend a local, public school program. Contact with his natural mother occurred one weekend a month and during six vacation periods scheduled throughout the year (over 50 days a year).

∞

This transition was possible because The May Institute provided a broad range of placement options and was not restricted to a single model of group residential services. In David's case, moving along a placement continuum from residential to specialized foster care provided a graduated approach to community placement. The foster placement allowed David to be part of a stable family environment while maintaining contact with his biological mother. It also buffered his mother from the day-to-day stressors associated with being a single parent of a child with autism. In the following case, the initial parent concerns and transitional goals were very similar to those for David; however, the placement outcomes were very different.

∞

At the time of his referral, 10-year-old Jason lived at home with his parents while attending a private, special-needs school. Jason's parents indicated that they could no longer keep him at home because of his tantrums and aggression. His behavior had become so difficult that they could no longer take him out in public. He also exhibited a significant sleep disorder, remaining awake many nights. His parents indicated that he was unable to play independently and that his attention to tasks and activities was poor.

With the high degree of structure offered by the residential program, Jason learned quickly, meeting all of his transitional priorities in less than a year. His parents participated in all aspects of the parent education program and were soon prepared to have Jason move back home. Because Jason had done so well in the residential program, his family strongly requested a day-school program with a similar approach to education and with a similar level of family support. Furthermore, now that he was an adolescent, they believed that he needed a full-year program with an emphasis on vocational training. The May Institute's day-school program near his home seemed most appropriate. The program (described earlier in this chapter) provided a 6-day school week and a school year without vacations.

Unfortunately, as the day for transition grew nearer, Jason's family expressed concern that they were not fully trained and requested a delay. A revised plan was developed and additional instruction occurred over the next 2 months. Eighteen months following admission to the residential program, Jason returned to his natural home. Approximately 3 years later, Jason remained in his home, continued to attend the same day-school program, and his parents continued to participate in parent training classes as they felt it was needed.

∞

We can only hypothesize that a combination of parent and child variables resulted in very different placement outcomes for David and Jason. Two obvious differences were the parent's marital status and extended family support. In David's case, his mother was never able to balance the duties of working, maintaining a home, and raising two children, one with a severe developmental disability. In Jason's case, the parents were supportive of each other, and they were able to call on a network of friends and family. Nevertheless, both transitions were possible, in large part, because of the Institute's continuum of services. Our specialized foster care program provided a family-based alternative to the more traditional community-based group home or institutional setting for David. Successful transition for Jason depended on ongoing parent training and a 12-month school program. In each case, the Institute's network of services was available to make the transition possible.

IMPORTANT PARAMETERS OF EFFECTIVE SERVICE PROGRAMMING

Setting Organizational Goals and Standards

In our experience, effective service programming for children with autism, as well as other developmental disabilities and behavior disorders, requires a systematic approach to organizational development. Development begins with a definition of the organization's mission, goals, and objectives and should provide a clear statement of the organization's commitment to identify and understand child and family needs, provide services specifically tailored to those needs, and thereby increase and maintain child and family self-sufficiency to the maximum extent possible. In other words, an effective organization understands that it is not enough to teach a new skill or reduce the frequency of some maladaptive behavior; behavior change must be generalized to and maintained in new settings (e.g., home and family, public school) so that the child is equipped to adjust to the demands of those settings with minimal dependence on service providers (Christian & Hannah, 1983; Christian, Hannah, & Glahn, 1984).

Staff Training and Supervision

Follow-through on this organizational commitment is best accomplished by using the most effective, progressive strategies in the training and supervision of staff who will be most responsible for day-to-day service delivery (i.e., teachers and residential staff) (Christian, 1983a, 1987). These strategies include (Thibadeau et al., 1982):

1. Developing standards for each staff member that specify tasks to be performed
2. Breaking down each task into a sequence of steps (the task-analyzed checklist) to facilitate training
3. Preparing supervisors to be on-the-job trainers

4. Using task-analyzed checklists for on-the-job, competency-based training of direct service staff by their supervisors
5. Using ongoing monitoring and performance appraisal to ensure that, once achieved, competent performance is maintained

Systematic Service Programming

This methodology enables an organization to develop "case management" competencies in its direct service staff. This is of particular importance to the residential treatment program if it is to become a springboard to less restrictive community-based living and educational settings. For example, a case manager, in consultation with other staff, is responsible for assessing the child's needs; setting service goals and objectives; planning, conducting, and evaluating the success of behavior change projects; documenting behavior change in the child's case record (e.g., graphical representations, progress notes); and assisting in transitional planning for the child's progress to ensure that his or her needs are being met and rights are being protected.

Behavior change projects addressing service plan objectives are the products or output of the case manager system. Each project includes the following (Christian & Reitz, 1986):

1. Baseline assessment of the child's behavior to indicate his or her treatment/educational needs as well as to serve as a basis for evaluating the change (or lack of change) in the child's behavior in response to service programming
2. Functional analysis to determine the environmental antecedents and consequences responsible for the baseline rate of the child's behavior
3. Determination of a goal for treatment with an explicit criterion for success
4. Utilization of an evaluation procedure sufficient to enable program staff to determine reliably if the treatment administered or service delivered actually had some effect on the child's behavior, and if change seen in the child's behavior or baseline condition was reliably a result of the treatment administered or service delivered
5. Implementation of a treatment procedure or delivery of a service using procedures of demonstrated effectiveness when used with other children with autism who present similar problems
6. Measurement, analysis, and documentation of the results of treatment or service delivery, with ongoing peer review provided by other members of the program staff and professional consultants
7. Maintenance and generalization of treatment results by continuing to monitor the child's progress and by enlisting the support of other program staff

Program Evaluation and Accountability

Although this kind of operational specificity and consistency promotes program accountability and quality control, ongoing program evaluation is also essential. In-house evaluation strategies include: staff observation and recording of client behavior; peer review (e.g., treatment team review, case record review); and client tracking systems. External evaluation is provided by individual consultants, professional advisory boards, and professional peer reviewers. Careful selection, planning, and performance contracting can help to ensure that the program gets maximum benefit from consultation and peer review (Christian & Romanczyk, 1986).

The cost effectiveness of a residential program can be determined by looking at the program's budget as a function of: 1) average length of stay for children in residence, and 2) number of children returning to residential placement following discharge (Christian, 1983a). Clearly, programs must be held accountable for the cost of services, and client transition and maintenance of therapeutic/educational benefit must be considered in any determination of cost-effectiveness.

IMPLICATIONS FOR FAMILIES, FUNDING AGENCIES, AND POLICY MAKERS

It has become increasingly clear that, by allocating resources to prevention and early intervention, we can significantly impact on the number of children placed out of home. Not only are children typically more responsive to intervention at an early age, but parents often have greater energy and motivation. Most parents welcome any information that will assist them in understanding their child's disability. They also want to acquire skills that will enable them to teach their child more effectively. By accomplishing this at an early point in the child's development, we may avoid the burnout that seems to occur in many families. It has been argued (Griest & Forehand, 1982) that, by helping parents to become better teachers, we may indirectly impact on a wider range of family adjustment issues as well. That is, parents may acquire improved skills in decision making, coping, and problem solving that impact beyond the expected child-centered objectives. In short, public policy should establish incentives for agencies to provide parent training aimed at developing effective teaching and behavior management skills. Fortunately, a myriad of behaviorally anchored parent training programs are now available to assist anyone who wants to accomplish this goal.

We also know that no single service will fit all families and their children with autism. Thus, a network of placement alternatives for school and home must be made available to parents. Services should be concerned with avoiding future problems by providing counseling, respite, support groups, and advocacy, as well as services to meet present crises (e.g., residential placement, parent training, out-of-home respite). To have significant impact on the problem of placement, we also need better trained teachers and respite providers, longer school days and school years, and more home- and community-based programs. Parents should be made aware of the range of services and properly counseled as to when these services should be accessed.

We also should develop policies that support the construction of a clear continuum of services throughout the lives of individuals with autism. Often professionals responsible for one part of the child's life span (e.g., under 3 years old) fail to communicate with another group at a different point in the child's life span (e.g., school age). Assignments to agencies often are made on the basis of the individual's age, the nature of the service, and the child's specific diagnoses, without a vision of how these services will be linked. Frequently the mission, approach, and amount of funding for each agency may differ radically, resulting in confusion for parents and gaps in the service continuum. Parents must have a single point of entry that minimizes confusion and allows an expedient response to the needs of families and children throughout the life span.

Public policy should support additional research in the area of family adjustment. We need to understand why some families are so resilient, even in the face of seemingly insurmountable odds. We also need to find better ways of helping parents to effectively reduce and tolerate the stress of living with a child with autism. One area of relevant study is to examine the importance of social supports among family members and to learn more about strengthening relationships that may enable parents to cope more effectively.

Finally, we need to insist that agencies serving children with autism meet fundamental standards of effective intervention. The point to be made here is that we know how to structure and operate an effective human services program, how to train and supervise staff, how to assess need and provide effective services, how to evaluate program effectiveness, how to transition individuals from residential programs to the community, and so forth. Over 20 years of research have established the professional standards; legislation and litigation since 1972 have established the legal and societal standards (Christian, 1983b; Christian et al., 1984; Fuoco & Christian, 1986). What remains is for parents and advocates to become more versed in the applicable standards; for human services managers and practitioners to become better trained with regard to these standards and how to comply with them; and for regulatory and funding agencies to insist that programs strictly adhere to these standards. Until this type of change occurs, individuals placed in residential programs will not routinely receive the types of services they require, and the goal of returning every individual to community, school, home, and family environments will not be achieved.

REFERENCES

American Psychiatric Association. (1987). *Diagnostic and statistical manual of mental disorders* (3rd ed., rev.). Washington, DC: Author.
American Psychiatric Association. (1994). *Diagnostic and statistical manual of mental disorders* (4th ed.). Washington, DC: Author.
Anderson, S.R. (1989). Autism. In B.L. Baker (Ed.), Parent training and developmental disabilities. *Monographs of the American Association on Mental Retardation, 13,* 137-153.
Anderson, S.R., Avery, D.L., DiPietro, E.K., Edwards, G.L., & Christian, W.P. (1987). Intensive home-based early intervention with autistic children. *Education and Treatment of Children, 10,* 352-366.
Anderson, S.R., Christian, W.P., & Luce, S.C. (1986). Transitonal residential programming for autistic individuals. *The Behavior Therapist, 9,* 205-211.
Anderson, S.R., Luce, S.C., Newsom, C.D., Gruber, B.K., & Kennedy-Butler, K. (1983, May). *Individualized treatment planning for autistic youth.* Paper presented at the meeting of the Association for Behavior Analysis, Milwaukee.
Anderson, S.R., & Schwartz, I.S. (1986). Transitional programming. In F.J. Fuoco & W.P. Christian (Eds.), *Behavior analysis and therapy in residential treatment environments* (pp. 76-100). New York: Van Nostrand Reinhold.
Baker, B.L. (1989). Parent training and developmental disabilities. *Monographs of the American Association on Mental Retardation, 13.*
Baker, B.L., Landen, S.J., & Kashima, K.J. (1991). Effects of parent training on families of children with mental retardation: Increased burden or generalized benefit. *American Journal on Mental Retardation, 96,* 127-136.
Bettelheim, B. (1967). *The empty fortress.* New York: The Free Press.
Bristol, M.M. (1984). Family resources and successful adaptation to autistic children. In E. Schopler & G.B. Mesibov (Eds.), *Issues in autism: The effects of autism on the family* (pp. 289-310). New York: Plenum Press.
Bronicki, G.J., & Turnbull, A.P. (1987). Family-professional interactions. In M.E. Snell (Ed.), *Systematic instruction of persons with severe handicaps* (pp. 9-35). Columbus, OH: Merrill Publishing Company.
Campbell, M., & Green, W.H. (1985). Pervasive developmental disorders of childhood. In H.I. Kaplan & B.J. Sadock (Eds.), *Comprehensive textbook of psychiatry* (4th ed., pp. 1672-1683). Baltimore: Williams & Wilkins.
Christian, W.P. (1983a). A case study in the programming and maintenance of institutional change. *Journal of Organizational Behavior Management, 5,* 99-153.
Christian, W.P. (1983b). Legal issues relevant to child development and behavior. In M.D. Levine, W.B. Carey, A.C. Crocker, & R.T. Gross (Eds.), *Developmental-behavioral pediatrics* (pp. 1175-1190). Philadelphia: W.B. Saunders Company.

Christian, W.P. (1987). Effective management of human service programs for individuals with developmental disabilities. In J. Mulick & R.F. Antonak (Eds.), *Transitions in mental retardation* (pp. 1–22). Norwood, NJ: Ablex Publishing Corporation.

Christian, W.P., & Hannah, G.T. (1983). *Effective management in human services.* Englewood Cliffs, NJ: Prentice-Hall.

Christian, W.P., Hannah, G.T., & Glahn, T.J. (Eds.). (1984). *Programming effective human services.* New York: Plenum Press.

Christian, W.P., & Reitz, A.L. (1986). Administration. In F.J. Fuoco & W.P. Christian (Eds.), *Behavior analysis and therapy in residential programs* (pp. 24–49). New York: Van Nostrand Reinhold.

Christian, W.P., & Romanczyk, R.G. (1986). Evaluation. In F.J. Fuoco & W.P. Christian (Eds.), *Behavior analysis and therapy in residential programs* (pp. 145–193). New York: Van Nostrand Reinhold.

Czyzewski, M.J., Christian, W.P., & Norris, M.B. (1984). Preparing the family for client transition: Outreach parent training. In W.P. Christian, G.T.Hannah, & T.J. Glahn (Eds.), *Programming effective human services* (pp. 177–202). New York: Plenum Press.

DeMyer, M.K., & Goldberg, P. (1983). Family needs of the autistic adolescent. In E. Schopler & G.B. Mesibov (Eds.), *Autism in adolescents and adults* (pp. 225–250). New York: Plenum Press.

Dunlap, G., & Robbins, F.R. (1991). Current perspectives in service delivery for young children with autism. *Comprehensive Mental Health Care, 1,* 177–194.

Education for All Handicapped Children Act of 1975, PL 94-142. (August 23, 1977). Title 20, U.S.C. 1401 et seq: *U.S. Statutes at Large, 89,* 773–796.

Education of the Handicapped Act Amendments of 1986, PL 99-457. (October 8, 1986). Title 20, U.S.C. 1400 et seq: *U.S. Statutes at Large, 100,* 1145–1177.

Fenski, E.C., Zalenski, S., Krantz, P.J., & McClannahan, L.E. (1985). Age at intervention and treatment outcome for autistic children in a comprehensive intervention program. *Analysis and Intervention in Developmental Disabilities, 5,* 49–58.

Folstein, S.E., & Priven, J. (1991). The etiology of autism: Genetic influences. *Pediatrics, 87,* 767–773.

Fox, T.J., & Williams, W. (1991). *Implementing best practices for all students in their local school.* Burlington, VT: Center for Developmental Disabilities.

Fuoco, F.J., & Christian, W.P. (Eds.). (1986). *Behavior analysis and therapy in residential programs.* New York: Van Nostrand Reinhold.

Griest, D.L., & Forehand, R. (1982). How can I get any parent training done with all these other problems going on?: The role of family variables in child behavior therapy. *Child and Family Behavior Therapy, 4,* 73–80.

Grossman, H.J. (Ed.). (1983). *Classification in mental retardation.* Washington, DC: American Association of Mental Deficiency.

Harris, S.L. (1983). *Families of the developmentally disabled: A guide to behavioral intervention.* New York: Pergamon Press.

Harris, S.L. (1988). Family assessment in autism. In E. Schopler & G.B. Mesibov (Eds.), *Diagnosis and assessment in autism* (pp. 199–210). New York: Plenum Press.

Harris, S.L., & Powers, M. (1984). Behavior therapists look at the impact of the family system. In E. Schopler & G.B. Mesibov (Eds.), *Issues in autism: The effects of autism on the family* (pp. 289–310). New York: Plenum Press.

Holroyd, J. & McArthur, D. (1976). Mental retardation and stress on the parents: A contrast between Down's syndrome and childhood autism. *American Journal of Mental Deficiency, 80,* 431–436.

Horner, R.H., Dunlap, G., & Koegel, R.L. (Eds.). (1988). *Generalization and maintenance: Life-style changes in applied settings.* Baltimore: Paul H. Brookes Publishing Co.

Individuals with Disabilities Education Act of 1990 (IDEA), PL 101-476. (October 30, 1990). Title 20, U.S.C. 1400 et seq: *U.S. Statutes at Large, 104,* 1103–1151.

Johnson-Martin, N.M. (1990). Early intervention as a preventive strategy. In S.M. Pueschel & J.A. Mulick (Eds.), *Prevention of developmental disabilities* (pp. 241–260). Baltimore: Paul H. Brooks Publishing Co.

Koegel, R.L., Schreibman, L., Loos, L.M., Dirlich-Wilhelm, H., Dunlap, G., Robbins, F.R., & Plienis, A.J. (1992). Consistent stress profiles in mothers of children with autism. *Journal of Autism and Developmental Disorders, 22,* 205–216.

Lovaas, O.I. (1987). Behavioral treatment and normal educational and intellectual functioning in young autistic children. *Journal of Consulting and Clinical Psychology, 55,* 3–9.

Lovaas, O.I., Koegel, R., Simmons, J.Q., & Long, J.S. (1973). Some generalization and follow-up measures on autistic children in behavior therapy. *Journal of Applied Behavior Analysis, 6,* 131–166.

Lovaas, O.I., Smith, T., & McEachin, J. (1989). Clarifying comments on the Young Autism Study: Reply to Schopler, Short, and Mesibov. *Journal of Consulting and Clinical Psychology, 57,* 165–167.

Luce, S.C. (1986). Residential behavior therapy with autistic children and adolescents. In F.J. Fuoco & W.P. Christian (Eds.), *Behavior analysis and therapy in residential treatment environments* (pp. 280–313). New York: Van Nostrand Reinhold.

Luce, S.C. & Christian, W.P. (1981). *How to reduce autistic and severely maladaptive behavior.* Austin, TX: PRO-ED.

Luce, S.C., Christian, W.P., Anderson, S.R., Troy, P.J., & Larsson, E.V. (1992). Development of a continuum of services for children and adults with autism and other severe behavior disorders. *Research in Developmental Disabilities, 13,* 9–25.

Luckasson, R., Coulter, D.L., Polloway, E.A., Reiss, S., Schalock, R.L., Snell, M.E., Spitalnik, D.M., & Stark, J.A. (1992). *Mental retardation: Definition, classification, and systems of supports.* Washington, DC: American Association on Mental Retardation.

McEachen, J.J., Smith, T., & Lovaas, O.I. (1993). Long-term outcome for children with autism who received early intensive behavioral treatment. *American Journal on Mental Retardation, 97,* 359–372.

Ornitz, E.M. (1985). Neurophysiology of infantile autism. *Journal of the American Academy of Child Psychiatry, 24,* 251–262.

Patterson, G.R., & Gullion, M.E. (1976). *Living with children: New methods for parents and teachers.* Champaign, IL: Research Press.

Rapin, I. (1991). Autistic children: Diagnosis and clinical features. *Pediatrics, 87,* 751–760.

Rousey, A., Blacher, B., & Hanneman, R. (1990). Predictors of out-of-home placement of children with severe handicaps: A cross-sectional analysis. *American Journal on Mental Retardation, 94,* 522–531.

Schreibman, L., & Britten, K.R. (1984). Training parents as therapists for autistic children: Rationale, techniques, and results. In W.P. Christian, G.T. Hannah, & T.J. Glahn (Eds.), *Programming effective human services* (pp. 295–314). New York: Plenum Press.

Schreibman, L., Koegel, R.L., Charlop, M.H., & Egel, A.L. (1990). Infantile autism. In A.S. Tellack, M. Hersen, & A.E. Kazdin (Eds.), *International handbook of behavior modification and therapy* (2nd ed., pp. 793–789). New York: Plenum Publishing Corporation.

Sherman, B.R. (1988). Predictors of the decision to place developmentally disabled family members in residential care. *American Journal on Mental Retardation, 92,* 344–351.

Stokes, T.F., & Baer, D.M. (1977). An implicit technology of generalization. *Journal of Applied Behavior Analysis, 10,* 349–367.

Thibadeau, S.F., Butler, K.K., Gruber, B.K., Luce, S.C., Newsom, C.D., Anderson, S.R., & Christian, W.P. (1982). *Competency-based orientation and training of human service personnel.* Paper presented at the Annual Convention of the Association for the Advancement of Behavior Therapy, Los Angeles.

Thibadeau, S.F., Murray, M., & Byrne, S. (1992, May). *Planned involvement of families in treatment programs and transitions: The May Institute's residential program.* Paper presented at the Annual Meeting of the American Association on Mental Retardation, New Orleans.

Turnbull, A.P., & Turnbull, H.R. (1982). Parent involvement in the education of handicapped children: A critique. *Mental Retardation, 20,* 115–122.

Turnbull, A.P., & Turnbull, H.R. (1990). *Families, professionals and exceptionality: A special partnership.* Columbus: Merrill Publishing Company.

10

Residential Treatment for Children with Dual Diagnoses of Mental Retardation and Mental Disorder

Steven I. Pfeiffer and Bruce L. Baker

This book considers the many reasons and ways that modern-day Dorothys find themselves uprooted from home. Mental retardation in a child presents severe challenges to the family system and an ever-present possibility that he or she will need to live elsewhere (Blacher, chap. 8, this volume). Mental disorder in a child creates family turmoil and a search for treatment, perhaps in a residential setting. If Dorothy were to have both mental retardation and a mental disorder, however, it is especially likely that her room at home would be empty. She would have landed in some strange and unaccommodating place, a service delivery Oz where she seems an oddity and the road back home is uncharted.

Our concern here is with children with dual diagnoses of mental retardation and a mental disorder. These children are among the most underserved and least understood of any group with disabilities (Campbell & Malone, 1991; Ellis, 1988; Jacobson & Ackerman, 1989; Reiss, Levitan, & McNally, 1982). Dual diagnosis presents unique diagnostic and treatment challenges and leaves youngsters at particular risk for unfavorable long-term life outcomes. Placement is more likely when youngsters with mental retardation have serious maladaptive behaviors that challenge the family's capacity to manage the child or adolescent effectively (Borthwick-Duffy & Eyman, 1990; Bromley & Blacher, 1991; Bruininks, Hill, & Morreau, 1988). Beyond placement, serious maladaptive behavior among persons with mental retardation predicts failure in community living arrangements, frequent moves, social isolation and rejection, and reduced employment prospects (Borthwick-Duffy & Eyman, 1990; Borthwick-Duffy, Widaman, Little, & Eyman, 1992; Bromley & Blacher, 1991; Bruininks et al., 1988; Reid, 1980).

We consider here the primary emphases in the literature on dual diagnosis—issues of diagnosis, epidemiology, and expression of mental disorder in mental retardation—in an attempt to understand who these children with dual diagnoses are. From there, we explore the challenges these children present to their families and the service delivery (non)system that awaits them. Then, in turn, we examine approaches directed toward keeping the child at home, treating the child in residential placement, and maintaining family involvement with the child wherever he or she might be living.

WHO ARE DUALLY DIAGNOSED CHILDREN?

∞

Juanita's childhood seemed happy enough, despite her mild to moderate mental retardation. The turmoils of adolescence, however, exceeded her immature coping skills and worsened her already low self-esteem. A breakup with her boyfriend, an agitated depression, slitting her wrist with a knife, and residential psychiatric placement followed in quick succession.

∞

Daniel had been a handful even as a young child. His family struggled to manage disruptive behavior in this boy with severe retardation and no speech. Now 16 years old and weighing 175 pounds, Daniel's explosive outbursts against other people and property had become destructive and frightening to his family and neighbors. The time had finally come to think seriously about residential placement.

∞

Definition

The term *dual diagnosis* embraces all levels of mental retardation (mild, moderate, severe, or profound), accompanied by one or more mental disorders (American Psychiatric Association, 1994).[1] Even though some authorities speak of "dual diagnosis" as if it were a diagnosis in and of itself (Reiss, 1993), it is obvious that the term refers to a number of quite different patterns of difficulties. Juanita and Daniel have in common some degree of mental retardation and evidence of mental disorder, but the similarities soon end.

The most challenging issue in defining dual diagnosis generally, as well as in diagnosing an individual case, is deciding what constitutes a co-morbid mental disorder rather than just problem behaviors associated with the mental retardation. Persons with mental retardation often exhibit a variety of maladaptive behaviors, such as stereotypies, self-injurious behavior, and poor anger management. The question is whether these behaviors are symptoms of an underlying psychiatric disorder rather than artifacts of the cognitive and adaptive limitations of mental retardation.

When it is clear that a person can be diagnosed with both mental retardation and mental disorder, a further difficulty arises if one attempts to distinguish between the primary and secondary diagnosis. There is often no rational basis for making this distinction. Moreover, because services usually are directed only to the primary disorder, the problem considered secondary may well go untreated (Reiss, 1993). For

---

[1]The American Psychiatric Association has a multiaxial classification system (American Psychiatric Association, 1994). Mental disorders are diagnosed on Axis I. Mental retardation, specific developmental disorders (e.g., developmental reading disorder), and pervasive developmental disorder (or autism) are diagnosed on Axis II. The term *dual diagnosis* has multiple meanings in the literature. In psychiatry it refers to two Axis I diagnoses, one of which is substance abuse. In the mental retardation field, and as we use it in this chapter, dual diagnosis refers to mental retardation (an Axis II diagnosis) and any Axis I mental disorder. Some writers also include under dual diagnosis the person with mental retardation and pervasive developmental disorder or autism, both Axis II diagnoses. In this book, these children are considered in Chapter 9.

While the American Psychiatric Association continues to classify mental retardation by the familiar categories of mild, moderate, severe, and profound, readers should be aware of a new definition from the American Association on Mental Retardation. The AAMR definition eliminates a deficit-oriented categorized approach in favor of an emphasis on four assumptions:
1. Valid assessment considers *cultural and linguistic diversity* as well as differences in communication and behavioral styles;
2. The existence of limitations in adaptive skills occurs within the *context of community environments* typical of the individual's age peers and is indexed to the person's individualized needs for support;
3. Specific adaptive *limitations often coexist with strengths* in other adaptive skills or other personal capabilities; and
4. With appropriate supports over a sustained period, the *life functioning* of the person with mental retardation *will generally improve* (American Association on Mental Retardation, 1992).

these reasons, the concept of dual diagnosis seems preferable, with its implication that both disorders require attention.

Diagnosis

The actual process of diagnosing mental disorder in a person with mental retardation is fraught with its own predicaments. One diagnostic problem has been termed *diagnostic overshadowing* (Reiss, Levitan, & Szyszko, 1982). Reiss and his colleagues found that the salience of the mental retardation often decreases the likelihood that the diagnostician will attend to accompanying abnormal behavior. In several studies, professionals were presented with case vignettes describing a person with a mental disorder (e.g., alcoholism, schizophrenia). When information was included that the person was mentally retarded, the mental disorder was rated as less serious than when this information was not included. Hence, the presence of the cognitive and adaptive limitations of the person often leads professionals to overlook or minimize the psychiatric problems or attribute them to intellectual impairment. As we shall see, diagnostic overshadowing is also reflected at a broader level in the unavailability of services for persons with dual diagnosis.

Psychological assessment also is hampered by a host of developmental factors (Borthwick-Duffy & Eyman, 1990; Matson & Barrett, 1982). The cognitive limitations of youngsters with mental retardation often make it difficult for them to express their feelings and inner experience in anything but concrete terms. This forces the clinician to rely heavily on diagnostic information gleaned from observing a youngster and from rating scales completed by others who have observed him or her. In Daniel's case, the diagnostician had to rely on observed behavior to infer an underlying mental disorder (explosive personality disorder), and others might question this inference. Even in children and adolescents with less severe mental retardation, such as Juanita, verbally reported perceptions and inner distress are not as accessible in the diagnostic process as they would be if retardation were not present. Relatedly, diagnostic questions that exceed the youngster's comprehension often lead to frustration, anxiety, withdrawal, and inattentiveness—possibly misinterpreted by the interviewer as a sign of psychopathology rather than as an adaptive response to a highly frustrating experience.

Prevalence, Expression, and Severity

It must be clear from the above definitional and diagnostic vagaries that exact prevalence rates for dual diagnosis have not been determined (Campbell & Malone, 1991; Matson & Frame, 1986; Nezu, Nezu, & Gill-Weiss, 1992). We do know, however, that the co-morbidity of mental retardation and psychiatric disorders is substantial. Estimates range from as low as 10%–12% (Borthwick-Duffy & Eyman, 1990; Bruininks et al., 1988) to 67% (Bregman, 1991; Campbell & Malone, 1991) and higher. Most investigators report prevalence rates four to five times those found in the normal population (Jacobson, 1982; Matson, 1984; Matson & Frame, 1986; Menolascino & Fleischer, 1991; Russell & Forness, 1985). A recent review of these studies sets an actual rate of incidence of mental illness among persons with mental retardation at 20%–35% (Nezu et al., 1992).

The full range of mental disorders have been diagnosed in persons with mental retardation. Menolascino and his colleagues (Eaton & Menolascino, 1982; Menolascino, 1988; Menolascino & Fleischer, 1991) carefully studied the types and frequency of psychiatric disorders. Among their many findings is the conclusion that persons with mental retardation manifest all of the psychoses, neuroses, personality disorders, behavior disorders, and adjustment reaction disorders found in the population without retardation.

The relative frequencies of mental disorder, however, are not the same as in persons without mental retardation. Myers (1987) studied a group of 113 adolescents (ages 10–21) with mental retardation who were referred for psychiatric evaluation to the primary child development center in Rhode Island. Prominent psychiatric problems included conduct disorder and marked social withdrawal. Drug and alcohol abuse, affective disorders, and neurotic symptoms occurred with relative infrequency. As Myers noted, however, there may have been a sampling bias wherein adolescents with disruptive behavior were more likely to be referred than those with subjective distress.

Differences in the prevalence of disorders may in part represent the accessibility of information to the diagnostician that we noted above. Szymanski (1988) posited that the reason for the underdiagnosis of depression in persons with mental retardation is that clinicians must rely on observed behavior and vegetative signs, because verbalizations of dysphoric mood and low self-image are not easily accessed. He further noted that psychotic and organic disorders are grossly overdiagnosed in persons with mental retardation. These diagnoses may rely on strange behavior such as self-stimulation and eating inedible objects—behaviors that often are associated directly with the cognitive impairment of mental retardation and not necessarily indicative of an underlying psychotic process. The diagnosis of conduct disorder may be relatively accurate, however, in that the criteria are observable.

Differences in prevalence also may represent actual differences in the expression of mental disorders. In persons with mild mental retardation, symptom expression may not differ appreciatively from that in persons without retardation. In individuals with more severe retardation, however, the expression of a psychiatric disorder such as depression, schizophrenia, or conduct disorder may differ. Pawlarcyzk and Beckwith (1987) found, for example, that depressed adults with mild to moderate mental retardation displayed dysphoric mood and feelings of worthlessness similar to those of depressed persons without mental retardation. However, these were less recognizable in adults with more severe mental retardation who were considered to be depressed, among whom common symptoms were sleep disturbance, psychomotor agitation, and appetite disturbance.

In any event, epidemiological studies suggest that persons with more severe retardation are more likely to develop a psychiatric disorder (Eaton & Menolascino, 1982; Matson & Frame, 1986; Pawlarcyzk & Beckwith, 1987). This is not unexpected given their increased vulnerability; they are more likely to have neurological impairment, restricted social opportunities, overprotective living situations, social stigma and rejection, and a limited ability to handle interpersonal situations effectively.

Who, then, are these children and adolescents with dual diagnoses? They are youngsters whose mental retardation placed them at heightened risk for behavioral and emotional difficulties and who present with a diagnosable mental disorder. Diagnosis is impeded, however, by professionals' tendency to overlook the mental problem, by the children's limitations in communicating their experiences, and by the way the disorder expresses itself differently with more severe retardation. The confusion of diagnosticians, however, is nothing compared to the distress of the child's family members.

CHALLENGES TO THE FAMILY

There is much evidence that initially well-functioning families who raise a child with mental retardation experience heightened stress and an ongoing challenge to their coping abilities that may well lead to placement (see Blacher, chap. 8, this volume). Whereas some parents cope remarkably well, it is not uncommon to find those who come to be preoccupied with this child; are consumed by feelings of anger, worry, or depression; experience little sense of parental competence; encounter increasing marital tension and distress—the list goes on. Although researchers have not studied how families cope with children with dual diagnoses, it seems reasonable that the mental disorder further heightens stress and brings with it a host of new challenges to even the most stable family.

In other circumstances, the child with mental retardation and mental disorder may be born into an existing dysfunctional family system. The special needs of the child, in this instance, can exacerbate an already problematic family situation and create, at times, a situation the parents experience as intolerable. Quite often the child will need placement in a residential or inpatient setting to provide an opportunity to help both the youngster and the family stabilize and learn new coping skills to reduce the level of stress and conflict that led to the placement, as well as to identify resources within the community to begin reconstructive family intervention.

Among the most challenging maladaptive behaviors that lead to residential placement are property destruction, physical aggression, inappropriate sexual behavior, self-abusive acts, suicidal threats, and chronic noncompliance. The precipitators of psychological problems are conceptualized by Levitas and Gilson (1989) as a series of predictable crises in the lives of people who are retarded (see Table 1). Life changes that are apt to lead to or exacerbate psychopathology include, for example, entering school, being surpassed in abilities by a younger sibling, or reaching puberty. Where does the family struggling with the child's cognitive limitations and emotional upheavals turn for help?

Table 1. Predictable crises in the lives of persons with mental retardation

When the diagnosis of retardation is finalized or realized
Birth of siblings
Starting school
Puberty and adolescence
Sex and dating
Being surpassed by younger siblings
Emancipation of siblings
End of education
Out-of-home placement and residential moves
Staff/client relationships
Aging, illness, and death of parents
Death of peers, loss of friends
Psychiatric illness

From Levitas, A., & Gilson, S. F. (1989). Psychodynamic psychotherapy with mildly and moderately retarded patients. In R. J. Fletcher & F. A. Menolascino (Eds.), *Mental retardation and mental illness: Assessment, treatment, and service for the dually diagnosed* (pp. 71–109). Lexington, MA: Lexington Books; reprinted by permission.

SOCIAL POLICY AND SERVICES

"Although our nation has developed a social policy for the mentally ill and another for the mentally retarded, there is no provision for community-based living for the dually diagnosed. . . . This is a social policy by omission" (Fletcher & Menolascino, 1989, p. 208). Robert Fletcher, founder and executive director of the National Association for the Dually Diagnosed, goes on to note that the social policy of de-institutionalization highlighted the plight of persons with dual diagnoses, many of whom had been kept in the back wards of institutions for persons with mental retardation or, less frequently, psychiatric hospitals.

The provision of integrated services that can speak effectively to both mental retardation and mental disorder is difficult within the existing structure of services. In most states there are separate departments administering mental retardation and mental health services. Mental retardation services, with staff oriented toward skill training, are often ill-suited to the disruption to routine caused by a person with an acute psychiatric disorder. Mental health services, with staff oriented to therapy, are equally ill-suited to the person whose intellectual limitations are perceived as posing difficulties for the therapist and, in any event, imply long-term intervention. Both departments, operating within budget constraints, have an economic disincentive for serving the patient with dual diagnoses whose total service plan is bound to be a costly one.

The schism is furthered by the structure of federal research funding. The National Institute of Mental Health supports research in mental health while the National Institute of Child Health and Human Development and the National Institute of Disability and Rehabilitation Research support research in mental retardation. Research on dual diagnosis is out of the mainstream of both agencies.

As a consequence of these schisms, few professionals are proficient in providing mental health services to people with mental retardation (Marcos, Gil, & Vazquez, 1986; Pfeiffer, 1992). Moreover, treatment facilities for children who have dual diagnoses are difficult to find. Szymanski (1987) reported a survey of 18 inpatient psychiatric services in a metropolitan area, wherein 17 "refused outright to hospitalize a severely retarded and agitated (but not dangerous) young woman. Reasons given included lack of experience with patients who have mental retardation and difficulty in working with nonverbal persons" (p. 217). One result of the sparsity of services is that children with dual diagnoses are more likely to be placed in large residential facilities, often quite far from the family home.

Frank Menolascino, long an advocate for persons with dual diagnoses, envisioned the creation of services to support these persons within the mainstream of family and community life. He argued that community-based programs, such as classrooms, workshops, or group homes, should not have policies that exclude disruptive children from their services. Moreover, such programs should work with specialized services such as community mental health centers and acute psychiatric care hospitals, which could provide backup in crisis situations, reducing the likelihood of long-term institutionalization. As we examine later, such local services could help to prevent placement. Failing that, there would be reduced risk of permanent placement and of the family detachment that often accompanies placement in distant facilities.

PREVENTING PLACEMENT

If treatment and support for the family and the child with dual diagnoses were to be located in the home community, what would it look like? Treatment would, of course, aim to replace the child's maladaptive and antisocial behaviors with a set of more age-appropriate, prosocial, and adaptive skills. At the same time, however, parents, and perhaps siblings, would be involved as partners in the treatment program. The particular approach to families would depend on the extent to which the family is well adjusted and can work in partnership with professionals to help the target child—or the family is dysfunctional and must be itself the focus of therapeutic intervention.

Parent Training

A blanket *preventive approach* is to enhance parenting skills in any family raising a young child with mental retardation. One could hypothesize that, if parents learn successful ways to teach their children and to manage problem behaviors, the likelihood will be reduced that such behaviors will ultimately lead to psychiatric disorder and to the need for inpatient or residential treatment.

Parent training programs are available in many early intervention services and have been widely studied (Baker, 1989). Although these programs vary considerably in their format and focus, they typically follow a curriculum based on principles of behavior modification. The focus of outcome has been primarily on the child's acquisition of skills or the reduction of specific problem behaviors. However, we do not have long-term follow-up studies that utilize psychiatric criteria to determine whether such programs actually reduce the prevalence of subsequent mental disorder, although this would be an important area for further study.

Moreover, we do not know if parent training programs increase the family's ability to cope with problems enough so that placement is avoided or delayed. We can imagine from a convergence of evidence, however, that this often may be the case. One thread of evidence is the repeated finding that problem behaviors are a primary precipitator of placement (Blacher, chap. 8, this volume), coupled with clear evidence that parent training programs lead to a reduction in problem behavior (Baker, 1989). Another thread is the finding that families place their children when the buildup of stress becomes intolerable (Blacher & Baker, 1994; Sherman, 1988), coupled with findings that stress and other indicators of parental maladjustment decrease following participation in parent training (Baker, Landen, & Kashima, 1991). A related thread is the finding that parents who ultimately place report that their attachment to the child was the primary factor delaying placement (Bromley & Blacher, 1991), coupled with the positive effects of early intervention programs on the mother–child relationship. Parental bonding with the infant seems to be increased, in part as the parent comes to understand and adapt to behaviors that might seem like rejection (e.g., stiffening when lifted, erratic sleep and feeding cycles).

A *high-risk intervention approach* is to target families that already have children and adolescents with dual diagnoses, in order to deter placement. One such specially designed family intervention is the Home Intervention Program (HIP) (Allin, 1988). The program was started in 1978 with initial funding from the Virginia Department of Mental Health and Mental Retardation. Adopting a consultation model, the goal of the HIP is to enhance parenting skills by providing direct instruction, modeling, and graduated practice in the youngster's natural environment—the home. Teams of male and female therapists visit the home, observe the client in his or her natural environment, develop a treatment plan in conjunction with the parents, and teach parents by coaching and demonstration. The program has been successful in working with depression, self-abusive behavior, obsessive compulsive behavior, aggression, suicidal threats, and inappropriate sexual acting out—those behaviors that are serious impediments to community living and most often lead to placement.

Family Therapy

Some parents of youngsters with dual diagnoses may be too dysfunctional to benefit from the services provided in a family-oriented psychoeducational program like HIP. For example, one or both parents may be contributing to the psychiatric symptoms of the child or adolescent, or the youngster's improvement may lead to symptoms or deterioration in another family member (Leahey & Wright, 1985).

Family therapy is often very helpful in enhancing family functioning in areas that may be awry in dysfunctional families: cohesiveness, openness to diverse opinions, clear and spontaneous communication, ability to work together in joint problem solving, clarity of family roles and rules, and warmth and optimism of the family mood. The two overarching goals are to help the family move toward a more effective, healthy, and satisfying lifestyle and to encourage new patterns of interaction within the family that support the launching of the adolescent with dual diagnoses toward more adaptive and independent functioning. Family therapy is a powerful intervention because it helps families appreciate that their difficulties are not unique and that they are not alone in their pain. Family therapy is also potent because it "reframes" or changes the meaning of family attitudes, beliefs, and recurrent transactions into a less malignant and more positive view. Behavioral family therapy can build from this foundation to include training in strategies of child behavior management.

If, despite prevention efforts, the child enters residential treatment, the intervention is of necessity focused more on the child. The ultimate aim is to facilitate noninstitutional living—ideally at home.

TREATING CHILDREN IN RESIDENTIAL PLACEMENT

Although the number of child inpatient hospitalizations for psychiatric treatment has actually increased nationally over the past decade (Kiesler, 1993), children with mental retardation and no accompanying mental disorder are less likely to be placed than in the past. The number of children in state institutions for persons with mental retardation dropped dramatically from 92,000 in 1965 to only 9,400 in 1989. Moreover, the number of children with mental retardation living in any out-of-home setting also dropped 50%, from 91,000 in 1977 to 46,000 in 1988 (Amado, Lakin, & Menke, 1990). Legal guarantees of school services, supports for families, and community-based alternative programs have somewhat diminished the need for placement. An antiplacement stance in professional circles, together with unavailability of funding, has been a further pressure on families to keep children at home longer.

Children with mild or even moderate retardation are not likely to be accepted for residential placement unless there are significant additional complications, such as mental disorder. They then typically are placed in a psychiatric facility. Children with severe mental retardation, as well, are increasingly likely to present with challenging behaviors such as aggression, self-stimulation, and autistic withdrawal. This is to say that our observations suggest that residential treatment of children and adolescents with mental retardation is becoming almost synonymous with treatment of dual diagnoses.

Treatment goals must be shaped within a long-term transition plan. Will children with dual diagnoses who are in residential placement be reunited with their families? Surprisingly, the answer is "not usually." For any number of reasons, some adolescents with mental retardation and mental disorders do not have families to whom to return (Allen & Pfeiffer, 1991; Itzkowitz, 1985). Moreover, in some instances their highly provocative behavior makes it difficult to find them foster placements, intensifying their low self-esteem, frustration, and tendency to act out. Allen and Pfeiffer (1991) examined the entire population of adolescents who were discharged over a 1-year period from 11 residential treatment facilities that are part of a nationwide nonprofit health care organization. The sample included a large number of youths with dual diagnoses. Only 31% of discharged adolescents returned to live with their parents with the expectation that this living arrangement would continue. Hence a sizable number of adolescents with mental retardation and psychiatric disorders require not only treatment for their mental disorder but also opportunities to learn independent living skills and social skills. Failure to learn these during adolescence can exacerbate or lead to later psychiatric problems, such as social isolation and depression (Allen & Pfeiffer, 1991; Crystal, 1986).

In some cases a clear psychiatric disorder is diagnosed and treatment is not very different from treatment for the same disorder in persons without mental retardation (e.g., major depression, bipolar disorder, schizophrenia) (Menolascino & Fleisher, 1991). Treatment with psychoactive drugs, although beyond our scope here, is an example of therapy in which effectiveness appears to be similar whether or not the mental disorder is accompanied by retardation (Matson & Frame, 1986). A wide range of psychotherapeutic interventions have been attempted with children who are dually diagnosed (Bregman, 1991; Fletcher & Menolascino, 1989; Matson & Frame, 1986; Menolascino, 1989; Menolascino & Fleischer, 1991; Ratey, 1991). Behavior therapies have effectively reduced problem behaviors across the range of mental retardation, whereas most reports of favorable outcome with verbal psychotherapies have involved persons with mild or sometimes moderate retardation (Reiss et al., 1982). We focus here on psychotherapy and group therapy, and primarily on their relationship-building feature, because close and trusting interpersonal relationships are often lacking and these may be the cornerstone for further effective intervention.

Psychotherapy

Levitas and Gilson (1989) noted that a person with retardation's first placement can be the result of a plan, long in the making, or a crisis. In either case, but especially in the latter:

> ... the chances are the placement has or had more to do with the needs of the family, the unavailability of in-home intervention or appropriate educational facilities, or some problem behavior, rather than with the wishes of the retarded person. ... Movements from home to the facility, facility to facility, and facility back to home have less to do with treatment than with agency, facility, or institutional imperatives. (Levitas & Gilson, 1989, p. 90)

The mental health worker must be highly cognizant of how a person's history of "services" may have contributed to the emotional problems.

The following case illustrates the type of circumstances that precede entry into psychotherapy in a residential setting. Therapy above all must provide an opportunity for bonding with another person and for empowerment.

∞

> Nicole was an 11-year-old girl referred to residential treatment because of mild mental retardation accompanied by self-destructive and explosive behavior at home. Nicole's family was highly dysfunctional and unable to manage her behavior. Her parents were unresponsive and disinterested in her, and had evidenced great difficulty caring for Nicole since she was a toddler. Her mother was described as having borderline mental retardation and was emotionally unstable, exceedingly passive, and sexually promiscuous. Her father was reported to have abused drugs and to have a history of antisocial behavior, marked by incarceration since Nicole was 4 years old.
>
> Nicole's parents' relationship was marked by little emotional spontaneity, extreme rigidity, and a fear of closeness. Her father was a powerful, fearful, and controlling figure and her mother childlike in her passivity and dependence. According to early records, a social worker had described Nicole's parents as distrustful, angry, and lacking in warmth. The parents, in turn, had described Nicole as an unresponsive, disinterested baby; Nicole was equally unhappy whether being held, rocked, or left in the crib or playpen. They were disappointed and frustrated that their daughter did not seem to develop a closeness either to them or their other children.
>
> School records recounted a developmental history marked by early speech and language delays, short attention span, hyperactivity, and social immaturity. Nicole was first identified as requiring special education in kindergarten, because of disinterest in school and aggressive and confrontational behavior with other students. Psychological testing at age 8 highlighted intellectual and adaptive functioning within the mild range of mental retardation, and significant behavioral diffi-

culties: temper tantrums, annoying and provoking others, failure to control her anger, argumentativeness, depression and discouragement, remaining alone and aloof, showing little interest in adult approval or praise, and withdrawing from or avoiding social contacts.

Subsequently, when Nicole arrived at the residential treatment center, she was perceived by both staff and peers as hostile, withdrawn, and distrustful. In transition planning, it seems unlikely that Nicole would be reunified with her family. A foster placement would not seem promising either, unless Nicole grew in her capacity to trust others.

∞

A useful framework for conceptualizing treatment is attachment theory (Bowlby, 1988), and in particular the notion of an internal working model—the child's expectations of how others will behave and his or her sense of self as deserving those behaviors. Nicole's case illustrates how expectations of negative behavior from others learned within a dysfunctional family can become self-fulfilling. Because Nicole had experienced considerable rejection since infancy, she remained emotionally distant. Nicole's behavior was indicative of an insecurely attached child whose early attachment needs were chronically ignored by her parents during her first years of life. In response to this early emotional neglect, and in conjunction with her intellectual limitations, Nicole developed an internal working model of others as unresponsive and herself as unworthy of affection. To cope with these painful expectations, Nicole adopted an "avoidant" attachment style—in order to avoid further rejection, she withdrew from her environment and literally gave up trying to interest the persons around her. Her confrontational and unfriendly behavior can be viewed as an elaboration of her avoidant style begun in infancy, based on her assumption that others will be unresponsive to her efforts to engage them. On entering treatment, Nicole again acted on the basis of her negative expectations and rebuffed her peers and staff, setting herself up to be rejected again but for the intervention of her therapist.

It is important to emphasize that internal models, although initially developed in infancy and stable over time, are not unchangeable and can be revised in childhood or adolescence. Three avenues through which revisions to internal working models of attachment can occur are: 1) changes in the early attachment relationship itself; 2) a series of other relationships each of which potentially disconfirms the earlier, dysfunctional model; and 3) one especially intense emotional attachment that disconfirms the earlier model (Ricks, 1985). While family therapy speaks to the first of these avenues, residential and inpatient treatment can be applied to the second and third, each of which relies on new attachments to disconfirm the early, maladaptive learning that occurred in the dysfunctional family.

∞

> Nicole eventually developed a close relationship with her primary therapist, who saw her in both individual and group counseling. The closeness was considered a major breakthrough for Nicole. The therapist was able, through the special relationship that she developed with Nicole, to support her and encourage her to address her problems in the residence and in the school program more adaptively.
>
> After several months of treatment, Nicole began to make significant progress. She rarely engaged in physical altercations with peers or adults and, with minimal verbal prompting, could effectively regain control of herself when her behavior did begin to deteriorate. Her mood became more elevated as she interacted more positively with peers and staff and as she attained more freedom and privilege on the unit.

∞

Group Approaches

Groups that involve counseling and social skills training are particularly helpful for working with children and adolescents with dual diagnoses. Groups, as do other psychotherapeutic approaches, instill hope and provide for catharsis/ventilation of emotions. However, groups also have four more unique therapeutic benefits:

A sense of relief in not feeling alone
Support and reassurance from group members
Learning new social skills, anger management strategies, and other coping techniques
Opportunity to try out new behaviors within the protective environment of the group

Prouty and Kubiak (1988) have developed a pretherapy procedure to develop readiness for therapy with more regressed and uncommunicative persons with dual diagnoses. The method is described as an extraordinarily concrete level of therapeutic reflection, supporting reality contact and communication. One of us (S.I.P.) has found the procedure useful during the initial preparatory stage of group counseling.

Careful patient selection for the group is extremely important, particularly with children who are dually diagnosed. For a group to be cohesive and task oriented, members must be motivated to attend, willing to remain for the entire session, and able to understand and adhere to the group rules. Persons who are poor candidates for group counseling are those who are unwilling to comply with group norms, extremely agitated, unable to tolerate group interaction, and likely to assume a deviant role (Yalom, 1985).

∞

> Michael was one of six adolescents who participated in a 12-week social skills training group that met twice weekly. Michael was 12 years old and was placed in residential treatment because of mild mental retardation and escalating physical aggression at home, poor impulse control, fire setting, eating inedible objects, and property damage at his school. His mother had a history of psychiatric problems and drug abuse, and his stepfather allegedly physically abused Michael.
> Michael frequently became agitated whenever another group member spoke, often overreacted to even friendly teasing, required a considerable amount of the group leader's attention, and did not accept feedback well from the group. Nonetheless, Michael made moderately good progress in the group. He learned a number of appropriate social skills and enjoyed participating in the "hands-on" activities reinforcing the group work. He particularly looked forward to observing himself on videotape and responded well to time out, response cost, and overcorrection procedures designed to suppress undesirable behavior during group.
> Group counseling proved to be particularly helpful for Michael, in part because it was coordinated with his overall residential program, which included his individual therapy, educational program, milieu and recreational program, and family work. Michael made a successful transition to a therapeutic foster care program in the community, where he is doing well.

∞

FAMILIES AND RESIDENTIAL TREATMENT

Only a generation ago, a child or adolescent could be placed residentially for reasons no more compelling than the family's inability to cope. Furthermore, placement often became a life sentence. Today, just as placements are fewer, they are also shorter, often a year or two at most. Psychiatric placements often are measured in weeks rather than years, and, although children and adolescents with dual diagnoses are apt to be placed for longer periods, there is usually an emphasis on transition—to less restrictive settings or to home. Well-planned family involvement would seem essential in order to promote both successful treatment and transition. With individuals who have mental retardation living in community-based residences, for example, family involvement in planning has been related to successful community adjustment (Bruininks et al., 1988).

Permanency planning provides both a philosophical and a legal impetus to supporting and involving families in treatment. This notion, originating in child welfare during the 1970s, has been defined as "the process of taking prompt, decisive action to maintain children in their own homes or place them permanently with other families" (Maluccio & Fein, 1983, p. 195). The Adoption Assistance and Child Welfare Act of 1980 codified permanency planning and extended it to encourage residential treatment facilities to shift their focus from child-centered care to family care, in order to move the child home as quickly as possible. Residential placement would be viewed as temporary, and elements of the child's home and community life would be incorporated into the treatment process (Jenson & Whittaker, 1989). Some residential agencies have begun to specify parents' rights, responsibilities, and opportunities for direct involvement in their child's treatment and aftercare, although these efforts still fall far short of the legal mandate.

There has been very little study of families and residential treatment for children with dual diagnoses. Three questions are of particular interest:

How does the family relate to the child and to the facility throughout residential treatment?
How does the family adjust to the child's placement?
When and to what extent is reunification of the child with the family desirable or successful?

We, together with Jan Blacher, have begun to study these questions, with several samples of children with mental retardation and/or mental illness who have been placed in a wide variety of residential facilities.

Family Involvement

For children with dual diagnoses, one might envision family involvement as embracing a range of activities, beginning before admission (e.g., cooperating in developing individual treatment plans), proceeding through treatment (e.g., participating in parent training, family therapy, or support groups; assisting in program planning), and extending to transition (e.g., carrying over programs into the home; participating in aftercare groups) (Jenson & Whittaker, 1989). The most essential involvement is contact with the child. Visitation, at the residential facility or at home, has been the most widely used measure of family involvement. Historically, however, when families have placed their children in residential care, most have maintained little involvement with the child or his or her program by any measure (Blacher & Baker, 1992).

We recently examined the involvement of families with 266 children with psychiatric disorders, mental retardation, or dual diagnoses who were in residential treatment programs (Baker, Blacher, & Pfeiffer, 1993). For the majority of children, involvement with families was quite low. Twelve percent of the children had no families and another 19% had no visits with their families, bringing to almost one third the proportion of children with no family contact. Examined another way, about half of the children had three or fewer contacts per year, or markedly insufficient contact for meaningful involvement of families in the program. Patterns of family involvement seemed to be established at the outset; the extent of involvement did not relate to the length of time the child had been in the placement, which for 90% of the sample ranged from 1 month to 3 years.

We further examined involvement by diagnostic status, a question that had received virtually no prior study. Children with dual diagnoses had significantly fewer contacts with their families than did either children with psychiatric disorder or those with mental retardation alone. Although we were tempted to theorize that children with dual diagnoses kept their families at bay with their multiple difficulties, further analyses proved otherwise. We found that lower socioeconomic status and greater distance from the facility were highly predictive of less family involvement. We also found that children with dual diagnoses were more likely to come from lower socioeconomic status homes that were far away. When we statistically controlled for socioeconomic status and distance, family involvement with the children with dual diagnoses was no longer different from family involvement with other children. Children with dual diagnoses in residential treatment, then, did have the least involved families, but this was attributable to other characteristics of the dual diagnosis group rather than to the child's functioning.

What are the implications for service delivery? Families with children with dual diagnoses may be least involved because their children are particularly difficult to place and are likely to end up in treatment far from home. Also, regardless of distance, these families are of lower socioeconomic status, with more limited resources for maintaining involvement (e.g., money, time, transportation, child care for other children). Family involvement would likely increase if a greater number of programs were available to children with dual diagnoses and if program staff facilitated access for families with limited resources.

As large institutions have downsized and developed smaller community-based facilities (see Blacher, chap. 8, this volume), there has been a tendency to locate these on the grounds or near the original institution. Although this may increase residents' access to friends and facilities at the institution, and may facilitate administration, it does little to facilitate family involvement or, in many cases, community integration. A network of small and widely dispersed programs has greater potential for maintaining meaningful contact with families.

Programs also could offer to families a variety of ways to be involved, so as to accommodate individual desires and resources. Indeed, in a study of children with mental retardation who were placed within 2 years of the interview, Baker and Blacher (1993) found that the strongest predictor of family involvement was the opportunities provided by the facility for such involvement. With families who have limited resources, opportunities must be made accessible. In one outpatient program, for example, Hispanic families, who traditionally underrutilize mental health services, maintained extraordinarily high participation when access was increased through personal invitations to participate, a specially tailored program, and the provision of bilingual staff, evening meetings, transportation reimbursements, and child care (Prieto-Bayard & Baker, 1986).

On a final note, although Baker, Blacher, and Pfeiffer (1993) found overall family involvement to be low, 20% of the children had 30 or more visits a year with families. For these families, who are already highly involved, treatment facilities should be challenged to maximize programs to make these frequent contacts even more beneficial to the child and family and to promote more successful family reunification.

Family Adjustment

How does the family system accommodate the placement of a family member? We do not know of reports of longitudinal data on family adjustment before and then following placement of a child. Therefore, we can only approach this question by asking how families retrospectively report their adjustment in the months and years following placement. Earlier studies of families from which a child was removed and placed in foster care found subsequent evidence of parental depression, guilt, and feelings of failure (Jenkins & Norman, 1975). Conversely, however, two recent studies of families who voluntarily placed a child with mental retardation indicated very positive adjustment.

In one study, we assessed the adjustment of 62 mothers who had placed their child with mental retardation in a variety of community residences in Southern California within 2 years of the interview. All but one mother readily stated advantages of placement to herself. These primarily included reduced parenting stress, a sense of freedom to pursue personal interests, and better family relationships (Blacher & Baker, 1994). Here is one family's story.

∞

> Placement of 6-year-old Eric had been exhausting. At first his mother Angela wouldn't let him go; then, as she began to explore placement, programs wouldn't take him. His severe mental retardation and autism were a combined ordeal; each day brought an endless series of outbursts, self-abuse, and learning failures. Each evening brought renewed arguments between Angela and her husband, Scott.
>
> There were three issues to be considered in placing Eric, and, although they were debated, they were hardly debatable. First, Scott, a busy executive, was totally exasperated with the lifestyle that Eric's behavior brought. Second, both parents agreed that their younger son Stephen was being ignored. Third, everyone acknowledged that even the best efforts to teach Eric had all but failed.
>
> Interestingly, a point that seemed pretty much overlooked in the decision to place was the considerable restriction that Eric's being at home had placed on Angela. Her former career abandoned, she was devoting her full time and even more energy to caring for her children. Within weeks of placement, she appeared more relaxed and had begun to talk of herself and her plans as if she were a person again. There was some guilt mixed with relief, as she experienced a household devoid of Eric; she once remarked wistfully, remembering Eric's eating habits, "The floor doesn't crunch anymore." Yet in time Angela, Scott, and Stephen became closer. Eric came home for reasonably successful visits and he began to show some gains in his group home. Angela felt that her life had begun again.

∞

In another study, we surveyed parents who had placed children with mental retardation, mental illness, or dual diagnoses into large private treatment facilities. We asked whether, in balance, the decision had positive or negative consequences for them, the child, and the family. Most respondents indicated that the net effect of placement was advantageous for themselves (94%), for the child (94%), and for the family (92%). Moreover, these advantages were viewed as greatest in families with a child with dual diagnoses (Blacher, Baker, & Pfeiffer, 1994).

Reunification

There have been implicit assumptions about placement, reflected in the programs that have evolved. In the past, when children with mental retardation, and to a lesser extent mental illness, were placed, they generally were considered to have left the home permanently. For children with mental retardation, despite today's professional advocacy that they should remain at home throughout childhood, it is typically the parents' view that placement, once initiated, is permanent. For children with mental illness, there is more of an expectation that residential treatment will end when the problems or the funding do. However, temporary treatment still may not imply reunification with the family. Allen and Pfeiffer (1991) noted that, although adolescents typically were discharged after less than 2 years of treatment, fewer than half of adolescents discharged from psychiatric facilities returned to live with their families and that many of these did so only temporarily.

We recently surveyed 268 staff in three residential treatment programs for children with mental retardation and/or mental disorder (Baker, Heller, Blacher, & Pfeiffer, in press). Our interest was in staff attitudes toward families and their involvement. One question asked about the percentage of children (under age 19) for whom the respondent thought that family reunification should be a goal. Surprisingly, the average was only about 50%, and many staff perceived the percentage to be much lower. The reunification score did not vary with whether the staff member primarily worked with residents who had mental retardation, mental disorder, or dual diagnoses. Hence, despite legislation and social policy encouraging permanency planning, the staff treating children in placement often do not see family reunification as an objective. There is clearly a need to make the concept of permanency planning and the processes of engaging families and programming for transition more salient for staff in residential programs.

IMPLICATIONS FOR RESEARCH AND POLICY

Children who are dually diagnosed are multiply victimized, by the incoherence of our policies and practices as well as by the limitations of our knowledge and training. There has been enormous progress in recent years in increasing awareness of this underserved population and promoting accurate diagnosis and effective treatment. We propose six priority areas for further policy, research, and service.

1. *Develop models for integrated service.* Planning should be encouraged, especially at the state level, to develop visionary models for service to children who are dually diagnosed. Such models would likely involve some administrative reorganization to prevent youngsters with dual diagnoses from being shuttled between mental health and mental retardation agencies. Within such a plan, we would imagine there would be diverse options, including small community-based facilities and larger treatment centers.

2. *Clarify legal rights in commitment and treatment.* Current laws regarding placement of persons with mental retardation are not nearly as uniform as those in the area of mental health, and differ considerably from the procedures for the commitment of persons with mental illness. For example, typical mental retardation placement statutes have no requirement for showing dangerousness to self or others (Ellis, 1988). There is a need to create a more carefully articulated legal mechanism and set of civil rights for the placement, treatment, and transition of persons with mental retardation, particularly when the concomitant psychiatric disorder may be the primary reason for the legal action.

3. *Support interdisciplinary professional training.* There is a growing recognition that the general level of expertise in the field of mental retardation is less than optimal (Matson & Frame, 1986). Psychiatric disorders greatly amplify this problem. Mental retardation professionals typically receive little training in mental disorder, and psychiatrists and clinical psychologists often receive no training in mental retardation. There is a clear need for more dually trained professionals.

4. *Support treatment research.* Federal and state agencies should be encouraged to establish lines of support for research on dual diagnosis. We need to know whether treatments that typically are employed with psychiatric disorders of children without retardation work as well with children who also have mental retardation. If not, then in what ways should they be adapted to accommodate the particular needs of the child with dual diagnoses? As one example, we need to understand the effectiveness of the psychotropic drugs that frequently are used to treat self-abuse, stereotypies, and poor impulse control. Too often, pharmacotherapy is prescribed to treat isolated symptoms rather than medication-responsive psychiatric disorders (Bregman, 1991).

5. *Expand family support services.* If outpatient and residential services were available in small facilities near where families live, family support services also would become more feasible. Prevention and intervention services that should be more widely extended to families include parent training, marital and family therapy, supportive

counseling, permanency planning, and transitional programs to help the child return to the home (Pfeiffer, 1992; Schalock & Lilley, 1986).

6. *Provide consultation and technical assistance to schools, residential centers, and health-care programs.* There is much that we already know about effective treatment, and we need to find better ways to disseminate this knowledge to frontline treatment settings. This might involve in-service training in the application of behavioral strategies to reduce maladaptive behaviors, to support community and in-home adaptation, and to encourage social interaction. It might involve helping staff develop ways to promote meaningful family involvement. It also might involve ways to protect caregivers from burnout and promote feelings of self-efficacy and positive self-esteem (Pfeiffer, 1992).

REFERENCES

Allen, J.P., & Pfeiffer, S.I. (1991). Residential treatment of adolescents who do not return to their families. *Comprehensive Mental Health Care, 1,* 209–222.

Allin, R.B. (1988). Intensive home-based treatment interventions with mentally retarded/emotionally disturbed individuals and their families. In J.A. Stark, F.J. Menolascino, M.H. Albarelli, & V.C. Gray (Eds.), *Mental retardation and mental health: Classification, diagnosis, treatment and services* (pp. 265–280). New York: Springer-Verlag.

Amado, A.N., Lakin, K.C., & Menke, J.M. (1990). *1990 Chartbook on services for people with developmental disabilities.* Minneapolis: University of Minnesota, Center for Residential and Community Services.

American Association on Mental Retardation. (1992). *Mental retardation: Definition, classification, and systems of supports* (special 9th ed.). Washington, DC: Author.

American Psychiatric Association. (1994). *Diagnostic and statistical manual of mental disorders* (4th ed.). Washington, DC: Author.

Baker, B.L. (1989). *Parent training and developmental disabilities.* Washington, DC: American Association on Mental Retardation.

Baker, B.L., & Blacher, J.B. (1993). Out-of-home placement for children with mental retardation: Dimensions of family involvement. *American Journal on Mental Retardation, 98,* 368–377.

Baker, B.L., Blacher, J., & Pfeiffer, S. (1993). Family involvement in residential treatment of children with psychiatric disorder, mental retardation, or dual diagnosis. *Hospital and Community Psychiatry, 44,* 561–566.

Baker, B.L., Heller, T., Blacher, J., & Pfeiffer, S. (in press). Attitudes of residential treatment staff toward family involvement. *Hospital and Community Psychiatry.*

Baker, B.L., Landen, S.J., & Kashima, K.J. (1991). Effects of parent training on families of children with mental retardation: Increased burden or generalized benefit? *American Journal on Mental Retardation, 96,* 127–136.

Blacher, J., & Baker, B.L. (1994). Out-of-home placement for children with retardation: Family decision making and satisfaction. *Family Relations, 3,* 10–15.

Blacher, J.B., & Baker, B.L. (1992). Toward meaningful family involvement in out-of-home placements. *Mental Retardation, 30,* 35–43.

Blacher, J., Baker, B.L., & Pfeiffer, S. (1994). *Families with a child in residential treatment: Advantages and disadvantages of placement.* Unpublished manuscript, University of California Riverside.

Borthwick-Duffy, S.A., & Eyman, R.K. (1990). Who are the dually diagnosed? *American Journal on Mental Retardation, 94*(6), 586–595.

Borthwick-Duffy, S.A., Widaman, K.F., Little, T.D., & Eyman, R.K. (1992). *Foster family care for persons with mental retardation.* Washington, DC: American Association on Mental Retardation.

Bowlby, J. (1988). Developmental psychiatry comes of age. *American Journal of Psychiatry, 145,* 1–10.

Bregman, J.D. (1991). Current developments in the understanding of mental retardation, Part II: Psychotherapy. *Journal of the American Academy of Child and Adolescent Psychiatry, 30,* 861–872.

Bromley, B.E., & Blacher, J. (1991). Parental reasons for out-of-home placement of children with severe handicaps. *American Journal on Mental Retardation, 29*(5), 275–280.

Bruininks, R.H., Hill, B.K., & Morreau, L.E. (1988). Prevalence and implications of maladaptive behaviors and dual diagnosis in residential and other services programs. In J.A. Stark, F.J. Menolascino, M.H. Albarelli, & V.C. Gray (Eds.), *Mental retardation and mental health: Classification, diagnosis, treatment and services* (pp. 3–29). New York: Springer-Verlag.

Campbell, M., & Malone, R.P. (1991). Mental retardation and psychiatric disorders. *Hospital and Community Psychiatry, 42,* 374–379.

Crystal, S. (1986). Psychosocial rehabilitation and homeless youth. *Psychosocial Rehabilitation Journal, 10,* 15–21.

Eaton, L.F., & Menolascino, F.J. (1982). Psychiatric disorders in the mentally retarded: Types, problems, and challenges. *American Journal of Psychiatry, 139,* 1297–1303.

Ellis, J.W. (1988). Residential placement of dual diagnosis clients. In J.A. Stark, F.J. Menolascino, M.H. Albarelli, & V.C. Gray (Eds.), *Mental retardation and mental health: Classification, diagnosis, treatment and services* (pp. 326–337). New York: Springer-Verlag.

Fletcher, R., & Menolascino F.J. (1989). *Mental retardation and mental illness: Assessment, treatment and service for the dually diagnosed.* Toronto, Ontario, Canada: Lexington Books.

Itzkowitz, A. (1985, July-August). Treating children in placement: Can you do family therapy when there's no family to do therapy with? *Family Therapy Networker,* pp. 15–17.

Jacobson, J.W. (1982). Problem behavior and psychiatric impairment within a developmentally disabled population. I: Behavior frequency. *Applied Research in Mental Retardation, 3,* 121–139.

Jacobson, J.W., & Ackerman, L.J. (1989). Psychological services for persons with mental retardation and psychiatric impairments. *Journal of Mental Retardation, 27,* 33–36.

Jenkins, S., & Norman, E. (1975). *Beyond placement: Mothers view foster care.* New York: Columbia University Press.

Jenson, J.M., & Whittaker, J.K. (1989). Partners in care: Involving parents in children's residential treatment. In R.D. Lyman, S. Prentice-Dunn, &

S. Gabel (Eds.), *Residential and inpatient treatment of children and adolescents* (pp. 207–227). New York: Plenum.
Kiesler, C.A. (1993). Mental health policy and the psychiatric inpatient care of children. *Applied & Preventive Psychology, 2,* 91–99.
Leahey, M., & Wright, L. (1985). Intervening with families with chronic illness. *Family Systems Medicine, 3,* 60–69.
Levitas, A., & Gilson, S.F. (1989). Psychodynamic psychotherapy with mildly and moderately retarded patients. In R.J. Fletcher & F.J. Menolascino (Eds.), *Mental retardation and mental illness: Assessment, treatment, and service for the dually diagnosed* (pp. 71–109). Lexington, MA: Lexington Books.
Maluccio, A.N., & Fein, E. (1983). Permanency planning: A redefinition. *Child Welfare, 62,* 195–201.
Marcos, L.R., Gil, R.M., & Vazquez, K.M. (1986). Who will treat psychiatrically disturbed developmentally disabled patients? A health care nightmare. *Hospital and Community Psychiatry, 37,* 171–174.
Matson, J.L. (1984). Psychotherapy with persons who are mentally retarded. *Mental Retardation, 22,* 170–175.
Matson, J.L., & Barrett, R.P. (Eds.). (1982). *Psychopathology in the mentally retarded.* New York: Grune & Stratton.
Matson, J.L., & Frame, C.L. (1986). *Psychopathology among mentally retarded children and adolescents.* Newbury Park, CA: Sage Publications.
Menolascino, F.J. (1988). Mental illness in the mentally retarded: Diagnostic and treatment issues. In J.A. Stark, F.J. Menolascino, M.H. Albarelli, & V.C. Gray (Eds.), *Mental retardation and mental health: Classification,, diagnosis, treatment and services* (pp. 109–123). New York: Springer-Verlag.
Menolascino, F.J. (1989). Overview: Promising practices in caring for the mentally retarded-mentally ill. In R.J. Fletcher & F.J. Menolascino (Eds.), *Mental retardation and mental illness: Assessment, treatment, and service for the dually diagnosed* (pp. 3–13). Lexington, MA: Lexington Books.
Menolascino, F.J., & Fleischer, M.H. (1991). Developmental concepts in mental retardation and mental illness. *Comprehensive Mental Health Care, 1,* 45–56.
Myers, B.A. (1987). Conduct disorders of adolescents with developmental disabilities. *American Journal on Mental Retardation, 25,* 335–340.
Nezu, C.M., Nezu, A.M., & Gill-Weiss, M.J. (1992). *Psychopathology in persons with mental retardation.* Champaign, IL: Research Press.
Pawlarcyzk, D., & Beckwith, B.E. (1987). Depressive symptoms displayed by persons with mental retardation: A review. *American Journal on Mental Retardation, 25,* 325–330.
Pfeifffer, S.I. (1992). Psychology and mental retardation: Emerging research and practice opportunities. *Professional Psychology: Research and Practice, 23,* 239–243.
Prieto-Bayard, M., & Baker, B.L. (1986). Parent training for Spanish speaking families with a retarded child. *Journal of Community Psychology, 14,* 134–143.
Prouty, G.F., & Kubiak, M. (1988). Pre-therapy with mentally retarded/psychotic clients. *Psychiatric Aspects of Mental Retardation Reviews, 7*(10), 62–66.
Ratey, J.J. (1991). *Mental retardation: Developing pharmacotherapy.* Washington, DC: American Psychiatric Association.

Reid, A. (1980). Psychiatric disorders in mentally handicapped children: A clinical and follow-up study. *Journal of Mental Deficiencies Research, 24,* 287–298.

Reiss, S. (1993). Assessment of psychopathology in persons with mental retardation. In J.L. Matson & R.P. Barret (Eds.), *Psychopathology in the mentally retarded* (pp. 17–40). Needham Heights, MA: Allyn & Bacon.

Reiss, S., Levitan, G.W., & McNally, R.J. (1982). Emotionally disturbed mentally retarded people: An underserved population. *American Psychologist, 37,* 361–367.

Reiss, S., Levitan, G.W., & Szyszko, J. (1982). Emotional disturbance and mental retardation: Diagnostic overshadowing. *American Journal of Mental Deficiency, 86,* 567–574.

Ricks, M.H. (1985). Social transmission of parental behavior: Attachment across generations. In I. Bretherton & E. Waters (Eds.), Growing points in attachment theory and research. *Monographs of the Society for Research in Child Development, 209*(1–2), 211–227.

Russell, A.J., & Forness, S.R. (1985). Behavioral disturbance in mentally retarded children in TMR and EMR classrooms. *American Journal of Mental Deficiency, 89,* 338–344.

Schalock, R.L., & Lilley, M.A. (1986). Placement from community-based mental retardation programs: How well do clients do after 8 to 10 years? *American Journal of Mental Deficiency, 90,* 669–676.

Sherman, B.R. (1988). Predictors of the decision to place developmentally disabled family members in residential care. *American Journal on Mental Retardation, 92,* 344–351.

Szymanski, L. (1987). Prevention of psychosocial dysfunction in persons with mental retardation. *Mental Retardation, 25,* 215–218.

Szymanski, L. (1988). Integrative approach to diagnosis of mental disorders in retarded persons. In J.A. Stark, F.J. Menolascino, M.H. Albarelli, & V.C. Gray (Eds.), *Mental retardation and mental health: Classification, diagnosis, treatment and services* (pp. 125–139). New York: Springer-Verlag.

Yalom, I.D. (1985). *The theory and practice of group psychotherapy* (3rd ed.). New York: Basic Books.

IV

RECONCEPTUALIZING PLACEMENT

The chapters of Part IV describe alternative conceptualizations of placement, alternative family support structures, and changes in legal and social policies that could produce better outcomes. The perspective on child placement in this country can be seen as rigid and restrictive from the viewpoints of other cultures, with policies regarding placement ill defined. The final chapter is a commentary, focusing on a redefinition of our nation's goals and the development of a coherent and flexible national policy that will help us to serve our children appropriately.

11

To Have and to Share
Culturally Constituted Fostering in Familial Settings

Janet E. Kilbride and Philip L. Kilbride

The practice of parents voluntarily sending their children away from their natal homes to be raised at least part of the time in someone else's home may seem unthinkable. For those familiar with the attachment theory of child psychology, thoughts of detrimental effects on a child's development as a result of the improper formation, the breaking, or the nonformation of parent–child bonds come to mind. Nevertheless, Valsiner (1989), a psychologist who has written a book that examines cultural influences on personality development, pointed out that for many centuries children have migrated from and back to their natal homes with "no detriment to the human species. Undoubtedly, such migration has on occasion created some complex psychological, legal, and social problems, but none of these has led to any lessening of the viability of *Homo sapiens*" (p. 109).

For various emotional, economic, lifestyle, or other reasons, parents may be unable or unwilling to be the sole caregivers of their children, especially those children with special needs. In the chapters in this volume, the reader has encountered diverse situations in which decisions have been made for the out-of-home residence of children with special needs. Lest such placements, in and of themselves, be construed as aberrant manifestations of modern times and a Western, capitalistic society, the present chapter concerns itself with some cross-cultural examples of normative fostering in familial settings. Examples of informal shared caregiving arrangements are presented to suggest to the reader alternative ways for more members of our society to truly *share* in the care of our children. American society most often views the child as the rightful possession of his or her birth or legal parents, a concept arguably not always in the best interests of the child, the parents, the professionals concerned with the welfare of the child, or even a healthy, functioning society.

Specific cases of fostering in different cultures serve to highlight different types of fostering as well as those conditions under which fostering is most likely to occur within the context of a particular society. First, we consider some reasons why a society might want to develop and encourage informal foster care arrangements. A more lengthy examination of fostering among the Abaluyia of Kenya, where the authors have done fieldwork over the past 16 years on a variety of topics related to family life, further illustrates situations in which informal shared childcare arrangements are feasible and desirable. We conclude with some implications for constructive change in an overburdened United States foster care system.

FUNCTIONS OF INFORMAL FOSTERING

There are many potential reasons why parents might consider it desirable or necessary to have their child fostered or indeed to become foster parents themselves. Thus, fosterage (the delegation of certain elements of the parental role; Goody, 1982, p. 23) takes different forms depending on such factors as the reasons for the fosterage; the age, personal characteristics, and birth order of the children being fostered; to whom they are fostered; and the cultural context in which fostering is practiced. Goody (1982), in her seminal work on fostering in West Africa, reminds us that, in order to define fosterage, we also must understand what it is not: "As used here, fosterage does not affect the status identity of the child, nor the jural [legal] rights and obligations this entails. Fosterage concerns the *process* of rearing, not the jural definition of status or relationships" (p. 23).

In the United States today, the type of fosterage that most frequently comes to mind is "crisis fostering" brought about because of circumstances that are potentially threatening to the health and well-being of the child, such as illness, poverty, death or divorce of the parents, or, in extreme cases, the neglect or abuse of the child. Alongside this relatively formal and institutionalized type of fostering is a less apparent and more flexible type of informal fostering that is entered into voluntarily. For example, a teenage, single parent may want her own parents or a married older sister to raise her child for her. Either party may initiate such an arrangement, which becomes acceptable to both under agreed-on conditions.

The ritualization, prevalence, and contractual nature of fosterage varies across and within cultures. Our selective perusal of the cross-cultural material on fostering indicates that the most common type of fostering is *kinship fostering* by the mother, father, sister, or brother of the parent. In other societies, some members of the community function as resources for foster care outside a kin group, or the entire community may accept care responsibilities for all of its children. However, foster care generally has specific functions in a given society. In the cultures of West Africa, the most common form of fostering during infancy and early childhood is that of "nurturant fostering," which entails "providing food and care and early socialization in control of impulses and bodily functions" (Goody, 1982, p. 23). Fostering of the school-age child and adolescent is typically for educational or apprenticeship purposes. A child also may be sent to a relative to alleviate loneliness or to help out with household chores. Other common reasons for voluntary fostering or the sharing of parental rights and duties include the birth of a child out of wedlock, the pursuit of education by the parent, or the need to work outside of the home in order to support one's family. Other cultures also provide crisis fostering as a means to avoid unfanticide or prevent or halt child abuse and neglect, or in cases of death of one or both parents. An informal fostering system is used in these situations as well.

Fostering as an Alternative to Infanticide and Child Abuse and Neglect

The killing of her own infant in cases of extreme helplessness and poverty is perhaps one of the most desperate cries for help that a mother can make. This is especially so in cultures such as that in the United States, where doing so is not only culturally unacceptable but a punishable crime. Infanticide, whether one likes to admit it or not, has been fairly widespread worldwide (Mull & Mull, 1987; Scrimshaw, 1984). Nevertheless, it is a practice in which most cultures engage only when circumstances provide no reasonable alternative. Informal fostering most likely has saved many children from this fate.

In times of relative prosperity, or at least a lack of severe deprivation, excess infants and infants with disabilities are allowed to survive and are even welcomed by both parents and foster parents. Traditionally among the Masai of East Africa the birth of twins, especially twin boys, was a source of joy. Typically, the mother kept only one of the twins, giving the other to a barren relative or to one of her co-wives to nurse. Today, however, with natural disasters such as severe droughts and a reduction in adequate grazing lands, twins are not seen as a blessing. Masai mothers will select the stronger male twin and give up the other to a barren relative for adoption if she does not let the infant die of neglect, as might be done for twin girls, a very sick newborn, or the illegitimate baby of an old and sick man (de Vries, 1987, p. 171). De Vries suggested that this shift in attitude and behavior toward offspring is related to economic and resource factors.

Scheper-Hughes (1987), in her discussion of maternal thinking and behavior as it relates to child survival in a shantytown of recent rural migrants in Northeast Brazil, stated that the accepted practice of circulating babies through informal adoption or abandonment most probably saved the lives of some children. Scheper-Hughes (1987) explained that mothers who cannot care for their infants may sometimes ask:

> ... a current or former employer to take their baby as a foster child or even as a future household servant. Young and unmarried women will sometimes leave a 5- to 6-month-old baby on the doorstep of an Alto woman known to be particularly tender-hearted. (p. 203)

Apparently, fostering or adoption is viewed by some societies as an alternative to infanticide.

Although infanticide of "obviously abnormal" newborns occurred traditionally among aboriginal New Guineans such as the Bena Bena, Langness (1981), for example, in a book by Korbin (1981) on cross-cultural perspectives of child abuse and neglect suggested that fostering may have lessened this practice in general. He reported that fostering (also called informal adoption but differing from adoption in that no legal rights to the child are exchanged) is common for both male and female children and may serve to guard against infanticide or child abuse because "if someone does not take immediately to a child another parent can readily be found" (p. 27). Langness (1981) went on to point out that even:

> ... small children are free to change residences, at least temporarily, if they become angry or feel mistreated. As they always have relatives nearby, it is a simple matter to sleep with grandmother, an uncle, or a cousin, and as the communities are small, the parents usually know where their children can be found. Thus a parent is never put into the situation of being the sole satisfier of a child's needs. (p. 27)

Another example of this type of temporary, informal fostering in the service of helping to prevent infanticide and child abuse is given by Johnson's fieldwork among the Machiguenga, a relatively nonviolent, egalitarian society in southeastern Peru. Although children are treated affectionately and spend most of the day with one or both of their parents being taught by example and patience to be obedient and helpful, control of family size and elimination of infants the mother deems unlikely to survive as a contributing member of society (i.e., physically malformed) may still be achieved by infanticide. Although fostering is not likely in these cases, the likelihood of abuse against older children who have been weaned may be lessened by the acceptance of the practice of informal fostering. Johnson (1981) reported that:

> In native South America the flexibility of the social structure enables parents to transfer responsibility for children of various ages for indefinite periods of time. In fact, the removal of a child, to be brought up elsewhere, is often a convenient solution to domestic difficulties. (p. 65)

This is also true for the Inuit. Two scenarios in which grandparents came to the rescue of their abused grandchildren are presented by Graburn (1987):

> Another girl, aged about five, was deemed to be stupid by her parents. She was treated badly, given ragged clothes, fed scraps and occasionally hit. Her parents seem to have given up on her, and they let her grandparents take her over. They too found her difficult to raise, but they did not mistreat her physically. At last report she was alive, but severely retarded socially, though no organic illness was obvious.
> A boy, aged five or six, who was similarly maltreated by his parents, appeared to be mentally retarded and undisciplined. Again he was given to his grandparents but could not talk by that age, and couldn't or wouldn't walk. They treated him very kindly and eventually he began to thrive, learned to talk and walk and grew up to be a "normal" if dull and somewhat non-social teenager. (p. 214)

With limited resources, these grandparents performed what they saw as their appropriate role as custodians of the family.

Fostering After the Death of a Parent

Informal fostering also provides care for children in cases involving the loss of a primary caregiver. In each society, emergency caregiving alternatives have developed within particular social contexts. For example, one solution to the death of a child's mother that is not available in the context of the American, monogamous family is an alternative for a polygamous family. A common domestic homestead for the Masai of Kenya is a man, his two or three wives, and their children. In cases in which one wife dies before her infant is weaned, one of her co-wives will breastfeed this infant, thereby making him or her, in their eyes, a blood relation of the co-wife's own children. "Foster children are thus held to be related by consanguinity" (de Vries, 1987, p. 171).

In his fieldwork among the Adaman Islanders in 1906–1908, Radcliffe-Brown noted that, when parents of a child less than 6 or 7 years of age died, that child was adopted by another family. This practice, which he called "orphan adoption," was different from the practice of a married couple (foster parents) "adopting" a child over the age of about 7 until he or she reaches adulthood even though the child's parents are still living and continue to visit the child periodically (Radcliffe-Brown, 1964, p. 72).

Fostering as an Exchange System

Thus far, we have considered fostering mainly in terms of its consequences for foster children and their natural parents, but this informal arrangement also should be considered as a mutual exchange system with consequences for foster parents as well. Grandparents as foster care providers present an excellent example of this arrangement.

Grandparents as Providers of Foster Care In many different cultures, grandparents are often the ones turned to for fostering. Weibel-Orlando (1990), in a chapter in which she identified five different grandparenting styles among Native Americans, offers cases in which grandparents by choice or necessity have taken over the primary caregiving responsibilities for one or more of their grandchildren. It is a long-established tradition for these Indian grandmothers to be primary caregivers for first- and second-born grandchildren in multigenerational households. When grandparents became old and feeble, they were, in turn, cared for by the family. When parents are going through a divorce, are working outside the home, are overburdened by too many children, or become ill or die, custodial grandparents provide needed care for their grandchildren. Weibel-Orlando (1990) surmised that custodial grandparenting may exist "across cultures where unanticipated family trauma (divorce, death, unemployment, abandonment, illness, neglect, or abuse) separates child and parents" (p. 119).

Contemporary American Indian groups also must deal with the problems of alcoholism and drug abuse, which force young grandparents to take on full custodial care of their grandchildren before they are ready. Weibel-Orlando (1990) gives as an example of this scenario the case of one grandmother who was caring for her daughter's three children, one son's child, plus a great-grandchild! "The custodial role essentially has been forced upon her by the misconduct or lack of interest of two of her children" (p. 120).

Whereas this 57-year-old grandmother who is experiencing role overload feels overburdened, there are other grandmothers who seek out foster grandchildren to care for because of the lack or absence of biological grandchildren. One 67-year-old Sioux woman from South Dakota, for example, undertook this "fictive grandparent" role, explaining her choice to Weibel-Orlando (1990) thusly:

> Well, I got to missing my grandchildren so much. And none of my kids would let me have one of their kids to take care of so I decided that I had to do something. And there's so much need out here... you know... with all the drinking, and wife abuse, and neglect of the children and all that... so I felt I could provide a good home for these pitiful Sioux kids whose families couldn't take care of them. So I applied for the foster parent license. (p. 118)

Although this grandparent sought a formal route to obtaining foster grandchildren, others foster children informally.

One 83-year-old woman had living with her a 25-year-old son whom she had informally adopted when he was 17 because he no longer wanted to live with his mother and his father's whereabouts were unknown. She had only one daughter, and this daughter worked away from the home all day and was practically blind. This Creek woman explained that her reasons for this informal fostering were that the boy needed a home and she needed someone to help her around the house and to drive her places to shop (Weibel-Orlando, 1990, p. 119).

Foster Parenting as Companionship and Assistance Foster children are welcome additions to many households because they offer companionship and service. The temporary exchange of children is seen as an advantage for both fostering adults and the children they foster. Aptekar (1988), in his study of street children from the city of Cali in Colombia, pointed out that among these children the fostering relationship sometimes was initiated by the child rather than the adult. In such cases, the child must convince the adult that he or she can be of value to the latter. For example, Aptekar (1988) described the enterprise of one child who always slept near the garage of a wealthy family, until they felt that they must indeed do something about him. He suggested that they might need him to guard their house, so they agreed to let him sleep inside the garage in exchange for this service. Gradually, he became part of their group of workers, enabling him to receive more benefits, such as food. In other cases, street children were informally adopted because they looked like a young relative who had died or because the benefactors had once been street children themselves (Aptekar, 1988, p. 40). These relationships were usually temporary and could be broken by either participant. Nevertheless, in most cases of fostering, the decision to enter into such a relationship is contracted among adults.

Fostering as a Bond Between Adults Aptekar (1988) also mentioned the tradition in Colombia of giving children as gifts (*regalitos*) to relatives such as grandparents, uncles, or aunts, or even nonrelatives who are close family friends, who are more economically blessed than the biological parents. Elsewhere, Aptekar (1991) stated that among lower-class Colombian women who had children as a result of premarital unions, neither the mother nor her child was stigmatized. Because of the instability of the male–female relationship among young adults, in part a result of the lack of long-term wage work for the male, "The children from these unions were taken care of by their mothers, by their mother's mother, by female relatives, or even by women friends of the mother or grandmother" (p. 338).

Among Colombians of all social strata, the family represents both social and self-identity. The *compadrazgo* system of appointing a friend as a type of fictive family member to help the family in times of need or unforeseen disasters serves as a safeguard when families can no longer care for their children. Aptekar (1988) described this system, which unfortunately does not work to help street children, who are without extended family or close family friends:

> It is common practice to appoint a special non-family member, known as the *comadre* or *compadre* (literally, the co-mother and co-father), who assumes a commitment to help the "adopted" child. This commitment is one of the most sacred between friends. The compadrazgo relationship begins at birth with church services and continues with community and church support throughout life. (p. 80)

Another category of women served very much as temporary or sometimes permanent foster mothers. Aptekar (1988) defined the *madre de crianza* as typically a female friend of the mother who assumes her parenting role. "Crianza means nursing, but these women were not wet nurses. Nor were they professional child caretakers, but rather women who for a variety of reasons raised children not their own" (p. 221).

Radcliffe-Brown (1964), in making mention of the Adaman Islands custom of fostering children older than 7, refers to the observation made by E. H. Man in 1882 that the custom of fostering was so widespread that it was unusual to find a child of 7 who was living with his or her biological parents. In fact, for a married man to ask a friend to allow him to "adopt" one of his children was considered to be a mark of friendship. Likewise, it was a sign of friendship and trust to allow one's friend to raise one's child. Parents also paid continual visits to their own child and "asked permission" to have their child stay with them for a few days periodically. Although theoretically a man was free to adopt as many children as he wished, he was required to treat these adopted children with kindness and care for them as he would his own children. The child, in turn, was expected to show filial piety toward his foster father. By the time Radcliffe-Brown did his fieldwork among the Adamanese between 1906 and 1908, the usual age of adoption was around 9 or 10 years or older (Radcliffe-Brown, 1964, p. 77).

Fostering as an Alternative to Childlessness Adoption of children belonging to a local group other than one's own also occurs and serves to increase the chances of peace between neighboring groups who may be friendly or unfriendly. Cipriani (1966) recalled that one Adamanese woman always had children with her even though she had no biological children of her own. It was only when he noticed that these children differed from year to year that he realized that these were "adopted" (foster) children (Cipriani, 1966, p. 64). He reported that these children were given lavish attention and kept for years or permanently if their parents did not request their return. This custom allows childless couples to declare these adopted children as their own.

Messing (1957) stated that the Amaraha, a patrilineal, patrilocal[1] society in Ethiopia, value children so much that a childless home is considered to be cursed. Children are viewed as a source of riches from childhood when they help with household tasks, and in adolescence and adulthood as defenders in times of wars, as well as being a source of comfort and security in old age. There are two degrees of fostering; one that is typically permanent and similar to informal adoption is called by the Amaraha "breast parenthood." Levine (1965) described the traditional ritual of the ceremony of the "breast mother or breast father" in which the honey-dipped nipples or thumb of the intended foster parent were sucked by the child to be adopted. He explained:

> Used metaphorically the image of sucking someone's breast is employed to indicate becoming close to or ingratiating oneself with a superior; breast-feeding is so explicitly connected with emotional security that people are inclined to allude to it when finding a new source of security. (p. 222)

The second form of fostering, called "bread parenthood," was viewed as more temporary and less secure. Messing (1957) stated that this relationship depended more on the good will of the bread mother for continued permanence. Therefore an adolescent orphan would try to acquire a breast parent rather than a bread parent. Situations in which the bread parent relationship might be initiated were at times of remarriage or divorce or when a father asked a friend to care for his child at the time of his death.

---

[1]In a patrilineal, patrilocal society, kinship is determined through the father's line, and at marriage a woman leaves her own kin group and goes to live with her husband's kin group (often this involves a move over some distance). Patrilocality acts to preserve the kinship lines of each group in a formalized way; the wife now belongs to her husband's kin group, as do their children.

KINSHIP FOSTERING

Descriptions of fostering in the various societies presented thus far suggest that informal fostering may work best when there is cooperation between natal and foster parents in the sharing of parenting, as well as ongoing contact between foster children and their biological and foster families. This situation is most likely to occur in the case of kinship fostering. Before turning to some examples of kinship fostering among the Abaluyia of Kenya, where the present authors have done fieldwork and where we can provide cultural context, we first consider case material from the United States from one ethnic group in which fostering has been extensive and richly described.

African American Examples

Stack (1975), in a now-classic study of African American family and kinship in a poverty-stricken neighborhood of a midwestern city, gave numerous examples of how fosterage or "child-keeping," as part of the larger practice of "swapping" goods and services, has become an adaptive strategy for survival under conditions of poverty and racism. She spoke of the intense domestic cooperation among individuals, both kin and fictive kin, who exchange and trade goods, resources, and the care of children in this community she calls "The Flats." These relationships are of such importance that, if one did not repay an exchange (eventually, since exchanges were rarely carried out simultaneously), it could mean that "someone else's child would not eat" (Stack, 1975, p. 28). Reminiscent of examples given previously for other cultures, these African Americans interpret temporary and mutual child exchanges as a symbol of trust. Stack (1975) viewed the informal circulation of children in The Flats as intertwined with an informal, but tacitly agreed on, distribution system of limited resources. Thus, in times of need, parental responsibility can be shared by close friends or kin of the mother or father of the child, or even transferred to them (see p. 29).

Similar to the acquiring of fictive kin in other societies, socially recognized kinship relations may be added to one's domestic circle by the satisfying of reciprocal obligations to one another. In exchange, one may be treated as and called a sister, brother, cousin, or daddy, for example. The composition of a "household" also might fluctuate from time to time. At any one time, a person might be a member of more than one household, sleeping in one, eating in another, and contributing resources to a third. With this flexibility in mind, Stack (1975) defined "family" in The Flats as "the smallest, organized durable network of kin and non-kin who interact daily providing domestic needs of children and assuring their survival" (p. 31). One's male genitor, therefore, need not be socially recognized as one's "daddy," the man predominantly involved in raising the child.

Likewise, when an unwed, teenage girl has her first child, she may continue to live in the same house as her baby and even share the same room, but the girl's mother, her mother's sister, or her older sister may take over the care of the infant and become the child's "mama." The mother and her firstborn daughter are in this case often raised as sisters. This same girl may, however, actively raise her second child, assuming the responsibilities of his or her "mama." Stack (1975) pointed out that, although a child raised by a close, female relative knows who his biological mother is, he reserves the label "mama" for the woman who "raised him up" (p. 47). Nevertheless, although the biological mother gives up some of her parenting rights, she does not give up all of them. In the Flats, 80% of the "mamas" are the natural mothers, and their children become part of their (real and fictive) kinship network.

For a child to become part of his or her biological father's kinship network, the father must acknowledge openly that he is responsible for the child, that "he own it" (Stack, 1975, p. 51). Even if the father is not in a position to help his child, his kin are expected to do so. If the latter actively participate in the raising of the child, they validate their parental rights. If a young woman is not able to care for her child, the father's close female relatives may claim parental rights. In fact, Stack reported that when 188 mothers receiving Aid to Families with Dependent Children were asked to rank order who would raise their children (1,000 total) if they died, one third listed their own mother first, one third listed their child's father or the father's mother first, and the remaining one third (second through fifth choices) chose their own kin, such as a maternal aunt, sister or brother, or daughter. In a crisis situation, then, both maternal and paternal kin are eligible to assume the responsibilities of legal parenthood (Stack, 1975, p. 53).

Stack (1975) found that most of the adults in her study had been fostered by kinsmen at one time or another. This practice has continued with their own children. "These alternatives enable parents to cope with poverty: they are possibilities that every mother understands" (p. 62). In a chapter devoted to the topic of "child-keeping," Stack stated that shared parental responsibility among kin has been one way in which the African American community has responded to poverty (p. 62). Sudarkasa's (1982) and our own and others' work among the Abaluyia suggest that this "solution" to poverty may, in part, be a culturally constituted strategy existing in societies in which children are valued both economically and emotionally. Sudarkasa argued that reliance on an extensive network of kin did not originate in "response to the adverse socioeconomic circumstances in which Blacks found themselves. The groups originated in Africa, where they had served many of the same purposes they came to serve in America" (1982, p. 154).

Spruill (1994) has done fieldwork among elderly African Americans living in a Main Line Philadelphia suburb. Her studies provide further examples of fosterage as a cultural response to crisis situations. In the course of her interviews, she discovered that the practice of informal adoption was quite common and served as a safeguard for children in times of marital disputes and divorce. Children were fostered temporarily or longer in order to get them away from marital conflict and until the custodial parent (usually the mother) could once again care for them. The fluidity of household boundaries is illustrated by Spruill (1994) with an example of one elderly woman who was raising her four nephews and a niece because their biological parents were having marital difficulties. The latter, who were the foster mother's brother and his wife, lived upstairs in the same apartment building as she, and she cooked meals for them and their children as well as for herself and her own husband. Another case involved a woman who adopted the son of her husband's sister-in-law. She explains that this sister-in-law and her husband separated when the son was very, very young so, "They asked me to take him."

Among typical African American values identified by Aschenbrenner (1983) are a high value placed on children and strong family bonds (p. 137). In keeping with these ideals, informal adoption or fosterage by friends and neighbors is common. Furthermore, African American children who are fostered are not made to feel at a disadvantage, because fostering is viewed as an extension of the extended family system, which traditionally has shared in the care of children and one another. Additionally, because orphaned or rejected children are taken in by families as a matter of course, legal adoption is not thought of as being crucial. Typically, such adoption does not disallow continued ties and interaction with the child's biological parents. Even in middle-class African American families, ties to the extended family are strong, with child care being part of this helping system. The live-in grandmother who babysits while both parents work, or a couple "doing well" who take a nephew or niece to live with them so the child can attend a better school, are examples of fostering that continue to exist. Children, in their turn, provide status and companionship.

In the course of obtaining life histories for a research project dealing with elderly living alone in the community (see Rubinstein, Kilbride, & Nagy, 1992), Janet Kilbride interviewed an elderly, middle-class African American, the widow of a medical doctor, who fostered a child. One of this woman's less economically fortunate, single neighbors was having difficulty caring for all of her children. This foster mother recounted the story of how her then–8-year-old foster son stopped by her house for lunch one day, then stayed all day and for supper. He decided to sleep there that night and continued to do so until he was a young adult. His mother agreed to this informal arrangement. Today he still visits his foster mother and his biological mother and siblings when he is in town. Another person interviewed was an African American widower who, with his wife, had informally fostered his sister's son and daughter. The sister, who was unmarried and had to work, still lives two blocks away and now helps take care of this brother, who is now legally blind.

Although fostering may occur for the convenience of adults, as in cases of alleviating the loneliness of an elderly relative, intensifying the bond between the parent and foster parent, or helping parents with a "problem" child, the transfer of a child occurring for reasons more directly affecting the child's welfare, such as better schooling or less crowded living conditions, also may motivate an informal adoption. Fostering does not mean that the child is abandoned; rather, the child, who is valued, becomes part of a larger system of shared responsibility for the welfare of family and friends. It is with this cultural heritage, which places much value on the rearing and sharing of children, in mind that we now turn to our final examples of fostering, this time in Africa, particularly among the Abaluyia of Kenya.

Fosterage as Part of a Shared Care System

In discussing the widespread practice of fostering in Africa, Kayongo-Male and Onyango (1991) stated that fostering traditionally has been and continues to be a common feature of African family life. Along with the custom of sending a child to an adult relative who has no children or to a grandparent whose children have grown and left home, they noted that fostering can take the form of an exchange of children among married brothers. Importantly, although foster children spend a good portion of their life away from their biological parents, these children still have contact with them and often call both set of parents "father and mother" (p. 21).

Davis and Davis (1989), in their study of adolescence in the Moroccan town of Zawiya, used the term *fostered* instead of *adopted* because "there is rarely a legal procedure, and the child recognizes and feels close to its biological parents" (p. 68). This distinction is an important one that tends to be characteristic of informal fostering in general. Some of the same reasons for fostering children mentioned previously for other societies are present in Zawiya. For example, if a woman is childless, she might ask her brother or sister for one of their children to raise as her own, because it is by having a child to raise that a woman becomes a full adult. A foster daughter is preferred by a woman because she will be able to help with the housework. Sometimes families that already have children take a cousin from the country to town to live with them and help with the chores. The already overburdened country family with many children is pleased to have this opportunity for one of their children. The foster child works hard, but she is ideally treated like a daughter, and her foster family may even help her find a husband and contribute toward her wedding (Davis & Davis, 1989, p. 68).

Davis and Davis (1989) also pointed out that these foster children remained in contact with their biological parents. They provided as an example the case of one family in which a grown daughter sent her eldest daughter and later her next eldest daughter to live with her parents when they needed help. The grandparents' home was only a block away from the parents, so they saw their mother and father daily. This living arrangement did not require a change of schools, and the younger daughter liked living with her grandparents because they encouraged her more in her schoolwork. The parents benefited by having one less child to feed and clothe without giving up contact with their child (Davis & Davis, 1989, p. 85). This sort of living arrangement was agreed on and useful for the families involved. "Thus the pattern of fostering children seems partly utilitarian, partly a duty to help relatives, and partly an outgrowth of people's pleasure in children" (Davis & Davis, 1989, p. 69).

Kayongo-Male and Onyango (1991) pointed out that a distinguishing characteristic of socialization in the African family is "the large number of agents of socialization" (p. 19). Included as socializing agents are older brothers and sisters, some of whom have been sibling caregivers. Weisner (1982), writing on the general topic of sibling interdependence and child caregiving, described the sharing of parental care as part of a "shared functioning family system and an affiliative rather than egoistic individualistic style of achievement and competence" (p. 316). Thus, fostering may be viewed in the context of adult interdependence, of which caregiving by children, who are most frequently 7–14 years of age, is an integral part. Where work and survival needs are shared by kin and community, training in the care of others tends to begin early (Whiting & Whiting, 1975). Weisner (1987) suggested that sibling care is most prevalent in situations in which "there are large, coresident families, customs encouraging fosterage, adoption, and exchange of children between households, higher fertility, and low use of birth control" (p. 246). Such conditions allow for more available household helpers. In his own fieldwork among the Abaluyia of Kenya, who typify this kind of shared care system, Weisner found that 74% of the 70 mothers he interviewed reported that, as children, they had done sibling care either in their natal homes or in the homes of relatives. Also, 54% of the mothers reported that relatives or hired maids helped in their childhood homes (Weisner, 1987, p. 261).

Likewise, Jensen and Juma (1989), in their study of women, childbearing, and nutrition, interviewed 65 predominantly (90%) Abaluyia women. Of this sample, about 30% have had at least one of their children living in a household other than their own, and 30% have children other than their own living in their households (p. 69). Similarly, Weisner (1987) reported that 38% of his sample of Abaluyia mothers reported that they themselves sent their own children to the homes of relatives to help with child care and other chores around the house. This practice might be declining somewhat because children are now attending school; however, it is still culturally accepted, as is the practice of sending children who are difficult to discipline to a relative in the hope that a change of environment will have a positive impact on the child (Weisner, 1987, p. 262). Other reasons mentioned for fostering include sending a child to a grandmother at weaning, especially if the mother is pregnant or to provide a better educational opportunity for the child (Jensen & Juma, 1989, p. 70).

Relating to the practice of fostering the child at weaning, Ainsworth (1967) reported that, among the Baganda of Uganda, the infant being weaned must be sent back to the mother on the third day after the initial separation and stay with the mother that third night lest he or she become ill or die. The child then might remain at home or be sent back to the grandmother. Southwold (1965), describing the above fostering practices for the Baganda, stated:

> Infants are often sent to grandparents, or to other kinsmen without children of their own, though such children frequently return at six or seven when school fees have to be found. But, at the same age, other children are sent to live with relatives who live near a good school; if this means living in Kampala, their parents will not only pay their school fees but also make a contribution to their keep. (p. 107)

Contemporary Foster Care in Kenya: A Study of the Abaluyia

Social change and modernization in Kenya have made more difficult the functioning of the type of sibling care society described by Weisner (1987) above and the maintenance of the extended family as a meaningful support group, which continues to be ideologically important as well. The concept of the value of children, the voluntary exchange of children (in many cases believed to be in the best interest of the child or at least the child's family), and the traditional fostering system itself seem to be undergoing revision and in need of outside support. In fact, when we arrived in Kenya in 1984 for a year of study of the Abaluyia family, members of the community urged us to look into the extent to which basic parenting responsibilities were being delegated to grandparents rather than shared with parents, as was traditionally the case.

In our own fieldwork in Kenya among the Abaluyia, we discovered cases of fostering in the course of our larger study of family life in East Africa (Kilbride & Kilbride, 1990). We now present a few of these cases in order to highlight how fostering cannot be understood apart from other cultural contexts of which it is a part; such a holistic approach is central to the practice of anthropology. Our foster parents of choice will be grandparents, because traditionally they have been, and still are, very much involved in fostering, especially crisis fostering.

One of the major reasons why a child might be living with grandparents is that he or she is the result of an unwed, teen pregnancy of which the father does not accept paternity.

∞

> A 19-year-old girl was interviewed when she went to her mother's home to visit her 2-year-old daughter. When she was in her ninth year of schooling, she became pregnant by a fellow student. She was "in love," and he was her first boyfriend. Because he was young and still in school, neither he nor his parents would accept responsibility for the pregnancy. She plans to marry someday, but if her husband will not allow her to take her daughter with her, she will leave the child with her mother to raise. The grandfather died in 1980, but there are about 10 acres of land and the home is a relatively prosperous one. Nevertheless, the grandmother is worried about her ability to support her granddaughter, particularly if she should die. Her own son lives with her, along with his wife and his wife's 1-year-old son. The son has agreed to keep (foster) this boy for several more years, after which the "owner" (the boy's maternal grandmother) will take (foster) him.

∞

Traditionally, a child born before a woman marries would be accepted (even welcomed) and raised (fostered) by the paternal grandparents and/or their son (the child's father) and his future wife, or by the future husband of the child's mother. Now this is less likely to be the case, as illustrated by the next case studies.

∞

> A 52-year-old man lives with his wife, six sons, and a daughter. Two other sons and two other daughters have married and live elsewhere, but one daughter-in-law lives at his home with her three children. Two children of his other daughters-in-law also live with him. He has,

however, a total of seven grandchildren living with him because each of the two daughters who have married out left behind a child born before their marriages. These two grandchildren were not accepted by their mothers' husbands. In each case, the alleged father denied in court his paternity. One was fined 3,000 shillings (about $200), but he never paid. These two children often call their grandfather "father," and he loves them as his own children. He is concerned, however, because his wife does not love them. She gives them less food and lots of work to do. He has told his wife to treat them better, but he feels that most grandmothers are like that and look down on such unwanted grandchildren. It should be noted that these relatively young grandparents still have seven of their own children living with them, a fact that may keep the grandmother overworked even without these added grandchildren. Nevertheless, they do not appear to be experiencing financial hardships in that they are not among the poorest residents of the community.

∞

A woman in her 50s is one of three wives.[2] She lives on several acres of land along with her co-wives. Still living at home are a total of 24 children among the three of them. Two sons live in the compound with their own families. Problems associated with school fees and clothing are acute in this compound because her husband is not a wealthy person. Our informant, in addition to her nine resident children, also supports two grandsons of 8 and 10 years of age. Her daughter had been made pregnant by two different men, one a teacher. These men "disappeared" long ago, and her daughter left the children behind when she married out. This daughter has three children with her present husband; the husband has forbidden her to visit her older sons, and she sends no help. The grandfather, already hard pressed, has paid school fees for these grandchildren, but clothing and bedding are a big problem.

∞

A woman in her 50s has been living with her two sons and a granddaughter since 1982. She is divorced and has another son who lives

---

[2]Among the Abaluyia, polygyny (the marriage of one man to more than one woman) has been, and continues to be, a cultural ideal. Nevertheless, the majority of families are monogamous as is always the case where polygyny is the ideal. In our research, between 5% and 10% of households were polygynous. Ideally, a polygynous man should be wealthy, having enough land and economic resources to support his wives and children, as well as to provide help to extended family members. At the same time, the agricultural work provided by his wives and their children should serve to increase the wealth of the family and their power and prestige in the community. The large family also provides protection against perceived, hostile outsiders. Today, however, as a result of a declining significance of cultural sanctions that once regulated the practice of polygyny and greater reliance on a monetary economy, an increasing number of men who lack the economic resources are, unfortunately, polygynous. This results in harsh circumstances of living for their wives and children.

elsewhere. The latter son is the father of her granddaughter. The granddaughter is a pretty, 10-year-old student who bears a scar on her forehead from when she was beaten with a cooking stick by her stepmother 3 years ago. In the 1970s, her father had lived in Mombasa, where he had three children (two are now dead) with a woman labeled as a "prostitute." He subsequently married another woman, with whom he has had a son and a daughter. This wife became jealous on those occasions when he would "sleep out" and would aggress against her husband's "outside" child. When interviewed, the child said she was beaten about four times a month but never when her father slept at home. She got along well with her siblings, but she was the only one ever beaten. Her father would beat her stepmother whenever he discovered that she had beaten his daughter. The stepmother was remorseful after beating the child, as indicated by her taking the child to a hospital for treatment. The child now lives with her grandmother, who was happy to take her because she has no daughters. Her stepmother sometimes brings her clothes, but neither she nor the father provides any other assistance. Her biological mother frequently visits but is closely monitored by the grandmother for fear that she will steal the child.

∞

A brother had been helping his now-divorced sister with boarding school fees for her 16-year-old daughter.[3] The daughter had been raised by her mother's barren co-wife and her father. She did not, however, get along with her stepmother. Eventually, perhaps because of a lack of school fees, she returned to the care of her mother. She became pregnant by a man she hardly knew, a married man visiting the rural area from the city. According to the girl, she did not even realize that she was pregnant for 7 months. After giving birth to the baby alone while at school, she waited for 30 minutes before deciding that the only solution to her problems (no husband, being kicked out of school if her pregnancy were discovered, losing all the money in school fees that her family had paid in the hope that one of them would do well, etc.) was to throw her baby into the boarding school's pit latrine! School officials, having been alerted by another student

---

[3]In patrilineal families such as the Abaluyia, among whom bridewealth is exchanged, the maternal brother has a special tie to the sister who provided him with the brideprice for his own marriage. Bridewealth is more technically referred to as "progeny price" because it bestows to a man and his natal family the rights of ownership of the children produced by the marriage. This practice occurs where marriage predominantly links families rather than individuals. Typically, the husband's family gives to the wife's family material items such as cattle, blankets, and money in exchange for the rights to the children the wife will produce in the marriage. If no children are produced, the husband's family has the option of requesting the return of the bridewealth given. Because a woman has the potential to bring in bridewealth, an illegitimate daughter may be more readily accepted by her mother's future husband than would be a son for whom land, now in decreasing supply, is needed.

who heard the baby crying, rescued the newborn. After much negative sanctioning from the community, the police, and the court, the girl was released under probation with her baby (who had first been hospitalized with his mother) to the care of her mother. Her mother's brother continues to help financially when he can. The child is now 7 years old and doing well. He is living with his grandmother, whom he calls "mother." His biological mother now works and lives in a distant village with another relative, where people do not know about her child or her past problems.

∞

The five cases above, derived from our fieldwork among the Abaluyia of western Kenya, illustrate how the extended family, concentrating in these cases on grandparents and maternal brothers, acts as a safety net in crisis situations. The traditional extended family fostering system, in which the fostered child was not expected to be kept permanently by the foster parents, still exists in Kenya today. It is most prevalent in the rural areas, where grandparents continue to be the most numerous category of foster parents.

In the summer of 1992, Philip Kilbride spoke with staff at Nangina Hospital in Samia Location about the Abaluyia practice of fostering as well as about any examples of this that they had seen among people seeking their social services. Agnes Okwaro Olalle, an assistant to the Director of Social Services at Nangina, described the occasions for fostering, from most to least common:

1. A child born out of wedlock will stay with his or her mother's parents, usually permanently; sometimes the child is accepted by the mother's husband when she marries.
2. At the death of one or both parents, a child may stay with a relative (uncle, aunt, etc.) after the funeral. Land is kept for a male child and, after growing up, he goes to it.
3. A child is sent to a better off relative but will visit his or her parents from time to time and will eventually return to live with them. The child helps with housework; a girl cooks and cleans, and a boy does less but works in the shamba (farm).
4. If living alone, one can request a child from a sister to alleviate loneliness, or to leave in the house while at work, on night duty, and so forth.

From her own experience, Mrs. Olalle sees fostering for one reason or another occurring commonly. She estimates that about one half of the children in Abaluyia society are fostered. This figure is comparable to that reported by Goody (1982) for the Gonja of Ghana, among whom she found that over 50% of both men and women have been fostered for part of their childhood (p. 39). The Abaluyia attach no stigma to being a foster child. As with any children in a family, some foster children are treated more favorably than others. Ms. Olalle reported, furthermore, that sometimes the child himself or herself asks to be fostered. In fact, it is not unusual for an older child or an adolescent to ask to go live with a favorite relative. She, for example, lived with her sister in Mombasa for 2 years of her schooling. With the exception of *ayahs* (babysitters, housegirls), who are taken into the city by nonrelatives, children are fostered by relatives.

Ms. Ollale also pointed out that, among the Abaluyia, the age at which fostering occurs varies in terms of to whom one is fostered and the specific circumstances surrounding the fostering. Children from infancy on up are fostered by grandparents; children are fostered to a wealthy relative from 5 years or older (school age); in cases of the death of a parent, children from infancy to age 18 are fostered; to alleviate loneliness, children 10 years or older are fostered. Both boys and girls may be fostered to relatives. Fostering to nonrelatives is extremely rare (our own observations and informal interviews support this contention). Boys are more frequently fostered out for education, girls to alleviate a relative's loneliness. Generally, grandparents prefer to keep girls because girls will not need land in adulthood, but they will keep either. In addition to the economic gain of bridewealth, girls provide needed help with housework, cooking, and the care of younger children, as well as potential help for elders. Whereas boys do less housework, they also help by fetching and working on the farm as they get older. Moreover, because they may own land, boys may be of economic help during the foster parents' old age. In cases of death of the parent(s), there is no preference. Children with disabilities are not fostered traditionally for fear that they may be mistreated, but instead are "spoiled" at home.

The most common recipients of foster children are grandparents, wealthy relatives, and childless relatives. Married sisters and brothers of the parents are likely choices too. The exact arrangements, in terms of economics and visitations, are discussed and agreed on by the parents and foster parents. They discuss the circumstances and maintain contact over time. The child visits his or her parents from time to time. If in school, these visits typically occur during holidays.

According to Ms. Ollale, people today do not cooperate as they did previously. For example, in the past, co-wives very much cooperated. It was common for a co-wife to cook for any of the children or to send any of them on errands. Also, a younger co-wife would foster one of her children to an older co-wife's son (her stepbrother) in much the same way that she would to her "real" (full) brother. Thus, the stepbrother helps his younger stepsister while he receives help from this child. Nevertheless, although she sees some problem areas, Ms. Olalle believes that the fostering system generally works as before.

People who come to her for help most frequently are aunts who have taken children at a parent's death and need assistance for the children's education, and grandparents, especially grandmothers, with grandchildren born out of wedlock. Grandfathers come to her for help only if the grandmother is dead because "today men rarely do anything but drink and roam about with women, so the grandmothers are the ones coming for help." Acquired immunodeficiency syndrome (AIDS) is not a problem among the cases she sees. She suspects that many people have died of AIDS-related diseases, but few have come for help. She knows of one case, in particular, in which both parents died of AIDS and four children, two boys and two girls, were left with their grandmother, who came for help. In another case, the mother of a 5-year-old boy died, so his maternal grandmother took the boy to live with her.

Cases of formal adoption were reported to be very rare. Sister Marianna Hulshoff, Director of Social Services at Nangina Hospital, knew of only one case. Whether a child is adopted (in most cases not in the formal, legal sense) depends on the child's needs, kinship obligations, requests by a dying parent, friendship, barrenness, and a man wanting to marry the child's mother. For the most part, it involves kin (especially patrilineal). In cases in which the mother and/or father die, the father's brother is most likely to be designated as the person who adopts.

Maria Cattell, who like ourselves, has done fieldwork among the Samia Abaluyia, reported that she found no specific Lusamia word for adoption. The terms used for taking care of another person's child are general terms meaning to "accept" or to "take care of." The foster parent is said to have "picked what's lost" (personal communication, November 11, 1992). M. Cattell asked 29 men and women (23 of whom were in their 60s to 70s) whether, in the "olden days," Samia men ever accepted responsibility for another man's child. All 29 respondents replied "yes." Nineteen of these 29 stated that they knew of actual cases in which this had happened. This was most likely to occur if the child was an orphan (13/29) or the mother had married or remarried (8/29). One person gave the example of a barren woman adopting. One of Cattell's elderly male informants stated that, unlike today, in the old days only an orphan could be adopted, and the adoptive parent would be a relative.

Ms. Olalle explained further that adoption is not common because "the child can have bad traits like stealing," and because the system of naming does not make it obvious that a natural child's status is different from that of his or her foster sibs. For example, when a women's child comes into the family, he or she need not use the woman's husband's name because the child has the mother's given name (circumstances of birth, etc.), a baptismal name, and his or her biological father's given name after the ancestors. However, because only the first two names typically are used, the foster child is not stigmatized as being obviously different from other children in the household. Nevertheless, adoption may occur for an out-of-wedlock child who stays with his or her maternal grandfather. Referred to in West Africa as a "house child" (Goody, 1982, pp. 102–103), he or she will be given this grandfather's name as a third name. In this case, the child is adopted. If the child is a girl, the grandfather gets the bridewealth at the time of her marriage (see Kilbride & Kilbride, 1990, for specific examples).

Mrs. Joyce Umbima, National Executive Officer of the Child Welfare Society of Kenya, addressing a workshop on foster care and adoption in Kenya, pointed out the importance of traditional foster care, which was built into the culture as a means of caring for weak and disadvantaged children. Grant (1991) reported on what Mrs. Umbima said about the built-in system of foster care within the extended family, clan, and community. When children were in need, it was the duty of clan members to foster these children. In explaining the fostering system, Mrs. Umbima stated:

> Clan members felt that they had blood obligations to each other and failure to respond to the needs of the weak in their midst could anger the spirits of the dead. The ancestral super-spirit enforced morality and social obligation to each other. (Grant, 1991, p. 3)

Mrs. Umbima believed that changes in society, such as Christianity, which emphasized "universal good without roots of the blood," colonial rule, urbanization, large-scale farming, industrialization, and the introduction of a money economy, have put strains on the traditional foster care system by adding "massive poverty, uncontrolled population growth, and the new phenomenon of single parenthood" (Grant, 1991, p. 3). In spite of these changes, she thinks that traditional elements of fostering are still present in rural Kenya today.

IMPLICATIONS FOR SOCIAL POLICY

As we have seen, there are a variety of informal fostering practices that have existed in the past, as well as many that continue to exist today. By presenting specific examples and case studies in this chapter, we have attempted to show how these various practices fit into the cultural systems of which they are a part. Some of these practices may have seemed strange to the reader at first, but we hope that, through the anthropological process of "making the strange familiar," the reader may conclude that some of our own culture's institutionalized fostering practices are indeed strange when compared to those of other cultures, such as those considered in this chapter.

Although there are striking similarities in fosterage beliefs and practices among the different societies, one difference that is most apparent is our culture's emphasis on the nuclear family as the sole and proper owner and caregiver of its children. We may, indeed, be considered strange when compared to cultures that are built on strong sibling bonds and extended families. Some of the severe social problems facing American families, such as child abuse and neglect, female victimization, substance abuse, and the feminization of poverty, which add to an increased number of children who overload our present foster care system, may be due in part to a breakdown in our informal helping networks.

We are also strange given our national preoccupation with "legal" solutions to human interactional problems. In actuality, noninstitutionalized, informal fostering thrives in many cultures precisely because there are no legal roadblocks to its formation. Although rules and regulations concerning the rights of the child, parents, and foster parents are necessary in extreme cases for the proper functioning of the institutionalized foster care system in the United States, they may also serve to jeopardize a viable, informal fostering system that is struggling to exist among certain ethnic groups or in situations of need. This system is one that needs more study in order to understand and to utilize its strengths.

As the above examples from various societies have illustrated, the practice of fostering often serves to solidify or enhance relationships between adults and to act as support networks for them and their children. Most frequently, such fostering occurs among kinfolk, especially in times of crisis or in situations of poverty, and among groups for whom fostering is a culturally acceptable way to share the rights and obligations of parenting. All parents need someone to turn to for help with child care, especially in crisis situations. As we have seen in this chapter, many societies make use of informal fostering systems as safety nets for children and resources for parents in need of help with parenting responsibilities. Fosterage also enables parents to share in the joys of raising children who are valued as companions, helpers, future security in old age, and sources of immortality.

It is important to note that such fostering is not viewed as a separation from one's parents but as an incorporation of additional caregivers into the family system. Frequent visiting occurs between foster children and their biological parents and, often, between the biological and foster parents. In this way, a child can feel enriched by the addition of parenting adults rather than deprived of his or her biological parents and siblings. Thus, the joys and responsibilities of parenting truly are shared. The present formal fostering system in the United States may be better able to function efficiently and humanely by emulating this aspect of informal fostering agreements. Too often conflicting with a genuine desire to help the foster child are issues of protectiveness, powerlessness, being judgmental, possessiveness, and jealousy. Truly sharing in the care of a child would be achieved most easily in situations in which there is an existing (or potential) interdependence and general agreement regarding childrearing practices and goals. This type of system is most feasible under conditions in which foster parents are kinfolk and live nearby the biological family. At times, nonkin may be incorporated into the fostering system by becoming fictive kin and, thereafter, labeled and treated as kin. As one of Carol Stack's African American informants told her, "We help each other out and that's what kinfolks are all about" (1975, p. 45).

In the United States today, with our strong emphasis on individualism and the rights of biological parents, the courts are more likely to award sole custody to the biological mother rather than to fostering kin, at times to the detriment of the child. As Stack (1975) discovered, there are folk sanctions concerning the transfer of rights in children that may be in conflict with publicly sanctioned state laws. In cases in which mothers have successfully taken fostering kinsmen, such as their own mother or aunt, to court to regain custody of their children, local communities that view children as a mutual responsibility of the kin group may not approve. As Stack explained:

> Children born to the poor in The Flats are highly valued, and rights in these children belong to the networks of cooperating kinsmen. Shared parental responsibilities are not only an obligation of kinship, they constitute a highly cherished right. Attempts of outside social agencies, the courts, or the police to control the residence, guardianship, or behavior of children are thwarted by the domestic group. Such efforts are interpreted in The Flats as attempts on the part of the larger society to control and manipulate their children. (1975, p. 89)

The view of the child as being the *sole* property and responsibility of his or her biological parents is a rarity worldwide and, in practice, may never have existed at all. Such an extreme form of individualism seems to be detrimental to the survival of the child, who must learn to adapt to individual developmental changes as well as societal changes.

Given the likelihood that informal fostering systems have been in place perhaps from the beginning of human existence, in many societies throughout the world, we would suggest that our formal, institutionalized foster care system attempt to become more aware of their existence in the communities they serve. Understanding the value and functioning of informal fostering systems might provide a valuable resource for their mission of helping children in need by finding suitable foster parents. As this chapter has suggested, informal fostering arrangements appear to work best when there is sharing of child care by both parents and foster parents and where there is open communication between the two so that the foster child is able to have continued contact with both birth and foster parents. A neighbor, friend, or relative living in the same community as that of the biological parents, or a nearby community, might better understand the problems with which the latter has to cope. The foster child would more likely have had previous contact with the foster parent, so that the fear of being sent to live with a stranger, however temporarily, would be lessened.

Although there is a great need for a formalized foster care system, especially in cases of child abuse and neglect, in other cases parents may seek and receive foster care for their children from people they already know and trust. A relative or friend might be more willing to foster a child if a national health care system were affordable to all, if psychological counseling and substance abuse treatment programs were affordable and available to all, and if the threat of being sued by the very people one is trying to help were not so possible. Our local, state, and national governments might provide financial, medical, and educational assistance to help poor foster children and foster parents who are part of this informal network of fostering. A greater understanding of those communities having the greatest need for foster care might help the formal foster care system to identify potential foster parents and to provide social supports for those who already are informally assuming this role. Grandparents who become foster parents to the children of their own children who have substance abuse/addiction problems might be a good place to start.

Foster parents who are nonkin might be recruited more easily if the system encouraged their voluntary, continued contact with the child's biological parents and the foster child both during and after placement. In some cases, the separation of foster child and foster parent may need to take place more gradually for the better adjustment of all concerned. As in our own case with our previous foster son, occasional phone calls, requested advice, visits, and presents continue as his biological family has graciously accepted us as fictive kin. As his mother said to us, "You're family." In the universal sense, all children are part of our family and yours, the family of humankind. Fostering, both formal and informal, allows us the responsibilities and joys of sharing the parenting role.

To reiterate, our major recommendation for the formal foster care system in the United States is to become more informed about both formal and informal foster care arrangements in other cultures as well as in subcultures within the United States. By doing so, those dedicated and overworked foster care professionals and foster parents, who are trying under difficult circumstances to provide care for our nation's foster children, may be able to apply to their own circumstances insights obtained from world-wide informal fostering systems that already exist. A major example would be to make better use of informal fostering arrangements by identifying and directing resources to help strengthen these informal arrangements. Some formalized support may help to increase the number of potential foster parents, thus serving to lessen the caseload and increase the quality of service provided by our formal foster care system. Strengthening informal support systems in the individual communities from which foster children come also may decrease the number of children that ever need be placed in the formal foster care system as it exists in the United States today.

REFERENCES

Ainsworth, M. (1967). *Infancy in Uganda: Infant care and the growth of love.* Baltimore: Johns Hopkins University Press.
Aptekar, L. (1988). *Street children of Cali.* Durham, NC: Duke University Press.
Aptekar, L. (1991). Are Colombian street children neglected? The contributions of ethnographic and ethnohistorical approaches to the study of street children. *Anthropology & Education Quarterly, 22,* 326–349.
Aschenbrenner, J. (1983). *Lifelines: Black families in Chicago.* Prospect Heights, IL: Waveland Press, Inc.
Cipriani, L. (1966). *The Adaman islanders* (T. Cox, assisted by L. Cole, Eds. and Trans.). New York: Praeger.
Davis, S., & Davis, D. (1989). *Adolescence in a Morrocan town.* New Brunswick, NJ: Rutgers University Press.
de Vries, M. (1987). Cry babies, culture, and catastrophe: Infant temperament among the Masai. In N. Scheper-Hughes (Ed.), *Child survival: Anthropological perspectives on the treatment and maltreatment of children* (pp. 165–185). Boston: D. Reidel Publishing Company.
Goody, E. (1982). *Parenthood and social reproduction: Fostering and occupational roles in West Africa.* New York: Cambridge University Press.
Grant, S. (1991, January/March). Fostering—do you have what it takes! *Sasa: The voice of the children* (pp. 2–5). Nairobi: The Child Welfare Society of Kenya.
Graburn, N. (1987). Severe child abuse among the Canadian Inuit. In N. Scheper-Hughes (Ed.), *Child survival: Anthropological perspectives on the treatment*

and *maltreatment of children* (pp. 211–225). Boston: D. Reidel Publishing Company.
Jensen, A., & Juma, M. (1989). *Women, childbearing and nutrition: A case study from Bungoma, Kenya.* Oslo: Norwegian Institute for Urban and Regional Research.
Johnson, O. (1981). The socioeconomic context of child abuse and neglect in native South America. In J. Korbin (Ed.), *Child abuse and neglect: Cross-cultural perspectives* (pp. 56–70). Berkeley: University of California Press.
Kayongo-Male, D., & Onyango, P. (1991). *The sociology of the African family* (3rd ed.). New York: Longman Group.
Kilbride, P., & Kilbride, J. (1990). *Changing family life in East Africa: Women and children at risk.* University Park: Pennsylvania State University Press.
Korbin, J. (1981). *Child abuse and neglect: Cross-cultural perspectives.* Berkeley: University of California Press.
Langness, L. (1981). Child abuse and cultural values: The case of New Guinea. In J. Korbin (Ed.), *Child abuse and neglect: Cross-cultural perspectives* (pp. 13–34). Berkeley: University of California Press.
Levine, D. (1965). *Wax and gold: Tradition and innovation in Ethiopian culture.* Chicago: University of Chicago Press.
Messing, S. (1957). *The highland-plateau Amahara of Ethiopia.* Doctoral dissertation, University of Pennsylvania. (Ann Arbor, MI: University Microfilms No. 23, 619.)
Mull, D., & Mull, J. (1987). Female infanticide and child neglect in rural north India. In N. Scheper-Hughes (Ed.), *Child survival: Anthropological perspectives on the treatment and maltreatment of children* (pp. 113–132). Boston: D. Reidel Publishing Company.
Radcliffe-Brown, A. (1964). *The Adaman islanders.* New York: Free Press.
Rubinstein, R., Kilbride, J., & Nagy, S. (1992). *Elders living alone: Frailty and the perception of choice.* New York: Aldine De Gruyter.
Scheper-Hughes, N. (1987). Culture, scarcity, and maternal thinking: Mother love and child death in northeast Brazil. In N. Scheper-Hughes (Ed.), *Child survival: Anthropological perspectives on the treatment and maltreatment of children* (pp. 187–208). Boston: D. Reidel Publishing Company.
Scrimshaw, S. (1984). Infanticide in human populations: Societal and individual concerns. In G. Hausfater & S. Hrdy (Eds.), *Infancy: Comparative and evolutionary perspectives* (pp. 439–442). New York: Aldine.
Southwold, M. (1965). The Ganda of Uganda. In J. Gibbs (Ed.), *Peoples of Africa* (pp. 81–118). New York: Holt, Rinehart & Winston.
Spruill, J. (1994). The role of the child in African American marital disputes: A study of the role of the extended family and the practice of informal adoption. In P. Kilbride & R. Washington (Eds.), *Afro-American ethnicity: Ethnographic encounters in an urban metropolitan area.* Nashville: University of Tennessee Press. Manuscript submitted for publication.
Stack, C. (1975). *All our kin: Strategies for survival in a Black community.* New York: Harper & Row.
Sudarkasa, N. (1982). African and Afro-American family structure. In J. Cole (Ed.), *Anthropology for the eighties: Introductory readings* (pp. 132–161). New York: Free Press.
Valsiner, J. (1989). *Human development and culture: The social nature of personality and its study.* Lexington, MA: Lexington Books (D.C. Heath and Company).

Weibel-Orlando, J. (1990). Grandparenting styles: Native American perspectives. In J. Sokolovsky (Ed.), *The cultural context of aging: Worldwide perspectives* (pp. 109–125). New York: Bergin & Garvey Publishers.

Weisner, T. (1982). Sibling interdependence and child caretaking: A cross-cultural view. In M. Lamb & B. Sutton-Smith (Eds.), *Sibling relationships: Their nature and significance across the lifespan* (pp. 305–327). Hillsdale, NJ: Lawrence Erlbaum Associates.

Weisner, T. (1987). Socialization for parenthood in sibling caretaking societies. In J. Lancaster, J. Altmann, A. Rossi, & L. Sherrod (Eds.), *Parenting across the lifespan: Biosocial dimensions* (pp. 237–270). New York: Aldine De Gruyter.

Whiting, B., & Whiting, J. (1975). *Children of six cultures: A psychocultural analysis*. Cambridge, MA: Harvard University Press.

12

Commentary
A Social Policy Perspective

Emmy E. Werner

"Men have forgotten this truth," said the fox. "But you must not forget it. You become responsible, forever, for what you have tamed."

Antoine de Saint-Exupéry (1943)

On September 29 and 30, 1990, the first World Summit for Children, sponsored by UNICEF, was held in New York. It became the forum for the ratification of the United Nations Convention on the Rights of the Child. This Convention represents the first comprehensive international law for children—a unique document in human history.

It affirms that the best interests of the child should prevail in all legal and administrative decisions, and enjoins the international community to establish the proper institutional standards for the care and protection of children (Article 3). It assures each child the right to live with his or her parents unless this is deemed incompatible with his or her best interests (Article 9). It calls for the protection of children by the state from all forms of physical or mental injury or abuse, neglect, and exploitation by parents or others, and for preventive and treatment programs for those abused and neglected (Article 19). It also proclaims the rights of children to receive special protection and assistance from the state when deprived of their family environment, including the provision of alternative care, such as foster care, adoption, or institutional placement (Article 20) (United Nations Commission on Human Rights, 1990).

This chapter was written with grant support from the University of California, Davis, Washington Center and the Center for German and European Studies at the University of California, Berkeley.

Although the Convention is *legally* binding only on member states that have ratified it, it exerts a *moral* pressure on *all* nations of the world to examine their current attitudes toward and treatment of the most vulnerable children among them—those who are the focus of this book.

NO PLACE TO CALL HOME

At present, the Convention on the Rights of the Child is only a blueprint of what *ought* to be rather than a reflection of everyday reality. It is a tragic fact that the number of abused, neglected, and homeless children in the United States has been increasing steadily, as have those who are in need of out-of-home care because of mental retardation and/or mental illness.

Current estimates of the number of children who are among the most at risk for placement have been provided in preceding chapters. They range from over 2.6 million children who reportedly have been abused or neglected to more than 650,000 juveniles admitted to detention centers, jails, or state training schools; an estimated 500,000 children in foster homes, group homes, or institutional settings; some 55,000 youngsters admitted to psychiatric facilities; and the 100,000 children who each night can be counted among the homeless (see Blacher, chap. 8, this volume; Children's Defense Fund, 1992; National Commission on Children, 1991).

Child advocates and legislators of every political persuasion in the United States agree that dramatic increases in the numbers of American children placed outside their homes have occurred during the decade of the 1980s, and are continuing to occur in the child welfare, juvenile justice, and mental health systems of our country (U.S. House of Representatives Select Committee on Children, Youth and Families, 1989). Reports of child abuse and neglect rose 259% between 1976 and 1989, and more than 50% of all placements today are for children who need protection from adults in their own homes. An analysis of multiple factors that place children at risk for maltreatment suggests that *family income* is consistently related to all types of abuse and neglect (National Commission on Children, 1991). Unfortunately, during much of the last two decades, poverty among U.S. children has been on the rise: In 1991, nearly one of four children under the age of 6 lived in families with incomes below the official poverty level. Forty-one percent of all African American children and 37% of all Hispanic children live in poor homes (Children's Defense Fund, 1992; Huston, 1991).

CHILDREN'S WELL-BEING: AN INTERNATIONAL COMPARISON

Cross-national comparisons of children's well-being show that the United States, even though it is among the richest nations in the world, has a higher poverty rate among children than the other major industrial countries, such as Canada, the United Kingdom, the Federal Republic of Germany, and Sweden. More children by far, both in number and in percentage, live in single-parent families in the United States than in other industrialized countries, and the gap between the United States and the other developed nations has widened in the past decade. The United States also has the highest rate of teenage pregnancies among the Western nations. The poverty rate of children in single (usually female-headed) families in the United States is four times higher than that of children living with *both* parents (U.S. House of Representatives Select Committee on Children, Youth and Families, 1990a).

In turn, children from poor and broken homes are making a disproportionately high contribution to placements, *both* in temporary and long-term foster care (see Davis & Ellis-MacLeod, chap. 5, and Massinga & Perry, chap. 6, this volume) and among youngsters found in juvenile detention centers (see Portwood & Reppucci, chap. 1, this volume). Our national shame, the homeless children on America's streets, comes overwhelmingly from female-headed families in extreme poverty (see Bassuk & Weinreb, chap. 2, this volume).

CHILD AND FAMILY POLICIES IN THE EUROPEAN COMMUNITY

The United States is at present one of the few industrialized nations in the world that does not have a family allowance. In contrast, all of the nations that make up the European Community (EC) have a system of cash transfer that subsidizes families with children, irrespective of labor force participation and family structure. Regular payments are made (usually on a monthly basis) for every child. Even in the 1980s, during an era of social retrenchment and economic decline, *no* EC country eliminated allowances for children.

The majority of the EC countries have updated their benefits in 1990–1991 (Dumont, 1992). With a few exceptions, they are now indexed to take into account rising costs of living. Child allowances tend to be linked to family size, and they are not subject to taxation. Some EC countries, such as Belgium, France, Luxembourg, Portugal, and the United Kingdom, also have birth allowances. Coupled with paid maternity leave and universal health care, this social insurance has led to a significantly lower poverty rate for children in the nations of the EC.

Family allowances, however, although meeting the basic needs for housing, food, and health care, have not totally eliminated child abuse and neglect. Even in a country with well-developed preventive social policies, such as Denmark, about 1% of all children under the age of 18 are placed outside the home, either in an institution, in a family commune, or in foster care, and about 10% of infants are at risk of abuse or neglect, with 4% subject to physical abuse/neglect (Christensen, 1993; Christoffersen, 1988). Danish social scientists have concluded from their nationwide surveys that the general preventive activities offered to all parents are not being used by about 10% of those with young children, and that these parents will need a more individually oriented intervention to prevent child abuse and neglect.

With respect to the increase in recognition of child abuse and neglect, the Council of Europe has recommended a dual strategy of immediate intervention coupled with prevention policy. It singles out four priority areas: prevention, early detection, management, and training of personnel. Unlike the EC's regulations concerning economic life, however, these recommendations are not yet directives; that is, they carry no binding obligations for the member states (Armstrong & Hollows, 1991).

Individual country reports from nations as diverse as Denmark, the Netherlands, Spain, and the United Kingdom indicate similar difficulties in implementing these recommendations. One is struck by their shared conclusion that, for any individual child, fragmented and poorly coordinated "systems" may result in confusion, delays, and lack of decisive action. A promising beginning in overcoming these obstacles is the Norwegian Ombudsman for Children Program, which assists in resolving problems surrounding cases of youngsters removed from or placed outside the home in a more personal way than through the traditional court system (Melton, 1991).

As in the United States, current training may not equip European professionals adequately for the particular challenges of child abuse work in their own cultural settings, let alone across ethnic and national boundaries. Increasing economic mobility of residents in EC member states means that professionals will deal more frequently with families from other member states and with immigrants and asylum seekers from developing countries.

In sum, although the nations of the EC generally have been more successful than the United States in providing for the basic needs of their children through income assistance (i.e., family and child allowances), their judicial, mental health, and social welfare systems are confronted with problems similar to those we encounter when dealing with families who, for a variety of social and psychological reasons, cannot provide a home for their children in which there is stable care and caring (see Davis & Ellis-MacLeod, chap. 5, Portwood & Reppucci, chap. 1, and Weisz, chap. 3, this volume).

CHILD AND FAMILY POLICY IN THE UNITED STATES

Evaluating Existing Legislation

In an evaluation of the American record of policies for children and families, Jacobs and Davies (1991) posed four questions that can assist us in understanding the focus of current legislation for children who need a stable, caring home.

Question 1: Does the Policy Focus on the Child or the Family? Jacobs and Davies concluded that, during the 1980s, families gained some prominence in child policy deliberations. The decade began with the passage of PL 96-272, the Adoption Assistance and Child Welfare Act of 1980, which acknowledged the needs of the "failed" families of abused and neglected children. This major piece of legislation proposed supporting and maintaining children in their families of origin as the primary strategy of intervention.

The Education of the Handicapped Act Amendments of 1986 (PL 99-457) provide state funds to serve infants and toddlers with developmental disabilities and those at risk for disabilities, in early intervention programs. Among the provisions of PL 99-457 is a requirement that programs develop an individualized family service plan in which the family is an active participant. This mandate assures parents of children with mental retardation and/or mental illness an important role in decision making regarding placement (Anderson, Thibadeau, & Christian, chap. 9, Blacher, chap. 8, and Pfeiffer & Baker, chap. 10, this volume).

During the 1980s, several state governments also began to embrace family-centered programs to stabilize the family unit, improve family functioning, increase parental competence, and prevent foster care placement. Among the first states to seize this initiative were Connecticut, Kentucky, Maryland, Minnesota, and Missouri (Family Impact Seminar, 1992). These state initiatives are promising signs that policies are developing that meet the needs of the total family unit while being mindful of the needs of individual children.

Question 2: Does the Policy Provide Families with Economic Support or Support for Caregiving and Nurturance? Americans tend to favor income security policies as the least intrusive way to offer assistance to "needy" families, rather than to concentrate on helping them fulfill their nurturance and caregiving role. The debate over policies dealing with homeless families illustrates this point. Whereas some maintain that homeless families only need low-cost shelter, others argue for a broader "economic package" that includes job training and job placement, and still others insist that they need a "caregiving" package that includes services such as home management training, support groups, and parent education (see Bassuk & Weinreb, chap. 2, this volume).

The 1980s saw increased attention to economic support policies and some public support for caregiving and nurturing policies. The Family Support Act of 1988 provides direct economic support to families through two mechanisms. One seeks to enforce noncustodial parents' child support contributions, and the other mandates states to provide job training and child care for parents receiving Aid to Families with Dependent Children (AFDC) who are trying to move from welfare dependency to employment.

Attention to the family's nurturing function is apparent in the federal Child Care and Development Block Grant's investment in broadening the access and improving the quality of state child care systems. In general, state legislators and public agency personnel appear more attuned to the noneconomic needs of families than is the federal government (Family Impact Seminar, 1992).

Question 3: Is the Policy Targeted or Universal? American child and family policy tends to be targeted rather than universal. In order to receive the benefits of *both* economic and caregiving support, children and families must be considered "needy," usually in the extreme. The United States relies to a far greater extent than other Western industrialized nations on income- and means-tested family programs (Dumont, 1992).

With the exception of the Family and Medical Leave Act that passed Congress and was signed by President Clinton into law in 1993, there has not been much sustained progress, at least on the federal level, in establishing universal child and family policies. States such as Hawaii, Minnesota, and Missouri have been more active in the pursuit of broader access. Jacobs and Davies (1991) suggested that the states, as more proximate, familiar governing units, are better able to convince their legislators and voters of the need for universal policies than is the federal government.

Question 4: Does the Policy Focus on Treatment or Prevention? United States child and family policies are overwhelmingly treatment oriented, with only individuals and families already in difficulty being eligible; as of this time, few preventive programs are broadly available. However, momentum is slowly building in favor of preventive strategies to address issues of child and family well-being. The 1980 federal Adoption Assistance and Child Welfare Act took a major step toward a prevention approach by explicitly favoring family preservation services over foster care placement. Also, one of the major principles for action adopted by the bipartisan National Commission on Children (1991), appointed by President Bush (which counted among its members the Governor of Arkansas, Bill Clinton), was that "preventing problems before they become a crisis is the most cost-effective way to address the needs of troubled families and vulnerable children" (p. xx).

On balance, Jacobs and Davies (1991) were cautiously optimistic about the future of child and family policy in the United States. Their analysis suggests that there has been a modest movement toward family-centered, preventive policies on the American scene (more so on the state than on the federal level) that support the caregiving and nurturing dimensions of family life. However, they also pointed to the urgent need to retain and strengthen those policies that consider the child's individual needs, offer necessary treatment to family members, and support families economically.

A Word of Caution

Before considering new federal policies and legislation on behalf of American children and their families, it is worth briefly examining a report published by the Select Committee for Children, Youth and Families of the U.S. House of Representatives (1990b). It is entitled *Federal Programs Affecting Children and Families, 1990*. One can read it not merely as a catalogue of child programs, but also as a primer about the American public policy process. So far, the U.S. Congress has created a maze of some 125 different programs for families and children that may well confuse and frustrate not only the "average" taxpayer (their estimated cost in 1990 was $426.7 billion, or 10.5% of the gross national product) but also the individuals and families who would be served.

When these programs are evaluated, they generally emphasize *process* rather than *client* outcomes. As uncertainty increases about how a program performs and how the individuals and families it is meant to serve are affected, Congress tends to give up choosing among alternatives and simply adds (or "layers") another program to the existing system.

Many of the new programs created in the 1980s, and much of the increased funding under previously existing programs, represents the cost to repair the negative consequences of abuse, neglect, and the malformation and dissolution of families. So far, most *federal* resources and program initiatives have been oriented toward crisis intervention rather than toward ensuring families' long-term economic security or preventing crises from occurring in the first place.

The minority view in this report reminds us that we should not take lightly the charge that the United States does *not* have a *national* policy on families and children, because we tend to confuse *national* with *federal* programs and policies. National policy is rooted in the constitutions of the federal and state governments, the functions of more than 83,000 units of local governments, and myriads of judicial decisions. The real problem in the United States today appears to be a conflict among competing policies, not the absence of policy.

New Legislation

The most significant legislation on behalf of abused and neglected children in more than a decade was approved by Congress and signed into law by President Clinton in August 1993 (U.S. House of Representatives, 1993). The new family preservation and support legislation will provide $1 billion in funds to the states over the next 5 years to strengthen, support, and preserve families and to improve federal foster care and adoption assistance. It reflects many of the policy recommendations made in the 1991 report by the bipartisan National Commission on Children and by a number of contributors to this present volume, notably Blacher (chap. 8), Davis and Ellis-MacLeod (chap. 5), Glidden (chap. 7), Massinga and Perry (chap. 6), Pfeiffer and Baker (chap. 10), and Weisz (chap. 3).

The new legislation offers annually increasing fiscal incentives and a wide range of options for:

1. Early support to families to prevent abuse and neglect
2. More intensive home-based services for families in crisis
3. Improvement in the quality of foster care and adoption assistance for children who cannot be protected at home
4. Enhancements in service delivery

In order to improve services to strengthen families and to prevent unnecessary placement of children in out-of-home care, some $930 million in capped entitlement funds will be made available to states and Indian tribal organizations over the next 5 years for a wide range of family support, family preservation, and family reunification services.

Funds are earmarked for family resource centers and home visiting programs, which get help to families early *before* problems develop and assist them to better protect and care for their children. States will have significant discretion in deciding where, how, and by whom intensive home-based crisis intervention services will be provided, and their agencies will be able to tailor new funds more flexibly to better serve children and families in crisis.

Improvements also are sought in the quality of foster care and adoption assistance for children who cannot be protected at home. Seventy-five percent federal matching funds are authorized for training of foster and adoptive parents. Increased funding is made available for respite care for foster and adoptive parents. Older teens who are preparing to leave foster care and live independently will receive increased federal assistance.

The new legislation also seeks to remove some of the major impediments to service delivery in the judicial, mental health, and social welfare systems that have been highlighted in preceding chapters (see Chapters 1, 4, and 5). It seeks to strengthen the functions of the court's role in implementing protective services for abused and neglected children and their families by grants to the highest state courts to assess court activities and to implement improvements. It seeks to enhance the quality of staff by providing federal matching funds for training and by authorizing demonstration grants designed to educate and support bilingual staff to deliver "culturally sensitive" child welfare services. Finally, it expands opportunities for coordinating services on the state level and for using federal funds more flexibly, but it also demands accountability for the effectiveness of the services provided to vulnerable children and their families. It mandates the establishment of a federal foster care and adoption assistance data system in order to monitor the quality of placement on a national level, and requires the Secretary of Health and Human Services to carry out regular evaluations of the effectiveness of family support and preservation programs.

BUILDING A PYRAMID OF SERVICES

In the best of all possible worlds, *all* American families would have access to decent jobs, housing, child care, schools, and health care to raise their offspring successfully. In addition, families need access to a continuum of services that can offer them assistance when they lack these basics or have particular problems to overcome.

The nation's most effective child advocacy group, the Children's Defense Fund, in its report on *The State of America's Children, 1992*, suggested that every community should make such family support programs available to *all* families, especially those with young children, to improve family functioning *before* crises develop. In addition, communities should offer targeted community-based services (e.g., mental health services) for families needing more intensive help with specific problems. Family preservation services are necessary for families already in crisis, and, finally, high-quality foster family care, therapeutic group care, and specialized residential treatment should be available for children whose families cannot meet their needs (Figure 1). When communities are able to offer a pyramid of assistance that matches the pyramid of family needs, the problems that have led to

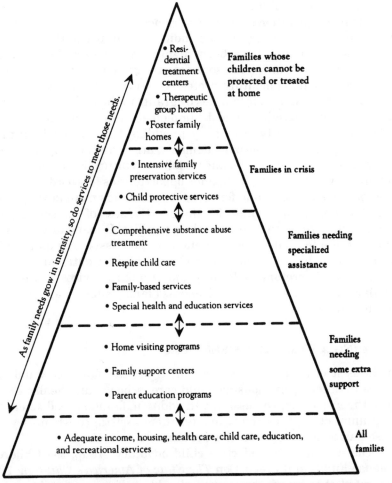

Figure 1. Building a pyramid of services. (From Children's Defense Fund. [1992]. *The state of America's children 1992*, p. 68. Washington, DC: Author; reprinted by permission.)

children's placement may, in the future, be solved or alleviated at earlier stages, when they are easier and less costly to address.

There is ample evidence from studies of the cost-effectiveness of early intervention programs for vulnerable children and families to suggest that appropriate services at any level of the pyramid reduce the demand for services at the next, more intensive and more costly level (Schorr, 1988). For example, the cost of a family preservation program, such as Michigan's Families First service, is about $4,500 *per family,* compared with the cost of maintaining *one child* in family foster care for a year, which is about $12,000. The saving is even greater if placement in detention or psychiatric facilities is avoided (Barthel, 1992).

To be effective, however, *all* services, as well as the systems that deliver them, must be flexible in considering the options that best meet the needs of vulnerable children and families (see Blacher, chap. 8, this volume). Ideally, all of the services provided by different agencies within and between each level of the pyramid should be coordinated, so children's and families' needs can be addressed comprehensively, and so that individuals can move back and forth between levels as circumstances dictate.

UNFINISHED BUSINESS

A glance at current federal legislation on behalf of vulnerable children and families in the United States suggests that most of the policies now in place aim to assist delivery of services in the middle levels of the pyramid, those delivered to families judged by the "helping professions" to need specialized assistance and families in crisis. Missing is the broad base of the pyramid: *income security.* In the beginning of this chapter, I noted that the United States is one of the few industrialized nations in the world that does not have a family allowance and that, with respect to children in poverty, our country bottoms out in comparison with other Western nations. In order to solve this pervasive problem, the United States must adopt some form of income redistribution that does not discriminate against the poorest of the poor in our midst —children in female-headed households.

In her book *Tyranny of Kindness* (1993), Theresa Funiciello—a former homeless welfare mother, and now a special assistant to the commissioner of New York's Department of Social Services and the New York State legislature—made a compelling argument that the time has come when the debate in our nation will shift to *what form* income redistribution should take, not *whether* it should be done at all. In her review of the history of guaranteed income in the United States, she noted that *both* President Johnson, a Democrat, *and* President Nixon, a Republican, attempted to introduce guaranteed income into U.S. domestic policy—and failed. More than two decades *after* the President's Commission on Income Maintenance (which consisted mostly of members of the business community) concluded that "Services cannot be a substitute for adequate income; they cannot pay rent or buy food for a poor family," the bipartisan National Commission on Children has reopened the public dialogue by urging the nation "to make the income security of families with children a high national priority during the 1990's" (1991, p. 80).

The expansion of the Earned Income Tax Credit in the Omnibus Budget Reconciliation Act of 1993 is an important starting point for future national debates on income security. Funiciello (1993) suggested that a family allowance may be the most politically viable form of income transfer on the horizon, but that a more equitable solution would be to establish a universal guaranteed adequate income. Such a guaranteed income would establish a bottom line of income security below which no family could fall. Conceptually, it would mean extending the principles of Social Security to everyone—especially to families with children.

PUBLIC AND PRIVATE RIGHTS AND RESPONSIBILITIES

The incremental and often halting progress of child and family policies in the United States depends, to a great extent, on widely differing notions among American citizens and among the representatives of the two-party system of what constitutes *public* and what are *private* rights and responsibilities for the well-being of their children and families. The line between "private" and "public" continues to be reexamined in policy debates and is no longer clearly demarcated in many social action programs on behalf of families and children. For example, community-based, private, nonprofit agencies, with public funds, provide the main share of emergency aid for social problems affecting families and children, such as homelessness and domestic violence, in the United States (Lipsky & Smith, 1989). Such organizations also assist in recruiting and training foster parents and adoptive parents for children with special needs (see Glidden, chap. 7, and Massinga & Perry, chap. 6, this volume).

At the same time, as we come to recognize that the ability of private families to care for their children is inextricably bound up with the public world of local, state, and federal policies, we also are learning the limits of formal legislation. The responsibility for our nation's children is collective. It "has not been (solely) reposed on Capitol Hill or 1600 Pennsylvania Avenue, but rather rests in the millions of homes, neighborhoods, schools, businesses, and churches across the country" (U.S. House of Representatives Select Committee on Children, Youth and Families, 1990b, p. 271).

GOVERNMENT AND A CIVIL SOCIETY

Formal government policies and programs on behalf of children must sustain (not replace!) what sociologist Alan Wolfe (1989) called a "civil society"—the web of extended families, friendship networks, neighborhoods, and volunteer groups that provide informal support in crisis and adversity. Harvard law professor R.H. Mnookin, in his book, *In the Interest of Children: Advocacy, Law Reform and Public Policy* (1985), has pointed out that there is a special paradox in any advocacy on behalf of vulnerable children and their families. On the one hand, these children have a greater need for advocates; on the other hand, they and their parents may have little power to control those who claim to speak for them—whether they are case workers, educators, judges, mental health professionals, or legislators! Such families have more control if care and caring are provided *not* on the basis of arbitrary eligibility criteria imposed by a bureaucratic system, but on the basis of reciprocity with kith and kin or by members of voluntary associations.

My comments relate to the lessons I have learned from our longitudinal study of a cohort of 698 multiracial children, born on Kauai (the westernmost county of the United States), whom we have followed from the prenatal period to adulthood. A third of the children on this Hawaiian island grew up in poverty and were exposed to multiple risk factors, such as perinatal stress, parental pathology, and a disorganized family environment. Their homes were troubled by discord and eventual breakup of the family, and/or by parental alcoholism or mental illness. Yet a third of these "high-risk" children managed to grow into competent, confident, and caring adults, and more than half of those who had developed problems in childhood or adolescence had recovered by the time they reached their mid-30s, and were responsible spouses, parents, and members of the work force (Werner & Smith, 1989, 1992).

A consistent thread runs through the interview responses (at ages 10, 18, and 32) of the men and women who "succeeded against the odds": These resilient individuals *all* had at least one competent person (not *necessarily* a biological parent) who accepted them unconditionally and provided consistent care and nurturance—especially in adversity and in transitional periods in their lives. Among such "alternate" parents were members of the extended family, such as grandparents, older siblings, aunts, or uncles; caring neighbors; teachers who became confidants and role models; youth leaders in church and voluntary organizations, such as the YMCA or YWCA, the Boy and Girl Scouts, or 4-H; and retired elder mentors.

Support from such an informal network of kin and neighbors and "ordinary" members of the community was more often sought and more highly valued by the "high-risk" children and their families in our study who overcame the odds than were the services of social agencies and mental health professionals—a refrain that has been echoed in other studies of African American and Caucasian families on the mainland (Kilbride & Kilbride, chap. 11, this volume; Werner, 1990).

Thus, in many contexts, it may make better sense, indeed, to strengthen *available informal* ties to kin and neighbors than to introduce additional layers of bureaucracy into the delivery of services for vulnerable children and their families. This viewpoint is perhaps best articulated by Daniel P. Moynihan in his book *Family and Nation:* "A credible family policy," he suggests, "will insist that responsibility begins with the individual, then the family, and only then the community, and in the first instance, the smaller and nearer rather than the greater and more distant community" (1987, p. 173). The U.S. Advisory Board on Child Abuse and Neglect (1991) called this a policy of "creating caring communities."

LESSONS OF SUCCESSFUL PROGRAMS

In *Within our Reach,* Lisbeth Schorr (1988) gave an inspiring account of her investigation of a broad range of health, education, and family support programs that have successfully prevented "rotten outcomes" for children who grew up in high-risk families. Schorr isolated a set of common characteristics of programs that succeeded in helping the children and their families: They were comprehensive, intensive, and flexible. They also shared an extra dimension: The nature of the services, the terms on which they were offered, the relationships with families— all took their shape from the needs of those they served rather than from the precepts, demands, and boundaries set by bureaucracy.

The staff members in these programs acted more like members of an extended family than "professionals" and were perceived by those they served as people who cared about them and respected them. They were ready to circumvent traditional bureaucratic limitations and to reduce barriers of money, time, fragmentation, and geographic and psychological remoteness. Their services were coherent and easy to use. None of the successful programs was the product of the normal functioning of a large system, and most were funded at least in part with foundation or government grants that did not carry the usual encumbrances.

Schorr pointed to the fundamental contradiction between the needs of vulnerable children and families and the traditional requirements of professionalism and bureaucracy that emerged in her findings—a contradiction that future attempts to build a pyramid of successful services must take into account. We need to recognize that many prevailing programs have been shaped by powerful political professional and administrative forces that are slow to change. Knowing that should be not a cause of despair, but a call for personal and collective action (Funiciello, 1993). In the final analysis, it is *not* new policies and programs, but the presence of caring people in a responsive community, that will make a lasting difference in the lives of the children for whom there is no place like home.

REFERENCES

Armstrong, H., & Hollows, A. (1991). Responses to child abuse in the EC. In M. Hill (Ed.), *Social work and the European Community* (pp. 142–161). London: Jessica Kingsley Publisher.

Barthel, J. (1992). *For the children's sake: The promise of family preservation.* New York: Edna McConnell Clark Foundation.

Children's Defense Fund. (1992). *The state of America's children, 1992.* Washington, DC: Author.

Christensen, E. (1993, March). *Neglected children: A Danish survey of children 0–1 year old.* Paper presented at the 4th European Conference on Child Abuse and Neglect, Padua, Italy.

Christoffersen, M.N. (1988, October). *Home is best—A sociological study of Danish children in foster care.* Paper presented at the International Meeting on Children at Risk: Future Development in Child Welfare and Family Policy, Prague, Czech Republic.

de Saint-Exupéry, A. (1943). *The little prince.* Orlando, FL: Harcourt Brace Jovanovich, Publishers.

Dumont, W. (Ed.). (1992). *National family policies in the EC countries.* Brussels: European Observatory of Family Policies.

Family Impact Seminar. (1992). *Keeping troubled families together—promising programs and statewide reforms.* Washington, DC: American Association for Marriage and Family Therapy.

Funiciello, T. (1993). *Tyranny of kindness.* New York: Atlantic Monthly Press.

Huston, A.C. (Ed.). (1991). *Children in poverty: Child development and public policy.* Cambridge, England: Cambridge University Press.

Jacobs, E.H., & Davies, M.W. (1991). Rhetoric or reality? Child and family policy in the United States. *Society for Research in Child Development Social Policy Report, V*(4).

Lipsky, M., & Smith, S.R. (1989). When social problems are treated as emergencies. *Social Science Review, 63*(1), 5–25.

Melton, G.B. (1991). Lessons from Norway: The children's ombudsman as a voice for children. *Journal of International Law, 23* (2), 198–254.
Mnookin, R.H. (1985). *In the interest of children: Advocacy, law reform and public policy.* New York: W.H. Freeman.
Moynihan, D.P. (1987). *Family and nation.* San Diego: Harcourt Brace Jovanovich, Publishers.
National Commission on Children. (1991). *Beyond rhetoric: A new American agenda for children and families.* Washington, DC: Author.
Schorr, L.B. (1988). *Within our reach: Breaking the cycle of disadvantage.* New York: Doubleday Anchor Press.
United Nations Commission on Human Rights. (1990). *U.N. convention on the rights of the child.* New York: United Nations.
U.S. Advisory Board on Child Abuse and Neglect. (1991). *Creating caring communities: Blueprint for an effective policy on child abuse and neglect.* Washington, DC: Author.
U.S. House of Representatives. (1993, August 4). Omnibus Budget Reconciliation Act (H.R. 2264, 103rd Congress, 1st session). *Congressional Record,* pp. H5878–H5881.
U.S. House of Representatives Select Committee on Children, Youth and Families. (1989). *No place to call home: Discarded children in America.* Washington, DC: Author.
U.S. House of Representatives Select Committee on Children, Youth and Families. (1990a). *Children's well-being: An international comparison.* Washington, DC: Author.
U.S. House of Representatives Select Committee on Children, Youth and Families. (1990b). *Federal programs affecting children and their families, 1990.* Washington, DC: Author.
Werner, E.E. (1990, October). *Civil society and human development.* Paper presented at the Law and Society Seminar, Harvard Law School, Cambridge, MA.
Werner, E.E., & Smith, R.S. (1989). *Vulnerable but invincible: A longitudinal study of resilient children and youth.* New York: Adams, Bannister, Cox.
Werner, E.E., & Smith, R.S. (1992). *Overcoming the odds: High risk children from birth to adulthood.* Ithaca, NY: Cornell University Press.
Wolfe, A. (1989). *Whose keeper? Social science and moral obligation.* Berkeley: University of California Press.

Index

Abaluyia (Kenya), contemporary foster care among, 315–322
Abandonment, children's coping strategies for, 142
Abuse and neglect, 7–14
  causes of, 65, 97
  of children with special needs, 139–141
  definition of, 7–8, 64–68
  emergency placement determinations with, 8–10, 81–82
  emotional, 67
  in European Community, 332
  fatalities from, 63
  foster care as alternative to, 304–305
  intervention for
    Native American families and, 75
    to preserve family unit, 74–81
  legal responses/processes in, 10–11, 69–89
    criminal prosecution for, 82–83
  physical, 65
  prevalence of, 63, 330
  prevention of, 141
    cross-cultural examples of, 304–305
  public policy and, 69–89, 98
  reporting, 8, 68–69
  reports, investigation of, 72–74
  research on, 153
  risk factors for, 330
  social responses/processes in, 69–89
  and substance abuse, 137–138
  substantiated versus unsubstantiated cases, 72–74
  termination of parental rights and, 11–13, 88–89, 93
  see also Abused child; Sexual abuse
Abused child
  adoption of, 93–95
  outcome, 199–200
  Bill of Rights, 92
  with disabilities, programs for, 78–81
  emergency removal from home, petitioning for, 8–10, 81–82
  foster care placement, 130
    adjudication, 82–84
    disposition hearing, 84–85
    factors affecting, 69–70
    long-term, 90, 96–97
    temporary, 90–93
  guardianship of, 95–96
  medical care for, 92
  mental health care for, 91–92
  out-of-home placement
    alternatives for, 89–97
    consequences of, 63–100
    order of preference for, 91
    psychosocial characteristics of, 91–92
  removal from home, 81–89
    adjudication, 82–84
    emergency, petitioning for, 8–10, 81–82
  residential treatment centers for, 97

Abused child—*continued*
  reunification with family, 86–88
  risk for long-term clinical dysfunction, 91–92
Academic difficulties, of children in foster care, 136–137
Acquired immunodeficiency syndrome, implications for foster care system, 138–139
Adjudication
  of foster care placement of abused child, 82–84
  in juvenile justice, 27–28
Adolescents, foster care placement, 127, 130
Adoptee(s)
  adoption's effect on, 192–196
  age at adoption, and outcome, 193–195, 199–200
  characteristics of, 187–191
  development of, 193–195
  older, 199–200
  psychosocial resources and issues for, 192–193
  socioeconomic status of, 192
Adoption, 181–209
  of abused child, 93–95
  advertising for, 188–189
  of children with disabilities, 200–201
  current practices, 184–191
  definition of, 93, 182
  disruption, 94
    definition of, 199
    with older child, 199–200
  dissolution, definition of, 199
  effects
    on adoptees, 192–196
    on adoptive parents, 197–198
    on birth parents, 196–197
    summary of, 198
  feasibility of, assessment and decision-making steps, 129–130
  of healthy infants, 191–198
  history of, 182–184
  incidence of, 184
  legal regulation of, 182–184
  motivations for, 182
  nonrelative, 181
    frequency of, 184
  of older children, 199–200

open, 189
optimization, recommendations for, 204–205
outcome, 145–149
  and child's age at adoption, 199–200
  clinical sample, 193–194
  nonclinical sample, 194–195
  with older child, 199–200
  types of, 199–200
prevalence of, 184
private, 189
relative, 181
special needs, 95, 183, 198–203
  motivations for, 190–191
termination of parental rights and, 13, 89, 93
transracial, 201–203
Adoption Assistance and Child Welfare Act (PL 96-272), 42, 69, 74, 90, 97, 126, 187–188, 289, 333, 335
  effects on child placement, 145–149
Adoption triangle, 191–198
Adoptive parents
  adoption's effects on, 197–198
  age of, 183
  characteristics of, 184–187
  gay, 184
  single, 183
  transition to parenthood, 192–193, 197–198
Adult court, prosecution of juveniles in, 28
African Americans
  kinship fostering among, 310–313
  see also Race
Aggressive behaviors, of homeless children, 49–50
Aid to Families with Dependent Children, 69, 75, 125, 334
Alameda Demonstration Project, 125
Alcohol consumption, during pregnancy, 68
Alternative families, *see* Adoption; Foster care
American Academy of Child and Adolescent Psychiatry, standards for inpatient treatment, 115–116
American Association on Mental Re-

INDEX 347

tardation, definition of mental retardation, 275
Anxiety, in homeless children, 46–47
Attachment behavior/processes
  of children with disabilities and their parents, 225–226
  and foster care placement, 90–91
  types of, 141–142
Attachment theory, 141–142, 301
Autism, child with
  behavior problems of, 248–250
  characteristics of, 247–250
  comprehensive school-based services for, 255–257
  dependency issues with, 248–250
  early intervention for, 252–253
  effect on family, 250–251
  family of, characteristics of, 251–252
  family support services and, 257–258
  foster care placement, 262–264
  home-based intervention for, 253–255
  parent training programs and, 253–255
  placement
    definition of, 246
    factors affecting, 246–258
    services affecting, 252–258
  residential placement, 258–264
  service programming for, 245–268
    accountability in, 266
    evaluation of, 266
    funding implications, 266–268
    goals and standards for, 264
    implications for families, 266–267
    public policy implications, 266–268
    staff training and supervision in, 264–265
  social deficits in, 248–250
  transitional residential programming for, 258–264

Behavioral problems
  of children in foster care, 136–137
  of child with autism, 248–250
  in homeless children, 46–47

Behavior disorders, inpatient treatment of, 112–113, 115
Bill of Rights, for children in out-of-home placement, 92
Birth parents, adoption's effects on, 196–197

Casey Family Program, The, 163–181
  attention to cultural identity, 175–179
  case planning factors in, 169–170
  children in
    acceptance criteria for, 168
    assessment of, 168–170
    characteristics of, 165
  collaboration with local individuals and organizations, 166–167
  Continuing Education and Job Training program, 171–173
  developmental issues addressed in, 175–179
  foster families in, 173–174
    characteristics of, 165–166
  kinship placements in, 174
  management views in, 164–168
  organizational values in, 164–168
  philosophy of, 164–168
  practice guidelines and services, 168–170
  rituals and traditions in, 175–179
  services for young adults, 170–173
  staff, 166, 174–175
Child abuse, *see* Abuse and neglect
Child Abuse Prevention and Treatment Act
  of 1974, 64, 68
  of 1988, 67
Child Care and Development Block Grants, 334
Child maltreatment
  definition of, 7–8
  see also Abuse and neglect
Child neglect, *see* Abuse and neglect
Child Protective Services, establishment of, 69
Children, well-being of
  international comparisons of, 331
  public and private rights and responsibilities for, 340–341

Children's Aid Societies, 124
Children's rights, 5–6
Child Welfare League of America, 127
Child witness, physical and psychological harm to, legal safeguards against, 10–11
Civil society, 341–342
Cognitive dysfunctions, of children in foster care, 136–137
Commitment, in mental illness cases, 18–24, 26–27, 29
  involuntary, 21–23, 27, 29
  voluntary, 19–20
Competency, of children
  in mental health treatment, 18–20
  to participate in custody decisions, 16–17
  to testify in court, 10
Conduct disorders, inpatient treatment of, 113–115
Consent, to medical and/or mental health treatment, children's participation in, 19–20
Coping strategies
  of abandoned children, 142
  of homeless children, 48–52
Counsel, juveniles' nonwaivable right to, 26
Courtroom proceedings
  with abuse and neglect, 10–11
  stress on child witness in, legal safeguards against, 10–11
Courts, *see* Juvenile courts; Legal policies
Coy v. Iowa, 11
Custody
  after divorce, legal considerations, 14–18
  transfer of, 11
  for mental health treatment, 23
  see also Joint custody

Depression
  of children in foster care, 136–137
  in homeless children, 46–47
DeShaney v. Winnebago County Department of Social Services, 9–10
Detention
  emergency, 27
  pretrial, of juveniles, 27

Developmental delays
  of children in foster care, 136–137
  in homeless children, 44–46, 54
Developmental disabilities, children with
  education services for, 253
  foster care placement for, 139–141
  see also Mental retardation; Special needs adoption
Diagnosis-related groups, 105–106
Diagnostic overshadowing, 276
Disabilities, children with
  abused or neglected, programs for, 78–81
  adoption of, 200–201
  foster care placement for, 139–141
Disposition hearing
  for foster care placement of abused child, 84–85
  in juvenile justice, 28–29
Divorce
  custody after
    best interests standard, 15
    child preference in, 16–17
    factors affecting, 15–18
    legal considerations, 14–18
    maternal preference standard, 14–15
    paternal preference standard, 14–15
  joint custody after, 17–18
Drug rehabilitation, and family preservation, 70
Dual diagnosis (of mental retardation and mental disorder) children with
  challenges presented by, 273–274
  characteristics of, 274–278
  effects on family, 278–279
  family adjustment to residential placement, 291–293
  family involvement in treatment of, 288–291
  family therapy and, 282–283
  group therapy for, 287–288
  out-of-home placement, prevention of, 281–283
  parent training programs and, 281–282
  permanency planning for, 289
  psychotherapy for, 285–287
  public policy and, 293–295

INDEX 349

research implications, 293–295
social policies and services for, 280–281
treatment of, in residential placement, 283–288
definition of, 274–276
diagnosis, 276
expression of, 276–278
prevalence of, 276–278
severity of, 276–278
Due process, 9, 12, 25

Early intervention
for children with disabilities, 78–81
for child with autism, 252–253
cost-effectiveness of, 339
Early Periodic Screening, Diagnosis, and Treatment Program (EPSDT), 80, 92
Earned Income Tax Credit, 340
Ecological theory, of behavior, 142
Educational problems, in homeless children, 47–48
Education for All Handicapped Children Act (PL 94-142), 217, 246
Education of the Handicapped Act
Amendments of 1986 (PL 99-457), 78, 253, 333
Amendments of 1991, 79
Education services, for child with autism, 253, 255–257
Emergency placement determinations, with abuse and neglect, 8–10, 81–82
Emotional disorders, inpatient treatment of, 113–114
Emotional maltreatment, definition of, 67
Emotional problems, of children in foster care, 136–137
EPSDT, see Early Periodic Screening, Diagnosis, and Treatment Program
Ethnic origin
and adoptive placement, 201–203
and out-of-home placement, 132–133, 164
research implications, 151
European Community, child and family policies in, 331–333

Family
alternative
see Adoption; Foster care
autonomy of, 4–5, 11–12
of child with autism, 251–252
involvement after residential placement of child, 261
support services for, 257–258
of child with dual diagnoses
adjustment to child's placement, 291–293
challenges to, 278–279
family therapy for, 282–283
parent training for, 281–282
and residential treatment, 288–291
reunification after residential treatment of child, 293
of child with mental retardation, 222–223
in-home assessment of, 76
privacy of, 4–5
reunification
after foster care placement of child, 86–88, 128–129, 145–149
after residential treatment of child with dual diagnoses, 293
practice and policy implications for, 153–154
support for, importance to civil society, 341–342
Family allowance(s)
in European Community, 331–332
in United States, 340
Family and Medical Leave Act, 334
Family and Nation (Moynihan), 342
Family libertarianism, 4–5
Family preservation
intervention for
in child abuse and neglect cases, 74–81
reasonable efforts criterion, 75–76, 83–84
legislative initiatives for, 333
and parent–child contacts, during foster care, 142–144
programs for, 76–78, 125
services, cost-effectiveness of, 338–339
Family services, building a pyramid of, 337–339, 343

Family Support Act, 334
Family Unification Program, 56
Family violence, research on, 153
Fare v. Michael C., 26
Federal Programs Affecting Children and Families, 1990 (Select Committee for Children, Youth and Families), 335
Fosterage, *see* Foster care
Foster care
  in Abaluyia society of Kenya, 315–322
  after death of parent, cross-cultural examples of, 305–306
  as alternative to abuse and neglect, 304–305
  as alternative to childlessness, cross-cultural examples of, 309
  as alternative to infanticide, 303–304
  as bond between adults, cross-cultural examples of, 307–309
  children in
    background characteristics of, 131–133
    coping strategies of, 142
    family contact with, 141–145
    goals for, 164
    mental health of, 136–137
    number of placements experienced by, 134–135
    numbers of, 163
    physical health of, 135–136
    psychosocial characteristics of, 150–151, 164
    racial/ethnic characteristics of, 132–133
    services provided to, 145–147
    socioeconomic status of, 131–132
    with special needs, 139–141
    special-risk populations, 137–141
  cross-cultural differences in, implications for social policy, 322–326
  cross-cultural examples of, 301–326
  definition of, 131, 302
  as exchange system, cross-cultural examples of, 306–309
  federal funding for, 74–75
  formal, recommendations for, 322–326
  forms of, 302
  grandparents as providers of, cross-cultural examples of, 305–307
  informal arrangements for, functions of, 302–303
  long-term, *see also* Casey Family Program, The
  number of children in, 130
  practice implications for, 153–154
  research, types of studies needed, 151–152
  research, since 1980, 131–149
  service delivery models, 152
  as source of companionship and assistance for providers, cross-cultural examples of, 307
  specialist, 126
  see also Foster care placement
Foster Care Mental Health Study, 151
Foster care placement
  of abused child, 89–97, 130
  adjudication, 82–84
  disposition hearing, 84–85
  long-term, 90, 96–97
  six-month review hearing, 85–86
  temporary, 90–93
  of adolescents, 127, 130
  agencies for, 126
  of child with autism, 262–264
  contraindications to, 127
  decision making in, research implications, 151–152
  description of, 126–130
  family services with, 128–129, 145–147
  see also Family preservation
  of HIV-infected children, 138–139
  length of stay in, 133–134, 164
  and parent–child contacts, 142–143
  long-term, 130
  outcome, 125, 145–149
  number of children in, 103
  permanency planning framework for, 125–126, 129–130

recidivism, 145–149
referral categories in, 130–131
of siblings, 144–145
  recommendations for, 127
  studies of, need for, 151–152
  substance abuse by parents and, 130–131, 137–138
temporary, 123–161
  discharge from, 145–149
  historical background of, 124–126
  outcome, 145–149
  purposes of, 123
  research implications, 150–153
Foster homes, types of, 126
Foster parents
  licensing of, 126–127
  role of, 126

General hospitals, psychiatric inpatient care in, 107–112
Grandparents, as foster care providers, cross-cultural examples of, 305–307
Group therapy, for children with dual diagnoses, 287–288
Guardian *ad litem*, for custody determinations, 18
Guardianship
  of abused children, 95–96
  in child placement decisions, 130, 149

Head Start program, 58, 70, 98
Health insurance
  expenditures for mental health care of children and youth, 106
  number of persons without, 103
  for special needs children, 95
Health passport, for children in out-of-home placements, 92
Health status, of children in foster care, 135–136
Home, definition of, 3–4
Homebuilders family reunification program, 164
Homeless children, 37–62
  aggressive behaviors of, 49–50
  coping strategies of, 48–52
  developmental delays in, 44–46, 54
  educational problems in, 47–48
  educational services for, 53–55
  emotional problems of, 46–47
  foster care placement, 38, 41–42, 55–56
    developmental effects of, 44–46
  medical problems of, 43–44
  mother–child relationship and, 40–41, 50–52
  mothering behaviors in, 50–52
  mothers of
    child welfare system and, 41–42
    programs and services for, 55
    psychosocial characteristics of, 41
  needs of, 43–48
    long-term responses to, 56–58
    program and policy responses to, 52–58
    short-term responses to, 53–56
  number of, 39, 103
  psychosocial characteristics of, 38–43
  regressive behaviors of, 48–49
  response to losing home, 39–40
  shyness in, 49–50
  social difficulties of, 46–47
  stable environment for, provision of, 53–54
  stresses on, 38–43
    in hotels, 40–41
    in shelters, 40
  trauma to, 42–43
  withdrawn behaviors of, 49–50
Homelessness
  effects on children, 103–104
  extent of problem, 37, 39, 103
  family intervention and, 42–43
  long-term responses to, 56–58
  origins of problem, 37–38
Housing, temporary versus stable, effects on children, 103–104
Human immunodeficiency virus infection, pediatric, 138–139

Income security, 339–340
Indenture System, 124
Indian Child Welfare Act of 1978 (PL 95-608), 75
  and adoption, 202
  and Casey Family Program, 167

Individuals with Disabilities Education Act, 79, 217, 246
Infanticide, fostering as alternative to, 303–304
Infant–Toddler Program of early intervention, 78
Infertility, and adoption, 185, 192–193
In re Angelia P., 93–94
In re Gault, 6, 25
In re Gregory K., 13
In re Sara K., 88–89
In re Shantelle, 83
In re Winship, 25, 28
In the Interest of Children: Advocacy, Law Reform and Public Policy (Mnookin), 341
In the matter of A.A.I., 30

Joint custody, after divorce, 17–18
Justice, individualized, for children, 24–25
Juvenile courts, 24–25
Juvenile delinquency, 24–30
Juvenile justice
  adjudication, 27–28
  discretion in, 28–29
  disposition, 28–29
  intake and pretrial proceedings, 25–27
  monitoring of placement and service provision, 29–30

Kent v. United States, 28
Kenya, contemporary foster care in, 315–322
Kidstart program, 58
Kinship care
  as foster care, 126–127
  reimbursement for, 126–127
Kinship fostering, 303
  cross-cultural examples of, 310–322
Kinship placements, in Casey Family Program, 174

Lassiter v. Department of Social Services, 12
Least restrictive alternative, 216–217

Legal policies, in child placement, 3–35
  future prospects, 30–31
  overview of, 3–4
  recommendations, 30–31
Legislation
  child and family policies in, evaluation of, 335–336
  existing, child and family policies in, evaluation of, 333–335
  new, child and family policies in, evaluation of, 336–337
  unfinished business not yet addressed by, 339–340
  see also Public policy; *specific legislation*

Maryland v. Craig, 11
May Institute, 247
  home-based intervention and parent training program, 254–255
  transitional residential placement program, 261–264
McKeiver v. Pennsylvania, 25
Medicaid
  for children in out-of-home placements, 92
  expenditures for mental health care of children and youth, 104, 106
  groups covered by, 105
  for special needs children, 95
Medical care, for children in out-of-home placements, 92
Medicare, Prospective Payment System, 105
Memory dysfunctions, of children in foster care, 136–137
Mental health, of children in foster care, 136–137
Mental health care
  for children, 137
  commitment for, 18–24
    children's rights in, 113
    involuntary, 21–23
    voluntary, 19–20
  need for, children's, 103
  see also Psychiatric inpatient care
Mental health policy, 101–118
  analysis of, 102

for children, special issues in, 102–104
Mental illness
  legal definition of, 22–23
  see also Dual diagnosis (of mental retardation and mental disorder)
Mental retardation
  children with, residential placement for, 213–243
    choice of facility, 230–231
    consequences of, 231–235
    as decision-making process, 220–221
    factors affecting, 219–220
    family involvement after, 218, 232–234
    full-scale inclusion and, 217–218
    historical background, 215–218
    natural home and, 217–218
    normalization principle and, 216–217
    prevention of, 223–229
    public policy implications, 235–237
    risk factors for, 221–223
    satisfaction with, 231
  definition of, 214, 248, 275
  family of children with
    adjustment after out-of-home placement, 234–235
    characteristics of, and out-of-home placement, 222–223
    plans to seek out-of-home placement, factors affecting, 224–227
    postplacement involvement, 218, 232–234
    resources for, 223–227
    respite care for, 224–227
    satisfaction with out-of-home placement, 231
    support system of, 223–226
  normalization principle and, 216–217
  prevalence of, 214
  see also Dual diagnosis (of mental retardation and mental disorder)
Meyer v. Nebraska, 5, 11

Miranda v. Arizona, 26
Mothering behaviors, in homeless children, 50–52
Mother's Pension Legislation, 125
Myers v. Morris, 8

National Institute on Mental Health, research on children's mental health services, 101, 118
Native Americans
  intervention for child abuse and neglect in, 75
  see also Indian Child Welfare Act
Neglect
  definition of, 66
  see also Abuse and neglect
Neuropsychiatric disorders, inpatient treatment of, 113
Newborn, toxicology screen of, 68
New York Children's Aid Society, 124
Normalization principle, and children with mental retardation, 216–217

Ohio v. Roberts, 10
Oregon Permanency Planning Project, 125, 145
Orphan trains, 124, 182
Out-of-home placement
  children at risk for, numbers of, 330
  children in, numbers of, 163, 330
  see also Adoption; Foster care; Residential placement; Residential treatment

Parens patriae, 4, 14
  and juvenile court, 29–30
Parental rights, termination of, 11–13, 88–89, 93
Parent–child contacts, and foster care placement, 142–144
Parents' rights, 5
Parent training
  and child with autism, 253–255
  and child with dual diagnoses, 281–282
Parham v. J.R., 21–22
Patrilineal society, 309, 318

Patrilocal society, 309
Pervasive developmental disorder, 248
Pierce v. Society of Sisters, 5, 11
PL 94-142, *see* Education for All Handicapped Children Act
PL 95-608, *see* Indian Child Welfare Act of 1978
PL 96-272, *see* Adoption Assistance and Child Welfare Act
PL 99-457, *see* Education of the Handicapped Act, Amendments of 1986
Polygyny, 317
Poverty
 and child abuse, 330
 children living in, number of, 330–331
 effects on children, 103–104
 and out-of-home placement, 131–132
 research implications, 151
 in United States, 103
Prevention, legislative initiatives for, 334–335
Prince v. Massachusetts, 5
Psychiatric disorders, of children and youths, classification of, 113
Psychiatric evaluation, of juvenile offenders, 28–29
Psychiatric hospitals, private, psychiatric inpatient care in, 107–112
Psychiatric inpatient care
 of adults, analysis of, 102
 bed occupancy rate for, 109
 beds available for, 108–109
 of children and youths, 101–118
 cost of, by treatment setting, 110–111
 effectiveness, 116
 funding, 106
 in general hospitals, 1980–1985, 105–107
 inappropriate versus necessary, 115–117
 indications for, 113
 lack of alternatives to, 115, 117
 legal issues in, 112–113
 national de facto system of, 107–109
 policy issues, 104–105
 quality of, 109–112
 referral patterns in, 113–115
 relationship to other policy issues for children, 112–115
 sites of, 106–107, 110
 staffing patterns, by treatment setting, 110–112
 without psychiatric disorders, 113–115
 for children with dual diagnoses, 283–288
Psychosomatic disorders, inpatient treatment of, 113
Psychotherapy, for children with dual diagnoses, 285–287
Public policy
 changes needed in, 117
 and child abuse and neglect, 69–89, 98
 and child with dual diagnoses, 293–295
 and foster care, 154, 322–326
 and homeless children, 52–58
 and psychiatric inpatient care of children, 113–115, 117
 and residential placement, for children with mental retardation, 235–237
 and service programming for children with autism, 266–268
 successful, elements of, 342–343
 and support for family networks, 341–342
 see also Legislation; Mental health policy
Pyramid of services, building, 337–339, 343

Quasi-units, psychiatric inpatient care in, 107–112

Race
 and adoptive placement, 201–203
 and out-of-home placement, 132–133, 164
 research implications, 151
Regressive behaviors, of homeless children, 48–49

INDEX 355

Residential placement, 211
 for child with autism, transitional, 258–264
 of children with mental retardation, 213–243
Residential treatment, for children with dual diagnoses, 273–298
Residential treatment centers
 for abused children, 97
 psychiatric inpatient care in, 107–112
Right to treatment, 216–217

Santosky v. Kramer, 12
Scatter hospitals, 106
Schall v. Martin, 27
Self-esteem, of children in foster care, 136–137
Sexual abuse
 causal factors in, 65–66
 criminal prosecution for, 82–83
 definition of, 65
 signs of, 66
Shyness, of homeless children, 49–50
Siblings
 contact, during foster care, 144–145
 foster care placement, 144–145
 recommendations for, 127
 placement patterns for, research implications, 151
 separation of, stress of, 124
Social relationships, impaired, of children in foster care, 136–137
Social services, building a pyramid of, 337–339, 343
Special needs, definition of, 198
Special needs adoption, 95, 183, 198–203
 frequency of, 198
 motivations for, 190–191
 research questions, 198
Special needs foster care placement, 139–141
Stanley v. Illinois, 11
State
 power to control activities of children, 5
 responsibility for protecting children from abuse, 9–10
The State of America's Children (Children's Defense Fund), 337
Stewart B. McKinney Homeless Assistance Act, 54–56
Strict scrutiny test, 12
Substance abuse
 and child abuse and neglect, 137–138
 maternal, foster care placement of children for, 83–84, 137–138
 prenatal exposure to, 67–68, 137–138
 reporting, 69
 prevalence of, 137
Substitute care, children in, numbers of, 163
Sullivan v. Zebley, 80
Supplemental Security Income, 79–80

Treatment, of juvenile offenders
 monitoring of, 29–30
 right to, 29
Tyranny of Kindness (Funiciello), 339

Uniform Marriage and Divorce Act, 15
United Nations Convention on the Rights of the Child, 329–330
United States, child and family policies in, 333–337
 existing legislation, evaluation of, 333–335

West Africa, fosterage in, functions of, 303
WIC, *see* Women, Infants and Children
Willie M. v. Hunt, 29
Wisconsin v. Yoder, 11
Withdrawn behaviors, of homeless children, 49–50
Within our Reach (Schorr), 342–343
Women, Infants and Children (WIC), 70, 98